Nomos Universitätsschriften

Recht

Band 1050

Natalia Subbotina

Biodiversity Protection Framework at the Intersection of Ethics, Law and Policy

The Case of Forest Ecosystems of the Ukrainian Carpathians

Nomos

Gefördert durch ein Stipendium der Begabtenförderung der Konrad-Adenauer-Stiftung.

The Deutsche Nationalbibliothek lists this publication in the Deutsche Nationalbibliografie; detailed bibliographic data are available on the Internet at http://dnb.d-nb.de

a.t.: Ukrainische Freie Universität, Diss., 2025

ISBN 978-3-7560-4161-9 (Print)
978-3-7489-6776-7 (ePDF)

Online Version
Inlibra

1st Edition 2026

PREFACE

The present work is a result of my doctoral studies in International Law at the Ukrainian Free University in Munich, from October 2021 until the defence of this dissertation in May 2025.

The idea of this study on biodiversity protection at the intersection of law, ethics and policy gradually emerged from my master's thesis on the human right to a healthy environment and an exchange semester at Tilburg University while pursuing the LLM in human rights at Ukrainian Catholic University in 2018. The course Catholic Social Thought at Tilburg introduced me to the encyclical letter Laudato Si' by Pope Francis and led to the creation of the Lviv Laudato Si' Chapter, whose activities inspired me to focus on the Carpathian forests.

I am deeply grateful to my scientific supervisor, Prof. Dr. Vasyl Nepyivoda, for his encouraging guidance during this academic journey, including our numerous discussions on law and sustainability and advice on my writing, for getting me in touch with the local residents of the Carpathian region, and literally guiding me through the forests in the area. I am also sincerely grateful to Prof. Dr. Myroslava Antonovych, who chaired the thesis defence committee and to the reviewers Prof. Dr. Halyna Mykhailiuk and Prof. Dr. Mykhailo Savchyn for their time and attention to my work. Furthermore, I would like to thank everyone who participated in the research interviews or helped to organise them, including Bohdan Kuchenko, Yehor Hrynyk, Oksana Omelchuk, Orsolya Decker, Kristin Biebl and many others who preferred to stay anonymous.

Likewise, I am grateful to all those who enabled this research and publication. I am particularly grateful to the Konrad Adenauer Foundation for supporting my doctoral studies in Germany in various ways. I would also like to thank the Bavarian State Library for providing access to academic literature and being my 'home' for the most of my desk research.

I am thankful to all those who encouraged and accompanied my studies, including Oleksandra Mudrak and Anastasiia Savchuk, who 'productively distracted' my writing process through our participation in several international law moot court competitions. I am also beyond grateful to the Ukrainian Greek Catholic Church, especially the communities of the Cathedral of the Intercession of the Mother of God and of St. Andrew the Firstcalled and of the Asam Church (St. John Nepomuk Church) in Munich, for being the source of hope, strength, and comfort throughout these turbulent times of war and challenging years of research and writing. My deepest gratitude goes to my family, especially my sister Olha, and my friends, especially Ivanna, Yuliia and Erika.

Finally, this work is dedicated to my mother, Olesya, whose love, care, and prayers surrounded me throughout all my studies, and is written in gratitude to God for all the magnificent creatures that dwell on Earth.

Munich, December 2025 *Natalia Subbotina*

Table of Contents

LIST OF ABBREVIATIONS

Abbrev.	Definition
ASCI	Areas of Special Conservation Interest
CBD	Convention on Biological Diversity
CBF	Carpathian Biodiversity Framework
CFREU	Charter of Fundamental Rights of the European Union
CITES	Convention on International Trade in Endangered Species of Wild Fauna and Flora
CMS	Convention on the Conservation of Migratory Species of Wild Animals
COP	Conference of the Parties
CST	Catholic Social Teaching
EAP	Environmental Action Programme
EIA	Environmental Impact Assessment
EPL	Environment-People-Law
EU	European Union
FAO	Food and Agriculture Organization of the United Nations
FRA	Global Forest Resources Assessment
FSC	Forest Stewardship Council
GBF	Global Biodiversity Framework
GPEC	Global Partnership on Ecological Connectivity
HRC	Human Rights Council
INDCs	Intended Nationally Determined Contributions
IPBES	Intergovernmental Science-Policy Platform on Biodiversity and Ecosystem Services
IPCC	Intergovernmental Panel on Climate Change
IPF	Intergovernmental Panel on Forests

Abbrev.	Definition
INC	Intergovernmental Negotiating Committee for a Convention on Biological Diversity
IUCN	International Union for Conservation of Nature
MEA	Multilateral Environmental Agreement
NAPPs	National Adaptation Program Plans
NBSAP	National Biodiversity Strategies and Action Plans
NGO	Non-Governmental Organisation
NRF	Nature Reserve Fund
OECD	Organisation for Economic Co-operation and Development
OECMs	Other Effective Area-Based Conservation Measures
SACs	Special Areas of Conservation
SAP	Strategic Action Plan
SBSTTA	Subsidiary Body on Scientific, Technical and Technological Advice
SDG	Sustainable Development Goal
SEA	Strategic Environmental Assessment
SEI	State Environmental Inspectorate of Ukraine
SFM	Sustainable Forest Management
SPAs	Special Protection Areas
SPMS	Strategic Plan for Migratory Species
TEU	Treaty on European Union
TFEU	Treaty on the Functioning of the European Union
UN	United Nations
UNCG	Ukrainian Nature Conservation Group
UNEP	United Nations Environment Programme
UNESCO	United Nations Education, Scientific and Culture Organization
UNFCCC	United Nations Framework Convention on Climate Change
UNGA	United Nations General Assembly
WWF	World Wildlife Fund

INTRODUCTION

Biological diversity or biodiversity is commonly defined in international law as variability among living organisms, including diversity within species, between species, and of ecosystems.[1] The relatively recent international concern for nature protection (and subsequently specifically biodiversity), which led to the conclusion of the international treaties in this sphere, dates to the 1970s, culminating in the adoption of the Convention on Biological Diversity at the 1992 United Nations Conference on Environment and Development in Rio de Janeiro. As of 2025, the present pace of biodiversity loss, often characterised as mass extinction, continues to be alarming, forming part of the so-called 'triple planetary crisis' and amounting to one of the most pressing global environmental issues of our time. Counteracting this trend requires research across various disciplines and action at multiple levels, with a particular focus on the areas that constitute biodiversity hotspots.

This work focuses on the forest ecosystems of the Ukrainian Carpathians, which are among the biodiversity hotspots in Ukraine and Europe. While constituting about 6 % of Europe's territory, Ukraine contains approximately 35 % of its species diversity.[2] The forests of the Ukrainian Carpathians harbour numerous species protected by key international biodiversity treaties, and the areas of old-growth forests here are among the largest in Europe. At the same time, this region is significantly understudied compared to other mountainous regions in Europe. Among all disciplines that deal with biodiversity, the present study focuses on the domains of law, ethics, and policy.

The relevance of the topic is further underscored by the need to analyse the most recent developments in global, regional, subregional, and Ukrainian legal regulations on biodiversity, which have not yet been comprehensively reflected in the scholarly literature. The quest for better legal

1 Cf. "Convention on Biological Diversity," opened for signature June 5, 1992, United Nations Treaty Series 1760 p. 79, https://treaties.un.org/pages/ViewDetails.aspx?src=TREATY&mtdsg_no=XXVII-8&chapter=27, Article 2 [CBD].

2 Ministry of Ecology and Natural Resources of Ukraine, *Fifth national report of Ukraine to the Convention on Biological Diversity*, (Kyiv, 2015), https://www.cbd.int/doc/world/ua/ua-nr-05-en.pdf, 3.

regulation of biodiversity is an ongoing process that warrants research on the current state of such regulation. One of the key global developments is the Kunming-Montreal Global Biodiversity Framework (GBF), adopted by the Conference of the Parties to the Convention on Biological Diversity in December 2022, which suggests renewed global directions of action on biodiversity. The GBF is also crucial to other global, regional, and subregional biodiversity treaties to ensure coordination and avoid duplication of efforts. Its impact, accordingly, extends to the Carpathian Convention, where, moreover, a separate Carpathian Biodiversity Framework (CBF) was created in 2023. At the national level, Ukrainian biodiversity-related legislation has undergone significant developments in recent years, particularly following the 2013–2014 Revolution of Dignity and the resulting strong focus on European integration, leading to the need to approximate its legislation to the EU law. Moreover, Russia's full-scale aggression against Ukraine brought new challenges to the protection of the biodiversity of the forest ecosystems of the Ukrainian Carpathians. Nevertheless, these developments have received scant attention in academic literature to date. Moreover, in light of the sustainable development paradigm, it is not enough to focus simply on the environmental aspect of biodiversity. Instead, a broader consideration of social and economic factors should be undertaken. All of these factors justify the need to generate knowledge on the framework for biodiversity protection at the intersection between ethical, legal and policy components as applicable to the forest ecosystems of the Ukrainian Carpathians as a territory with shared environmental, legal, socio-political, cultural and religious backgrounds.

In the present work, it was endeavoured to analyse biodiversity protection of the forest ecosystems of the Ukrainian Carpathians in an interdisciplinary way at the intersection of law (international law and Ukrainian law), ethics (including Christian environmental ethics), and policy. The legal perspective of biodiversity protection constitutes the primary focus of the present thesis. At the same time, the perspective of ethics is studied both as a foundation for the development of legal provisions, informing their interpretation, and as a factor contributing to their implementation. The policies for biodiversity protection are studied as approaches reflected in the laws currently in force[3] and as possible future directions of action to enhance biodiversity protection based on the best practices, identified at global, regional, and subregional levels. Within the domain of Public In-

3 As of December 2024.

ternational Law, the present work contributes to conceptualising the novel area of International Biodiversity Law by analysing (customary) principles, provisions of the global and regional instruments, and recent strategic documents adopted by the Conferences of the Parties of these instruments. From the perspective of Ukrainian law, it presents the analysis of the most recent legislative changes in nature protection legislation and forestry as they relate to the Ukrainian Carpathians and expands the understanding of the current stage of Ukraine's implementation of international obligations on biodiversity. Exploration of the concepts of Christian environmental ethics (focusing on the teachings of the Catholic Church and the Orthodox Church of Ecumenical Patriarchate) in conjunction with their practical implications also potentially offers novel interdisciplinary insights. Although the breadth of the subject matter does not allow for a fully exhaustive analysis of all the components within these three dimensions, an attempt was made to construct a framework encompassing essential elements within them at the current stage.

The central research question of the present dissertation is: What framework for biodiversity protection in the forest ecosystems of the Ukrainian Carpathians, comprising ethical, legal, and policy components, is currently in place, and how could it be improved against the background of best practices on a global, regional, and subregional level?

The following research objectives were identified as means for expanding the understanding of the framework at the intersection of ethics, laws, and policies on biodiversity protection applicable to the forest ecosystems of the Ukrainian Carpathians:

- to explore the ethical foundations of biodiversity protection in environmental ethics and international law;
- to describe laws and policies on biodiversity protection on the global, regional, and subregional levels as applicable to the Ukrainian Carpathians;
- to characterise the biodiversity of forest ecosystems in the Ukrainian Carpathians in a socio-economic context;
- to depict legal and institutional landscapes of the biodiversity protection of forest ecosystems in the Ukrainian Carpathians according to Ukrainian legislation;
- to identify specific issues, risks, threats, and challenges to biodiversity protection in the forest ecosystems of the Ukrainian Carpathians;
- to assess the implementation of the international obligations of Ukraine according to the key biodiversity treaties;

- to present an overview of the best practices and recommendations on biodiversity protection in the forest and mountainous ecosystems, including the existing practices in the national parks within the German federal state of Bavaria;
- to investigate the potential synergies between biodiversity protection and related legal regimes, including climate change and human rights;
- to portray Christian environmental ethics as a potential moral underpinning of biodiversity protection in the Ukrainian Carpathians;
- to suggest the lines of change in the legal, policy, and ethical components for enhanced protection of the biodiversity of forest ecosystems of the Ukrainian Carpathians.

The following methodological approach has been applied. The qualitative research methodology constitutes the basis of this study, including mainly case studies and analytical methods. The case study has been used as an overarching method to gain a comprehensive understanding of biodiversity protection in the forest ecosystems of the Ukrainian Carpathians at the intersection of ethics, law, and policy. The research has been conducted based on both primary and secondary data. The primary data has been collected by means of semi-structured research interviews. In particular, 24 semi-structured research interviews were conducted in September 2022 with various actors involved in biodiversity protection in the Ukrainian Carpathians, including local residents in villages in the vicinity of Kolomyia (Kosiv district of the Ivano-Frankivsk region, Ukraine), employees of the National Natural Park "Hutsulshchyna", high-ranking civil servants of the Ivano-Frankivsk Regional Forestry and Hunting Management Authority and Lviv Regional Forestry and Hunting Management Authority, foresters working in the commercially-exploited biodiversity-rich areas of the Ukrainian Carpathians, and experts from the leading nature-protection non-governmental organisations in Ukraine. In addition, semi-structured interviews with three employees of the two national parks in Bavaria (Berchtesgaden and Bavarian Forest) were conducted in December 2023. In accordance with the preferences of the interviewees, the majority of the interviews have been anonymised. The list of the typical questions and the categories of interviewees are presented in Annex A and Annex B accordingly. These semi-structured interviews were used to understand the status quo of biodiversity protection in the Ukrainian Carpathians in the socio-economic context, including ethical attitudes of different actors, the institutional landscape for biodiversity protection, issues deserving special attention, and risks, threats, and challenges to the biodiversity protection in the specific context of the Ukrainian Carpathians as well as for studying the existing practices in the Bavarian national parks. The collected data has been mainly analysed qualitatively. Doctrinal legal research and document analysis methods have been applied to establish current legal and policy frameworks for biodiversity protection as applicable to the forest ecosystems of the Ukrainian Carpathians. Document analysis and content analysis methods have also been used to explore the ethical foundations of biodiversity protection in environmental ethics, international law, and Christian environmental ethics. Document and policy analysis methods have been utilised to choose the most suitable practices among the range of best practices and recommendations on forest and mountainous biodiversity at the global, regional, and subregional levels.

This manuscript comprises three chapters, where Chapter I primarily addresses the international setting, Chapter II is dedicated to Ukrainian realities, and Chapter III interweaves both international and domestic dimensions. The chapters are structured as follows:

Chapter I begins by covering the ethical foundations of biodiversity protection in environmental ethics and international law, provides an overview of the (customary) principles and key provisions of the international treaties governing biodiversity and applicable to the Ukrainian Carpathians, and sketches the EU laws and policies on biodiversity.

Chapter II depicts the environmental and socio-economic contexts of the Ukrainian Carpathians, presents the current legal and institutional landscape of biodiversity protection in the forest ecosystems of the Ukrainian Carpathians based on the Ukrainian legislation and highlights the specific issues, risks, threats, and challenges to biodiversity protection in the forest ecosystems of the Ukrainian Carpathians.

Chapter III summarises the state of implementation of the key international obligations regarding Carpathian forest biodiversity in Ukraine and explores best practices, recommendations, and trends that could be applicable to the forest biodiversity of the Ukrainian Carpathians. These include, among others, examples of national parks in Bavaria, the search for synergies between biodiversity protection and related legal regimes, and the ideas of Christian environmental ethics. Finally, the lines of change for enhancing the protection of the biodiversity of forest ecosystems of the Ukrainian Carpathians are suggested.

CHAPTER 1. AN OVERVIEW OF THE ETHICS, LAWS AND POLICIES INFORMING THE BIODIVERSITY PROTECTION OF FOREST ECOSYSTEMS IN THE UKRAINIAN CARPATHIANS

1.1. Preliminary remarks

Humanity's concern for the environment in general and biodiversity in particular is a relatively recent phenomenon. Although some efforts to conserve what is now called 'biodiversity' have been there for thousands of years or could be traced at least to the late nineteenth century, it was not until the early 1970s that the concern for nature preservation became a widely discussed issue on a global scale.[4] Thus, international environmental law as such and 'international biodiversity law' in particular are much 'younger' areas compared, for instance, to diplomatic and consular law, international humanitarian law, or the law of the sea. Not focusing on the full picture of historical developments in the international regulation of biodiversity, well described in the scholarly literature,[5] this chapter deals primarily with the laws, policy directions and ethics behind biodiversity protection contained in the contemporary international law instruments applicable to the Ukrainian Carpathians.

The term 'biological diversity' or its shortened version 'biodiversity' is even more recent than concern for the environment as such. The contemporary understanding of 'biodiversity' used in this thesis stems from Article 2 of the 1992 Convention on Biological Diversity (CBD), where 'biological diversity' is defined as "variability among living organisms from all sources, including inter alia, terrestrial, marine and other aquatic ecosystems and

4 Braulio Ferreira de Souza Dias and Kathryn Garforth, "Historical perspectives on the challenge of biodiversity conservation," in *Biodiversity and Nature Protection Law*, ed. Elisa Morgera and Jona Razzaque (Cheltenham: Edward Elgar, 2017), 14; Alexander Gillespie, *Conservation, Biodiversity and International Law,* New horizons in environmental and energy law (Cheltenham: Edward Elgar, 2011), 3.

5 See Dias and Garforth, "Historical perspectives on the challenge of biodiversity conservation"; David Hunter, James Salzman, and Durwood Zaelke, *International Environmental Law and Policy*, 6th ed., University Casebook Series (St. Paul, MN: Foundation Press, 2022), 976 – 977.

the ecological complexes of which they are part; this includes diversity within species, between species and of ecosystems".[6]

Conceptually, the term 'biodiversity' has emerged mainly as the term 'wildlife' was regarded as too narrow, whereas the term 'nature' was regarded as too vague.[7] While being a proxy for 'nature', 'biodiversity' has the advantage of being objectively measured, demonstrating nature's economic value, thus ensuring political will for conserving all life.[8] As a result of the CBD's wide acceptance, 'biodiversity' became a new key concept to address 'all living organisms and their intricate interdependence' and regulate human actions towards it.[9]

This seemingly succinct term, however, contains a whole range of conceptual and practical challenges, which are well described in the scholarly literature.[10] Moreover, humanity's knowledge, even about the number of species (not to mention all the intricacies of their mutual interactions and interdependencies), remains far from being complete.[11]

The term 'protection' is used in this work as a generic or overarching term encompassing more narrow notions of 'conservation' and 'preservation' of biodiversity, as well as mitigation of threats to biodiversity.

---

6 CBD, Article 2.

7 Daniel P. Faith, "Biodiversity", in *The Stanford Encyclopedia of Philosophy*, ed. Edward N. Zalta and Uri Nodelman, Fall 2023 (Metaphysics Research Lab, Stanford University, 2023), https://plato.stanford.edu/archives/fall2023/entries/biodiversity/; See also Uta Eser, „Naturschutz," in *Handbuch Umweltethik*, ed. Konrad Ott, Jan Dierks, and Lieske Voget-Kleschin (Stuttgart: J.B. Metzler Verlag, 2016), 45–46; Thomas Potthast und Margarita Berg „Biodiversität" in *Handbuch Umweltethik*, ed. Konrad Ott, Jan Dierks, and Lieske Voget-Kleschin (Stuttgart: J.B. Metzler Verlag, 2016), 240–242.

8 Hunter, Salzman, and Zaelke, *International Environmental Law and Policy*, 978, 980.

9 Alexandre Charles Kiss and Dinah L. Shelton, *Guide to International Environmental Law* (Leiden: Nijhoff, 2007), 178.

10 See Georg Toepfer, "On the Impossibility and Dispensability of Defining 'Biodiversity'," in *From Assessing to Conserving Biodiversity: Conceptual and Practical Challenges*, ed. Elena Casetta, Jorge Marques da Silva, and Davide Vecchi (Cham: Springer International Publishing, 2019), 341–51; Yves Meinard, Sylvain Coq, and Bernhard Schmid "The Vagueness of 'Biodiversity' and Its Implications in Conservation Practice," in *From Assessing to Conserving Biodiversity: Conceptual and Practical Challenges*, ed. Elena Casetta, Jorge Marques da Silva, and Davide Vecchi (Cham: Springer International Publishing, 2019), 353–74; Sahotra Sarkar "What Should 'Biodiversity' Be?," in *From Assessing to Conserving Biodiversity: Conceptual and Practical Challenges*, ed. Elena Casetta, Jorge Marques da Silva, and Davide Vecchi (Cham: Springer International Publishing, 2019), 375–99; Faith, "Biodiversity".

11 Kiss and Shelton, *Guide to International Environmental Law*, 179.

The international treaties subject to the analysis in this work have been selected on the basis of Ukraine's membership in them and their relevance to the biodiversity of the forest ecosystems in the Ukrainian Carpathian Mountains. Ukraine is a State Party to a number of the biodiversity-related international instruments or 'biodiversity treaties'.[12] Among them, those that are of immediate relevance to the protection of biodiversity of the forest ecosystems of the Ukrainian Carpathians include: the Convention on Biological Diversity, the Convention on International Trade in Endangered Species of Wild Fauna and Flora (CITES or Washington Convention), the Convention on the Conservation of Migratory Species of Wild Animals (CMS or Bonn Convention), the Convention Concerning the Protection of the World Cultural and Natural Heritage (World Heritage Convention), the Convention on the Conservation of European Wildlife and Natural Habitats (Bern Convention), and the Framework Convention on the Protection and Sustainable Development of the Carpathians (Carpathian Convention). In addition, out of the global biodiversity treaties, Ukraine is a State Party to the Convention on Wetlands of International Importance especially as Waterfowl Habitat (Ramsar Convention), as some of the Ramsar Sites are located in the Ukrainian Carpathians.[13] However, as this convention is centred on the wetlands, its discussion is not included in this thesis, which focuses on forest ecosystems' biodiversity. Furthermore, on the regional level, the Council of Europe Landscape Convention, the Convention for the Protection of Human Rights and Fundamental Freedoms (European Convention on Human Rights) and the European Social Charter are of some relevance for the protection of biodiversity, but they do not establish direct obligations in this regard, and accordingly, are not described in detail in this thesis.

Within the ambition to join the European Union (EU), Ukraine has undertaken to approximate its legislation to a number of legislative acts of

12 The term 'biodiversity treaties' is used throughout dissertation in the meaning suggested by Veit Koester, denoting "international treaties that are concentrated on the protection or conservation (leaving aside the definition of those terms) of biodiversity or specific components of biodiversity". See Veit Koester "Environmental principles and concepts in biodiversity treaties," in *Principles of Environmental Law*, ed. Ludwig Krämer and Emanuela Orlando, (Cheltenham: Edward Elgar, 2018), 539.

13 See "Ukraine," The Convention on Wetlands, accessed November 11, 2024, https://www.ramsar.org/country-profile/ukraine.

the EU, including those in the environmental domain.[14] Even though this is still an ongoing process and the accession of Ukraine to the EU remains a future perspective, EU legislation and policies are gradually gaining relevance for Ukraine. They, therefore, are also examined in this chapter as part of the normative framework on a regional level.

This Chapter begins by exploring various grounds of biodiversity protection in environmental ethics and philosophy, paying attention to a broader category of 'nature' and a neighbouring category of 'wilderness'. After that, the focus narrows to analysing the ethical grounds behind biodiversity protection, as enshrined in international law on biodiversity. Ultimately, the provisions of the global and regional biodiversity treaties applicable to the Ukrainian Carpathians, as well as the EU legislative acts and policies, are examined.

1.2. An overview of the ethical foundations of biodiversity protection in environmental ethics and international law

1.2.1. The key traditional and emerging ethical foundations of biodiversity protection

Before delving into the specific legal norms and policies on biodiversity protection, it is crucial to explore its ethical foundations, answering the question of why humanity cares about biodiversity. The differing answers to this question can have different practical implications, leading to differences in legal norms and policy designs, as well as varied approaches to their implementation.[15] The clear ethical justifications seem to be beneficial for building a public consensus as to the protection of biodiversity. Moreover, as Sahotra Sarkar points out, in cases where the mere argument is not enough, the measures needed to conserve biodiversity may require coercion, and accordingly need to be supported by good ethical justifications.[16]

---

14 See "Environment", Mission of Ukraine to the European Union, April 15, 2021, https://ukraine-eu.mfa.gov.ua/en/2633-relations/galuzeve-spivrobitnictvo/ohorona-dovkillya.

15 Cf. Andrew Bosworth et al., *Ethics and biodiversity,* Ethics and Climate Change in Asia and the Pacific (ECCAP) Project, Working Group 16 Report (UNESCO Bangkok, 2011), 9.

16 Sahotra Sarkar, *Biodiversity and Environmental Philosophy: An Introduction* (Cambridge, UK: Cambridge University Press, 2005), 46.

The question of 'why conserve biodiversity' has traditionally been at the core of environmental ethics.[17] Since the emergence of environmental ethics as an academic field in 1960–1970s,[18] various grounds for biodiversity protection have been suggested in doctrine and mentioned in the international legal instruments on biodiversity.[19] The main broad categories of biodiversity's value and reasons for its protection have been framed as a contrasting juxtaposition of anthropocentric and non-anthropocentric arguments[20] or of instrumental and intrinsic value.[21] Apart from that, mixed approaches have been identified.[22] Furthermore, the belonging of particular concepts to these broad groups and the meaning of these terms can vary, as can the understanding of the 'value' itself.[23]

The instrumental value of nature (sometimes also called 'pragmatic value'[24]) is the least questioned category (especially in comparison with the 'intrinsic value').[25] It denotes the value deriving from the human use of biodiversity, such as food, medicinal properties, or timber production.[26] This category is based on the anthropocentric premise, where humanity acts as the valuer towards nature ('the valuee') and is entitled to exploit it.[27]

17 Sarkar, *Biodiversity and Environmental Philosophy*, 45.

18 Kristin Schrader-Frechette, "Environmental Ethics," in *The Oxford Handbook of Practical Ethics*, ed. Hugh LaFollette, Oxford University Press, (Oxford New York, NY: Oxford University Press, 2003), 189; Andrew Brennan and Norva Y. S. Lo, "Environmental Ethics", *The Stanford Encyclopedia of Philosophy* (Summer 2024 Edition), ed. Edward N. Zalta and Uri Nodelman, Fall 2023 (Metaphysics Research Lab, Stanford University, 2024), https://plato.stanford.edu/archives/sum2024/entries/ethics-environmental/.

19 The international legal instruments are addressed in the next subchapter.

20 Alexander Gillespie, *International Environmental Law, Policy, and Ethics*, 2nd ed. (Oxford: Oxford University Press, 2014), 2–3.

21 Mattia Fosci and Tom West, "In Whose Interest? Instrumental and Intrinsic Value in Biodiversity Law," in *Research Handbook on Biodiversity and Law*, ed. Michael Bowman, Peter G. G. Davies, and Edward Goodwin (Cheltenham: Edward Elgar Publishing, 2016), 55.

22 Schrader-Frechette, "Environmental Ethics," 189–91; Sarkar, *Biodiversity and Environmental Philosophy*, 75–105.

23 Bosworth et al., *Ethics and biodiversity*, 24–26.

24 Thomas E. Lovejoy, "Biodiversity: An inordinate fondness for living things," in *Routledge Handbook of Religion and Ecology*, ed. Willis Jenkins, Mary Evelyn Tucker, and John A. Grim, (Abingdon New York (N. Y.): Routledge Earthscan from Routledge, 2017), 250.

25 Joshua S. Duclos, *Wilderness, Morality, and Value* (Lanham (Md.): Lexington books, 2022), 57.

26 Fosci and West, "In Whose Interest?," 55.

27 Fosci and West, "In Whose Interest?," 55.

Instrumental value is said to either comprise only material and productive use of biodiversity, or it can also include non-productive, non-material uses and non-uses (such as aesthetic, religious, cultural, recreational and psychological considerations).[28] One of the notable implications of the instrumental value is the ability to measure the nature protection interest against other societal objectives, allowing for the evaluation of benefits to humans in the decision-making process.[29]

The valuation process itself, however, might be challenging, facing both methodological and cognitive limitations and thus not leading to a balanced outcome.[30] Economic valuation, being mostly focused on the financial worth of the resources used in productive activities, falls short of defining the whole instrumental value of nature.[31] One of the approaches to better assess the instrumental value of nature is the concept of 'ecosystem services', encompassing a broader range of factors, including non-excludable and non-rivalrous ecological benefits.[32] While this approach might also be criticised for 'putting a price on nature', it is helpful for taking nature's value into account during decision-making.[33] The cognitive limitation concerns humans' "limited capacity to anticipate the environmental consequences of certain activities", such as the cumulative impact of numerous individual actions, or the impact caused over time.[34] This is particularly true with regard to biodiversity, where it might be hard to predict future negative consequences, coupled with a temptation to disregard them altogether for the sake of immediate economic gain. As science advances, however, so might also be the protection of species justified by the instrumental value. In particular, as interconnections among different organisms are better understood by scientists and explained to the public and decision-makers, even those species not directly useful to humans or the whole network should be considered, especially in light of the precautionary approach.[35]

28 Fosci and West, "In Whose Interest?," 55–56.
29 Fosci and West, "In Whose Interest?," 61.
30 Fosci and West, "In Whose Interest?," 62.
31 Fosci and West, "In Whose Interest?," 62–63.
32 Fosci and West, "In Whose Interest?," 64.
33 Lovejoy, "Biodiversity: An inordinate fondness for living things," 251–252.
34 Fosci and West, "In Whose Interest?," 65.
35 Fosci and West, "In Whose Interest?," 65–66.

Intrinsic value is one of the most problematic concepts in environmental ethics.[36] The concept of intrinsic value (or sometimes the interchangeably used notion 'inherent value'[37]) could be traced back to George Edward Moore or even to Immanuel Kant.[38] Interestingly enough, Moore suggested a definition of it (although not in the context of environmental protection) back in 1922,[39] yet the search for understanding and defining it remained relevant for another hundred years, which is evidenced, for instance, by the 2022 contribution to this topic by Joshua Duclos.[40] As Mattia Fosci and Tom West note, despite its common use and general understanding of intrinsic value as of value possessed by nature without regard to human considerations, there is no agreed-upon definition of it in environmental ethics.[41] Sarkar also notes that this term has been used in the environmental ethics literature 'sloppily'.[42] There are indeed numerous ways to define and understand intrinsic value, and these are not spared from critique. According to John O'Neill, there are three meanings of 'intrinsic value': non-instrumental value, that is, an end in itself; value related to intrinsic proprieties as opposed to extrinsic ones; and objective value, the one that exists independently from a human valuer.[43] Fosci and West combine these three meanings into one definition for the sake of clarity while discussing biodiversity law.[44] Duclos takes a different approach and suggests four distinct types of intrinsic value while talking of the intrinsic value of the wilderness.[45] These are: (1) intrinsic value as ultimate, non-instrumental value; (2) intrinsic value as morally considerable; (3) intrinsic value as non-relational value; and (4) intrinsic value as value independent of valuers.[46] Duclos aptly explains why the third and fourth of these meanings are not suitable for justifying wilderness preservation (mainly due to methodologi-

36 Duclos, *Wilderness, Morality, and Value*, 47, 57.

37 See Michael Bowman, "Biodiversity, Intrinsic Value, and the Definition and Valuation of Environmental Harm," in *Environmental Damage in International and Comparative Law: Problems of Definition and Valuation*, ed. Michael Bowman, and Alan Boyle (Oxford: Oxford University Press, 2002), 41–61.

38 Gillespie, *International Environmental Law, Policy, and Ethics*, 113.

39 Gillespie, *International Environmental Law, Policy, and Ethics*, 113.

40 Duclos, *Wilderness, Morality, and Value*, 45–74.

41 Fosci and West, "In Whose Interest?," 56.

42 Sarkar, *Biodiversity and Environmental Philosophy*, p. 53.

43 John O'Neill, "The Varieties of Intrinsic Value," *The Monist*, 75, Issue 2, (April 1992): 119 https://doi.org/10.5840/monist19927527.

44 Fosci and West, "In whose interest?," 56.

45 Duclos, *Wilderness, Morality, and Value*, 48–50.

46 Duclos, *Wilderness, Morality, and Value*, 48–50.

cal and epistemic difficulties).[47] Even though 'wilderness' is a different category than 'biodiversity', the logic behind this argumentation on intrinsic value may well apply *mutatis mutandis* to biodiversity.[48]

In the case of biodiversity, those advocating for it based on the 'intrinsic value', treat species or other components as a 'repository of intrinsic value' that have to be spared from harm, and conclude that all of the biodiversity components deserve protection regardless of whether they bring any direct or indirect value to humans.[49] Sarkar talks of the two concepts of 'intrinsic value' in this regard, that may also be used simultaneously: the first one (similar to O'Neill's second meaning and Duclos's third meaning) is related to the entity's internal proprieties as contrasted with the extrinsic ones (to the extrinsic dimension belong relations with other entities); and the second one is the entity's value irrespective of its usefulness for other entities, that is contrasted with the instrumental value (and bears similarity to the first meaning of O'Neill and first and second meanings of Duclos combined).[50] According to Sarkar, the first concept of intrinsic value could support the justifications for biodiversity protection based on such characteristics as morphological or behavioural complexity, endangerment, endemism, fragility or rarity, but it is questionable whether it simultaneously carries any ethical implications, so that it can assist in formulating the ethical obligations vis-a-vis biodiversity.[51] Therefore, the second sense has been more widespread and has been viewed from a variety of angles. Different theories have been suggested with respect to locating the value,[52] that is, explaining to what non-human creatures and how exactly it applies, as well as what ethical implications it entails, especially in light of its parallel to the inherent human dignity.[53] It could mean, for instance, a demand for equal treatment of all the entities endowed with this type of value or, for example, the need for action to rectify a harm caused to such an entity, so

47 Duclos, *Wilderness, Morality, and Value*, 56–61.

48 'Wilderness' might be understood as one of the dimensions of biodiversity, as it is mentioned in the CBD among the conservation targets for biodiversity – See Annex I to CBD. It should not be used as a synonym to biodiversity though – See Sarkar, *Biodiversity and Environmental Philosophy*, 38.

49 Sarkar, *Biodiversity and Environmental Philosophy*, 55.

50 Sarkar, *Biodiversity and Environmental Philosophy*, 53–55.

51 Sarkar, *Biodiversity and Environmental Philosophy*, 56–58.

52 See Fosci and West, "In whose interest?," 68 [the search for 'locus of valuational activity'].

53 See Sarkar, *Biodiversity and Environmental Philosophy*, 58–74, Gillespie, *International Environmental Law, Policy, and Ethics*, 114.

that it can continue to 'pursue its own good'.[54] The practical implications of the intrinsic (inherent) value remain to be a subject of debate, and their consequences for international environmental law have not been clearly established yet.[55]

The characterisation of the intrinsic value in the second sense described by Sarkar and Duclos (as morally considerable) is closely related to the debate on anthropocentrism and non-anthropocentrism. Anthropocentrism in a strict sense assumes moral superiority of humans over other beings, and thus human value and the value of humans are considered to be paramount.[56] Non-anthropocentrism does not assume general moral superiority of humans over other beings and does not hold that all moral deliberations should be concerned with what is valuable for human beings. There are three main versions of non-anthropocentrism in environmental ethics: sentientism, biocentrism and ecocentrism.[57] A concise overview of these concepts is provided below, drawing principally from the analysis presented by Duclos.

Proponents of sentientism hold that only sentient beings are morally considerable. There are at least three versions of it: according to Peter Singer capacity to experience pleasure and pain is a decisive factor for moral considerability. Joel Feinberg and Tom Regan use more restrictive approaches. According to Feinberg, a category of interest is important for moral standing, requiring at least some cognitive capacity to consciously imagine and aim at a being's future. For Regan, morally considerable creatures have to fulfil his 'subject of life' criterion, involving feelings, memories, desires, a sense of one's future and the capacity to care about one's own welfare.[58]

Biocentrism is the view that all living beings are morally considerable. It is broader than sentientism, as it includes nonsentient organisms. In a broad sense, biocentrism means moral consideration of all life and is related to Albert Schweitzer's principle of 'reverence for life'.[59] One of its subtypes, associated with Paul Taylor and holding that all living beings are worthy of the same respect as human beings, received the name of

54 Gillespie, *International Environmental Law, Policy, and Ethics*, 115.

55 Cf. Fosci and West, "In whose interest?," 72.

56 Duclos, *Wilderness, Morality, and Value*, 51.

57 Duclos, *Wilderness, Morality, and Value*, 51–52.

58 Duclos, *Wilderness, Morality, and Value*, 52–53; See also Gillespie, *International Environmental Law, Policy, and Ethics*, 111–113.

59 Bosworth et al., *Ethics and biodiversity*, 12.

'biocentric egalitarianism'.[60] Other proponents of biocentrism include Kenneth Goodpaster and Robin Attfield.[61] Biocentrism criticises sentientism by treating sentience as only one of the possible types of biological adaptation and by rejecting sentientists' stance that the capacity for experiencing is an inevitable condition for having interests. For biocentrists, every being has an interest in having its good satisfied without regard to being conscious of this good; thus, for instance, a plant has an interest in having access to water, nutrients, and sunlight.[62]

Ecocentrism attributes moral considerability to ecosystems. It is different from biocentrism as it is concerned with the good of some ecological system as a whole as an essential factor of the good of individual organisms. Ecocentrism takes into account the interconnectedness of life and the well-being of a community, which comprises elements like soil, water, plants, and animals. Its followers include Aldo Leopold (with his famous 'land ethic') and Holmes Rolston. Interestingly, in Rolston's view, intrinsic/instrumental classification is inadequate to describe the value of ecosystems, and he suggests 'systemic value' instead. In his view, an ecosystem is a 'value producer' rather than a 'value owner' as it contributes to organismic life, but also 'the stability, integrity and beauty of biotic communities are what are most fundamentally to be conserved'.[63]

While biocentrism criticises sentientism, biocentrism and ecocentrism are also subject to critique. Biocentrism is criticised for its interpretation of the 'interest', as it might potentially end up including all sorts of objects that have good of their own.[64] Furthermore, neither sentientism nor biocentrism suggests a sound practical approach to prioritising in case of a collision of interests.[65] Practical concerns associated with ecocentrism include, for instance, vagueness of the 'ecosystem', artificiality of understanding ecosystems as independent entities, and 'environmental fascism', meaning that the good or right of an individual becomes subservient to the good or

---

60 Bosworth et al., *Ethics and biodiversity*, 13.

61 Duclos, *Wilderness, Morality, and Value*, 53–54.

62 Duclos, *Wilderness, Morality, and Value*; See also Fosci and West, "In whose interest?," 68–70.

63 Duclos, *Wilderness, Morality, and Value*, 54–56, See also Fosci and West, "In whose interest?," 70–72.

64 Duclos, *Wilderness, Morality, and Value*, 61–66.

65 Christopher D. Stone, "Ethics and International Environmental Law," in *The Oxford Handbook of International Environmental Law*, ed. Daniel Bodansky, Jutta Brunnée, and Ellen Hey, 1st ed. (Oxford: Oxford University Press, 2012), 299–300.

right of the ecosystem.[66] Apart from that, all three approaches seem to be difficult or even impossible to maintain literally.[67]

In addition, other approaches have been described in scholarly literature, including 'enlightened' or 'prudential' anthropocentrism, which attributes 'eudaemonic intrinsic value' to nature;[68] 'holism' as related to ecocentrism, but sometimes identified as a separate category;[69] 'deep ecology' as a set of principles distinguishing it from the 'shallow' one;[70] and 'cosmocentrism'.[71]

There have been various attempts to present a coherent scheme of the linkages among various ideas on nature's value, for instance, 'Map of nature ethics' by Angelika Krebs.[72] After the initial division of nature's value into instrumental and intrinsic, the latter is further divided into the categories of eudemonic intrinsic value and moral intrinsic value. Eudemonic intrinsic value comprises three categories: aesthetic value, holiness (sense of life), and "Heimatwert" (in German) – the one dealing with identity and sense of home. Moral intrinsic value is divided into three arguments: based on the suffering of nature (that is, sentientism), purposefulness or teleology of nature (similar to biocentrism), and the entire nature (which could be equated to ecocentrism or holism). According to this scheme, instrumental value is interpreted narrowly and includes 'basic needs of humanity', whereas aesthetic appreciation and other eudemonic dimensions of value are considered to form a part of nature's intrinsic rather than instrumental value. These two categories are, however, grouped together into the 'anthropocentric value' while the three categories of 'moral intrinsic value' are grouped into 'physiocentric' (non-anthropocentric) value. This scheme aptly captures what is meant by 'enlightened' anthropocentrism.

There is, however, a question in a recent scholarly debate as to the extent to which anthropocentrism can be expanded or reconciled with the intrin-

66 Duclos, *Wilderness, Morality, and Value*, 66–70.

67 Cf. Stone, "Ethics and International Environmental Law," 300.

68 Bosworth et al., *Ethics and biodiversity*, 11–12, citing Angelika Krebs and Bernard Williams, *Ethics of Nature: A Map*, Perspektiven Der Analytischen Philosophie 22 (Berlin: W. de Gruyter, 1999).

69 Jan Dierks „Holismus," in *Handbuch Umweltethik*, ed. Konrad Ott, Jan Dierks, and Lieske Voget-Kleschin (Stuttgart: J.B. Metzler Verlag, 2016), 177–183.

70 Bosworth et al., *Ethics and biodiversity*, 14–15; Terence Ball, "Deep Ecology," *Encyclopedia.com.* (May 2018), https://www.encyclopedia.com/environment/encyclopedias-almanacs-transcripts-and-maps/deep-ecology.

71 Bosworth et al., *Ethics and biodiversity*, 15.

72 As depicted in Markus Vogt, *Christliche Umweltethik: Grundlagen und zentrale Herausforderungen*, (Freiburg: Herder, 2022), 328.

sic value of nature. Uta Eser considers an anthropocentrism that allows for "an intrinsically motivated protection of nature 'for its own sake'" among the possible approaches.[73] Leonie Bossert and Lena Schlegel criticise this approach, mainly by holding that anthropocentrism is, by definition, a human-centred perspective.[74] Marcus Vogt uses the term 'anthroporelational approach' to describe a relation in which humans are understood as subjects of responsibility and at the same time the recognition of the intrinsic value of animals, plants and ecosystems is not excluded. This approach is also close to Christian environmental ethics.[75] Vogt provides ten characteristics of the 'ecological enlightenment of anthropocentrism', describing the anthropocentric ethic that goes in the direction of anthroporelational approach, that is, tries to circumvent the metaphor of centre and periphery.[76] Without listing all the principles here, we would like to draw attention to the way in which nature's intrinsic or inherent value ('Eigenwert' in German) is linked there with human appreciation. The perception of nature's beauty, the preservation of nature's diversity, and the respect for the conditions needed for nature's development are, at the same time, treated as a matter of human harmony with oneself, including one's identity and self-esteem. The aesthetic, mystical and ontological qualities that are often said to be those representing nature as such are considered here to be culturally specific, as they are closely related to human perception.[77]

When it comes to Christianity in general, it has been famously criticised by Lynn White in 1967 for contributing to the ecological crisis through its anthropocentric approach.[78] There are, however, several answers to this criticism. One of the possible replies is that the problem is not anthropocentrism as such, but rather its secularised understanding, which

---

73 Uta Eser „Mit Umweltethik Gegen Pandemien? Zum Unterschied von Ethik Und Politik," *GAIA – Ecological Perspectives for Science and Society* 30, no. 4 (16 December 2021): 226, https://doi.org/10.14512/gaia.30.4.3.

74 Leonie N. Bossert and Lena M. Schlegel „Anthropozentrismus (in) Der Krise: Warum Probleme Nicht Mit Der Denkweise Gelöst Werden Können, Die Sie Auch Hervorgerufen Hat," *GAIA – Ecological Perspectives for Science and Society* 31, no. 1 (31 March 2022): 14–15, https://doi.org/10.14512/gaia.31.1.5.

75 Vogt, *Christliche Umweltethik*, 53–54.

76 Vogt, *Christliche Umweltethik*, 333–336.

77 Cf. Vogt, *Christliche Umweltethik*, 333–336.

78 Ernst M. Conradie, "Christianity: An ecological critique of Christianity and Christian critique of ecological destruction," in *Routledge Handbook of Religion and Ecology*, ed. Willis Jenkins, Mary Evelyn Tucker, and John A. Grim, (Abingdon New York (N. Y.): Routledge Earthscan from Routledge, 2017), 70.

boils down to the purely instrumental understanding of nature. Instead, in Christian anthropocentrism, the human as *Imago Dei* (image of God) shall be understood as the one endowed with the responsibility for other creatures, and not the one who can exploit nature without any limits.[79] Such a criticism, however, was helpful for exploring, revitalising and reinterpreting the forgotten meaning, for it invigorated theological debate on this matter, attempting to "retrieve the ecological wisdom embedded in the Christian tradition".[80] 'Ecological reformation' has been taking place in all of the main branches of Christianity, with a recent example being Pope Francis' encyclical letter Laudato Si' (2015), which builds on other similar statements, including those of Patriarch Bartholomew.[81] In fact, the number of publications in this field has proliferated to more than 10.000 books, articles and essays, so that various undercurrents within the environmental discourse in Christianity could be identified, yet the journey remains ongoing.[82] Chapter III of this thesis deals with the Orthodox (Ecumenical Patriarchate, relevant also for the Orthodox Church of Ukraine) and Catholic (Roman Catholic, relevant also for the Ukrainian Greek-Catholic Church) teachings, reflected in the statements of the heads of these Churches and official documents.

Some of the other interesting and relatively recent ideas in the domain of environmental ethics include the concept of 'retinity', 'new anthropocentrism' and '*homo mundanus*'. The term 'retinity', which stems from the Latin word 'rete' meaning the 'net', was coined by Wilhelm Korff to describe the general interconnectedness between the development of human civilisation and nature.[83] It includes numerous facets of connections between social, economic and natural components and avoids the model of center and periphery.[84] The concept of the 'new anthropocentrism' is related to the properties of the Anthropocene – a new geological epoch, where humanity is a power capable of shaping the earth.[85] This fact as a status quo is distinguished from the normative claim of a human to be ruler of the

---

79 Cf. Vogt, *Christliche Umweltethik*, 334.

80 Conradie, "Christianity," 71; Christian Hardmeier and Konrad Ott, „Biblische Schöpfungstheologie," in *Handbuch Umweltethik*, ed. Konrad Ott, Jan Dierks, and Lieske Voget-Kleschin (Stuttgart: J.B. Metzler Verlag, 2016), 184.

81 Conradie, "Christianity," 72.

82 See Conradie, "Christianity," 73–77.

83 Vogt, *Christliche Umweltethik*, 337.

84 Vogt, *Christliche Umweltethik*, 338–339.

85 Vogt, *Christliche Umweltethik*, 339.

Earth. Clive Hamilton wittingly admits that "[t]he problem is not that we are anthropocentric, but that we are not anthropocentric enough", denoting the irrational and unrestricted human behaviour, putting humanity itself at risk.[86] The present circumstances require, however, to restrain and restrict human activities, taking account of their environmental impact. This approach distinguishes itself from 'anthropo-supremacism', but highlights human specialness related to both power and danger, implying accompanying obligations.[87] To a certain extent, this approach is concordant with Immanuel Kant's ideas of treating animals decently for a human's sake and with David Schmidtz's view on the duties of humans towards other creatures being driven by markedly human aspirations.[88] The '*homo mundanus*' concept elaborated by Wolfgang Welsch suggests a certain extension of humanism ("from homo humanus to homo mundanus") to overcome dualistic division or disparity between a human and the world.[89]

Overall, even though the ethical stances of humanity towards biodiversity (and related broader or narrower categories) have been debated in the scholarly literature over a period of nearly 60 years, the new approaches continue to emerge, and the old ones are being redefined and reframed. A trend towards abandonment of ideas centred on an extreme narrow aspect and instead of a search for a more holistic approach, underlining human responsibility is observed. The emergence of new approaches in the philosophical domain may potentially form a ground for subsequent developments in the legal regulation of nature protection, the actual status of which is explored in the ensuing subchapters.

1.2.2. Justifications of biodiversity protection in international environmental law

The ethical stances described above are highly relevant for understanding legal instruments in the domain of international environmental law, as their development was invigorated by the ever-greater awareness of human im-

86 Clive Hamilton, *Defiant Earth: The Fate of Humans in the Anthropocene*, (Cambridge: Polity, 2017), 43, quoted in Vogt, *Christliche Umweltethik*, 339.

87 Cf. Hamilton, *Defiant Earth*, 49, 54, quoted in Vogt, *Christliche Umweltethik*, 340.

88 See Stone, "Ethics and International Environmental Law," 300–301.

89 Cf. Vogt, *Christliche Umweltethik*, 343–347; See Wolfgang Welsch, *Homo mundanus: jenseits der anthropischen Denkform der Moderne* (Weilerswist: Velbrück Wissenschaft, 2012).

pact on the natural environment. The questions like "what obligations does humankind, as a whole, owe to the natural world" belong to the fundamental types of ethical or value-centred questions, accompanying international efforts to conserve biodiversity.[90] The sources informing the answer to this question are often found outside of the strictly legal or political domain, and are related to other disciplines, in the first instance, philosophy and religion. As Alexander Gillespie puts it, the "debates about the ethical values which are utilised in this area have moved from the journals of philosophy in the 1970s to the international levels in the 1990s".[91] As Dinah Shelton notes, religious and philosophical concepts "are relevant to understanding current law and to creating new approaches to environmental protection."[92] Some kind of guidance on human stance towards the environment may be found in all major religious traditions, including Judeo-Christian tradition, Islam, and Buddhism as well as in the religious beliefs of the indigenous peoples.[93] The religious and philosophical concepts often imply individual responsibility for various reasons, such as "the benefit of other persons, of future generations, of other species, or of the processes and life-support systems of the biosphere", and this dimension of responsibility found its reflection in Principle 1 of the 1972 Declaration on the Human Environment (Stockholm Declaration).[94]

Christopher Stone talks about three ways of application of the ethics to international environmental law: issues related to the human obligations to the non-human environment; ethics among the states; and ethics among generations. He calls the first type proper 'environmental ethics', the second 'inter-national ethics' and the third 'inter-generational ethics'. In addition, Stone aptly observes the grounds for the relevance of the ethics to the

90 Farhana Yamin, "Biodiversity, Ethics and International Law," *International Affairs (Royal Institute of International Affairs 1944-)* 71, no. 3 (July 1995): 529, https://doi.org/10.2307/2624839.

91 Gillespie, *International Environmental Law, Policy, and Ethics*, 1.

92 Alexandre Kiss and Dinah L. Shelton, *International Environmental Law*, 3rd ed (Ardsley, NY: Transnational Publ, 2004), 11.

93 Kiss and Shelton, *International Environmental Law*, 11–14; See an overview of the Judeo-Christian sacred texts in Dinah Shelton, "Nature in the Bible," *Man and the Environment: Essays In Honor of Alexandre Kiss,* (Frison-Roche, 1998): 63–79, https://ssrn.com/abstract=1028357; see also Christopher D. Stone, "Do Morals Matter? The Influence of Ethics on Courts and Congress in Shaping U.S. Environmental Policies," *U.C. Davis Law Review* 37 (1) (November 2003): 42–43 https://environs.law.ucdavis.edu/sites/g/files/dgvnsk15356/files/media/documents/ENV-27-1-stone.pdf.

94 Kiss and Shelton, *International Environmental Law*, 20.

international environmental law and policy: first, as a guidance in moral reasoning when there is a need to choose among policy alternatives, second as an instrument of persuasion to choose certain option, and third as a justification of imposing a legitimate rule on others, even if they do not share the same opinion.[95]

In scholarly literature, ethical justifications behind biodiversity protection in international law are classified in various ways. For instance, Shelton, while describing the foundations of biosphere protection by means of international environmental law, groups them into categories of 'religion and philosophy', 'science', and 'economics'. The foundations belonging to the first category are further divided into religious sources, utilitarianism (or anthropocentric orientation), and equity, which comprises intra-generational, inter-generational equity (rights of future generations) and inter-species equity. The discussion on intrinsic value is placed here among the inter-species equity.[96] Gillespie, in one of his works, singles out six distinctive arguments within the anthropocentric framework: self-interest, economics, religion, aesthetics, culture and future generations, and four categories of non-anthropocentric arguments: interests of other sentient beings, all organisms that are alive, endangered species and ecosystems as a whole.[97] In another contribution, Gillespie classifies self-interest, culture, economic values, aesthetics and future generations as anthropocentric values, and sentience and humane considerations, existence values and ecosystem values as non-anthropocentric ones.[98] Accordingly, in international law, both intrinsic and instrumental value are combined.[99]

In the biodiversity treaties, the rationales for biodiversity protection are usually presented as lists of notions without their subsequent definition or detailed description. For instance, the CBD that provides one of the most exhaustive lists of justifications, admits consciousness of "the intrinsic value of biological diversity and of the ecological, genetic, social, economic, scientific, educational, cultural, recreational and aesthetic values of biological diversity and its components", "the importance of biological diversity

---

95 Stone, "Ethics and International Environmental Law," 292.

96 Kiss and Shelton, *International Environmental Law*, 11–26.

97 See Gillespie, *International Environmental Law, Policy, and Ethics.*

98 Alexander Gillespie, "Ethical Considerations," in *The Oxford Handbook of International Environmental Law*, ed. Lavanya Rajamani and Jacqueline Peel, 2nd ed. (Oxford: Oxford University Press, 2021).

99 See also Hunter, Salzman, and Zaelke, *International Environmental Law and Policy*, 982–983.

for evolution and for maintaining life sustaining systems of the biosphere" and links the conservation and sustainable use of biodiversity with "the benefit of present and future generations".[100] The 1979 Bern Convention, which has a somewhat narrower scope of subject matter and geographical application, similarly recognises that "wild flora and fauna constitute a natural heritage of aesthetic, scientific, cultural, recreational, economic and intrinsic value that needs to be preserved and handed on to future generations" and "the essential role played by wild flora and fauna in maintaining biological balances".[101] Thus, both CBD and Bern Convention recognise in their preambles the intrinsic value of biodiversity, and Bern Convention is regarded as the first international legally binding instrument to do so.[102]

The CITES recognises that "wild fauna and flora in their many beautiful and varied forms are an irreplaceable part of the natural systems of the earth which must be protected for this and the generations to come" and mentions its value "from aesthetic, scientific, cultural, recreational and economic points of view". Interestingly enough, the attribute 'ever-growing' is used to describe this value, as if it were to gain greater significance overtime.[103] The CMS uses quite similar wording to the CITES. It recognises that "wild animals in their innumerable forms are an irreplaceable part of the Earth's natural system which must be conserved for the good of mankind" and that each human generation holds the resources for future generations and thus it "has an obligation to ensure that this legacy is conserved and, where utilized, is used wisely". The CMS's authors are also conscious of the "ever growing value" of wild animals from "environmental, ecological, genetic, scientific, aesthetic, recreational, cultural, educational, social and economic points of view".[104]

Most of the justifications for biodiversity protection in international law remain anthropocentric and reflective of an instrumental approach to biodiversity. Even such instruments as CBD and Bern Convention, despite

100 CBD, Preamble.

101 "Convention on the Conservation of European Wildlife and Natural Habitats," opened for signature September 19, 1979, *European Treaty Series* No. 104, https://rm.coe.int/1680078aff, Preamble [Bern Convention].

102 Kiss and Shelton, *International Environmental Law*, 19.

103 "Convention on International Trade in Endangered Species of Wild Fauna and Flora," opened for signature March 3, 1973, *United Nations Treaty Series* 993 p. 243, https://cites.org/eng/disc/text.php, Preamble [CITES].

104 "Convention on the Conservation of Migratory Species of Wild Animals," opened for signature June 23, 1979, *United Nations Treaty Series*, 1651, https://www.cms.int/en/convention-text, Preamble [CMS].

mentioning the 'intrinsic' value, cannot be overall regarded to be 'non-anthropocentric' if their substantive provisions are analysed.[105] For instance, much of the text of the CBD refers to 'biological resources'.[106] In addition, the mention of intrinsic value in several legal sources does not resolve the lack of clarity as to its practical implications, as these instruments lack guidance on the meaning of these concepts. Such a situation opens a room for discussion as to the meaning of intrinsic value in international law through the lens of the philosophical framework described above – at least of sentientism, biocentrism and ecocentrism, none of which presents a coherent system of prioritisation in case of conflicting interests among several entities endowed with intrinsic value. It is, however, common to other areas of international law, such as human rights law, that the problem of prioritisation[107] or the disagreement on the reasons behind the protection exist.[108] The sober look at the intrinsic value might, moreover, mean that certain degree of suffering and death should be accepted as part of the natural processes, where the death of some of the constituents is inevitable for the continuous existence of the ecosystem.[109]

There are also concerns as to the dominance in the international environmental law instruments, such as CBD and CITES, of the protection of groups, such as species or ecosystems, over the individuals, as species is itself a human-defined category, the subtle boundaries of which are prone to changes and redefinitions.[110] The definition of 'biodiversity' through 'variability' among living organisms is also not free from ambiguity, making it challenging to attribute intrinsic value to it.[111]

The concepts of instrumental and intrinsic values may be closely related and mutually complementary. Indeed, neither instrumental nor intrinsic value is capable of providing an "entirely convincing ethic" on its own.[112] The intrinsic value may be translated into the need for protection and conservation of species, given the interconnectedness of "all parts of the natural web", to which humans also belong.[113] At the same time, the in-

105 Cf. Stone, "Ethics and International Environmental Law," 299.
106 Stone, "Ethics and International Environmental Law," 299.
107 See Fosci and West, "In whose interest?," 74.
108 Kiss and Shelton, *International Environmental Law*, 20.
109 Fosci and West, "In whose interest?," 75.
110 Stone, "Ethics and International Environmental Law," 298.
111 Stone, "Ethics and International Environmental Law," 299.
112 Fosci and West, "In whose interest?," 76.
113 Kiss and Shelton, *International Environmental Law*, 20.

terrelations within an ecosystem might be understood as relying on the instrumental value of its various elements, so that not only humans, but also other species benefit from the instrumental value of certain elements or processes within nature.[114] The instrumental approach in a limited sense, which tries to "evaluate everything with a common metric", is, moreover, not able to encompass all the value of nature.[115] As natural objects have not been granted a separate legal status, the integrated approach, combining nature's inherent value and features useful to humanity, could be the best foundation for environmental protection.[116] This approach, common to several international legal instruments, is particularly clearly articulated in the non-binding 1982 World Charter for Nature. Within it, the anthropocentric aim of human survival remains, but human beings are viewed as an interdependent part of the natural world, and thus all the "indispensable elements of the interrelated system" must be considered.[117]

Except for the intrinsic value and various utilitarian values of biodiversity, there are several other related legal terms of art featuring in the international instruments on biodiversity and pertaining to the anthropocentric foundations of biodiversity protection: the generations to come (future generations), common concern of mankind (humanity) and common heritage of mankind (humanity). These concepts are also occasionally classified as principles of international environmental law.[118]

The common concern (or interest) of mankind (or humanity) has been enshrined in a wider range of sources of international environmental law than those that are directly applicable to the Ukrainian Carpathians.[119] Among the sources relevant for the Ukrainian Carpathians, the cited above CMS mentions "good of mankind" as a reason for conserving the wild animals, and the CBD affirms that "the conservation of the biological diversity

114 Fosci and West, "In whose interest?," 75–76.

115 Fosci and West, "In whose interest?," 76.

116 Kiss and Shelton, *International Environmental Law*, 19–20.

117 Kiss and Shelton, *International Environmental Law*, 20.

118 Koester, "Environmental principles and concepts in biodiversity treaties," 540; Isabelle Michallet, "Equity and the interests of future generations," in *Principles of Environmental Law*, ed. Ludwig Krämer and Emanuela Orlando, (Cheltenham: Edward Elgar Publishing, 2018), 150–160; Prue Taylor "Common heritage of mankind and common concern of humankind," in *Principles of Environmental Law*, ed. Ludwig Krämer and Emanuela Orlando, (Cheltenham: Edward Elgar Publishing, 2018), 303–322.

119 Kiss and Shelton, *International Environmental Law*, 32–33.

is a common concern of humankind".[120] The recently adopted within the CBD Kunming-Montreal Global Biodiversity Framework complements this thought by stating that "reversing the loss of biological diversity, for the benefit of all living beings, is a common concern of humankind".[121] The wording of 'common concern of humankind' is also used in another Rio Convention – the Framework Convention on Climate Change.[122] This concept is said to establish "the general basis for the concerned community to act" rather than entailing specific obligations, and it must also be balanced with respect for national sovereignty.[123]

The concept of common heritage of mankind denotes certain elements beneficial to humanity as a whole, including certain objects both beyond and under national jurisdiction.[124] This concept features in the Preamble of the 1972 UNESCO Convention, which states that "parts of the cultural or natural heritage are of outstanding interest and therefore need to be preserved as part of the world heritage of mankind as a whole".[125] According to Shelton, even though this principle is not explicitly mentioned in the CBD, it is incorporated in the provisions of its Articles 6–10, which require State Parties to take measures for the conservation and sustainable use of biodiversity on their territories.[126]

---

120 CMS, Preamble; CBD, Preamble; Kiss and Shelton, *International Environmental Law*, 33–34.

121 Conference of the Parties, *Kunming-Montreal Global Biodiversity Framework*, CBD COP Decision 15/4, CBD/COP/DEC/15/4 (2022) https://www.cbd.int/doc/decisions/cop-15/cop-15-dec-04-en.pdf, Annex, Section C, § 7 (k) [*Kunming-Montreal Global Biodiversity Framework*].

122 Kiss and Shelton, *International Environmental Law*, 34; "United Nations Framework Convention on Climate Change," opened for signature May 9, 1992, *United Nations Treaty Series* 1771, p. 107, https://treaties.un.org/pages/ViewDetailsIII.aspx?src=TREATY&mtdsg_no=XXVII-7&chapter=27&Temp=mtdsg3&clang=_en [UNFCCC].

123 Kiss and Shelton, *International Environmental Law*, 34.

124 Edwin Egede, "Common Heritage of Mankind," in *Oxford Bibliographies Online: International Law*, ed. Anthony Carty (July 2014), https://doi.org/10.1093/obo/9780199796953-0109.

125 "Convention concerning the Protection of the World Cultural and Natural Heritage," opened for signature November 16, 1972, *United Nations Treaty Series* 1037 p.151, https://whc.unesco.org/en/conventiontext/, Preamble [World Heritage Convention].

126 Kiss and Shelton, *International Environmental Law*, 36.

The gradual emergence of the concern for 'future generations' in international law could be traced back to the Charter of the United Nations.[127] It was first applied in the environmental context in the 1946 Convention on Regulation of Whaling, became popularised at the 1972 Stockholm Conference, and was eventually enshrined in a number of international environmental instruments.[128] It is reflected in the non-binding World Charter for Nature, and in the legally-binding biodiversity treaties.[129] For instance, the CMS utters awareness that "each generation [...] holds the resources of the earth for future generations and has an obligation to ensure that this legacy is conserved and, where utilized, is used wisely".[130] The Bern Convention and the CBD cited above, refer to future generations in a similar manner in their preambles. In the UNESCO Convention, moreover, this concept is placed among its operative provisions, amounting to a duty to transmit cultural and natural heritage to future generations.[131] Importantly, the concern for future generations is at a core of the concept of 'sustainable development'.[132] Interestingly, the link between sustainable development and biodiversity protection has been noted at least since the 1987 Brundtland Report, which is widely regarded to have coined the term 'sustainable development' as such.[133] The following dimensions of biodiversity's significance are mentioned in the Brundtland Report:

---

127 "We, the people of the United Nations, determined to save succeeding generations from the scourge of war" – "Charter of the United Nations," opened for signature June 26, 1945, *UNCIO* XV, p. 335, https://treaties.un.org/pages/ViewDetails.aspx?src=IND&mtdsg_no=I-1&chapter=1&clang=_en, Preamble; Gillespie, *International Environmental Law, Policy, and Ethics*, 102.

128 Gillespie, *International Environmental Law, Policy, and Ethics*, 102–103; See also Stephen Humphreys, "Against Future Generations," *European Journal of International Law* 33, no. 4 (December 2022): 1061–92, https://doi.org/10.1093/ejil/chac068.

129 Kiss and Shelton, *International Environmental Law*, 34.

130 CMS, Preamble.

131 World Heritage Convention, Article 4.

132 World Commission on Environment and Development, *Report of the World Commission on Environment and Development "Our Common Future"* A/42/427, New York, NY: UN Headquarters, August 4, 1987, https://digitallibrary.un.org/record/139811?v=pdf [Brundtland report]; Alexander Gillespie, *International Environmental Law, Policy, and Ethics*, 103–104.

133 Philippe Sands, Jacqueline Peel, Adriana Fabra, and Ruth MacKenzie, *Principles of International Environmental Law*, 4th ed. (Cambridge: Cambridge University Press, 2018), 218.

> The diversity of species is necessary for the normal functioning of ecosystems and the biosphere as a whole. The genetic material in wild species contributes billions of dollars yearly to the world economy in the form of improved crop species, new drugs and medicines, and raw materials for industry. But utility aside, there are also moral, ethical, cultural, aesthetic, and purely scientific reasons for conserving wild beings.[134]

Within relationships between sustainable development and future generations, two models are identified (and these might be in conflict with one another): the welfarist model (claiming an obligation to leave future generations a certain level of general welfare) and the preservationist one (to leave future generations some specific assets, such as tropical forests).[135] The relevance and effectiveness of the concept of 'future generations' in environmental context has been also criticized, mainly because of its vagueness.[136]

In conclusion, a variety of justifications of biodiversity protection, has been incorporated into international law. These grounds are both anthropocentric and non-anthropocentric ones, with the prevalence of the former category. This dominance as such, however, shall not hinder biodiversity protection at least for two reasons. First, anthropocentric arguments for the nature preservation may be as valid and useful as non-anthropocentric (and they may even better satisfy logical soundness and enjoy greater credibility among wider society) and second, these broad categories do not exclude one another and may be applied simultaneously. In fact, various justifications may appeal to a greater or lesser extent to different people, and thus the enlisting of the plethora of them in the international legal sources remains beneficial. In the subsequent chapters of the present dissertation, among the various currents of ethical justifications behind biodiversity protection, closer attention will be paid to those embedded in Christianity insofar as these are of relevance to the population of the regions comprising the Ukrainian Carpathians.

---

134 Brundtland report, § 53.

135 See Stone, "Ethics and International Environmental Law," 308–311.

136 See Humphreys, "Against Future Generations," 1061–1092.

1.3. An overview of the laws and policies on biodiversity protection on the global level, as applicable to the Ukrainian Carpathians

1.3.1. Principles and customary rules of international environmental law relevant for the biodiversity protection in the Ukrainian Carpathians

Principles of international environmental law constitute a varied and dynamic category. They may be found in the non-binding sources such as the 1972 Stockholm Declaration and the 1992 Rio Declaration on Environment and Development, in the preambles or main normative provisions of the international treaties, and in the domestic law. Some of the principles are widely recognised and are believed to have entered the category of customary international law, while other principles are emerging and being debated. Sometimes, there are terminological uncertainties as to framing a particular idea as a 'principle', a 'concept', an 'objective', a 'framework' or an 'approach'.[137] One of the famous examples in this respect would be the precautionary principle or precautionary approach.[138] The characterisation of principles may also differ, including such adjectives as 'general', 'fundamental', orienting', 'instrumental' or 'operational' principles.[139] Although the contested nature and legal status, indeterminate nature and open-endedness of the principles and related ideas might seem to be problematic, it could also be beneficial for the purposes of negotiations and policy-making.[140] Even though it has been claimed that no environmental principle (or most probably the way this principle has been applied) "has succeeded in causing a significant reduction or stop to the loss of biological

137 Ludwig Krämer and Emanuela Orlando, "Introduction to Volume VI" in *Principles of Environmental Law*, ed. Ludwig Krämer and Emanuela Orlando, (Cheltenham: Edward Elgar Publishing, 2018), 2–4.

138 See Jacqueline Peel, "Precaution," in *The Oxford Handbook of International Environmental Law*, ed. Lavanya Rajamani and Jacqueline Peel, 2nd ed. (Oxford: Oxford University Press, 2021); Yoshifumi Tanaka, *The International Law of the Sea*, 2nd ed (Cambridge: Cambridge University Press, 2015), 252–256; Jonathan B Wiener "Precautionary Principle," in *Principles of Environmental Law*, ed. Ludwig Krämer and Emanuela Orlando, (Cheltenham: Edward Elgar Publishing, 2018).

139 Gilles J Martin, "Principles and rules, "in *Principles of Environmental Law*, ed. Ludwig Krämer and Emanuela Orlando, (Cheltenham: Edward Elgar Publishing, 2018), 14.

140 Krämer and Orlando, "Introduction to Volume VI" in *Principles of Environmental Law*, 3.

diversity" until today, principles may lay foundations for future positive developments.[141]

The significance of the principles is also related to their 'linking' function. They are claimed to help translate the values and ideas into the legal language, especially once they are incorporated into treaties or policy instruments. Thus, they are an 'ideal bridge between ideals and duties, values and rules' as well as a link between the 'morality of aspiration' and 'morality of duty'.[142] They have also been described as 'policy ideas', an intersection between policy and law with the potential to lead to the further development of environmental norms.[143] The principles also serve the aim of connecting domestic and international law, and contribute to the internal coherence within the regimes of environmental protection, including biodiversity protection.[144]

There is a variety of interlinkages between principles and rules in environmental law. Although there is no settled criterion to draw a firm line of distinction between principles and rules, it is possible to distinguish them by function. The rules' function is slightly easier to define (for instance, to impose, authorise or prohibit) while principles' function is less precise (such as orienting, symbolic, programmatic, and strategic one).[145] At the same time, the principles support the rules by initiating or legitimising them, giving coherence to a set of rules or helping to interpret the rules. Using the metaphor of Gilles Martin, principles are "the basic linen on which the rules are written and to the evolution of which they contribute".[146] As Philippe Sands notes, the *Iron Rhine* case and the *Gentini* case present examples of the otherwise scarce judicial practice on the distinction between principles and rules of international environmental law.[147] In the *Iron*

---

141 Krämer and Orlando, "Introduction to Volume VI" in *Principles of Environmental Law*, 7.

142 Krämer and Orlando, "Introduction to Volume VI" in *Principles of Environmental Law*, 2–3; Jonathan Verschuuren, "Sustainable Development and the Nature of Environmental Legal Principles," *Potchefstroom Electronic Law Journal*, 9, no. 1 (2006): 1- 57, https://ssrn.com/abstract=899537.

143 Krämer and Orlando, "Introduction to Volume VI" in *Principles of Environmental Law*, 3; Eloise Scotford, *Environmental Principles and the Evolution of Environmental Law* (London, Oxford: Bloomsbury Publishing Hart Publishing, 2017), 6.

144 Krämer and Orlando, "Introduction to Volume VI" in *Principles of Environmental Law*, 3; See also Martin, "Principles and rules," 17–18.

145 Martin, "Principles and rules," 14, 17–18, 22.

146 Martin, "Principles and rules," 19–22.

147 Sands, Peel, Fabra, and MacKenzie, *Principles of International Environmental Law*, 199.

Rhine, the arbitral tribunal aptly described the lack of clarity in the distinction between the principles and rules and their status,[148] but confirmed the existence and applicability of the "principles of international environmental law".[149] In the *Gentini* case, the principles were said to express a general truth guiding the action, while rules were said to have a more practical and binding nature, thus positive rules of law may be understood as "practical formulation of the principles".[150]

The principles of international environmental law, being applicable "in respect of the protection of all aspects of the environment", naturally also apply to the sphere of biodiversity.[151] In Daniel Bodansky's view, the three most relevant to biodiversity principles are the precautionary principle, the principle of intergenerational equity, and the principle of differentiated responsibilities.[152] Alessandro Fodella mentions that for mountain biodiversity, the examples of the relevant principles would include "the no-transboundary environmental harm or preventive principle, the principles of cooperation (particularly management of shared resources), sustainable development (especially the integration principle), precaution, and public participation".[153]

The principles may be found in the preambles or operative parts of the biodiversity treaties, in the decisions of the governing bodies of these agreements, documents of international conferences (such as Stockholm and Rio Conferences), and in the jurisprudence of international courts and

---

148 *Iron Rhine Arbitration (Belgium v Netherlands)* (2005), Permanent Court of Arbitration ICGJ 373, Award of 24 May 2005, § 58 [The tribunal noted "considerable debate as to what, within the field of environmental law, constitutes 'rules' or 'principles'; what is 'soft law'; and which environmental treaty law or principles have contributed to the development of customary international law"].

149 *Iron Rhine Arbitration*, § 223.

150 Sands, Peel, Fabra, and MacKenzie, *Principles of International Environmental Law*, 199 [referring to to *Gentini case (Italy v Venezuela) (1903)* 10 RIAA 551, in Jackson H. Ralston and Doyle, W. T. Sherman Doyle, Venezuelan Arbitrations of 1903 Etc. (1904), 720, 725, cited in Bin Cheng, *General Principles of Law as Applied by International Courts and Tribunals* (London: Stevens, 1953, reprinted 2006), 376].

151 Sands, Peel, Fabra, and MacKenzie, *Principles of International Environmental Law*, 198; Daniel M. Bodansky, "International Law and the Protection of Biological Diversity," *Vanderbilt Journal of Transnational Law*, 28 Issue 4 (October 1995), 627.

152 For the description of these principles see: Bodansky, "International Law and the Protection of Biological Diversity," 627–628; see also supra note 119.

153 Alessandro Fodella, "Mountain biodiversity," in *Biodiversity and Nature Protection Law*, ed. Elisa Morgera and Jona Razzaque (Cheltenham: Edward Elgar Publishing, 2017), 171.

tribunals.[154] For instance, in the preamble of the CBD, it is noted that "it is vital to anticipate, prevent and attack the causes of significant reduction or loss of biological diversity at source", echoing the due diligence and prevention principles.[155] Article 3 of the CBD mentions the principle of states' sovereignty over their natural resources and the responsibility to ensure that activities within their jurisdiction or control do not cause damage to other States or to areas beyond the limits of national jurisdiction, that is no-harm principle or principle of preventive action.[156] Moreover, Article 14 of the CBD incorporates environmental impact assessment (EIA), which can also be considered as a principle.[157] The decisions of the Conference of the Parties of the CBD establish a set of complementary and interlinked principles on the 'ecosystem approach'.[158] Interestingly enough, according to Eloise Scotford, the CBD in its entirety represents an application of the principle of 'conservation of biological diversity'.[159]

It is, however, not common for the biodiversity treaties to contain explicit provisions on the 'classical principles' such as "prevention, precaution, environmental impact assessment, integration, and polluter-pays" principles.[160] This might be so as either the biodiversity treaties usually do not purport to regulate the activities threatening the biodiversity, relying here on other treaties, or as the principles are perceived as "the backcloth against which treaty regimes concerning wildlife conservation must necessarily be viewed" and thus are taken for granted.[161] There have, however, been differences among the states as to the understanding of the role of the principles

154 Sands, Peel, Fabra, and MacKenzie, *Principles of International Environmental Law*, 199.

155 Cf. Alice Ollino, "The Scope and Content of Due Diligence Obligations," in *Due Diligence Obligations in International Law*, (Cambridge University Press, 2022), 135, https://doi.org/10.1017/9781009053082.

156 CBD, Article 3; See Legality of the Threat or Use of Nuclear Weapons (Advisory Opinion), ICJ Rep 226, ICGJ 205 (1996), 241 § 27; Koester, "Environmental principles and concepts in biodiversity treaties," 540; Sands, Peel, Fabra, and MacKenzie, *Principles of International Environmental Law.*

157 CBD, Article 14.

158 See subchapter 1.3.2.

159 Scotford, *Environmental Principles and the Evolution of Environmental Law*, 70.

160 Koester, "Environmental principles and concepts in biodiversity treaties," 538–540.

161 Koester, "Environmental principles and concepts in biodiversity treaties," 540; Michael Bowman, Peter Davies, and Catherine Redgwell, *Lyster's International Wildlife Law*, 2nd ed. (Cambridge: Cambridge university press, 2010), 48; See also Patricia W. Birnie, Alan E. Boyle, and Catherine Redgwell, *International Law and the Environment*, 3d ed. (Oxford: Oxford University Press, 2009).

mentioned in the international treaties on the issue of whether they may be interpreted broadly and imply additional obligations not mentioned explicitly in the treaty or whether principles shall be used only narrowly to interpret obligations enshrined in the treaty text.[162]

It is often far from clear whether a certain principle has acquired a status of customary international law, so that it could be treated on par with treaty provisions. There is, however, a consensus as to the customary status of such principles of international environmental law as states' sovereignty over their natural resources coupled with a responsibility not to cause transboundary environmental damage ('no-harm' principle), the principle of preventive action (a due diligence duty of prevention), the principle of cooperation (including notification and consultation), and the environmental impact assessment (if it is understood as a principle and not merely as a technique for implementing certain standards).[163] The status of some other principles relevant to biodiversity, like common heritage of mankind and common concern of mankind, intra- and inter-generational equity, equitable access to benefit-sharing, public participation in decision-making or access to justice, is less clear.[164] The specific meaning and legal status of the principles may depend on a particular legal setting and may be clarified in the judicial practice.[165] One interesting aspect of further research that extends beyond the scope of this study might be to compare the normative meaning of the principles of international environmental law relevant to biodiversity protection, as enshrined in international treaties and as pertaining to the domain of customary international law.

Regardless of the principles' status, however, they "represent an orientation or framework for international discussion of environmental issues",

162 See Sands, Peel, Fabra, and MacKenzie, *Principles of International Environmental Law*, 200 [For example, "the amendment of the Article 3 of the Climate Change Convention to limit application of the principles to informing obligations under Convention based on the position of the USA and some other 'common law' delegations"; "the UK's Declaration upon signing the CBD purporting to limit the principles in a similar way to the Climate Change Convention, even though the Article 3 of the CBD is worded differently"].

163 Krämer and Orlando, "Introduction to Volume VI" in *Principles of Environmental Law*, 4; Koester, "Environmental principles and concepts in biodiversity treaties," 540; Sands, Peel, Fabra, and MacKenzie, *Principles of International Environmental Law*, 198–199.

164 Koester, "Environmental principles and concepts in biodiversity treaties," 540.

165 Krämer and Orlando, "Introduction to Volume VI" in *Principles of Environmental Law*, 4–5.

thus informing the law and policy of biodiversity protection.[166] Moreover, the principles of international environmental law not only influence international cooperation, but also impact activities on a national level, that can be harmful to other states, as the principle of the sovereignty over natural resources has been closely linked (at least since the 1972 Stockholm Declaration) to the responsibility not to cause damage to the environment of other states or areas beyond national jurisdiction.[167] Moreover, the common concern of humanity with respect to certain aspects of the environment further restricts the activities of a state within its own jurisdiction, and a general trend towards integrated protection of the environment is observed, requiring states to "exercise broad control over activities which can harm the environment" and in this way limiting their freedom of action.[168] In a biodiversity context, activities of a state within its jurisdiction, especially in the biodiversity-rich areas belonging to several national jurisdictions and hosting migratory species (such as the Carpathians) could easily negatively impact the environment of other states, and thus, require cautiousness of each among such neighbouring states on their respective national levels. It also follows that even without the context of direct extraterritorial impact, a state shall take measures to prevent the loss of biodiversity elements that are characterised as common heritage of humanity.

In addition, the principle of sustainable development is also not limited by the international cooperation but entails guidelines for organising the life within a state to achieve a balance between social, environmental, and economic components. The key legal elements of sustainable development, according to Sands, include: preservation of natural resources for the benefit of future generations, that is intergenerational equity; exploitation of

166 Bodansky, "International Law and the Protection of Biological Diversity," 627; for the description of principles and their relation to the wildlife applicable *mutatis mutandis* to biodiversity, see Bowman, Davies, and Redgwell, *Lyster's International Wildlife Law*, 48–60.

167 Sands, Peel, Fabra, and MacKenzie, *Principles of International Environmental Law*, 201; United Nations Environment Programme, *Stockholm Declaration: Declaration on the Human Environment* (1972), https://wedocs.unep.org/bitstream/handle/20.500.11822/29567/ELGP1StockD.pdf?sequence=1&isAllowed=y, Principle 21 [Stockholm Declaration]; United Nations Conference on Environment and Development, *Rio Declaration on Environment and Development*, A/CONF.151/26 Vol. I (1992), https://www.un.org/en/development/desa/population/migration/generalassembly/docs/globalcompact/A_CONF.151_26_Vol.I_Declaration.pdf, Principle 2 [Rio Declaration]; this principle is sometimes called jointly Principle 21/Principle 2.

168 Kiss and Shelton, *International Environmental Law*, 27–28, 36.

natural resources in a 'sustainable', 'rational', 'prudent', 'wise' or 'appropriate' manner, that is sustainable use; 'equitable' use that takes account of the needs of other states, that is intragenerational equity; and integration of environmental considerations into economic and other development plans, and consideration of development needs during the application of environmental objectives, that is the principle of integration.[169] The 'sustainable development' is often referred to as a 'principle', however other categories such as 'concept', 'framework', 'paradigm', or 'objective' have been used to characherise it.[170] Interestingly enough, among the treaties subject to analysis in this study, only the Carpathian Convention explicitly mentions 'sustainable development', and the CBD mentions it only narrowly with respect to the areas adjacent to protected areas.[171] The Carpathian Convention regime, moreover, includes protocols, focused on certain aspects of sustainability, including the Protocol on Sustainable Forest Management and the Protocol on Sustainable Tourism.[172]

The most recent international document on sustainable development, albeit adopted as the UN General Assembly resolution and thus non-binding as such, is the 2030 Agenda for Sustainable Development, containing 17 Sustainable Development Goals (SDGs).[173] Among them, SDG 15 on life on land – "Protect, restore and promote sustainable use of terrestrial ecosystems, sustainably manage forests, combat desertification, and halt and reverse land degradation and halt biodiversity loss," – is directly relevant to the protection of forest biodiversity. Its substantive targets encom-

169 Sands, Peel, Fabra, and MacKenzie, *Principles of International Environmental Law*, 218 219.

170 Virginie Barral, "The Principle of Sustainable Development," in *Principles of Environmental Law*, ed. Ludwig Krämer and Emanuela Orlando, (Cheltenham: Edward Elgar Publishing, 2018), 105–106.

171 "Framework Convention on the Protection and Sustainable Development of the Carpathians," opened for signature May 22, 2003, http://www.carpathianconvention.org/convention/framework-convention/, Preamble, Article 2, Article 5, Article 13 Article 16 [Carpathian Convention]; CBD, Article 8 (e); Koester, "Environmental principles and concepts in biodiversity treaties," 541.

172 "Protocol on Sustainable Forest Management," opened for signature May 27, 2011, http://www.carpathianconvention.org/convention/protocols/protocol-on-sustainable-forest-management/ [Protocol on Sustainable Forest Management]; "Protocol on Sustainable Tourism," opened for signature May 27, 2011, http://www.carpathianconvention.org/convention/protocols/protocol-on-sustainable-tourism/; Sands, Peel, Fabra, and MacKenzie, *Principles of International Environmental Law*, 218.

173 *Transforming our world: the 2030 Agenda for Sustainable Development,* General Assembly Resolution 70/1, A/RES/70/1 (25 September 2015) (www.un.org/ga).

pass, for example, conservation, restoration, sustainable use and management of ecosystems and their services, in particular forests and mountains, reduction of extinction and natural habitats' degradation, ending of poaching and trafficking of protected species, introduction of measures against impacts of invasive alien species, and the integration of ecosystem and biodiversity values into national and local planning.[174] As the SDGs are interconnected, SDG 15 is said to be especially closely linked to SDGs 1 (no poverty), 2 (no hunger), 3 (good health), 5 (gender equality), 8 (good jobs and economic growth), 9 (industry, innovation and infrastructure), 10 (reduced inequalities), 13 (climate action), 14 (life below water), and 16 (peace and justice).[175]

In sum, various principles of international environmental law of different legal status (including those amounting to customary international law and non-binding ones) are of relevance to biodiversity protection. They are often reflected in biodiversity treaties and continue to emerge. In the remaining subchapters of Chapter I, more detailed legal norms, often based on the principles mentioned above, will be explored.

1.3.2. The Convention on Biological Diversity

The CBD enjoying almost universal membership,[176] is the first global instrument, creating a 'general framework' or 'normative umbrella' in the field of biological diversity,[177] using comprehensive rather than sectoral approach.[178] It originates from the establishment of the Ad Hoc Working Group of Experts on Biological Diversity in 1987 by the United Nations Environment Programme (UNEP), charged with a task to harmonise existing

174 *Transforming our world: the 2030 Agenda for Sustainable Development*, GA, Goal 15.

175 SDG Academy, "How SDG 15 Links With Other SDGs", video by Jeffrey D. Sachs, 11:18, August 6, 2019, https://sdgacademylibrary.mediaspace.kaltura.com/media/How+SDG+15+Links+With+Other+SDGs/1_j0kpb2iw.

176 "Convention on Biological Diversity: Status", United Nations, https://treaties.un.org/pages/ViewDetails.aspx?src=TREATY&mtdsg_no=XXVII-8&chapter=27#1 [196 Parties as of September 2024].

177 Kiss and Shelton, *Guide to International Environmental Law*, 177–178; Bodansky, "International Law and the Protection of Biological Diversity," 630.

178 Lyle Glowka et al., *A Guide to the Convention on Biological Diversity: A Contribution to the Global Biodiversity Strategy*, IUCN Environmental Policy and Law Paper 30 (Gland Cambridge: IUCN the World Conservation Union, 1994), 1.

conventions related to biodiversity.[179] The formal process of negotiations began in 1991, when the Ad Hoc Working Group was renamed the Intergovernmental Negotiating Committee for a Convention on Biological Diversity (INC).[180] The CBD was eventually adopted by the INC at the Nairobi Conference in May 1992, opened for signature a month later at the United Nations Conference on Environment and Development in Rio de Janeiro and entered into force on 29 December 1993.[181] Ukraine has signed the CBD in 1992 and ratified on 7 February 1995.[182] The CBD has attracted a significant amount of scholarly attention,[183] however, as it remains the

---

179 UNEP Governing Council, *Rationalization of International Conventions on Biological Diversity*, Decision 14/26, proceedings of the Governing Council at its 14th session, UNEP/GC/DEC/14/26 (1987); Secretariat of the Convention on Biological Diversity, ed., *Handbook of the Convention on Biological Diversity*, prepared by Ruth Mackenzie, Sam Jonson and Martin Jenkins (London: Earthscan Publications, 2001), xvii.

180 Marine Yzquierdo, "The 1992 Convention on Biological Diversity," in *Multilateral Environmental Treaties*, ed. Malgosia Fitzmaurice, Attila Tanzi, and Angeliki Papantoniou, (Cheltenham: Edward Elgar Publishing, 2017), 11.

181 "Convention on Biological Diversity", United Nations, https://treaties.un.org/pages/ViewDetails.aspx?src=TREATY&mtdsg_no=XXVII-8&chapter=27#1.

182 "Convention on Biological Diversity", United Nations, https://treaties.un.org/pages/ViewDetails.aspx?src=TREATY&mtdsg_no=XXVII-8&chapter=27#1.

183 See Alan E. Boyle, "The Convention on Biological Diversity," in *The Environment after Rio: International Law and Economics*, ed. Luigi Campiglio et al., 1. publ, International Environmental Law and Policy Series (London: Graham & Trotman/Martinus Nijhoff, 1994) 111–130; Glowka et al., *A Guide to the Convention on Biological Diversity*; Bodansky, "International Law and the Protection of Biological Diversity," 623–634; Michael Bowman and Catherine Redgwell, *International Law and the Conservation of Biological Diversity*, International Environmental Law and Policy Series (London: Kluwer Law International, 1996); Rosemary Rayfuse, "Biological Resources," in *The Oxford Handbook of International Environmental Law*, ed. Daniel Bodansky, Jutta Brunnée, and Ellen Hey, 1st ed. (Oxford: Oxford University Press, 2012), 362–93; Kiss and Shelton, *Guide to International Environmental Law*; Yzquierdo, "The 1992 Convention on Biological Diversity," 9 – 24; Sands, Peel, Fabra, and MacKenzie, *Principles of International Environmental Law*, 384–409; Michael Bowman, Peter G. G. Davies, and Edward Goodwin, *Research Handbook on Biodiversity and Law* (Cheltenham: Edward Elgar Publishing, 2016); Elisa Morgera and Elsa Tsioumani, "Yesterday, Today, and Tomorrow: Looking Afresh at the Convention on Biological Diversity," *Yearbook of International Environmental Law* 21, no. 1 (1 January 2010): 3–40, https://doi.org/10.1093/yiel/yvr003; Stuart R. Harrop and Diana J. Pritchard, "A Hard Instrument Goes Soft: The Implications of the Convention on Biological Diversity's Current Trajectory," *Global Environmental Change* 21, no. 2 (May 2011): 474–80, https://doi.org/10.1016/j.gloenvcha.2011.01.014; Bowman, Davies, and Redgwell, *Lyster's International Wildlife Law*, 585–629; Chidi Oguamanam, "Biodiversity, Biosafety and Bioprospecting," in *Routledge Handbook*

main global framework for biodiversity protection, it will be explored in this study in a relatively detailed manner.

1.3.2.1. The analysis of the CBD provisions

The preamble of the CBD, even though not legally binding, is remarkable as it sets a particular matrix of understanding the biodiversity and approaches to it under international law. It begins by explaining the value of biodiversity (or rather, as mentioned above, simply listing, and for that matter requires external sources of interpretation, such as philosophical or religious ones), first the intrinsic one followed by ecological, genetic, social, economic, scientific, educational, cultural, recreational and aesthetic value of biodiversity and its components.[184] Among other things, the preamble also recognises biodiversity's importance for maintaining life-sustaining systems of the biosphere, and state's sovereign rights over their biological resources coupled with the responsibility to use them in sustainable manner and conserve biodiversity. Importantly, the issue of biodiversity conservation is not left solely to the sovereign domain of the states, but for the first time in the human history is affirmed to be a 'common concern of humankind'.[185] The conservation and sustainable use of biodiversity are also recognised as crucial for ensuring food, health and other needs, and should be pursued for the benefit of present and future generations.[186]

The operative provisions of the CBD serve the achievement of the three main objectives: the conservation of biological diversity, the sustainable use of its components, and the fair and equitable sharing of the benefits arising out of the utilization of genetic resources.[187] The balance among these three components constitutes the "heart of the political agreement upon which the Convention is founded".[188]

---

of International Environmental Law, Erika J. Techera et al., 2nd ed. (London: Routledge, Taylor & Francis Group, 2021) 101 – 115; Annecoos Wiersema, "Wildlife," in *The Oxford Handbook of International Environmental Law*, ed. Lavanya Rajamani and Jacqueline Peel, 2nd ed. (Oxford: Oxford University Press, 2021) 554–573; Hunter, Salzman, and Zaelke, *International Environmental Law and Policy*, 996–1047.

184 CBD, Preamble.

185 Glowka et al., *A Guide to the Convention on Biological Diversity*, 3.

186 CBD, Preamble.

187 CBD, Article 1.

188 Glowka et al., *A Guide to the Convention on Biological Diversity*, 15.

Article 2 provides the meaning of terms, first and foremost of the 'biological diversity' itself, cited in the Preliminary remarks above. The CBD is remarkable in being the first international agreement encompassing all three levels of biodiversity: ecosystems, species and genetic resources.[189] Importantly, 'biodiversity' is distinguished from the 'biological resources' (the latter meaning "genetic resources, organisms or parts thereof, populations, or any other biotic component of ecosystems with actual or potential use or value for humanity"[190]) as it is "an attribute of life" while resources are "tangible biotic components of ecosystems" and only those of value to humans.[191]

Another crucial term is an 'ecosystem', defined as "a dynamic complex of plant, animal and micro-organism communities and their non-living environment interacting as a functional unit".[192] The human knowledge about functioning of the ecosystems is fragmented. It is unclear, how different ecosystems may interact with each other and what exact role individual species may play in the ecosystems (for instance, some species are the 'keystone species' crucial for the ecosystem's stable functioning, some other species might be 'umbrella species' ensuring adequate habitat for other species, still others could be 'sentinel species' indicating the health of an ecosystem[193]). What is suggested by scientists is, however, the correlation between species diversity and the stability of an ecosystem.[194] The definition might cover ecosystems of any levels, as functional units might exist even on micro levels, comprising, for instance, tree trunk cavity and moreover the ecosystems might exist within the ecosystems. It is, however, more likely that the CBD is mostly concerned with larger units, such as particular forests, as it is practicable for the purposes of conservation.[195]

The substantive provisions are contained in Articles 6 – 20.[196] In particular, Article 6 establishes obligations on general measures for conserva-

---

189 Yzquierdo, "The 1992 Convention on Biological Diversity," 11; Glowka et al., *A Guide to the Convention on Biological Diversity*, ix; Katrina Brown et al., *Economics and the Conservation of Global Biological Diversity*, Working Paper, no. 2 (Washington, DC: Global Environment Facility, 1993), 3–5 cited in Hunter, Salzman, and Zaelke, *International Environmental Law and Policy*, 979.

190 CBD, Article 2.

191 Glowka et al., *A Guide to the Convention on Biological Diversity*, 16.

192 CBD, Article 2.

193 Hunter, Salzman, and Zaelke, *International Environmental Law and Policy*, 980.

194 Glowka et al., *A Guide to the Convention on Biological Diversity*, 20.

195 Glowka et al., *A Guide to the Convention on Biological Diversity*, 20–21.

196 Secretariat, *Handbook of the Convention on Biological Diversity*, xxiii.

tion and sustainable use, such as developing national strategies, plans or programmes on conservation and sustainable use of biodiversity and integrating these into relevant cross-sectoral documents. This is one of the foundational articles of the CBD as it concerns planning, and is related to numeorus other substantive articles.[197] The wording of this article, is, however, rather 'soft', as the development and integration required by this article are to be undertaken "in accordance with the particular conditions and capabilities of the Parties" and "as far as possible and appropriate". The latter language softener is also present in articles 7, 8, 9, 10, 11, 14, creating a significant leeway for the Parties, that may potentially claim impossibility or inappropriateness of the implementation of these provisions and continue 'business as usual' instead of introducing changes.

Article 7 establishes obligations of identification and monitoring of biodiversity, in particular a Party shall identify components of biodiversity, important for its conservation and sustainable use, for which purpose it shall consult Annex I, providing indicative categories. These identified components should be monitored through sampling or other techniques. Special attention during monitoring should be paid to the components of biodiversity requiring urgent conservation and those offering greatest potential for sustainable use. In addition, the processes and categories of activities that may negatively affect conservation or use of biodiversity should be identified, and their effects should be monitored. Data from all mentioned types of monitoring and identification should be maintained and organized.[198] This also means that information derived from data should be disseminated, for instance to the policy-makers, managers or educators, in a usable form.[199] The obligations under Article 7 are of a great relevance for those under Article 8, requiring taking action on the identified processes or activities, as it allows to track success or failure of the introduced measures.[200]

Article 8, on *in-situ* conservation, that is "conservation of ecosystems and natural habitats and the maintenance and recovery of viable populations of species in their natural surroundings and, in case of domesticated or cultivated species, in the surroundings where they have developed their

---

197 Glowka et al., *A Guide to the Convention on Biological Diversity*, 29.
198 CBD, Article 7.
199 Glowka et al., *A Guide to the Convention on Biological Diversity*, 36.
200 Glowka et al., *A Guide to the Convention on Biological Diversity*, 36.

distinctive properties",[201] covers a wide range of issues[202] and provides the central set of obligations on biodiversity conservation.[203]

The first of its sub-topics, 'protected areas' (Article 8 (a)–(c)) constitute the central element of the national biodiversity conservation strategy.[204] 'Protected areas' might include, for instance, national parks, nature reserves, heritage sites, wilderness areas etc. The meaning of the phrase "areas where special measures need to be taken to conserve biological diversity" which is distinguished from 'protected areas' by conjunction 'or' in paragraph (b) is less clear. Protected areas are supposed to form a system, implying a logically organised network based on a plan allowing to formulate the objectives, identify the gaps and action needed to fill them. Implementation of these paragraphs requires to have necessary legislation in place, as well as a conservation strategy and management plans, ideally created by involvement of various actors. The considerations of climate change should also be taken into account, meaning for instance, establishment of larger protected areas and corridors among them to allow for movement of species as the climate changes. The protected areas in the meaning of this article encompass also those designated on a basis of other international agreements, such as the World Heritage Convention or regional instruments.[205] Paragraph (c) requires regulation and management of biological resources both within and outside protected areas, implying a broad obligation to control all activities that directly or indirectly affect the biological resources considered. Such activities include, for example, hunting, harvesting, tourism, and pollution.[206]

The sub-topic of 'protected areas' has been recognised by the Conference of the Parties (COP) as closely related to forest biodiversity.[207] For instance, among objectives of the work programme on forest biodiversity within the CBD there is a task "to identify the contribution of networks of protected areas to the conservation and sustainable use of forests biological diversity".[208] The COP has also emphasized the importance of the establishment

201 CBD, Article 2.
202 Secretariat, *Handbook of the Convention on Biological Diversity*, 105.
203 Glowka et al., *A Guide to the Convention on Biological Diversity*, 39.
204 Glowka et al., *A Guide to the Convention on Biological Diversity*, 39.
205 Glowka et al., *A Guide to the Convention on Biological Diversity*, 39–40.
206 Glowka et al., *A Guide to the Convention on Biological Diversity*, 40–41.
207 Secretariat, *Handbook of the Convention on Biological Diversity*, 109.
208 Conference of the Parties, *Forest biological diversity*, Decision IV/7, UNEP/CBD/COP/DEC/IV/7 (1998) annex, § 3 (h).

and management of protected areas, and its integration into national forest and land-use plans.[209]

Article 8 (d) deals with protection of ecosystems, natural habitats and viable populations of species in natural surroundings. It encompasses areas both within and outside the protected areas, including those on private land.[210]

Article 8 (e) calls on to promote sustainable development of areas adjacent to the protected areas. One of the possible models is the creation of biosphere reserves, promoted by the UNESCO. Such reserves include three types of areas: core area enjoying strict protection, a buffer zone allowing only for activities compatible with conservation, and a transition zone, where sustainable resource management is practiced.[211] Adjacent areas are of particular relevance to the forest biodiversity in the context of habitat fragmentation and population viability.[212]

Rehabilitation and restoration of degraded ecosystems and recovery of threatened species required by Article 8 (f) includes development and implementation of plans or other management strategies. The obligation to restore stipulated in this paragraph, is novel compared to other international conventions, requiring only to protect.[213] The COP has also encouraged strengthening the capacities for restoration of forests.[214]

Article 8 (g) deals with biosafety and is related to the Cartagena Protocol on Biosafety. It primarily relates to the agriculture and aquatic biodiversity and is of lesser importance in the context of forests.

Article 8 (h) is dedicated to the cross-cutting issue of alien species, which is included into several programme areas in the work programme on forest biodiversity.[215] Parties to the CBD have been encouraged to develop national and supra-national projects to address this issue and incorporate

---

209 Conference of the Parties, *Forests and biological diversity*, CBD COP Decision II/9 (1995) annex,
§ 13; Conference of the Parties, *Programme of work for terrestrial biological diversity: forest biological diversity*, CBD COP Decision III/12 (1996) annex.

210 Secretariat, *Handbook of the Convention on Biological Diversity*, 111; Glowka et al., *A Guide to the Convention on Biological Diversity*, 41.

211 Glowka et al., *A Guide to the Convention on Biological Diversity*, 42–43.

212 Secretariat, *Handbook of the Convention on Biological Diversity*, 112; Conference of the Parties, *Forest biological diversity*, CBD COP Decision IV/7 (1998) annex, § 53.

213 Glowka et al., *A Guide to the Convention on Biological Diversity*, 44.

214 Conference of the Parties, *Progress report on the implementation of the programme of work for forest biological diversity*, CBD COP Decision V/4 (2000), § 10.

215 Secretariat, *Handbook of the Convention on Biological Diversity*, 117.

it into biodiversity strategies and action plans.[216] Prevention of introduction of alien species is generally regarded as an easier and cheaper measure than their eradication.[217]

Article 8 (i) relates to the compatibility between the conservation and sustainable use of biodiversity. The wording of this paragraph is, however, somewhat unclear.[218]

Article 8 (j) addresses traditional knowledge and practices of the indigenous and local communities, a broad topic, touched upon also in other CBD provisions. It is closely related to the forest biodiversity, for instance in context of the identification of traditional systems of conservation and sustainable use of forest biodiversity, promotion of wider application of traditional forest-related knowledge in sustainable forest management and understanding the role of traditional knowledge in ecosystem management to minimize or mitigate negative influences.[219]

Article 8 (k) requires developing or maintaining legislation and other regulatory provisions to protect threatened species and populations. Laws dealing with protection of individual species were an initial strategy of many states, which, however, proved not always to be an effective tool, and currently the better approach is to prevent destructions of habitats. The legislative provisions needed to comply with this article might also concern the use of incentives, planning constraints, land-use controls, environmental impact assessments and recovery plans.[220]

Article 8 (l) refers to the adverse effect determined pursuant to Article 7 and calls the Parties to regulate or manage those threats. It is also linked to Articles 10 and 14 of the CBD. Within the work programme on forest biodiversity, research is intended to find options to minimise or mitigate negative human influences on forest biodiversity and promote positive ones.[221] Parties have been encouraged by the COP to include mitigation

216 Conference of the Parties, *Report and recommendations of the third meeting of the Subsidiary Body on Scientific, Technical and Technological Advice, and instructions by the Conference of the Parties to the Subsidiary Body on Scientific, Technical and Technological Advice*, CBD COP Decision IV/1 (1998) C, § 3, 4.

217 Glowka et al., *A Guide to the Convention on Biological Diversity*, 47.

218 Glowka et al., *A Guide to the Convention on Biological Diversity*, 47.

219 Secretariat, *Handbook of the Convention on Biological Diversity*, 125–126.

220 Glowka et al., *A Guide to the Convention on Biological Diversity*, 49–50.

221 Secretariat, *Handbook of the Convention on Biological Diversity*, 130.

measures to the environmental impact assessments and minimise risks to biodiversity associated with tourism.[222]

Article 8 (m) deals with cooperation, which could be financial or other, such as support in monitoring, research or training, public education, or technical knowledge. The key focus of this provision is the support provided to the developing countries on a bilateral basis rather than within multilateral cooperation.[223]

Article 9 regulates *ex-situ* conservation, meaning the "conservation of components of biodiversity outside their natural habitat".[224] It is supposed to complement the *in-situ* measures.[225] *Ex-situ* conservation includes techniques such as gene banks or captive breeding undertaken by institutions such as botanical gardens, zoos and research centres. It should be primarily undertaken in a country of origin, allowing for the reintroduction of species and ensuring genetic constituency. These measures should also be implemented in a way not harmful for the ecosystems and *in-situ* populations of species. Similar to the *in-situ* conservation, cooperation and support between states are encouraged.[226]

Article 10 on sustainable use of components of biodiversity is closely related to the number of the CBD provisions and has been considered by the COP as a cross-cutting issue.[227] 'Sustainable use' is defined as the "use of components of biological diversity in a way and at a rate that does not lead to the long-term decline of biological diversity, thereby maintaining its potential to meet the needs and aspirations of present and future generations"[228] and relates to each thematic work programme.[229] This article encourages anticipatory rather than reactive inclusion of conservation and sustainable use considerations into national decision making (paragraph a), as well as adoption of other measures, needed to avoid or minimise harm to biological diversity (paragraph b). Special attention is being paid to the cus-

222 Secretariat, *Handbook of the Convention on Biological Diversity*, 130.; Conference of the Parties, *Impact assessment, liability and redress*, CBD COP Decision V/18 (2000) part I, § 2(b); Conference of the Parties, *Biological diversity and tourism*, CBD COP Decision V/25 (2000) § 4(b).

223 Glowka et al., *A Guide to the Convention on Biological Diversity*, 50–51.

224 CBD, Article 2.

225 CBD, Article 9.

226 Glowka et al., *A Guide to the Convention on Biological Diversity*, 52–56.

227 Conference of the Parties, *Sustainable use as a cross-cutting issue*, CBD COP Decision V/24 (2000).

228 CBD, Article 2.

229 Secretariat, *Handbook of the Convention on Biological Diversity*, 135.

tomary use of biological resources in accordance with traditional cultural practices, however only those compatible with the CBD objectives (paragraph c). Governments should support local populations in implementation of remedial action, as local populations are best suited to ensure the success of remediation (paragraph d). Local communities might establish partnerships with other actors, such as banks, universities, religious groups and non-governmental organizations. The need of cooperation between governmental authorities and private sector is also underscored (paragraph e).[230]

Under Article 11, the Parties are encouraged to adopt measures serving as incentives for conservation and sustainable use. Such incentives might be direct (in cash or in-kind) or indirect (fiscal, service or socially based). Imposition of disincentives that discourage undesired behaviour should also be considered as well as identification of the perverse incentives with a view to eliminate or minimise their negative impact.[231] In the Subsidiary Body on Scientific, Technical and Technological Advice (SBSTTA) and COP's documents, incentives are closely related to the valuation of biodiversity, initially being the economic ones and then extended to "market and non-market values of biological diversity" and "economic, cultural and ethical valuation".[232] Based on this article, the Parties have been encouraged to ensure incorporation of various values of biodiversity into their plans, strategies and impact assessments, to develop training programmes and promote private sector initiatives in this area.[233] Furthermore, the Parties have been called to identify threats to biodiversity and perverse incentives, and develop supportive legal and policy frameworks for the design and implementation of the incentive measures.[234]

Article 12 is dedicated to research and training with special attention to the needs of developing countries. This is one of the cornerstones of the CBD, as it addresses human capacity-building needed to overcome the

230 Glowka et al., *A Guide to the Convention on Biological Diversity*, 57–62.

231 Glowka et al., *A Guide to the Convention on Biological Diversity*, 63–64.

232 Secretariat, *Handbook of the Convention on Biological Diversity*, 138; SBSTTA, *Agenda item 3.11: Economic valuation of biological diversity*, SBSTTA recommendation II/9 (1996); Conference of the Parties, *Incentive measures*, COP Decision III/18 (1996) § 4; Conference of the Parties, *Measures for implementing the Convention on Biological Diversity*, COP Decision IV/10 (1998), § 1(c).

233 COP, Decision III/18.

234 COP, Decision IV/10, A.

knowledge gaps and implement other substantive obligations under this Convention.[235]

Article 13 deals with public education and awareness, which constitutes an integral component of all items under the programme of work of the CBD.[236] The Parties have been encouraged to promote education on biodiversity at different levels and by involving various stakeholders.[237] Formal and informal public education concerns might be incorporated into the national biodiversity strategy and biodiversity education plan. The process of preparation of such documents may uncover cultural, traditional and religious values as well as knowledge and practices, helpful for the future implementation.[238]

Article 14 regulates four areas: the environmental impact assessment (EIA); transboundary cooperation by means of reciprocal notifications, consultations and exchange of information with regard to activities likely to adversely affect biodiversity, and immediate notification in case of imminent or grave danger or damage; emergency planning; and examination of the issue of liability and redress for damage to biodiversity.[239]

The nuances of Articles 15 to 21, dealing with access to genetic resources, access to and transfer of technology, exchange of information, technical and scientific cooperation, handling of biotechnology and distribution of benefits, financial resources and financial mechanism are of lesser interest to the subject of the present thesis, and are considered at length in other sources.[240]

Article 22 regulates relationship with other international conventions, stating that CBD's provisions should not affect rights and obligations of the parties deriving from other agreements, however, adding a reservation "except where the exercise of those rights and obligations would cause a serious damage or threat to biological diversity".[241] This wording requires, however, further guidance on the threshold of damage or threat that triggers application of the CBD.[242]

---

235 Glowka et al., *A Guide to the Convention on Biological Diversity*, 65.

236 Conference of the Parties, *Education and public awareness*, CBD COP Decision V/17 (2000) § 5.

237 COP, Decision IV/10, B, § 1.

238 Glowka et al., *A Guide to the Convention on Biological Diversity*, 68.

239 Glowka et al., *A Guide to the Convention on Biological Diversity*, 71.

240 See Secretariat, *Handbook of the Convention on Biological Diversity*, 152–197; Glowka et al., *A Guide to the Convention on Biological Diversity*, 76–108.

241 CBD, Article 22.

242 Glowka et al., *A Guide to the Convention on Biological Diversity*, 109.

The set of articles that follow regulates the institutional mechanism of the CBD. Article 23 establishes COP and envisions its main functions, needed to "steer and supervise the implementation of the Convention",[243] also leaving some room to "consider and undertake any additional action that may be required for the achievement of the purposes of this Convention".[244] Since its establishment, COP has adopted a number of decisions. Of particular significance for the advancement in achieving its goals among them is the decision to prepare a Strategic Plan for the Convention,[245] which resulted in a substantive clarification of the key contemporary goals and directions of action under the CBD. This plan has been adopted initially for a period of 2002 – 2010,[246] revised and updated for the period of 2011 – 2020 (including the Aichi Biodiversity Targets)[247] and has recently been replaced with the new Kunming-Montreal Global Biodiversity Framework, establishing vision, goals and targets until 2030 and 2050.[248]

Article 24 establishes the Secretariat, with the main tasks of arranging the meetings of the COP and other bodies of the Convention, as well as to coordinate with other international bodies. On the first COP, UNEP (today UN Environment) had been designated to carry out the functions of the Secretariat before the Secretariat has been subsequently established in Montreal, Canada.[249] The Secretariat plays an active role in achieving the cooperation and synergy with other conventions. The Memoranda of Cooperation have been concluded with various conventions and institutions, which contributed to the harmonization of reporting of biodiversity-related conventions.[250] In addition to inter secretariat cooperation, COP has adopted decisions on cooperation on other levels, including calling national

243 Glowka et al., *A Guide to the Convention on Biological Diversity*, 111.
244 CBD, Article 23, § 4 (i).
245 Conference of the Parties, *Operations of the Convention*, CBD COP Decision V/20 (2000), § 10–16.
246 Conference of the Parties, *Strategic Plan for the Convention on Biological Diversity*, CBD COP Decision VI/26 (2002).
247 "Inputs to the process of revising and updating the CBD Strategic Plan 2002–2010," Convention on Biological Diversity, March 29, 2017, https://www.cbd.int/sp/inputs/.
248 "COP15: Final text of Kunming-Montreal Global Biodiversity Framework," Convention on Biological Diversity, December 27, 2022, https://www.cbd.int/article/cop15-final-text-kunming-montreal-gbf-221222; *Kunming-Montreal Global Biodiversity Framework*.
249 Secretariat, *Handbook of the Convention on Biological Diversity*, 204–205; Conference of the Parties, *Location of the Secretariat*, CBD COP Decision II/19 (1995).
250 Secretariat, *Handbook of the Convention on Biological Diversity*, 205–206.

focal points of biodiversity-related conventions to "cooperate on implementation and avoid duplication of effort".[251] CBD Secretariat has been active in promoting cooperation with other biodiversity-related conventions since its entry into force. Gradually, a Liaison Group of Biodiversity-related Conventions was established,[252] uniting secretariats of seven biodiversity conventions with the aim to assist cooperation and coordination among them.[253]

Article 25 establishes the SBSTTA with the task to provide the COP and other subsidiary bodies with the timely advice on implementation of the CBD. The SBSTTA recommended the COP to establish the ad hoc technical expert groups on thematic areas to assist its work. One of the groups approved by the COP deals with forest biological diversity. In addition, the COP founded a roster of experts in various areas, including the forest biological diversity. The SBSTTA takes part in cooperation with equivalent bodies of other biodiversity-related conventions, institutions and processes.[254]

Article 26 establishes the Party's obligation to report on the implementation of the Convention. Intervals and requirements of this reporting are established and modified by the COP. Sometimes Parties are invited to prepare detailed thematic reports. Secretariat is preparing synthesis of information contained in the national reports for the consideration of the COP and SBSTTA.[255] So far, the Parties have been invited to submit six national reports, the seventh and eighth reports are due in 2026 and 2029 respectively.[256] COP usually provides guidelines before the next series of

---

251 Secretariat, *Handbook of the Convention on Biological Diversity*, 207.

252 Conference of the Parties, *Cooperation with other conventions and international organizations and initiatives*, CBD COP Decision VII/26 (2004); Conference of the Parties, *Cooperation among multilateral environmental agreements and other organizations*, CBD COP Decision IX/27 (2008); Conference of the Parties, *Cooperation with other conventions and international organizations and initiatives*, CBD COP Decision X/20 (2010).

253 Sands, Peel, Fabra, and MacKenzie, *Principles of International Environmental Law*, 409; Liaison Group of Biodiversity-related Conventions https://www.cbd.int/blg/.

254 Secretariat, *Handbook of the Convention on Biological Diversity*, 212; Conference of the Parties, *Progress report on the implementation of the programme of work for forest biological diversity*, CBD COP Decision V/4 (2000), § 4–6.

255 Secretariat, *Handbook of the Convention on Biological Diversity*, 215.

256 "National Reports," Convention on Biological Diversity, accessed September 20, 2024, https://www.cbd.int/reports.

reports is due to ensure comparability and relevance of the information presented in those reports.[257]

Articles that follow (27–42) regulate rather technical legal issues, including settlement of disputes, adoption of protocols, amendment of the Convention and protocols, adoption and amendment of annexes, right to vote, relationship between the Convention and its protocols, signature, ratification, acceptance or approval, accession, entry into force, reservations, withdrawals, secretariat interim arrangements, depositary, and authentic texts.

Annex I establishes criteria on identification and monitoring (related to Article 7), and Annex II deals with arbitration and conciliation.

Three protocols to the CBD have been adopted so far: the Nagoya Protocol on Access to Generic Resources and the Fair and Equitable Sharing of Benefits Arising from their Utilization, the Cartagena Protocol on Biosafety and the 2010 Nagoya – Kuala Lumpur Supplementary Protocol to the Cartagena Protocol on Biosafety. They are, however, of lesser relevance to the focus of the present thesis, therefore will not be considered in this study. Of greater relevance here apart from the text of the CBD, are instead the following concepts: the 'ecosystem approach' as a general framework under the CBD, the thematic area of 'forest biodiversity' and the recent strategic plans to the CBD, that are addressed below.

Being a framework agreement, the CBD leaves the decisive role in its implementation to the level of national governments (moreover, unlike some other treaties in this field, the CBD does not contain any definitive lists of species or sites to be protected).[258] Therefore, it is sometimes described in the scholarly literature as "a hard instrument implemented within a soft framework".[259] Such a situation, on the one hand, allows for a broad acceptance of this convention, but on the other hand, negatively affects the effectiveness of its implementation. This situation is, however, mitigated by the numerous thematic-specific guidelines and strategies adopted by the COPs for a specific timeframe.

---

257 "Background," Convention on Biological Diversity, October 13, 2023 https://www.cbd.int/reports/national.shtml.

258 Glowka et al., *A Guide to the Convention on Biological Diversity*, 1, 6.

259 Yzquierdo, "The 1992 Convention on Biological Diversity," 13.

1.3.2.2. The ecosystem approach under the CBD

Since the second COP, the 'ecosystem approach' has been regarded as a primary framework of action under the CBD.[260] Not being enshrined in the CBD directly, the 'ecosystem approach' is a concept or even a "fully-fledged system of soft-law principles and guidelines" developed by normative activity of the COP based on the legal concept of 'ecosystem' found in Article 2 of the CBD.[261] Its content, having been subject to the varying views of the Parties to the CBD, has been gradually clarified at the meetings and discussions, resulting in points on operational guidance and guiding principles.[262] In particular, 'ecosystem approach' has been defined as "a strategy for the integrated management of land, water and living resources that promotes conservation and sustainable use in an equitable way".[263] It is based on consideration of the "levels of biological organization, which encompass the essential structure, processes, functions and interactions among organisms and their environment", which is consistent with the definition of the 'ecosystem' in Article 2 of the CBD and means that it "can refer to any functioning unit at any scale".[264] It requires adaptive management, able to facilitate the dynamic nature of ecosystems in the situations of uncertainty, that is "when some cause-and-effect relationships are not yet fully established scientifically".[265] Importantly, the 'ecosystem approach' allows a significant leeway in its application in a particular situation, as it depends on particular conditions on various levels from local to global and as it does not preclude the use of other management and conservation

---

260 Conference of the Parties, *Preliminary consideration of components of biological diversity particularly under threat and action which could be taken under the Convention*, CBD COP Decision II/8 (1995), § 1.

261 Elisa Morgera, "The ecosystem approach and the precautionary principle," in *Biodiversity and Nature Protection Law*, ed. Elisa Morgera and Jona Razzaque (Cheltenham: Edward Elgar Publishing, 2017), 71.

262 Secretariat, *Handbook of the Convention on Biological Diversity*, 254;
Conference of the Parties, *Report and recommendations of the third meeting of the Subsidiary Body on Scientific, Technical and Technological Advice, and instructions by the Conference of the Parties to the Subsidiary Body on Scientific, Technical and Technological Advice*, CBD COP Decision IV/1 (1998) B; Conference of the Parties, *Ecosystem approach*, CBD COP Decision V/6 (2000); Conference of the Parties, *Ecosystem Approach*, CBD COP Decision VII/11 (2004).

263 COP, Decision V/6, section A, 1.

264 COP, Decision V/6, section A, 2–3.

265 COP, Decision V/6, section A, 4.

approaches, "such as biosphere reserves, protected areas, and single-species conservation programmes" and could integrate these.[266]

There are twelve complementary and interlinked principles on ecosystem approach. According to the first principle, the objectives of management are a matter of social choice, and the management should take both cultural and biological diversity into account, including rights and interests of indigenous peoples and other local communities. Ecosystems thus are to be managed for both their intrinsic value and benefits for humans.[267] The second principle requires decentralisation of the management to the lowest possible level, as it helps to increase the responsibility, accountability, participation and use of local knowledge. In line with the third principle, the managers should consider the effects of their activities on other (adjacent and not only) ecosystems. For this purpose, the changes in the organisation of institutions and decision-making might be needed. The fourth principle takes economic context into account, suggesting the reduction of market distortions negatively affecting biodiversity, aligning incentives to promote conservation and sustainable use of biodiversity and possible internalization of costs and benefits. The fifth principle calls on to conserve ecosystem structure and functioning, that is "a dynamic relationship within species, among species and between species and their abiotic environment, as well as the physical and chemical interactions within the environment", attributing to it greater long-term significance compared to simple protection of species. The sixth principle promotes awareness of the limits of the ecosystem functioning, calling for the cautious management. The seventh principle suggests bounding the ecosystem approach by the spatial and temporal scales, appropriate to the objectives and defined operationally by relevant stakeholders. It also means that the connectivity between areas should be promoted, where needed. The eighth principle promotes long-term management objectives and consideration of the lag-effects as opposed to the short-term gains and immediate benefits. The ninth principle requires the adaptivity of management to the changes. The tenth principle calls on to seeking the balance between conservation and use of biodiversity, encouraging to shift from the strict division on protected and non-protected components of biodiversity to more flexible approaches. The eleventh principle is dedicated to the consideration of information from all sources to achieve a better understanding of ecosystem

266 COP, Decision V/6, section A, 5.
267 COP, Decision V/6, section B, 6.

functions and the impact of human use, and further suggests sharing this information with all stakeholders and actors. Finally, the twelfth principle suggests involvement of all relevant sectors of society at various levels and from various scientific disciplines due to the complexity of biodiversity management and associated side-effects and implications.[268] The five points of operational guidance are the following: "focus on the functional relationships and processes within ecosystems"; "enhance benefit-sharing"; "use adaptive management practices"; "carry out management actions at the scale appropriate for the issue being addressed, with decentralization to lowest level, as appropriate"; and "ensure intersectoral cooperation".[269]

The Decision VII/11 endorsed the Decision V/6, adding refinement and elaboration on the ecosystem approach based on experience of its practical application. In particular, it added annotations to the rationale contained in decision V/6 as well as implementation guidelines.[270] With regard to the forests, Decision VII/11 draws attention to the 'sustainable forest management' (SFM) as reflected in the Rio Forest Principles, stating that it "can be considered as a means of applying the ecosystem approach to forests".[271] It promotes enhanced cooperation to integrate the concepts of ecosystem approach and the SFM, and suggests in this respect placing greater emphasis within the SFM on inter-sectoral collaboration, interactions between forests and other biome/habitat types within a landscape and biodiversity conservation issues.[272] Furthermore, it underscores the need of good governance at all levels for successful application of the ecosystem approach and, accordingly, for achieving sustainable use and conservation of biodiversity, where intersectoral cooperation and integration of ecosystem approach into forestry is considered necessary.[273] Annex II explains the issue of relationship between ecosystem approach and the SFM in a greater detail, pointing to the interplay between them and room for development of both concepts. The key themes for the well-managed forests, including "[m]ultiple use, stakeholder participation, good information and monitoring systems, and

268 COP, Decision V/6, section B, 6.

269 COP, Decision V/6, section C; COP, Decision VII/11.

270 COP, Decision VII/11, § 8–18.

271 COP, Decision VII/11, § 7; See United Nations Conference on Environment and Development, *Forest Principles: Non-legally Binding Authoritative Statement of Principles for a Global Consensus on the Management, Conservation and Sustainable Development of All Types of Forests* A/CONF.151/26/Rev.1(Vol.I) (1992) https://digitallibrary.un.org/record/160453?v=pdf [Rio Forest Principles].

272 COP, Decision VII/11, § 11.

273 COP, Decision VII/11, § 18–19.

good governance" are recognised to be the key issues for the ecosystem approach.[274]

Elisa Morgera justly groups the central ideas of the 'ecosystem approach' into the concepts of integration, priority of conservation, emphasis on equity, and fair and equitable benefit-sharing.[275] She also notes the interaction between the ecosystem approach and precautionary principle in the light of adaptive management (that follows from the aforementioned Principles 6 and 9), and succinctly notes the few reflections of the scholarship on this topic.[276] Furthermore, 'ecosystem approach' creates a room for mutual supportiveness among the CBD and other international agreements, such as those on climate change or human rights.[277] In addition, an important issue for the development of international law in this context it whether 'ecosystem approach' should be treated as a principle of international environmental law, and whether by its means international environmental law's focus should be shifted to the needs of ecosystem integrity not based on sovereign interests of the states.[278] It is also unclear, whether ecosystem approach entails legally binding obligations for states.[279]

1.3.2.3. The thematic area of forest biodiversity

Turning to the thematic area of 'forest biodiversity', it is worth noting that the CBD does not contain the definition of 'forest', and for this purpose largely bases its forest-related definitions on those of the Food and Agriculture Organization of the United Nations (FAO).[280] In the same vein, in the issue of reporting and monitoring of forest biodiversity, CBD relies on the Global Forest Resources Assessment (FRA) process under FAO.[281] Nevertheless, significant attention is being paid to forest biodiversity under the CBD, as forests, being both habitats for the *in-situ* conservation and a source for various sustainable uses of biodiversity, are particularly

274 COP, Decision VII/11, Annex II, § 18.
275 Morgera, "The ecosystem approach and the precautionary principle," 72–73.
276 Morgera, "The ecosystem approach and the precautionary principle," 76–77.
277 Morgera, "The ecosystem approach and the precautionary principle," 77–78.
278 Morgera, "The ecosystem approach and the precautionary principle," 78.
279 See Koester, "Environmental principles and concepts in biodiversity treaties," 550.
280 SBSTTA, *A Background Report on Improving Forest Biodiversity Monitoring and Reporting*, UN Doc UNEP/CBD/SBSTTA/16/INF/25 (2012), 13.
281 SBSTTA, *A Background Report on Improving Forest Biodiversity Monitoring and Reporting*, 13.

important for the achievement of the CBD's objectives.[282] Therefore, it is no surprise that forest biodiversity is included among the thematic work programme under the CBD. It has been on the agenda since the beginning of the functioning of the institutional mechanism. In particular, SBSTTA 1 noted, upon request by the COP 1 (as to how the COP could consider biodiversity components, including those under threat), the establishment of the Intergovernmental Panel on Forests (IPF) and recommended the COP to consider input into the IPF process. Subsequently, COP 2 adopted a statement to the IPF on biodiversity and forests, COP 3 requested the Secretariat to develop work programme on forest biodiversity, COP 4 endorsed a work programme on forest biodiversity and COP 5 reviewed its implementation, drawing attention of the relevant actors to it, invited Parties to submit a detailed report on forest ecosystems, established an ad hoc technical expert group on forest biological diversity and noted that Parties' work on conservation and sustainable use of forest biological diversity should contribute to the work of the United Nations Forum on Forests.[283] The elements of the work programme initially included *inter alia* "holistic and inter-sectoral ecosystem approaches that integrate the conservation and sustainable use of biological diversity, taking account of social, cultural and economic considerations" and "comprehensive analysis of the ways in which human activities, in particular forest-management practices, influence biological diversity and assessment of ways to minimize or mitigate negative influences".[284] Documents and activities within this work programme serve as a means to operationalise and interpret Parties' obligations under the CBD.[285] Moreover, the forest management under the CBD is considered to constitute application of the ecosystem approach to forests, both within and outside the protected areas.[286]

---

282 Annalisa Savaresi, "Forest Biodiversity," in *Biodiversity and Nature Protection Law*, ed. Elisa Morgera and Jona Razzaque (Cheltenham: Edward Elgar Publishing, 2017), 210.

283 Secretariat, *Handbook of the Convention on Biological Diversity*, 230–232; CBD COP Decisions on forest biodiversity include: Decision II/9 (1995); Decision III/12 (1996); Decision IV/7 (1998); Decision V/4 (2000); Decision VI/22 (2002); Decision VII/1 (2004); Decision VIII/19 (2006); Decision IX/5 (2008); Decision X/36 (2010); Decision XI/19 (2012); and Decision XIII/7 (2016).

284 Secretariat, *Handbook of the Convention on Biological Diversity*, 231–232.

285 Savaresi, "Forest Biodiversity," 210.

286 Savaresi, "Forest Biodiversity," 210; SBSTTA, *Ecosystem approach: further elaboration, guidelines for implementation and relationship with sustainable forest management*, SBSTTA Recommendation IX/6 (2008) Annex II.

1.3.2.4. The recent strategic documents on biodiversity

When it comes to recent strategic documents on biodiversity, the Strategic Plan for Biodiversity 2011 – 2020, including Aichi Biodiversity Targets, was remarkable as it provided "a useful flexible framework" relevant not only to the CBD, but also "to all biodiversity-related conventions".[287] Its vision extended to 2050, its mission covered the period until 2020, and its 20 headline targets have been planned until 2015 or 2020 and grouped into 5 strategic goals. Among them, the most relevant for the forest biodiversity are targets 5 (bringing to zero or at least halving the rate of loss of natural habitats including forests, and reducing the degradation and fragmentation), 7 (areas under forestry are managed sustainably, ensuring conservation of biodiversity) and 11 (conserving at least 17 per cent of terrestrial areas through the system of protected areas and other effective area-based conservation measures).[288] In addition, targets not mentioning forests specifically, but addressing the general issues relevant for the forest ecosystems include 9 (on control and eradication of invasive alien species), 12 (on prevention of extinction of known threatened species) and 15 (on ecosystem resilience, contribution of biodiversity to carbon stocks, and restoration of ecosystems).[289] The progress with the achievement of the Aichi Targets has been reflected in the fifth edition of the Global Biodiversity Outlook.[290] Unfortunately, none of the 20 targets have been fully achieved on the global level.[291] As to the specific targets, closely related to the forest biodiversity, the success is partial. For instance, there has been some progress on target 5, as the rate of deforestation has been lower than during the previous decade, however loss, degradation and fragmentation remain high and wilderness areas continue to decline.[292] The same is true for the target 7, although some progress is acknowledged, it was not sufficient to meet this target. The situation is better with targets 9 and 11, that have status 'partially achieved', as some progress (especially with the identi-

287 Conference of the Parties, *The Strategic Plan for Biodiversity 2011–2020 and the Aichi Biodiversity Targets*, CBD COP Decision X/2, UNEP/CBD/COP/DEC/X/2 (2010), Preamble [*Strategic Plan for Biodiversity 2011–2020*].

288 Savaresi, "Forest Biodiversity," 211; *Strategic Plan for Biodiversity 2011–2020.*

289 *Strategic Plan for Biodiversity 2011–2020.*

290 Secretariat of the Convention on Biological Diversity, *Global Biodiversity Outlook 5* (Montreal, 2020) www.cbd.int/GBO5 [*Global Biodiversity Outlook 5*].

291 *Global Biodiversity Outlook 5*, 10.

292 *Global Biodiversity Outlook 5*, 13.

fication of invasive alien species, understanding of the risk they present and eradicating them) is evident, however only with respect to the limited scope of cases, and the new introductions of alien species remain unresolved. Concerning target 11, the proportion of protected areas is close to the target, however the criteria of them being ecologically representative, connected to one another and to the wider landscape and effectively managed have not been fulfilled.[293] The progress on targets 12 and 15 was limited, as wild animal populations continue to decline, and the ambitious projects on the restoration of ecosystems remain to be seen as fully implemented.[294]

The succeeding and the most recent strategic document on biodiversity is the Kunming-Montreal Global Biodiversity Framework, adopted in 2022 after a series of discussions.[295] It builds upon the Strategic Plan for Biodiversity 2011 – 2020[296] and serves as a strategic plan for the implementation of the CBD and its Protocols during the period of 2022 – 2030.[297] Its implementation is, in turn, supported by other recent decisions of the COP, including on monitoring framework for it,[298] on planning, monitoring, reporting and review;[299] on resource mobilization;[300] on capacity-building and development and technical and scientific cooperation;[301] on digital sequence information on genetic resources;[302] and on cooperation with other Conventions and international organizations.[303] The Kunming-Montreal Global Biodiversity Framework also acknowledges its linkages with sustainable development, human rights and principles of the Rio Declara-

293 *Global Biodiversity Outlook 5*, 14–15.

294 *Global Biodiversity Outlook 5*, 15–16.

295 "Preparations for the Post-2020 Biodiversity Framework," Convention on Biological Diversity, accessed September 20, 2024, https://www.cbd.int/conferences/post2020.

296 *Kunming-Montreal Global Biodiverpsity Framework*, Annex, § 3.

297 *Kunming-Montreal Global Biodiverpsity Framework*, § 8.

298 Conference of the Parties, *Monitoring framework for the Kunming-Montreal Global Biodiversity Framework*, CBD COP Decision 15/5 (2022).

299 Conference of the Parties, *Mechanisms for planning, monitoring, reporting and review*, CBD COP Decision 15/6 (2022).

300 Conference of the Parties, *Resource mobilization*, CBD COP Decision 15/7 (2022).

301 Conference of the Parties, *Capacity-building and development and technical and scientific cooperation*, CBD COP Decision 15/8 (2022).

302 Conference of the Parties, *Digital sequence information on genetic resources*, CBD COP Decision 15/9 (2022).

303 Conference of the Parties, *Cooperation with other conventions and international organizations*, CBD COP Decision 15/13 (2022).

tion on Environment and Development.[304] The Kunming-Montreal Global Biodiversity Framework establishes the 2050 vision and 2030 mission. Its vision (identical to that contained in the 2011 – 2020 Strategic Plan) is a world where "by 2050, biodiversity is valued, conserved, restored and wisely used, maintaining ecosystem services, sustaining a healthy planet and delivering benefits essential for all people."[305] Its mission, which is closely related to the CBD goals, is:

> To take urgent action to halt and reverse biodiversity loss to put nature on a path to recovery for the benefit of people and planet by conserving and sustainably using biodiversity and by ensuring the fair and equitable sharing of benefits from the use of genetic resources, while providing the necessary means of implementation.[306]

There are 4 long-term goals, corresponding to the 2050 vision and 23 action-oriented global targets to be initiated immediately and implemented until 2030. The goals include enhancement, maintenance and restoration of the ecosystems' integrity, connectivity and resilience combined and increase of the area of natural ecosystems, halting human-induced extinction of threatened species and maintenance of the genetic diversity of wild and domesticated species populations (Goal A); sustainable use and management of biodiversity and maintenance of the ecosystem functions and services (Goal B); fair and equitable sharing of benefits from the utilization of genetic resources and traditional knowledge (Goal C); securing the adequate means of implementation, including financial resources, capacity-building, technical and scientific cooperation and access to technologies to all Parties (Goal D). The 23 targets are grouped into 3 categories: "reducing threats to biodiversity" (targets 1 – 8); "meeting people's needs through sustainable use and benefit-sharing" (targets 9 – 13); and "tools and solutions for implementation and mainstreaming" (targets 14 – 23).

Target 1 deals with ensuring that all areas are under "participatory, integrated and biodiversity inclusive spatial planning and/or effective management processes addressing land- and sea-use change", which is important for stopping the loss of areas of high biodiversity importance. At the same time, the rights of indigenous peoples and local communities should be respected. Target 2 suggests restoring by 2030 at least 30 per cent of the

304 *Kunming-Montreal Global Biodiversity Framework*, Annex, Section C, § 7 (g), (k), Section D, § 8.
305 *Kunming-Montreal Global Biodiversity Framework*, Annex, Section F, § 10.
306 *Kunming-Montreal Global Biodiversity Framework*, Annex, Section F, § 11.

degraded ecosystems. Target 3 calls on to ensure and enable by 2030 effective conservation and management of at least 30 per cent of terrestrial (and other) areas, especially those of particular importance for biodiversity and ecosystem functions, including through the systems of protected areas and other effective area-based conservation measures, and ensuring that any sustainable use of such areas is consistent with the conservation outcomes. The connectivity of these areas, integration into wider landscapes and respect of the rights of indigenous and local populations should also be taken into account for the purposes of this target. Target 4 urges to ensure management actions to halt human induced extinction and for recovery and conservation of species, as well as to maintain the genetic diversity for the purposes of adaptive potential of wild and domesticated species, and to manage effectively human-wildlife interactions to minimize the conflict for coexistence. Target 5 deals with the harvesting and trade of wild species, requiring them to be safe and legal and preventing overexploitation; it also mentions ecosystem approach and respect of the sustainable use by indigenous peoples and local communities. Target 6 addresses the issue of invasive alien species, calling to identify and manage pathways of their introduction and eradicating or controlling them. Target 7 advocates reduction of pollution from all sources and its negative impacts. Target 8 sensitizes to the impact of climate change on biodiversity, calling to increase resilience through the mitigation, adaptation, and disaster risk reduction actions.[307]

Out of the next set of the targets, targets 9, 10 and 11 are particularly relevant to the forest biodiversity, requiring the sustainable management and use of wild species, which provide environmental benefits to people; sustainable management of areas under forestry; and restoration, maintenance and enhancement of nature's contribution to people, including ecosystem functions and services respectively.[308]

Among the third set of targets, of particular relevance to the forest biodiversity are: target 14 requiring full integration of biodiversity and its values into policies, regulations, planning and development processes, strategic environmental assessments, environmental impact assessments and other documents within all levels and sectors of government as well as progressive alignment of all relevant public and private activities and fiscal and financial flows with the goals of this framework; target 15 encouraging

---

307 *Kunming-Montreal Global Biodiversity Framework*, 9–10.
308 *Kunming-Montreal Global Biodiversity Framework*, 10–11.

business to reduce negative and increase positive impacts on biodiversity; target 16 dealing with the people's sustainable consumption choices; target 18 on elimination of incentives harmful to biodiversity; target 19 on progressive increase of the level of financial resources to implement national biodiversity strategies and action plans; target 21 on availability and accessibility of data, information and knowledge to guide effective and equitable governance, integrated and participatory management of biodiversity and on awareness-raising, education, monitoring, research and knowledge management.[309]

1.3.3. The Convention on International Trade in Endangered Species of Wild Fauna and Flora

One of the oldest biodiversity-related international treaties is the CITES, which was concluded in 1973 and entered into force in 1975. The idea behind this convention was promoted by the International Union for Conservation of Nature (IUCN) since 1960s.[310] As its name says, CITES is dedicated to regulating a narrow issue of international trade in endangered species, and unlike some other international law instruments focusing on protection of habitats, this convention uses a species-based conservation approach.[311] Its initial scope was limited to the instances of trade crossing the border of states, leaving the matters within the states, such as domestic harvest of these species, to be internalized by the state sovereignty.[312] It was, however, from the very beginning grounded on a "trade response to the perceived limitations of sovereignty-based protection of biodiversity".[313] Furthermore, during the years of operation of this convention, its requirements evolved beyond the original language of a mere international trade.[314]

309 *Kunming-Montreal Global Biodiversity Framework*, 11–13.

310 Dias and Garforth, "Historical perspectives on the challenge of biodiversity conservation," 17.

311 Annalisa Savaresi, "Forest biodiversity," 209.

312 Erika J. Techera "Species-based conservation," in *Biodiversity and Nature Protection Law*, ed. Elisa Morgera and Jona Razzaque (Cheltenham: Edward Elgar Publishing, 2017), 101.

313 Christine Willmore, "Sovereignty, conservation and sustainable use," in *Biodiversity and Nature Protection Law*, ed. Elisa Morgera and Jona Razzaque (Cheltenham: Edward Elgar Publishing, 2017), 37–38.

314 Hunter, Salzman, and Zaelke, *International Environmental Law and Policy*, 1082, 1102.

It could be noted that the preamble of the CITES implies biodiversity (its wildlife component) without referring to this word directly, that is by using the wording "wild fauna and flora in their many beautiful and varied forms" instead. It recognises that wild fauna and flora constitute the "irreplaceable part of the natural systems of the earth" and have to be protected for the sake of present and future generations. It also notes their value from the aesthetic, scientific, cultural, recreational and economic points of view. According to preamble, peoples and states are supposed to be the best protectors of their own wild fauna and flora, but international cooperation is also needed, especially to protect the species from over-exploitation related to international trade.[315]

The key instrument of protection of the species under the CITES is their listing into the three appendices, depending on the status of the species, and entailing different procedures. Appendix I includes species threatened with extinction[316] which are or may be affected by trade. It grants the highest protection possible by requiring strict regulation and stating that trade in specimens of these species must only be authorised in exceptional circumstances. It requires advise and consent of the Scientific and Management Authorities by both export and import States, as well as in the cases of re-export or introduction from the sea. It also excludes the possibility of import for primarily commercial purposes.[317]

Appendix II comprises species not necessarily currently threatened with extinction, but having probability to become so unless trade in their specimens is subject to strict regulation. It also covers other species, which may influence trade in the specimens covered by the general rule of this Appendix. Trade in specimens of Appendix II species requires advise and consent of the Scientific and Management Authorities of the exporting State, re-export State and a State of introduction from the sea. This Appendix,

---

315 CITES, Preamble.

316 The CITES does not provide a definition of 'threatened with extinction', however, this issue has been clarified by means of Bern critera and later by means of the Fort Lauderdale criteria; See Azra Dizdarevic, "Convention on international Trade in Endangered Species of Wild Fauna and Flora 1973," in *Multilateral Environmental Treaties*, ed. Malgosia Fitzmaurice, Attila Tanzi, and Angeliki Papantoniou, (Cheltenham: Edward Elgar Publishing, 2017), 72; Conference of the Parties, *Criteria for amendment of Appendices I and II*, CITES COP Resolution Conf. 9.24 (Rev. CoP17), Annex 1.

317 CITES, Article II, Article III; Hunter, Salzman, and Zaelke, *International Environmental Law and Policy*, 1085.

thus, does not require a separate import permit and does not include the criterion of the exclusion of the primarily commercial purposes of trade.[318]

Appendix III includes species identified by a particular State Party to be subject to regulation within its jurisdiction and requiring cooperation with other Parties to control the trade to this end. The export from a State that included certain species in Appendix III required granting of export permit. However, unlike for Appendices I and II, only Management Authority is involved (without participation of Scientific Authority).[319]

While granting the permits, Scientific Authority needs to consider a number of factors, including those associated with phrases "detrimental to the survival of that species" and "maintain that species throughout its range at a level consistent with its role in the ecosystems in which it occurs", used in Articles III and IV of the CITES. These concepts have been jointly named 'non-detriment findings' (NDFs) and addressed in Resolution 16.7.[320]

The CITES has detailed enforcement provisions, in comparison with many other environmental treaties.[321] The enforcement measures under the CITES include penalties, confiscation and designated ports of exit and entry. However, there are still unresolved practical issues such as the determination of the level of penalties.[322] The CITES COP has also developed a compliance system, where Standing Committee serves as a compliance committee empowered to handle matters regarding monitoring and assessment of compliance.[323] Other convention bodies, including the COP, Secretariat, and the Animal and Plants Committees also contribute

318 CITES, Article II, Article IV; Hunter, Salzman, and Zaelke, *International Environmental Law and Policy*, 1085.

319 CITES, Article II, Article V; Hunter, Salzman, and Zaelke, *International Environmental Law and Policy*, 1085.

320 Dizdarevic, "Convention on international Trade in Endangered Species of Wild Fauna and Flora 1973," 70–71; see Conference of the Parties, *Non-detriment findings*, CITES COP Resolution Conf. 16.7 (Rev. CoP17).

321 See Sands, Peel, Fabra, and MacKenzie, *Principles of International Environmental Law*, 416.

322 Dizdarevic, "Convention on international Trade in Endangered Species of Wild Fauna and Flora 1973," 74; CITES, Article VIII.

323 Dizdarevic, "Convention on international Trade in Endangered Species of Wild Fauna and Flora 1973," 75; Conference of the Parties, *CITES compliance procedures*, CITES COP Resolution Conf. 14.3 (Rev. CoP19), § 12, 29.

to the compliance procedure.[324] Non-complying countries may be subject to the "suspension of commercial or all trade in specimens of one of more CITES-listed species", which proved to be an effective measure to return countries to compliance.[325] The parties also have an obligation to submit periodic reports on the implementation of the CITES and make them available to the public, where it is not inconsistent with their legislation.[326]

Apart from CITES provisions as such, the institutional mechanism created by the CITES contributes to the greater flexibility of its application (in particular, through the use of annotations, quotas or working groups) and to the creation of the new conservation strategies within the CITES framework, even though these were not initially envisaged in the text of the convention.[327]

Moreover, the synergy with other relevant conventions, including the CBD and the CMS should be achieved, as was noted in the CITES Strategic Vision 2008 – 2020.[328] With respect to biodiversity, this strategic document specifically contained a component to "contribute to significantly reducing the rate of biodiversity loss and to achieving relevant globally-agreed goals and targets by ensuring that CITES and other multilateral instruments and processes are coherent and mutually supportive".[329]

The subsequent Strategic Vision 2021 – 2030 reiterates the linkages and the need for mutual supportiveness among the CITES and other international instruments, processes and actions, recognising the contribution of the CITES' aim to achievement of the Sustainable Development Goals and the post-2020 global biodiversity framework, that is the Kunming-Montreal

324 Dizdarevic, "Convention on international Trade in Endangered Species of Wild Fauna and Flora 1973," 75; Conference of the Parties, *CITES compliance procedures*, Resolution Conf. 14.3 (Rev. CoP19) § 10, 13, 14.

325 Dizdarevic, "Convention on international Trade in Endangered Species of Wild Fauna and Flora 1973," 75–76; Conference of the Parties, *CITES compliance procedures*, Resolution Conf. 14.3 (Rev. CoP19),
§ 30.

326 CITES, Article VIII (7), (8).

327 Hunter, Salzman, and Zaelke, *International Environmental Law and Policy*, 1102; see also Sands, Peel, Fabra, and MacKenzie, *Principles of International Environmental Law*, 415–416.

328 Conference of the Parties, *CITES Strategic Vision: 2008–2020*, CITES COP Resolution Conf. 16.3 (Rev. CoP17).

329 Dizdarevic, "Convention on international Trade in Endangered Species of Wild Fauna and Flora 1973," 76–77; Conference of the Parties, *CITES Strategic Vision: 2008–2020*, Goal 3.

Global Biodiversity Framework described above.[330] Besides the international dimension, the Strategic Vision envisages national action to achieve conservation and sustainable use of the species, stating that "Parties improve the conservation status of the CITES-listed specimens, put in place national conservation actions, support their sustainable use".[331] Parties are further encouraged to achieve "synergies in their implementation of CITES, other biodiversity-related conventions and other relevant multilateral environmental, trade and development agreements".[332]

The CITES regime is directly relevant to some of the species of the Ukrainian Carpathians. For instance, the Carpathian Biosphere Reserve is known to host 67 flora and fauna species listed in CITES appendices.[333] Among the species listed in Appendix I to the CITES, animal species such as the peregrine falcon (*Falco peregrinus*) and the European otter (*Lutra lutra*) are found in the Ukrainian Carpathians.[334] The "Checklist of CITES Species" database[335] or "Species +" database[336] might be consulted for the full list of the CITES species found in Ukraine.

330 Conference of the Parties, *CITES Strategic Vision: 2021–2030*, CITES COP Resolution Conf. 18.3, Goal 4, Objective 4.2; Goal 5, Objective 5.2 [*CITES Strategic Vision: 2021–2030*].

331 *CITES Strategic Vision: 2021–2030*, Goal 1, Objective 1.5.

332 *CITES Strategic Vision: 2021–2030*, Goal 5, Objective 5.1, Indicator 5.1.1.

333 "Carpathian Biosphere Reserve," Bern Convention, accessed September 20, 2024, https://www.coe.int/en/web/bern-convention/-/carpathian-biosphere-reserve.

334 Anatolii Poluda et al,. eds, *Encyclopaedia of migratory species of wild animals of Ukraine (Kyiv, 2018),* https://mepr.gov.ua/wp-content/uploads/2023/05/Entsyklopediya-migruyuchyh-vydiv-dykyh-tvaryn-Ukrayiny-3.pdf, 235; Wiesław Król et al., eds., *Carpathian List of Endangered Species* (Vienna : Krakow: WWF International Danube-Carpathian Programme; Institute of Nature Conservation, Polish Academy of Sciences, 2003) https://archive.nationalredlist.org/files/2012/08/Carpathian-List-of-Endangered-Species-2003.pdf, 24.

335 "Checklist of CITES Species: Ukraine," CITES, accessed September 20, 2024, https://checklist.cites.org/#/en/search/country_ids%5B%5D=211&cites_appendices%5B%5D=I&cites_appendices%5B%5D=II&cites_appendices%5B%5D=III&output_layout=alphabetical&level_of_listing=0&show_synonyms=1&show_author=1&show_english=1&show_spanish=1&show_french=1&scientific_name=&page=1&per_page=20.

336 "About Species+," Species+, accessed September 20, 2024, https://speciesplus.net/about.

1.3.4. The Convention on the Conservation of Migratory Species of Wild Animals

The 1979 Bonn Convention provides the framework for cooperation of states to protect species, which migrate from one country to another. Its conclusion was catalysed by the 1972 Stockholm conference.[337] Similarly to the CITES, CMS uses a species-based conservation approach.[338]

The fundamental principles of the CMS include the recognition of the importance of the conservation of the migratory species, and the need to take action individually or in cooperation to conserve such species and their habitat with the Range States agreeing to take action to this end, paying special attention to the species with unfavourable conservation status. The particular modes of action include research related to the migratory species; provision of immediate protection for migratory species included in Appendix I; and conclusion of agreements covering the conservation and management of the species included in Appendix II.[339]

Appendix I lists endangered migratory species, that is where the reliable evidence indicates "that the migratory species is in danger of extinction throughout all or a significant portion of its range", where 'range' means "all the areas of land or water that a migratory species inhabits, stays in temporarily, crosses or overflies at any time on its normal migration route".[340] The obligations of the Range States comprise conservation and restoration of the habitats that are of importance in removing the species from danger of extinction; prevention, removal, compensation for or minimisation of the adverse effects of activities or obstacles that seriously impede or prevent the migration of species; and prevention, reduction or control of the factors that are endangering or are likely to further endanger the species, such as strictly controlling the introduction of the exotic species. Range states should also prohibit the taking of animals belonging to such

337 Melissa Lewis and Arie Trouwborst, "Bonn Convention on the Conservation of Migratory Species of Wild Animals 1979," in *Multilateral Environmental Treaties*, ed. Malgosia Fitzmaurice, Attila Tanzi, and Angeliki Papantoniou, (Cheltenham: Edward Elgar Publishing, 2017), 25–26; United Nations, *Report of the United Nations Conference on the Human Environment,* UN Doc A/CONF.48/14/Rev.1 (Stockholm, 5–16 June, 1972), https://digitallibrary.un.org/record/523249?v=pdf, Chapter II, Recommendation 32.

338 See Techera, "Species-based conservation," 102–103.

339 CMS, Article II.

340 CMS, Articles III, I.

species (with the several exceptions based on the purpose of the taking).[341] The problematic aspect as regards the obligation with respect to species listed in the Appendix I, lies however, in the use of the wording, such as 'shall endeavour to', 'where feasible and appropriate', 'as appropriate' or 'to the extent feasible and appropriate', making the nature of obligations less strict and clear. The only 'unqualified' obligation is the prohibition of taking of animals.[342]

Appendix II lists migratory species which have an unfavourable conservation status and a conservation status which would significantly benefit from the international cooperation. Unlike Appendix I, it does not provide for particular obligations of the State Parties with respect to those species, leaving the determination of these to the "AGREEMENTS", which are to be concluded by the Range States. However, there remains a possibility for the migratory species to be listed simultaneously in both Appendix I and Appendix II.[343] It is worth noting that the same Article IV of the CMS dedicated to the Appendix II species, establishes a possibility of concluding agreements with respect to a wider category of species, not being 'migratory' in the narrow meaning of this word. In particular, Article IV (4) encourages the Parties to conclude agreements for "any population or any geographically separate part of the population of any species or lower taxon of wild animals, members of which periodically cross one or more national jurisdiction boundaries".[344] Besides, the interpretation of the elements of the definition of 'migratory species' under the CMS, including terms 'cyclically and predictably' (where 'cyclically' refers to a cycle of any nature, such as astronomical, climatic or life, and of any frequency and 'predictably' means the possibility to predict the recurrence of phenomenon, though not necessarily regularly in time),[345] implies the possibility of listing in the CMS Appendices more species that would have been possible under a stricter interpretation of this term.[346]

341 CMS, Article III.

342 Cf. Lewis and Trouwborst, "Bonn Convention on the Conservation of Migratory Species of Wild Animals 1979," 27.

343 CMS, Article IV.

344 CMS, Article IV (4); Lewis and Trouwborst, "Bonn Convention on the Conservation of Migratory Species of Wild Animals 1979," 27–28.

345 Conference of the Parties, *Guidelines for the Application of Certain Terms of the Convention*, UNEP/CMS/Resolution 02.02 (1988).

346 Lewis and Trouwborst, "Bonn Convention on the Conservation of Migratory Species of Wild Animals 1979," 31–32.

As with the CBD and the CITES, the key lines of action are outlined in the strategic document, until recently, the Strategic Plan for Migratory Species (2015 – 2023) (SPMS).[347] This plan was characterised as "a 'migratory species cut' of the Strategic Plan for Biodiversity", meaning that it not only serves the achievement of the aims of the CMS, but also helps to evaluate progress towards strategic documents under the CBD, and the related Sustainable Development Goals.[348] Moreover, it relied on the Strategic Plan for Biodiversity and its Aichi Biodiversity Targets (relevant until 2020 and later substituted by the Kunming-Montreal Global Biodiversity Framework) as on a framework to keep the SPMS consistent with the United Nations General Assembly resolutions calling for mainstreaming of the Aichi Biodiversity Targets and enabling the States to logically integrate migratory species targets into their National Biodiversity Strategies and Action Plans.[349] The SPMS's vision is clearly related to the wider category of biodiversity: "Living in harmony with nature – where populations and habitats of migratory species (along with all biodiversity) are valued, conserved, restored and wisely used, thereby contributing to global sustainability." Its mission is more specifically centred on migratory species: "To promote actions to ensure the favourable conservation status of migratory species and their habitats, and to ensure the ecological integrity, connectivity and resilience of migration systems."[350] The Plan itself comprises 5 Goals and 16 Targets. These goals and targets, focused on migratory species, and at the same time highly relevant for the biodiversity protection in general, include for instance: the need to address the causes of decline of migratory species by mainstreaming conservation and sustainable use priorities across government and society; reduction of the direct pressures on migratory species and their habitats; improvement of the ecological connectivity and resilience of the migratory species' habitats; and enhancement of the benefits to all from the favourable conservation status of migratory species and enhancement of the implementation of the norms.[351]

347 Conference of the Parties, *Strategic Plan For Migratory Species 2015–2023*, UNEP/CMS/Resolution 11.2 (2014), Annex 1.

348 Conference of the Parties, *Strategic Plan For Migratory Species 2015–2023*, UNEP/CMS/Resolution 11.2 (Rev.COP12) (2017), Preamble [*Strategic Plan For Migratory Species 2015–2023*].

349 *Strategic Plan For Migratory Species 2015–2023*, 6.

350 *Strategic Plan For Migratory Species 2015–2023*, 9.

351 *Strategic Plan For Migratory Species 2015–2023*, Goals 1–5.

The implementation of the SPMS was closely monitored by the CMS Secretariat, and the final report on its implementation contains detailed information based on the countries' national reports to COP14 (even though it is noted that the reporting rate was low so that doubts as to the representativeness of global implementation remain). The key findings indicate, that some progress on mainstreaming migratory species across government and society has been achieved (Goal 1), however, reduction of direct pressures has not been sufficient (Goal 2). Moreover, the conservation status of many species remains to be "unfavourable", and populations continue to decline (Goal 3). In addition, some moderate progress on Goal 4 and Goal 5 has been observed. It was concluded that more individual and collaborative efforts of the Parties are needed to achieve CMS' aims and the wider global goals on biodiversity conservation, as well as protection and restoration of natural ecosystems.[352]

Based on the information on implementation of the SPMS, the new Strategic Plan was adopted by the parties at the COP 14 (2024) in Samarkand. The Samarkand Strategic Plan for Migratory Species 2024 – 2032 comprises 6 Goals and 23 targets, where Goals 4, 5, and 6 support the achievement of Goals 1, 2, and 3 on improving the conservation status of migratory species; maintenance and restoration of the habitats and ranges of migratory species, supporting their connectivity; and elimination or reduction of threats affecting migratory species. All of the Goals serve the achievement of the vision "By 2032, migratory species are thriving and live in fully restored and connected habitats".[353]

The range of a number of migratory species, mainly birds and bats, runs through the Ukrainian Carpathians. For instance among Appendix II birds species, at least the following are present in the Ukrainian Carpathians: *Anthus spinoletta, Anthus trivialis, Aquila chrysaetos, Ciconia nigra, Clanga pomarina, Luscinia megarhynchos, Milvus migrans, Monticola saxatilis, Motacilla cinerea, Phylloscopus sibilatrix, Phylloscopus trochilus, Regulus ignicapilla, Regulus regulus, Scolopax rusticola, Tringa ochropus, Turdus tor-*

352 CMS Secretariat, *Implementation of the Strategic Plan for Migratory Species 2015–2023*, UNEP/CMS/COP14/Doc.14.1 (2023), § 10–11; Annex.

353 Conference of the Parties, *Samarkand Strategic Plan for Migratory Species 2024–2032*, UNEP/CMS/Resolution 14.1 (2024), Annex.

quatus.[354] Forests of the Ukrainian Carpathians host about 22 bat species.[355] It is worth noting that bats are specifically protected by one of the Agreements on the species included in the Appendix II – the Agreement on the Conservation of Populations of European Bats (EUROBATS), to which Ukraine is a Party since 1999.[356] The full list of the CMS species in Ukraine may be found on the "Species +" database.[357]

1.3.5. The Convention concerning the Protection of the World Cultural and Natural Heritage

The World Heritage Convention, created under the auspices of the United Nations Educational, Scientific and Cultural Organization (UNESCO) was opened for signature in 1972 and is regarded as "the most prominent UNESCO convention".[358]

The UNESCO as such historically played a remarkable role in consolidating the international response to the protection of ecosystems and representative habitats, by convening the 1968 Conference on the Use and Conservation of the Biosphere and initiating the Man and Biosphere (MAB) programme.[359] The MAB programme, paying attention to the habitats that are rare, unique or threatened, to the biological hotspots in general and forests in particular and having a strong interest in the 'flagship' species, has resulted in the Network of Biosphere Reserves including over 700 sites in

354 See Poluda, *Encyclopaedia of migratory species of wild animals of Ukraine*; "Species+: CMS: Ukraine", Species+, accessed September 20, 2024, https://speciesplus.net/species#/taxon_concepts?taxonomy=cms&geo_entities_ids=211&geo_entity_scope=cms&page=1.

355 Andriy-Taras Bashta, *Bat population status survey in the Ukrainian Carpathians Mts. (Ukraine)*, Final report, (Lviv: Bat Research and Protection Group, 2007), https://ruffordorg.s3.amazonaws.com/media/project_reports/03.06.05%20Detailed%20Final%20Report.pdf.

356 "Ukraine," UNEP/EUROBATS, accessed September 20, 2024, https://www.eurobats.org/about_eurobats/parties_and_range_states/ukraine.

357 "Species+: CMS: Ukraine".

358 Stefan Gruber, "Convention concerning the Protection of the World Cultural and Natural Heritage 1972" in *Multilateral Environmental Treaties*, ed. Malgosia Fitzmaurice, Attila Tanzi, and Angeliki Papantoniou, (Cheltenham: Edward Elgar Publishing, 2017), 60.

359 Gillespie, *Conservation, Biodiversity and International Law*, 175.

over 130 countries.[360] Several biosphere reserves among them are located on the territory of the Ukrainian Carpathian Mountains or in the immediate vicinity, including the Carpathian Biosphere Reserve (since 1992); East Carpathians Transboundary Biosphere Reserve (Poland/Slovakia/Ukraine) (since 1998) and Roztochya (since 2011, since 2019 transboundary biosphere reserve with Poland).[361] The designation and review of the MAB is based on the soft legal framework comprising the Statutory Framework of the World Network of Biosphere Reserves and Seville Strategy for Biosphere Reserves.[362] The category of biosphere reserves is related to the world heritage site as the latter sites might be located within the former, as is the case in the Ukrainian Carpathians with biosphere reserves mentioned above hosting territories belonging to the heritage site "Ancient and Primeval Beech Forests of the Carpathians and Other Regions of Europe".[363]

The World Heritage Convention was one of the first convention to recognise the principle of common heritage of humankind and is unique in combining concern for cultural and natural heritage simultaneously.[364] The present thesis is focused on the natural heritage and mixed cultural and natural heritage (cultural landscapes) aspects.

'Natural heritage', as defined in Article 2 of the World Heritage Convention, comprises three categories: natural features of outstanding universal value from the aesthetic or scientific point of view; geological and physiographical formations and precisely delineated areas constituting habitats of threatened species of animals and plants of outstanding universal value from the point of view of science or conservation; and natural sites or

360 Gillespie, *Conservation, Biodiversity and International Law*, 175–176; Dias and Garforth, "Historical perspectives on the challenge of biodiversity conservation," 17; "Biosphere reserves," UNESCO, accessed September 20, 2024, https://www.unesco.org/en/mab/map?hub=66369.

361 "Biosphere reserves – Ukraine," UNESCO, accessed September 20, 2024, https://www.unesco.org/en/mab/map?f%5B0%5D=countries%3A501c7f7d-f0c7-5ac3-a3e8-86ec665c6528&f%5B1%5D=dataset_filters%3A6c254c17-2986-4f89-aa10-17d38a33454c&f%5B2%5D=regions%3A53da4dd6-bdd0-433d-bbb3-476f12b4cc32&hub=66369#toggle-facets.

362 "Designation and Review Process," UNESCO, accessed September 20, 2024, https://www.unesco.org/en/mab/wnbr/designation.

363 See "East Carpathians," UNESCO, accessed September 20, 2024, https://www.unesco.org/en/mab/east-carpathians-0?hub=66369; "Carpathian," accessed September 20, 2024, https://www.unesco.org/en/mab/carpathian?hub=66369.

364 Hunter, Salzman, and Zaelke, *International Environmental Law and Policy*, 1150; World Heritage Convention, Preamble.

precisely delineated natural areas of outstanding universal value from the point of view of science, conservation or natural beauty.[365]

'Cultural landscapes' represent "combined works of nature and of man" designated in Article 1 of the Convention. They are "illustrative of the evolution of human society and settlement over time, under the influence of the physical constraints and/or opportunities presented by their natural environment and of successive social, economic and cultural forces, both external and internal" and are selected on the basis of their outstanding universal value and their representativity of a certain geo-cultural region. The three main types of cultural landscapes include landscape designed and created intentionally by people; organically evolved landscape; and associative cultural landscape.[366]

The elements of the definitions and criteria for inscription on the "World Heritage List" have been clarified in the Operational Guidelines for the Implementation of the World Heritage Convention. Thus, 'outstanding universal value' means "cultural and/or natural significance which is so exceptional as to transcend national boundaries and to be of common importance for present and future generations of all humanity."[367] One of the criteria for the assessment of outstanding universal value is directly dedicated to biodiversity, namely that the property shall "contain the most important and significant natural habitats for *in-situ* conservation of biological diversity, including those containing threatened species of Outstanding Universal Value from the point of view of science or conservation".[368] The property should also meet conditions of integrity[369] and/or authenticity,[370] and must have an adequate management and protection system in place (including legislative, regulatory, institutional and/or traditional protection and management to ensure their safeguarding).[371]

The World Heritage Convention establishes the regulatory regime that combines national and international protection. Each State Party is primarily responsible for ensuring the identification, protection, conservation,

365 World Heritage Convention, Article 2.
366 UNESCO World Heritage Centre, *Operational Guidelines for the Implementation of the World Heritage Convention*, WHC.17/01 (2017), § 47–48 [*Operational Guidelines*].
367 *Operational Guidelines*, § 49.
368 *Operational Guidelines*, § 77 (x).
369 *Operational Guidelines*, § 87–95.
370 *Operational Guidelines*, § 79–86.
371 *Operational Guidelines*, § 78; 96–119.

presentation and transmission to future generations of the heritage sites, situated within its territory.[372] The particular duties of the State Parties include adoption of a general policy that would give the cultural and natural heritage a function in the life of the community and integration of the protection of that heritage into comprehensive planning programmes; the creation of services for the protection, conservation and presentation of the heritage; development of scientific and technical studies that will enable State to counteract the dangers that threaten its heritage sites; taking legal, scientific, technical, administrative and financial measures for the identification, protection, presentation and rehabilitation of the heritage; and support of the national or regional training centres dealing with protection, conservation and presentation of the heritage.[373] While nominating a property, the State Party shall demonstrate its full commitment to preserve the heritage at issue.[374]

While fully respecting the national sovereignty, the World Heritage Convention pronounces that the protection of the world heritage is a duty of the international community as a whole.[375] The international cooperation and assistance within this Convention are established to support the States Parties in their activities on conservation and identification of the heritage.[376]

The Convention's protection mechanism comprises three key elements: listing of the natural and cultural heritage sites in the World Heritage List, recognition of the heritage in danger by inscribing it on the List of World Heritage in Danger and providing financial support for the maintenance and restoration of the sites.[377] The main conventional body for this purpose is the Intergovernmental Committee for the Protection of the Cultural and Natural Heritage of Outstanding Universal Value or "the World Heritage Committee".[378] In its work, the World Heritage Committee is assisted by the International Centre for the Study of the Preservation and Restoration of Cultural Property (Rome Centre), International Council of Monuments and Sites (ICOMOS) and the International Union for Conservation of Nature and Natural Resources (IUCN). With respect to the natural heritage,

372 World Heritage Convention, Article 4; Hunter, Salzman, and Zaelke, *International Environmental Law and Policy*, 1145.
373 World Heritage Convention, Article 5.
374 World Heritage Convention, Article 11; *Operational Guidelines*, § 53.
375 World Heritage Convention, Article 6.
376 World Heritage Convention, Article 7.
377 Hunter, Salzman, and Zaelke, *International Environmental Law and Policy*, 1145.
378 World Heritage Convention, Articles 8–14.

the role of the IUCN is to evaluate the properties nominated by the States Parties for the inscription on the World Heritage List, to monitor the state of conservation of the natural properties, to review the Parties' requests for international assistance and to support capacity building activities.[379]

The World Heritage Convention does not establish any enforcement mechanism as such, however there is a system of periodic reporting by the State Parties and monitoring by the IUCN and ICOMOS.[380] In addition, when the conditions of ascertained or potential danger to the heritage are present, it may be inscribed on the List of World Heritage in Danger.[381] Together with consideration of this inscription, the World Heritage Committee shall develop in consultation with the State Party concerned the desired state of conservation for the removal of property from that list and a programme of corrective measures.[382] The regular review allows then to take further action: to identify additional measures, to remove the property from the List of World Heritage in Danger or to remove it from both this list and the World Heritage List if the property loses the characteristics based on which in was inscribed there.[383]

Certain areas of the Ukrainian Carpathians are designated as natural heritage sites, belonging to the transnational property Ancient and Primeval Beech Forests of the Carpathians and Other Regions of Europe.[384] Six Ukrainian sites were initially inscribed on this list in 2007, and other nine sites were added in 2017.

The names, location, coordinates, and square of all the items presently belonging to this property within Ukraine is outlined in Annex C to this thesis.

The locations of the initially nominated sites are depicted on the nomination file's map.[385]

In the nomination of these sites, their role as outstanding examples representing significant on-going ecological and biological processes in the

---

379 *Operational Guidelines*, § 37, 71, 122, 143–151, 247–254.

380 Gruber, "Convention concerning the Protection of the World Cultural and Natural Heritage 1972," 64.

381 World Heritage Convention, Article 11 (4).

382 *Operational Guidelines*, § 183–184.

383 *Operational Guidelines*, § 191.

384 "Ancient and Primeval Beech Forests of the Carpathians and Other Regions of Europe," UNESCO, accessed September 20, 2024, https://whc.unesco.org/en/list/1133/.

385 "Nomination file 1133: Executive Summary," Ukraine, Slovak Republik (2007), https://whc.unesco.org/uploads/nominations/1133.pdf, 5.

development of terrestrial (forest) ecosystems and communities of their plants and animals, their aesthetic value as well as relevance for biodiversity were noted.[386] The latter was described in the following way:

> The beech primeval forests of the nominated series also contain genetic pools and provide habitats for numerous endangered species, including xylobiotic fungi, insects, hollow-nesting birds and large mammals, such as brown bear, wolf, lynx, wisent and others.[387]

1.4. Biodiversity protection on a regional level, as applicable to the Ukrainian Carpathians

1.4.1. The Convention on the Conservation of European Wildlife and Natural Habitats

The 1979 Bern Convention was concluded under the auspices of the Council of Europe and entered into force in 1982.[388] This Convention is aimed at the conservation of wild flora and fauna and their natural habitats, especially those whose conservation requires cooperation of several states and paying special attention to the endangered and vulnerable species.[389] Article 2 establishes a general obligation of states to take "requisite measures to maintain the population of wild flora and fauna at, or adapt it to, a level which corresponds in particular to ecological, scientific and cultural requirements", also stating that economic and recreational requirements and the needs of sub-species, varieties or forms at risk locally shall be considered. The parties to the Bern Convention, similarly to the CBD, are required to promote national policies for conservation of wild flora, fauna and natural habitats and to have regard on their conservation in the planning, development policies and measures against pollution.[390] As

386 "Nomination file 1133: Executive Summary," Ukraine, Slovak Republik (2007), https://whc.unesco.org/uploads/nominations/1133.pdf, 6–10.

387 "Nomination file 1133: Executive Summary," Ukraine, Slovak Republik (2007), https://whc.unesco.org/uploads/nominations/1133.pdf, 6.

388 "Convention on the Conservation of European Wildlife and Natural Habitats," opened for signature September 19, 1979, *European Treaty Series* no. 104 https://www.coe.int/en/web/conventions/full-list?module=treaty-detail&treatynum=104 [Bern Convention].

389 Bern Convention, Article 1.

390 Bern Convention, Article 3.

Nicolas de Sadeleer observes, this Convention has certain limitations from the biodiversity protection perspective as it "does not extend to the whole spectrum of biodiversity".[391] It is however, considered to be an effective instrument at least because it establishes substantive obligations for the parties rather than just vague goals.[392] It also played a crucial role in the development of the EU legislation regarding conservation of species, habitats and ecosystems including the Birds Directive and the Habitats Directive.[393]

With respect to protection of habitats, the Bern Convention requires its parties to introduce necessary legislative and administrative measures. This obligation in principle concerns all habitats of wild flora and fauna species, regardless of their scarcity,[394] however, it also calls for special attention to the species listed in Appendices I and II and to the conservation of endangered natural habitats.[395] In accordance with Article 4 (1), policies on planning or development shall take into account the habitat protection to avoid or minimise the deterioration in the protected areas. Special attention should be given to the areas that are important for the migratory species listed in Appendices II and III. The parties also undertake to coordinate their efforts for the protection of natural habitats located in the frontier areas.[396]

Regarding the protection of species, the Bern Convention establishes differing regimes based on the different Appendices.[397] With respect to the species of wild flora specified in Appendix I, the deliberate picking, collecting, cutting, and uprooting, as well as possession or sale shall be pro-

391 Nicolas de Sadeleer, "European Union in Biodiversity and nature protection law," in *Biodiversity and Nature Protection Law*, ed. Elisa Morgera and Jona Razzaque (Cheltenham: Edward Elgar Publishing, 2017), 414.

392 Cf. Kiss and Shelton, *Guide to International Environmental Law*, 184.

393 Directive 2009/147/EC of the European Parliament and of the Council of 30 November 2009 on the conservation of wild birds, *Official Journal of the European Union*, L 20, 26.1.2010, p. 7–25, http://data.europa.eu/eli/dir/2009/147/oj [Birds Directive]; Council Directive 92/43/EEC of 21 May 1992 on the conservation of natural habitats and of wild fauna and flora, *Official Journal of the European Union,* L 206, 22.7.1992, p. 7–50, http://data.europa.eu/eli/dir/1992/43/oj [Habitats Directive]; de Sadeleer, "European Union in Biodiversity and nature protection law," 419.

394 Sands, Peel, Fabra, and MacKenzie, *Principles of International Environmental Law*, 444.

395 Bern Convention, Article 4.

396 Bern Convention, Article 4.

397 Cyrille de Klemm and Clare Shine, *Biological Diversity Conservation and the Law,* (Gland, Switzerland and Cambridge, UK: IUCN, 1993), 30–31.

hibited.[398] As regards wild fauna species specified in Appendix II, they shall be afforded a special protection by means of legislative and administrative measures. A number of activities is prohibited in relation to these species, including deliberate capture and killing; deliberate damage to or destruction of breeding or nesting sites; deliberate disturbance, particularly during the period of breeding, roaring and hibernation; deliberate destruction or taking of eggs from the wild; possession of and internal trade in these species, alive or dead, including any readily recognisable part or derivative.[399] Some ambiguities of these provisions are noted in the literature, for instance, regarding the wording "deliberate damage or destruction", if these are analysed together with the interpretative documents. It is suggested that, construction works such as road-building, not having damage or destruction as their primary purpose, will still fall under the category of deliberate damage or destruction and have to be assessed against the background of Article 9 regulating the exceptions.[400] For the species of wild fauna specified in Appendix III, the protection is less stringent than for those specified in Appendices I and II, and certain exploitation is allowed given that it is regulated to keep the populations out of danger. Measures to this extent might include closed seasons and/or procedures regulating the exploitation, temporary or local prohibition of exploitation to restore the levels of population, and regulation of sale of live and dead wild animals.[401] The parties shall also introduce restrictions as to the means of capture or killing of Appendix III species to prohibit the use of all indiscriminate means and the use of means capable of causing local disappearance of, or serious disturbance to, population of species (this also applies by analogy to the Appendix II species when exceptions under Article 9 are applied).[402] Article 9 allows the parties to make exceptions from the provisions of Articles 4, 5, 6, 7 and 8 for certain reasons, given that there is no other satisfactory solution, and that this exception is not detrimental to the survival of the relevant population.[403] Migratory species listed in Appendices II and III shall be subject to additional efforts of protection under Article 10 by the range states. The parties further undertake to cooperate, encourage and

398 Bern Convention, Article 5.

399 Bern Convention, Article 6.

400 Sands, Peel, Fabra, and MacKenzie, *Principles of International Environmental Law*, 445–446.

401 Bern Convention, Article 7.

402 Bern Convention, Article 8.

403 Bern Convention, Article 9.

coordinate research and reintroduction of native species when it would be acceptable, and to control the introduction of non-native species.[404]

The institutional mechanism of the Bern Convention consists of the Standing Committee, the Bureau of the Standing Committee, and the Secretariat of the Bern Convention.[405] The Standing Committee is the primary body responsible for following the application of the Convention. It may review the provisions of the Convention, make recommendations to the parties on measures to be taken for the purposes of the Convention and make any proposals for improving the effectiveness of the Convention.[406] The Bureau "takes administrative and organisational decisions in between meetings of the Standing Committee", while the Secretariat provided by the Council of Europe "supplies administrative and other services that may be required by the Standing Committee".[407]

The establishment of the Standing Committee is regarded as a major progress compared to earlier regional treaties,[408] and the Standing Committee has been actively exercising its functions. One of the prominent examples of its activities is the creation of the network of Areas of Special Conservation Interest (ASCI), known as the Emerald Network. Starting from 1989, the Standing Committee has adopted numerous resolutions and recommendations to this extent.[409] This includes Resolution No. 1 (1989) on the provisions relating to the conservation of habitats, which defined certain notions including "habitat", "natural habitat", "conservation", and the meaning of the wording of Article 6b;[410] Recommendation No. 14 (1989) on identifying the species and habitats requiring special con-

---

404 Bern Convention, Article 11.

405 "Institutions of the Bern Convention," Bern Convention, accessed September 20, 2024, https://www.coe.int/en/web/bern-convention/institutions.

406 Bern Convention, Articles 13 and 14.

407 "Institutions of the Bern Convention," Bern Convention, accessed September 20, 2024, https://www.coe.int/en/web/bern-convention/institutions.

408 Kiss and Shelton, *Guide to International Environmental Law*, 184.

409 Group of Experts on Protected Areas and Ecological Networks, *The Emerald Network: A Network of Areas of Special Conservation Interest for Europe*, Explanatory document and compilation of relevant texts T-PVS/PA (2016) 4 (Strasbourg, 2016), https://rm.coe.int/168074669d, 4; See also Olena Bevz, "Legal Regulation of the Emerald Network: National and Global Aspects," *Journal of Vasyl Stefanyk Precarpathian National University*, 5, no. 2 (2018): 93–94, https://doi.org/10.15330/jpnu.5.2.91-98.

410 Standing Committee, *Resolution No. 1 (1989) of the standing committee on the provisions relating to the conservation of habitats*, (June 9, 1989) https://search.coe.int/democracy?i=0900001680746be2.

servation measures;[411] Recommendation No. 16 (1989) suggesting parties to designate ASCI and ensure their management as well as establishing criteria for their designation.[412] Due to political developments in Europe around 1990s, leading to the expansion of membership in the Bern Convention, as well as due to the European Community's implementation of the Bern Convention in a form of adoption of the Habitats Directive, that created the European ecological network of special areas of conservation known as "Natura 2000", the work on the ASCI's creation was somewhat delayed.[413] It was reinvigorated in 1996, when the Standing Committee resolved to create a network of ASCI giving it a name "Emerald Network".[414]

Other important decisions of the Standing Committee, serving the purpose of creation of the Emerald Network, include Resolution No. 4 (1996) listing endangered natural habitats requiring specific conservation measures; Resolution No. 5 (1998) concerning the rules for the Network of Areas of Special Conservation Interest (Emerald Network); Resolution No. 6 (1998) listing the species requiring specific habitat conservation measures (including revised Annex I to Resolution No. 6 (1998), adopted in 2011 by the Standing Committee); Resolution No. 8 (2012) on the national designation of adopted Emerald sites and the implementation of management, monitoring and reporting measures; Revised Recommendation No. 157 (2011) on the status of candidate Emerald sites and guidelines on the criteria for their nomination (revised in 2019); and Recommendation No. 172 (2014) interpreting certain provisions of Resolution No. 6 (1998) of the Standing Committee.[415]

The states of the Eastern Europe and the South Caucasus were subject to a special attention of the Standing Committee in their effort to establish

---

411 Standing Committee, *Recommendation No. 14 (1989) of the standing committee on species habitat conservation and on the conservation of endangered natural habitats*, (June 9, 1989) https://search.coe.int/democracy?i=09000016807464c9.

412 Standing Committee, *Recommendation No. 16 (1989) of the standing committee on areas of special conservation interest*, (June 9, 1989) https://search.coe.int/democracy?i=0900001680746c25.

413 Group of Experts on Protected Areas and Ecological Networks, *The Emerald Network*, 4.

414 Standing Committee, *Resolution No. 3 (1996) concerning the setting up of a pan-European Ecological Network*, (January 26, 1996), https://search.coe.int/democracy?i=09000016807467d3; See Group of Experts on Protected Areas and Ecological Networks, *The Emerald Network*, 4–5.

415 "Reference documents," Bern Convention, accessed September 20, 2024, https://www.coe.int/en/web/bern-convention/documentsl.

a fully operational Emerald Network, including a road map until 2020.[416] The construction and operation of this network remains challenging in Ukraine and is discussed in Chapter II of this thesis.

The Bern Convention also has a strong monitoring system, developed mostly based on the decisions of the Standing Committee. It comprises a reporting system and a case-file system.[417] Within the reporting system there are several types of reports: the obligatory biannual reports that a contracting party submits in case it makes exceptions from certain provisions based on Article 9 and the general reports on the national implementation of the Convention, that parties submit every 4 years on a voluntary basis. In addition, the Group of Experts undertakes a monitoring of implementation of the Bern Convention and Recommendations to it with a focus on specific conservation challenges or the conservation status of species or habitats. There is also a possibility of a Standing Committee to review implementation of the Convention in a contracting party through an analysis of the reports prepared by the independent experts.[418] The case-file system allows a 'concerned stakeholder' such as an NGO, a private person or a contracting party to submit a complaint on an alleged violation of the Bern Convention.[419] These are received and processed depending on their substance by the Bureau, the Secretariat or the Standing Committee. This mechanism proved to be a flexible and a successful instrument and is considered to be a unique example of a biodiversity treaty compliance mechanism incorporating cutting edge public participation standards.[420]

416 See Standing Committee, *Three Dimensional Road Map for Achieving a Fully Operational Emerald Network in 7 Countries of Central and Eastern Europe and the South Caucasus*, Document agreed at the Final Conference of the EU/CoE Joint Programme "Emerald Network of Nature Protection Sites, Phase II" and compiled by Mr Dave Pritchard T-PVS/PA (2016) 10 (Strasbourg, 2016) https://rm.coe.int/16807464ae.

417 "Monitoring set up under the Bern Convention," Bern Convention, accessed September 20, 2024, https://www.coe.int/en/web/bern-convention/monitoring.

418 "Monitoring set up under the Bern Convention."

419 See Secretariat of the Bern Convention, *Case-File System: Summary of General Procedures for the Processing of Complaints – a Resource for the Bern Convention Stakeholders*, T-PVS/Inf(2022)27 (Strasbourg, 2022), https://rm.coe.int/inf27e-2022-cfreflection-summary-of-general-procedures-for-processing-/1680a7bca7.

420 "Monitoring set up under the Bern Convention"; Antonio Cardesa-Salzmann, "Monitoring and compliance mechanisms," in *Biodiversity and Nature Protection Law*, ed. Elisa Morgera and Jona Razzaque (Cheltenham: Edward Elgar Publishing, 2017), 461.

Overall, Bern Convention decisions are regarded in literature as amounting to the 'subsequent agreements between the parties' that might be used for treaty interpretation within the meaning of the 1969 Vienna Convention on the Law of Treaties.[421]

The current direction of strategic developments related to the Bern Convention is outlined in the Vision for the period to 2030.[422] It admits an accelerating decline of biodiversity and suggests using 'renewed energies' to overcome this challenge, including by strengthening investment in conservation, improving quality and management of the Emerald Network, reinforing link between conservation, sustainable use of nature and other areas including "human rights, democracy, landscape, climate change, cultural heritage, health and major hazards", and by effective use of the various Convention mechanisms.[423] This document seeks to ensure coordination and avoid duplication with the strategic document under the CBD – Global Biodiversity Framework, aiming to contribute to its implementation in the pan-European context. To this end, four key goals are identified: an increase in the area connectivity, integrity and resilience of natural and semi-natural ecosystems; improvement of the conservation status of the threatened species and abundance of native species as well as reduction of the human-induced extinctions; valuing, maintenance and enhancement of the contributions of wild flora and fauna and their natural habitats to a safe, clean, healthy and sustainable environment;[424] and allocation of sufficient resources.[425]

1.4.2. The Framework Convention on the Protection and Sustainable Development of the Carpathians

The 2003 Framework Convention on the Protection and Sustainable Development of the Carpathians ("Carpathian Convention") is one the most

421 Koester, "Environmental principles and concepts in biodiversity treaties," 552.

422 Standing Committee, *Vision for the Bern Convention for the Period to 2030*, Document prepared by the Mr Dave E Pritchard, T-PVS(2021)14 ((Strasbourg, 2021), https://rm.coe.int/tpvs14e-2021-vision-final/1680ada0f0 [*Vision for the Bern Convention for the Period to 2030*].

423 *Vision for the Bern Convention for the Period to 2030*, 1.

424 It is worth noting that the wording used here ecoes to the wording used for naming a substative human right to the enrironment of certain quality (human right to a healthy environment).

425 *Vision for the Bern Convention for the Period to 2030*, 2.

recent biodiversity treaties, and the most specific in addressing the subject matter of this dissertation. It was negotiated based on the initiative of Ukraine with the facilitation of the United Nations Environment Program (UNEP) and with the support by the Presidency of the Alpine Convention, states, international organisations, non-governmental organisations, and academic institutions.[426] This sub-regional convention received far less attention in the scholarly literature in comparison with other biodiversity treaties described above. What is, however, noted in the literature on Carpathian Convention, is the explicit incorporation of the ecosystem approach and an emphasis on the creation of a transboundary ecological network.[427]

The Preamble of the Carpathian Convention begins by describing the Carpathians as "a unique natural treasure of great beauty and ecological value", "an important reservoir of biodiversity", "an essential habitat and refuge for many endangered species of plants and animals", and "Europe's largest area of virgin forests".[428] It also recognises the experience of the 1991 Convention on the Protection of the Alps (Alpine Convention) as a successful model, and indeed follows it.[429] The Carpathian Convention uses the Framework Convention and Protocol approach, where the Convention contains general provisions, and the Protocols contain more specific substantive obligations, thus serving as a key means of implementation of the Convention.[430] All of the protocols adopted to date are of some degree of relevance to the issue of the protection of the forest biodiversity of Ukrainian Carpathians, however the two protocols stand out among them, and will therefore be described here: the Protocol on Conservation and Sustainable Use of Biological and Landscape Diversity ("Protocol on Biodiversity") and the Protocol on Sustainable Forest Management.

The Carpathian Convention has the following general objectives: "improving quality of life, strengthening local economies and communities, and conservation of natural values and cultural heritage".[431] It lists the general principles that have to be promoted, while taking measures under

426 "History of the Convention," Carpathian Convention, accessed September 20, 2024, http://www.carpathianconvention.org/convention/history/.
427 Fodella, "Mountain biodiversity," 169.
428 Carpathian Convention, Preamble.
429 Fodella, "Mountain biodiversity," 169.
430 "Framework Convention," Carpathian Convention, accessed September 20, 2024, http://www.carpathianconvention.org/convention/framework-convention/.
431 Carpathian Convention, Article 2.

the substantive articles of the Convention to achieve its objectives: the precaution and prevention principles, the 'polluter pays' principle, public participation and stakeholder involvement, transboundary cooperation, integrated planning and management of land and water resources, a programmatic approach, and the ecosystem approach.[432]

Article 4 of the Carpathian Convention directly refers to the biodiversity, obliging parties to "pursue policies aiming at conservation, sustainable use and restoration of biological and landscape diversity throughout the Carpathians". The key aspects that have to be ensured include protection of natural and semi-natural habitats, their continuity and connectivity, protection of species being characteristic to the Carpathians, as well as particular protection of the endangered species, endemic species and large carnivores.[433] This article in a way mirrors some of the provisions of the CBD and Bern Convention, succinctly weaving them into one article and tying them to the context of Carpathian region. In particular, it calls for an adequate maintenance of semi-natural habitats, the restoration of degraded habitats, and support of the development and implementation of relevant management plans; prevention of introduction of invasive alien species and genetically modified organisms, their control or eradication; development of compatible monitoring systems, coordinated regional inventories of species and habitats and scientific research; cooperation in developing an ecological network in the Carpathians as part of the Pan-European Ecological Network; enhancement of conservation and sustainable management in the areas outside protected areas; integration of the biodiversity conservation and sustainable use objectives into sectoral policies.[434]

Protocol on Biodiversity, while building upon the provisions of the Convention, in particular, Article 4, provides more detailed content of the obligations or explanation of their logic (which is especially the case with Chapter III of the Protocol on "Specific measures"). Its objectives, beyond the conservation, restoration and sustainable use of bio- and landscape diversity of the Carpathians, include benefits to present and future generations. It provides a remarkably lengthy list of definitions. The key general obligations under the Protocol on Biodiversity include development and implementation of the relevant national policies and strategies by each party, taking into consideration those developed by other parties (Article

432 Carpathian Convention, Article 2.
433 Carpathian Convention, Article 4.
434 Carpathian Convention, Article 4.

4); integration of objectives of this Protocol into sectoral policies including agriculture and forestry, transport and infrastructure, tourism and other sectors (Article 5); encouragement of cooperation between institutions and regional and local authorities, and their shared responsibility (Article 6) as well as cooperation of authorities of all types at the international level (Article 7). Specific measures (Articles 8 – 20) oblige Parties to take measures on a wide range of activities, serving the objectives of the Protocol, and to cooperate on these activities. Furthermore, some actions to be taken by the Conference of the Parties are outlined, including adoption of a list of endangered natural and semi-natural habitat types that are native to the Carpathians (Carpathian Red List of Habitats) and adoption of the terms of reference of the Carpathian Network of Protected Areas. While the Protocol serves the aim of implementation of the Convention, the implementation of the Protocol, is in turn enhanced by the Strategic Action Plan (SAP) for its implementation envisaged in Article 21. The most recent SAP covers period from 2011 to 2023, and outlines objectives, actions and expected results.[435] Monitoring and compliance with Parties' obligations is exercised by the Conference of the Parties and Implementation Committee by means of collection, assessment, and analysis of information, including through the Parties' reports. Conference of the Parties is entitled to adopt or recommend measures to enhance compliance.[436]

Relatively recently, another action plan relevant to the biodiversity protection was adopted by the decision of the Conference of the Parties: Action Plan on conservation of large carnivores and ensuring ecological connectivity in the Carpathians.[437] Unlike Convention, and the Protocols,

---

435 Conference of the Parties, *Strategic Action Plan for the Implementation of the Protocol on Conservation and Sustainable use of Biological and Landscape Diversity*, UNEP/CC/COP4/DOC7 (Mikulov, 2014) http://www.carpathianconvention.org/tl_files/carpathiancon/Downloads/03%20Meetings%20and%20Events/COP/2014_COP4_Mikulov/WORKING%20DOCUMENTS/DOC7_Biodiversity%20Protocol%20SAP_Corrigendum.pdf.

436 "Protocol on Conservation and Sustainable Use of Biological and Landscape Diversity," opened for signature June 19, 2008, http://www.carpathianconvention.org/convention/protocols/protocol-on-biodiversity/, Article 28.

437 Cristian R. Papp, Harald Egerer, Klaudia Kuraś and Gabriella Nagy, *International Action Plan on Conservation of Large Carnivores and Ensuring Ecological Connectivity in the Carpathians*, UNEP Vienna Programme Office – Secretariat of the Carpathian Convention, WWF Romania, CEEWeb, Eurac Research (2020), http://www.carpathianconvention.org/tl_files/carpathiancon/Downloads/02%20Activities/Large%20carnivores/CC%20COP6_DOC9P_Int%20Action%20Plan%20Large%20Carnivores%20and%20Ecological%20Connectivity_ADOPTED.pdf.

it is not legally binding, but it is called to assist the implementation of those legally binding instruments. This Action Plan specifically covers large carnivores of the Carpathians, namely brown bear (*Ursus arctos*), grey wolf (*Canis lupus*), and Eurasian lynx (*Lynx lynx*). Its strategic objectives include: standardization of monitoring procedures of large carnivores in the Carpathians; prevention of habitat fragmentation and ensuring ecological connectivity; improving coexistence of humans with large carnivores; improving law enforcement with respect to instances of illegal killing of large carnivores; improving communication and cooperation between all relevant stakeholders; strengthening of institutional capacity-building; and decreasing impacts of climate change on large carnivores and their habitats.

Another sub-issue of a great importance for the biodiversity protection of the forest ecosystems of the Ukrainian Carpathians is sustainable forestry, addressed in Article 7 of the Carpathian Convention, and in the Protocol on Sustainable Forest Management. According to Article 7, the state parties shall pursue policies in line with internationally agreed principles of sustainable forest management, apply sustainable mountain forest management practices in the Carpathians, pursue policies aiming at designating protected areas in natural forests (especially virgin forests) in sufficient size and number to restrict or adapt their use in accordance with the objectives of conservation and promote environmentally sound forestry measures to assure appropriate retention of the precipitation in the mountains.[438]

The objective of the Protocol on Sustainable Forest Management is "to promote the sustainable management and protection of the Carpathian forests, bringing benefits to present and future generations".[439] To achieve this objective, this Protocol lists 17 areas of action and cooperation, including maintenance or enlargement of the forest cover, improving the health and vitality of forests, improving the conservation and sustainable use of components of forest biological diversity and identification and protection of natural, especially virgin forests.[440] Similarly to the Protocol on Biodiversity, the Protocol on Sustainable Forest Management obliges state parties to develop and implement corresponding policies and strategies on their national territory (Article 2) as well as to integrate the objectives of sustainable management and protection of the Carpathians forests into sectoral policies (Article 3). The best level of coordination and cooperation

438 Carpathian Convention, Article 7.
439 Protocol on Sustainable Forest Management, Article 1.
440 Protocol on Sustainable Forest Management, Article 1.

between national institutions and regional and local authorities for the purposes of the implementation of this Protocol should be defined (Article 4), and active international cooperation on various institutional levels is encouraged (Article 5). Article 7 provides definitions, such as "sustainable forest management", "close to nature forestry", "natural forests" and "virgin forests". The specific measures are contained in Articles 8 – 19. For the purposes of biodiversity protection, the most relevant obligations include taking measures to identify and protect "natural, especially virgin forests of the Carpathians, by establishing Protected Areas in sufficient size and number and implementing other specific measures of protection", to include sufficient areas of natural forests from Carpathian region in Protected Areas and to take measures for the preservation of genetic resources of natural, especially virgin forests (Article 10). Furthermore, states have to ensure coherence between the protected areas management plans and the forest management plans within protected areas (Article 11). In addition, the Protocol contains quite an unusual provision (compared to other biodiversity-related treaties) about sustainable wildlife management methods requiring "control of population size of hoofed animals so that it allows a natural regeneration of forests, and monitoring and management of large carnivores within the carrying capacities of the forests ecosystem."[441] The provisions on implementation, monitoring and compliance evaluation are quite similar to the Protocol on Biodiversity, and the Strategic Action Plan (SAP) is used as a means of implementing the Protocol.[442] The current SAP for the Implementation of the Protocol on Sustainable Forest Management covers a period of 2015 – 2026.[443] It includes 18 objectives, each of which includes actions and expected results.[444] An additional document

441 Protocol on Sustainable Forest Management, Article 16.

442 Protocol on Sustainable Forest Management, Article 20–26.

443 Carpathian Convention Working Group on Sustainable Forest Management, *Strategic Action Plan for the Implementation of the Protocol on SFM to the Carpathian Convention*, Presentation, (Zvolen, 2019), http://www.carpathianconvention.org/tl_files/carpathiancon/Downloads/03%20Meetings%20and%20Events/Working%20Groups/Sustainable%20Forest%20Management/7th%20meeting/presentations/Strategic%20Action%20Plan%20-Forest%20Protocol%20CC_M.Schwarz.pdf.

444 Conference of the Parties, *Strategic Action Plan for the Implementation of the Protocol on Sustainable Forest Management*, UNEP/CC/COP4/DOC11/REV1 (Mikulov, 2014), http://www.carpathianconvention.org/tl_files/carpathiancon/Downloads/03%20Meetings%20and%20Events/COP/2014_COP4_Mikulov/Follow%20Up/DOC11_Forest%20SAP%20FINAL_26SepCOP4.pdf [*Strategic Action Plan for the Implementation of the Protocol on Sustainable Forest Management*].

assisting the implementation of the provisions of the Protocol regarding virgin forests is the set of criteria and indicators for their identification.[445]

Some other provisions of the Carpathian Convention, while not addressing biodiversity or forest management directly, regulate closely related areas, capable of influencing biodiversity. For instance, Article 8 on sustainable transport and infrastructure draws Parties' attention to the protection of sensitive areas such as biodiversity-rich areas, migration routes or areas of international importance and the protection of biodiversity and landscapes within the policies on sustainable transport and infrastructure planning and development.[446] Other related areas include sustainable tourism (Article 9), industry and energy (Article 10), and traditional knowledge (Article 11). The procedural obligations of various types: risk assessments, environmental impact assessments, and strategic environmental assessments, as well as obligations related to monitoring and research are contained in Article 12.

The institutional mechanism of the Carpathian Convention comprises Conference of the Parties,[447] Secretariat, Implementation Committee[448] and various thematic working groups, including working groups on biodiversity and on sustainable forest management.[449] The State Parties also in turn exercise the responsibility of Presidency of the Convention, working on certain priorities and exercising the Programme of Work that guides implementation of the Convention.[450]

With respect to the cooperation with other global and regional treaties, the Carpathian Convention's activities on biodiversity protection seek to

---

445 Conference of the Parties, *Criteria and indicators for selection of virgin forests in the Carpathians*, adoped by the Decision COP4/4 Sustainable agriculture, rural development and forestry Article 7 of the Carpathian Convention (Mikulov, 2014) http://www.carpathianconvention.org/tl_files/carpathiancon/Downloads/03%20Meetings%20and%20Events/COP/2014_COP4_Mikulov/Follow%20Up/DOC13_Criteria_Indicators_virginforests_FINAL_26SEP.pdf.

446 Carpathian Convention, Article 8.

447 "COP Decisions," Carpathian Convention, accessed September 20, 2024, http://www.carpathianconvention.org/cop/.

448 "The Carpathian Convention Implementation Committee," Carpathian Convention, accessed September 20, 2024, http://www.carpathianconvention.org/organization/organizational-structure/.

449 "Working Groups," Carpathian Convention, accessed September 20, 2024, http://www.carpathianconvention.org/organization/working-groups/.

450 "The Presidency of the Carpathian Convention," Carpathian Convention, accessed September 20, 2024, http://www.carpathianconvention.org/organization/organizational-structure/.

support the implementation of the CBD and the Kunming-Montreal Global Biodiversity Framework at the level of Carpathians. In October 2023, the Carpathian Biodiversity Framework (CBF), that is a separate strategic document that adjusts the Kunming-Montreal Global Biodiversity Framework to local situation of the Carpathians was adopted by the Conference of the Parties. With its adoption, the Carpathian Convention became the first regional instrument in the world that has a distinct regional biodiversity framework.[451] In addition, in the light of the new global biodiversity framework, the CBD, the Alpine Convention, and the Carpathian Convention have renewed the trilateral Memorandum of Cooperation. Furthermore, the national biodiversity strategies and action plans of the Carpathian countries shall reflect the work of Carpathian Convention to avoid isolation and allow for efficient integrated approach.[452]

1.4.3. Biodiversity-related laws and policies of the European Union

Although Ukraine is not yet a member of the European Union (EU), so that the EU legislation and policies are not directly applicable to the biodiversity protection of the Ukrainian Carpathians, after concluding the Association Agreement with the EU, Ukraine undertook to approximate its legislation. A significant array of norms that need to be transposed into Ukrainian legislation in line with the Association Agreement is related to the environmental protection (although not necessarily precisely biodiversity).[453] With a view of the long-term perspective of becoming a member of the EU, which has been chosen as one of the strategic directions of Ukraine,[454] the biodiversity-legislation of the EU shall be taken into account during the development of Ukraine's legislation and strategic documents in this sphere.

---

451 "Carpathian Biodiversity Framework," CBD, October 14, 2023, https://www.cbd.int/article/carpathian-biodiversity-framework.

452 "Biodiversity," Carpathian Convention, accessed September 20, 2024, http://www.carpathianconvention.org/topics/biodiversity/.

453 Association Agreement between the European Union and its Member States, of the one part, and Ukraine, of the other part, Document 22014A0529(01), *Official Journal of the European Union,* L 161, 29.5.2014, p. 3–2137, http://data.europa.eu/eli/agree_internation/2014/295/oj, Annex XXX [Association Agreement between the EU and Ukraine].

454 *Constitution of Ukraine*, Document 254k/96-VR, Bulletin of the Verkhovna Rada of Ukraine, No. 30, p. 141 (1996) https://zakon.rada.gov.ua/laws/show/254%D0%BA/96-%D0%B2%D1%80#Text, Preamble, Article 85, 102, 116.

Similarly to the public international law, in the EU (the then European Economic Community), the environmental concerns were not addressed until the early 1970s. Indeed, the economic spheres of coal and steel industry forming a basis of future economic union were far from focusing on their environmental footprint in the 1950s. The development of the EU environmental norms was to a significant extent inspired by the global and regional international environmental law developments, including 1972 Stockholm conference, the 1979 Bern Convention, the 1992 Rio conference, and the CBD. The historical development of the EU environmental legislation is well addressed in the literature.[455]

In the present-day EU, the basis for the environmental protection is found in Article 3 (3) of the Treaty on European Union (TEU), Article 11 and Title XX of the Treaty on the Functioning of the European Union (TFEU), and Article 37 of the Charter of Fundamental Rights of the European Union (CFREU).[456] Article 3 (3) of the TEU directly ties internal market to the sustainable development, and mentions "a high level of protection and improvement of the quality of the environment" among its aims.[457] Article 192 (2) of the TFEU enshrines environmental principles, including precautionary principle, the principle of prevention ('preventive action should be taken'), rectification at source principle ('environmental damage should as a priority be rectified at source'), and polluter pays principle ('polluter should pay').[458] Article 11 of the TFEU – on integration of environmental protection requirements into the definition and implementation of all EU policies and activities, is said to contain one more principle

455 Suzane Kingston, "Environmental Policy," in *The Law of the European Union*, ed. Pieter Jan Kuijper et al., 5th ed. (Alphen aan den Rijn, the Netherlands: Wolters Kluwer, 2018), 1165–1169; Charlotte Burns and Neil Carter, "Environmental Policy," in *The Oxford Handbook of the European Union*, ed. Erik Jones, Anand Menon, and Stephen Weatherill, (Oxford: Oxford University Press, 2012), 512–516; David Benson, Viviane Gravey, and Andrew Jordan, "Environmental Policy," in *European Union Politics*, ed. Michelle Cini and Nieves Perez-Solorzano Borragan, 6th ed. (Oxford: Oxford University Press, 2012) 373–376; David A. O. Edward and Robert C. Lane, *Edward and Lane on European Union Law* (Cheltenham, UK Northampton, MA, USA: Edward Elgar, 2013), 881–882.

456 Edward and Lane, *Edward and Lane on European Union Law*, 882–883.

457 Consolidated version of the Treaty on European Union, Document 12016M/TXT, *Official Journal of the European Union*, C 202/1, http://data.europa.eu/eli/treaty/teu_2016/oj.

458 Consolidated version of the Treaty on the Functioning of the European Union, Document 12016E/TXT, *Official Journal of the European Union*, C 202/1, http://data.europa.eu/eli/treaty/tfeu_2016/oj.

– the 'integration principle'.[459] Article 37 of the CFREU echoes Article 11 of the TFEU, requiring the integration of "high level of environmental protection and the improvement of the quality of the environment" into the EU policies.[460] Thus, some of the nature protection norms are based on the 'genuine environmental legal basis', while others are called to integrate biodiversity-relevant provisions into other spheres, including common agricultural policy, the internal market and the common commercial policy.[461] The two most prominent directives related to the biodiversity protection are Directive 2009/147/EC on the conservation of wild birds (Birds Directive) and the Directive 92/43/EC on the conservation of natural habitats and of wild fauna and flora (Habitats Directive).

The Birds and Habitats directives constitute the cornerstones of the EU biodiversity-related legislation and policy.[462] They are closely related to and elaborate on the obligations under the Bern Convention.[463] While Birds Directive covers all avifauna in the EU, the scope of Habitats directive is restricted to the 'natural habitats and species of wild fauna and flora of Community interest'.[464] Together, these two instruments create the Natura 2000 network, a coherent European ecological network (and world's largest network of protected areas), which comprises 'special protection areas' (SPAs) under Birds Directive and 'special areas of conservation' (SACs) under the Habitats Directive.[465]

The Birds Directive originates from 1979, however was amended several times and codified in 2009 in the interests of clarity and rationality.[466] It

459 Kingston, "Environmental Policy," 1171; for an explanation of all mentioned principles see 1172–1176.

460 Charter of Fundamental Rights of the European Union, Document 12012P/TXT, *Official Journal of the European Union*, C 326, 26.10.2012, p. 391–407, http://data.europa.eu/eli/treaty/char_2012/oj, Article 37.

461 de Sadeleer, "European Union in Biodiversity and nature protection law," 418.

462 "The Birds Directive," European Commission, accessed September 20, 2024, https://environment.ec.europa.eu/topics/nature-and-biodiversity/birds-directive_en.

463 de Sadeleer, "European Union in Biodiversity and nature protection law," 419.

464 Habitats Directive, Article 2; de Sadeleer, "European Union in Biodiversity and nature protection law," 421–422.

465 Habitats Directive, Article 3; de Sadeleer, "European Union in Biodiversity and nature protection law," 422; "The Habitats Directive," European Commission, accessed September 20, 2024, https://environment.ec.europa.eu/topics/nature-and-biodiversity/habitats-directive_en; "Natura 2000: The largest network of protected areas in the world," European Commission, accessed September 20, 2024, https://environment.ec.europa.eu/topics/nature-and-biodiversity/natura-2000_en.

466 Birds Directive, Preamble.

applies to all naturally occurring birds in the wild state in the European territory of the EU Member States (including birds' eggs, nests, and habitats).[467] It requires Parties to take requisite measures to maintain birds' populations at a certain level in line with ecological, scientific and cultural requirements while also paying attention to the economic and recreational requirements.[468] For this purpose, the preservation, maintenance or re-establishment of a sufficient diversity and area of birds' habitats are required, which may include measures such as creation of protected areas, management of habitats inside and outside protected areas, creation of biotopes or re-establishment of destroyed biotopes.[469] While all birds are protected based on this Directive, some particularly vulnerable categories of birds are afforded special protection and listed in Annex I, resulting in the obligation of Member States to designate certain land and sea territories as SPAs for their conservation; additionally, some migratory birds not listed there should enjoy similar conservation measures.[470] Under the general system of protection for all species of birds, certain activities, including deliberate killing, destruction of or damage to nests and eggs, deliberate disturbance of birds, particularly during the period of breeding and rearing shall be prohibited.[471] There are, however, numerous exceptions, allowing lawful hunting, killing and capture (subject to the restrictions as to the means), and a possibility to derogate from the provisions of Articles 5 to 8.[472]

The 1992 Habitats Directive is dedicated to protecting biodiversity through the conservation of natural habitats of wild flora and fauna.[473] It is aimed at maintenance and restoration of natural habitats and species of Community interest, whereby 'species of Community interest' include endangered, vulnerable, rare or endemic species while 'natural habitat types of Community interest' include those in danger of disappearance in their natural range, those having a small natural range and those presenting outstanding examples of one or more of the certain biogeographical regions.[474]

467 Birds Directive, Article 1.
468 Birds Directive, Article 2.
469 Birds Directive, Article 3.
470 Birds Directive, Article 4.
471 Birds Directive, Article 5.
472 Birds Directive, Articles 6–9.
473 Habitats Directive, Article 2.
474 Habitats Directive, Article 2, Article 1 (g), (c).

Another related concept, specifying the protected elements is 'site of Community importance'.[475]

The components of Natura 2000 under Habitats Directive – the SACs – are sites of Community importance designated by Member States, where necessary conservation measures are applied for the maintenance or restoration of the natural habitats and/or populations of the species.[476] Natura 2000 comprises sites hosting the natural habitat types listed in Annex I and habitats of species listed in Annex II. These sites are proposed by Member States based on the criteria from Annex III and scientific information, and in case of insufficiency of the national list in a view of the Commission, the matter shall be resolved by consultations or ultimately decision of the Council.[477] For SACs, the necessary conservation measures, such as management plans or other development plans, statutory, administrative or contractual measures shall be developed by the Member States.[478] Appropriate steps shall be taken also to avoid disturbance of the species in these areas and deterioration of the habitats.[479] Plans or projects that are likely to have significant effect on the sites of Community interest, shall be assessed with a view to analyse their implications. If the negative assessment is established, but "imperative reasons of overriding public interest, including those of a social or economic nature" require implementation of such plans or projects, Member States shall take compensatory measures to protect the overall coherence of Natura 2000. In cases where the sites at issue host 'priority' habitats or species, a more restrictive approach is taken.[480] In addition, the requirement of the assessment was interpreted by the European Court of Justice in the light of the precautionary principle.[481]

The strict protection of species under the Habitats Directive, in particular, animal species listed in Annex IV, is similar to the general protection under the Birds Directive. The Member States are to take requisite measures to establish a system of strict protection, prohibiting all forms of deliberate capture or killing, disturbance of these species, particularly dur-

475 Habitats Directive, Article 1 (k).
476 Habitats Directive, Article 1 (l), Article 3.
477 Habitats Directive, Articles 4–5.
478 Habitats Directive, Article 6.
479 Habitats Directive, Article 6.
480 Habitats Directive, Article 6.
481 Kingston, "Environmental Policy," 1183; *Landelijke Vereniging tot Behoud van de Waddenzee and Nederlandse Vereniging tot Bescherming van Vogels v Staatssecretaris van Landbouw, Natuurbeheer en Visserij*, C-127/02 [2004] ECR I-07405, § 45.

ing the period of breeding, rearing, hibernation and migration, destruction or taking of eggs from the wild, deterioration of breeding sites or resting places, as well as keeping, transport and sale or exchange of these species.[482] For plant species it should be prohibited to deliberately pick, collect, cut, uproot or destroy them in their natural range in the wild and to keep, transport and sale or exchange them.[483] For specimens of species of wild flora and fauna listed in Annex V taking or exploitation is allowed, but should be compatible with their favourable conservation status and to this end might be subject to various managerial measures.[484] As in the Birds Directive, derogation is allowed under certain conditions, and means of capture or killing are restricted.[485]

The application of Birds and Habitats Directives overlaps to a significant extent and is quite complex overall. Moreover, the level of their implementation differs across the EU.[486] Implementation and enforcement of the EU environmental policy as such remains quite a challenge.[487] In 2017, the tool of "Environmental Implementation Review" was introduced to assist implementation of the EU environmental law.[488]

Apart from the mentioned directives, the EU's common agenda for environmental policy is adopted by the European Parliament and Council of the Union in accordance with the ordinary legislative procedure in a form of Environmental Action Programme (EAP).[489] Currently in force is the 8th EAP, adopted in 2022, covering a period until 2030 and being in line with EU long-term vision until 2050.[490] One of its objectives – "protecting, preserving and restoring biodiversity" – directly addresses biodiversity, while other objectives, such as "reducing environmental and cli-

482 Habitats Directive, Article 12.
483 Habitats Directive, Article 13.
484 Habitats Directive, Article 14.
485 Habitats Directive, Article 16, Article 15.
486 de Sadeleer, "European Union in Biodiversity and nature protection law," 422; *Commission v France* C-96/98 [1999] ECR I-8531; *Commission v France* C-2220/99 [2001] ECR I-5831.
487 Burns and Carter, "Environmental Policy," 516–517.
488 Kingston, "Environmental Policy," 1178; "Environmental Implementation Review," European Commission, accessed September 20, 2024, https://environment.ec.europa.eu/law-and-governance/environmental-implementation-review_en.
489 de Sadeleer, "European Union in Biodiversity and nature protection law," 418; "Environment action programme to 2030," European Commission, accessed September 20, 2024, https://environment.ec.europa.eu/strategy/environment-action-programme-2030_en.
490 European Commission, "Environment action programme to 2030".

mate pressures" might indirectly serve the aim of biodiversity protection.[491] The 8th EAP builds on the European Green Deal, that is the European Commission's "roadmap for making the EU's economy sustainable".[492] The Commission has also created the EU Biodiversity strategy for 2030 as the core part of the Green Deal.[493] In the sphere of forest biodiversity, there is a New EU Forest Strategy for 2030, the European Green Deal and the EU 2030 Biodiversity Strategy.[494] In addition, in March 2023, the Commission published two sets of guidelines on forests: Guidelines on Biodiversity-Friendly Afforestation, Reforestation and Tree Planting and Guidelines for Defining, Mapping, Monitoring and Strictly Protecting EU Primary and Old-Growth Forests.[495] Moreover, in May 2023, the new regulation aiming at minimisation of EU contribution to global deforestation and forest degradation was adopted.[496]

---

491 European Commission, "Environment action programme to 2030"; Decision (EU) 2022/591 of the European Parliament and of the Council of 6 April 2022 on a General Union Environment Action Programme to 2030, PE/83/2021/REV/1, Document 32022D0591, *Official Journal of the European Union, L 114, 12.4.2022, p. 22–36*, http://data.europa.eu/eli/dec/2022/591/oj, Article 2.

492 European Commission, "Environment action programme to 2030"; "The European Green Deal sets out how to make Europe the first climate-neutral continent by 2050, boosting the economy, improving people's health and quality of life, caring for nature, and leaving no one behind," European Commission, December 11, 2019, https://ec.europa.eu/commission/presscorner/detail/en/ip_19_6691.

493 European Commission, "Environment action programme to 2030", "EU Biodiversity Strategy for 2030: Bringing nature back into our lives," Communication from the Commission to the European Parliament, the Council, the European Economic and Social Committee and the Committee of the Regions, COM/2020/380 final, (May 20, 2020) https://eur-lex.europa.eu/legal-content/EN/TXT/?uri=celex%3A52020DC0380.

494 "New EU Forest Strategy for 2030," Communication from the Commission to the European Parliament, the Council, the European Economic and Social Committee and the Committee of the Regions, COM/2021/572 final, (July 16, 2021) https://eur-lex.europa.eu/legal-content/EN/ALL/?uri=COM%3A2021%3A572%3AFIN.

495 European Commission, "Environment action programme to 2030".

496 "Fighting deforestation and forest degradation," European Union, accessed December 31, 2024, https://eur-lex.europa.eu/legal-content/EN/LSU/?uri=CELEX:32023R1115#:~:text=The%20regulation%20sets%20out%20binding%20rules%20for%20European,to%20greenhouse%20gas%20emissions%20and%20global%20biodiversity%20loss; Regulation (EU) 2023/1115 of the European Parliament and of the Council of 31 May 2023 on the making available on the Union market and the export from the Union of certain commodities and products associated with deforestation and forest degradation and repealing Regulation (EU) No 995/2010, *Official Journal of the European Union*, L 150, 9.6.2023, p. 206–247, http://data.europa.eu/eli/reg/2023/1115/oj [EUDR].

Conclusions to Chapter 1

The ethical stances of humanity towards biodiversity (and related broader or narrower categories) have been debated in the scholarly literature over a period of nearly sixty years. This process is ongoing as new approaches continue to emerge, and the old ones are being redefined and reframed. The ethical approaches to biodiversity could be grouped into the broad categories of anthropocentric and non-anthropocentric arguments or those based on instrumental and on intrinsic value. Within the group of anthropocentric arguments and instrumental value, an idea of 'ecosystem services' has recently emerged as a practical tool to express the value of natural processes and, therefore, make biodiversity materially present in the decision-making process. Compared with the anthropocentric arguments and those based on instrumental value, the categories of non-anthropocentric arguments and intrinsic value are far more diverse and controversial. There is no commonly accepted definition of intrinsic (inherent) value in environmental ethics and at least four ways to understand it. Moreover, the next step after comprehending the notion of the intrinsic value of biodiversity as such and establishing that it should then lead to the category 'morally considerable' is to understand its practical implications. The debate as to them remains open. It is closely related to differences within various sub-currents of the non-anthropocentric argument such as sentientism, biocentrism, and ecocentrism. A trend towards abandonment of ideas centred on a certain narrow aspect and instead of a search for a more holistic approach, underlining human responsibility is observed. Among such ideas, there are, for instance, 'enlightened anthropocentrism', 'anthroporelational approach' or 'retinity'.

The religious and philosophical idea of human responsibility for nature and understanding of nature's value invigorated the development of international environmental law. Obligations of humankind towards the natural world belong to the fundamental ethical questions accompanying international efforts to conserve biodiversity. Ethics may inform moral reasoning of alternatives in international environmental law and policy and serve as a tool of persuasion or justification of specific options.

Biodiversity treaties, in describing value and justifications for biodiversity protection, rely on both anthropocentric and non-anthropocentric arguments, even though the former prevail. Among the anthropocentric ideas, the special role in international environmental law is played by the concepts of concern for future generations, a common concern of mankind and a common heritage of humanity, sometimes also listed among the principles of this area of law. Various examples of instrumental value, such as economic, educational, cultural, recreational or aesthetic, are mentioned in treaty instruments. Some instruments, such as the Bern Convention and the CBD, also explicitly mention intrinsic value, albeit leaving the question of its definition open. The dominance of anthropocentric ideas shall not be viewed as disadvantageous for biodiversity as the anthropocentric arguments remain valid, and they do not exclude non-anthropocentric arguments but may be applied simultaneously, ensuring wider outreach and reception of the grounds for biodiversity protection in societies.

Principles of international environmental law, whether reflected in the treaties, pertaining to the domain of customary international law or mentioned in the soft-law sources, perform an important function of linking values and rules, policy and law, and international and domestic law. Some principles are enshrined in the biodiversity treaties while others are taken for granted as part of the broader area of international environmental law. Some of the most relevant principles for biodiversity protection include the precautionary principle, intergenerational equity, no-harm, cooperation, public participation, environmental impact assessment, and sustainable development.

Ukraine is a State Party to a number of international treaties relevant to biodiversity protection in the Ukrainian Carpathians. Based on their geographical scope, these treaties pertain to the global level, including the CBD, CITES, CMS, and World Heritage Convention; regional level that is Bern Convention and the subregional level – the Carpathian Convention. Furthermore, the norms of the European Union are relevant to Ukraine within its ambition to join the EU, involving the need to approximate legislation. Each of the biodiversity treaties establishes a peculiar protection regime and institutional mechanism.

The CBD is the most comprehensive agreement on biodiversity protection in terms of the subject matter. Being a framework agreement and using several 'language softeners' pertaining to the state's capacity and appropriateness of action, it leaves the decisive role in its implementation to the level of national governments. Unlike some other treaties in this field, CBD does not contain any definitive lists of species or sites to be protected, suggesting simply a list of indicative categories in Annex I. The key obligations and policy areas are contained in Articles 6 – 20. The central obligations include strategic planning, identification and monitoring of biodiversity, *in-situ* conservation entailing a broad range of actions, sustainable use of biodiversity, public education and awareness, and environmental impact assessment. In addition to the provisions of this Convention, numerous thematic-specific guidelines, including those on forest biodiversity, have been adopted by the COPs, and some concepts that are not directly mentioned in the provisions, such as the 'ecosystem approach' became the primary framework of action almost inevitable for the implementation of this instrument. The institutional mechanism of the CBD provides a fruitful discussion space where the global strategies for biodiversity protection are designed. Following the expiration of the famous Aichi Biodiversity Targets, the new ambitious Kunming-Montreal Global Biodiversity Framework was developed as a global road map in this sphere.

The CITES regulates international trade in endangered species and follows a species-based conservation approach. The mechanism of species protection under the CITES is based on listing species into three appendices, which entails various degrees of protection and procedures. Appendix I includes species threatened with extinction, the trade in specimens of which is possible only in exceptional circumstances based on the consent of relevant authorities and not for primarily commercial purposes. Appendix II species are not necessarily threatened with extinction but may become so unless the trade in their specimens is regulated; the procedure of trade in them requires the consent of the relevant authorities (but unlike Appendix I species, the separate import permit is not required). Appendix III lists species designated by a particular State Party, which entails the need to grant export permits. The procedure for granting them is, however, slightly less complex than for Appendix II species. One of the peculiarities of the CITES in comparison with other biodiversity treaties is its robust compliance system. The current strategic documents on the implementation of the CITES aim to contribute to the implementation of the post-2020 global biodiversity framework and Sustainable Development Goals, require conservation action at the national level and encourage Parties to achieve synergies in implementing CITES and other biodiversity-related conventions.

The CMS is concerned with protecting species that migrate from one state to another. Similarly to the CITES, CMS uses a species-based conservation approach and lists species that require special protection. Appendix I includes migratory species in danger of extinction. The Range States of Appendix I species are obliged, in particular, to conserve and restore habitats of such species, to prevent or reduce factors that might further endanger such species and to prohibit taking of animals belonging to such species (with some exceptions). Appendix II lists species with unfavourable conservation status and those that will benefit from international cooperation. It does not entail any specific obligations for the Range States but suggests a possibility of concluding special agreements on the conservation of these species. Interestingly, the species might be simultaneously included in both Appendix I and Appendix II. The strategic documents created within the CMS's institutional mechanism are focused on biodiversity protection and seek to reinforce the realisation of the Kunming-Montreal Global Biodiversity Framework.

UNESCO helped to consolidate international efforts on the protection of remarkable natural sites in several ways, including by creating the Network of Biosphere Reserves and through the World Heritage Convention. According to the World Heritage Convention, the natural sites of outstanding universal value, as defined on the basis of several factors, may be designated as natural heritage or mixed heritage (i.e. cultural landscapes). The criteria for the assessment of outstanding universal value include the presence of important natural habitats for *in-situ* conservation of biological diversity. The protection regime under this Convention includes national and international efforts, where states are primarily responsible for ensuring the protection of the sites and their transmission to future generations. Within the Ukrainian Carpathians, several areas belong to the natural heritage Ancient and Primeval Beech Forests of the Carpathians and Other Regions of Europe, which represent significant ongoing ecological and biological processes in the development of forest ecosystems, are highly relevant for biodiversity protection and possess aesthetic value.

On a regional level in Europe, the Bern Convention is one of the key instruments for biodiversity protection that also inspired the development of EU legislation. The Bern Convention aims to conserve wild flora and fauna and their natural habitat, paying special attention to endangered and vulnerable species and natural habitats. It obliges states to introduce necessary legislative and administrative measures and calls for special attention to the species listed in Appendices I and II, prohibiting their deliberate picking, collecting, cutting, uprooting, possession and sale (with some exceptions). It also requires special protection of migratory species listed in Appendices II and III. Based on a series of resolutions of the Standing Committee, a network of Areas of Special Conservation Interest, known as the Emerald Network, has been created in Europe. The reporting and case-file systems have also been developed, enabling broad public participation. The strategic documents of the Bern Convention set precise directions for conservation efforts in Europe and seek to contribute to the implementation of the Global Biodiversity Framework in the pan-European context.

The Carpathian Convention obliges parties to pursue policies on conservation, restoration and sustainable use of biodiversity in the Carpathians. It pays special attention to the natural and semi-natural habitats, their continuity and connectivity, and the protection of species characteristic to the Carpathians, endangered species, endemic species and large carnivores. It also explicitly incorporates the ecosystem approach. Its Protocol on Conservation and Sustainable Use of Biological and Landscape Diversity and the Protocol on Sustainable Forest Management establish a set of norms most directly relevant to the protection of biodiversity of the Ukrainian Carpathians, and each of these protocols is accompanied by the strategic action plans on their implementation that provide further guidance. Importantly, with the adoption of the Carpathian Biodiversity Framework based on the Kunming-Montreal Global Biodiversity Framework, the Carpathians became the first region in the world to have a distinct regional biodiversity framework.

The EU legislation, similarly to public international law, initially had no provisions on environmental protection. Currently, however, the basis for environmental protection is found in key normative sources of the EU, including the Treaty on European Union (Article 3 (3)), the Treaty on the Functioning of the European Union (Article 11 and Title XX) and the Charter of Fundamental Rights of the European Union (Article 37). The key principles of international environmental law are reflected in the EU legislation, including the principle of integration of environmental concerns into various sectors of the economy. The cornerstones of the EU biodiversity legislation and policy are the Birds Directive (2009/147/EC) and Habitats Directive (92/43/EC). They are based on the Bern Convention and form a legal basis for the Natura 2000 network that comprises 'special protection areas' under the Birds Directive and 'special areas of conservation' under the Habitats Directive. In addition, the Environmental Action Programme adopted by the European Parliament and Council of the Union reflects the EU's common agenda for environmental policy. Objectives of such a Programme currently in force include protection, preservation and restoration of biodiversity. It builds on the European Green Deal and is related to the EU Biodiversity Strategy for 2030, which is the core part of the Green Deal. In addition, in the sphere of forest biodiversity, there is a New EU Forest Strategy for 2030, the related Guidelines on Biodiversity-Friendly Afforestation, Reforestation and Tree Planting, Guidelines for Defining, Mapping, Monitoring, and Strictly Protecting EU Primary and Old-Growth Forests as well as a new regulation aimed at fighting deforestation and forest degradation.

In conclusion, there is a robust international legal framework for protecting biodiversity in the Ukrainian Carpathians, further enhanced by the EU norms.

CHAPTER 2. THE STATUS QUO OF THE BIODIVERSITY PROTECTION OF FOREST ECOSYSTEMS IN THE UKRAINIAN CARPATHIANS FROM THE LEGAL, POLICY AND ETHICAL PERSPECTIVES

2.1. Main characteristics of the biodiversity of forest ecosystems in the Ukrainian Carpathians in a socio-economic context

As was outlined in Chapter I, the Ukrainian Carpathians, hosting species, habitats and sites enlisted in various inventories that stipulate their special protection, are of recognised importance for biodiversity from the global, regional (Europe) and subregional (Carpathian ecoregion) viewpoint. The Carpathian ecoregion has been called "Europe's largest territory with undisturbed forests".[497] The present subchapter aims to set the biodiversity protection of the Ukrainian Carpathians in a local context, that takes account of the sustainable development paradigm, combining environmental, social and economic considerations.

The area of the Ukrainian Carpathians constitutes approximately 24.000 square kilometres, amounting to nearly 4 per cent of the total area of Ukraine.[498] Within Ukraine, the Carpathian Mountains are situated in the Western part of the country, being partly located in four regions ('oblast'): Transcarpathia, Ivano-Frankivsk, Lviv, and Chernivtsi. The percentage of mountain areas within these regions is estimated to be 69.5 per cent, 37.5 per cent, 18.6 per cent and 15.8 per cent, respectively.[499] Within the

497 Anatoliy Smaliychuk and Uli Grabener, eds, *Natural forests of Ukrainian Carpathians,* (Lviv: Carty i Atlasy, 2018), 9; Carpathian Convention, Preamble.

498 "Geographical location," Carpathian Heritage, accessed September 20, 2024, http://carpathian-heritage.org.ua/ua/geograph.

499 Ministry of Ecology and Natural Resources of Ukraine, *National Report of Ukraine on the Implementation of the Protocol on the Conservation and Sustainable Use of Biological and Landscape Diversity to the Framework Convention on the Protection and Sustainable Development of the Carpathians*, (Kyiv, 2017), http://www.carpathiaconvention.org/tl_files/carpathiancon/Downloads/02%20Activities/Biodiveristy/National%20report%20Biodiversity%20Ukraine.pdf, 5, [*National Report of Ukraine on the Implementation of the Biodiversity Protocol*].

Carpathian ecoregion, comprising seven more states: Austria, Check Republic, Hungary, Poland, Romania, Serbia and the Slovak Republic and covering over 200.000 square kilometres, Ukrainian Carpathians account for approximately 10 per cent of the total area of this ecoregion.[500] Even though Ukraine's numerical share in the surface area of the Carpathian ecoregion is relatively small, its practical role in biodiversity conservation is significant. In particular, the Ukrainian Carpathians serve as an ecological corridor, assisting animal migration and plant distribution. They also host the largest massifs of the primeval beech forests in Europe.[501]

The Ukrainian Carpathians consist of a series of parallel mountain ranges of low (up to 1000 metres above sea level) and medium-high (1500 – 2061 metres above sea level) altitude. These ranges run from northwest to southeast and are divided by transversal river valleys. The Ukrainian Carpathians are located within the temperate continental climate zone and act as a climatic barrier, separating colder Precarpathian region (lying on the northeast) from the warmer Transcarpathian lowland (lying on the southwest). Accordingly, besides the altitudinal climatic differences, the southwestern macro-slope is slightly warmer and more humid in comparison with the northeastern one.[502] The altitudinal zonation is well-defined and follows the pattern of decrease of temperature and increase of precipitation with the elevation.[503] The climatic characteristics and other physio-geographical factors affect the vegetation of the Carpathians, based on which seven bioclimatic zones have been distinguished: a very warm altitudinal belt of oak forests; a warm beech-oak forest belt; a warm temperate belt of beech forests; a cool temperate belt of spruce-beech forests; a cool belt of spruce forests; a temperate cool belt of subalpine crooked woodland and a cold belt of genuine alpine meadows.[504] Among these zones, the genuine alpine meadows can be found only on the Chornohora Massif, and the subalpine crooked woodland is present only on the upper slopes and peaks of the highest mountain ranges. The dominant zones are the warm temperate belt of beech forests (dominant on the southwestern macro-slope) and a cool temperate belt of spruce-beech forests (dominant

500 Smaliychuk and Grabener, *Natural forests of Ukrainian Carpathians*, 9.
501 Smaliychuk and Grabener, *Natural forests of Ukrainian Carpathians*, 9.
502 Smaliychuk and Grabener, *Natural forests of Ukrainian Carpathians*, 9.
503 Smaliychuk and Grabener, *Natural forests of Ukrainian Carpathians*, 13.
504 For the characteristics of each bioclimatic region see: Smaliychuk and Grabener, *Natural forests of Ukrainian Carpathians*, 13–15.

on the northeastern macro-slope).[505] Apart from the bioclimatic zones, smaller units with shared biocenosis have been identified in the literature, namely the 33 territorial units, micro- and meso-ecoregions.[506]

The Carpathians have been characterised as 'biodiversity hotspots' representing the "one of the world's key Palaearctic montane ecoregions" and hosting the largest montane populations of brown bear, wolf and lynx.[507] The fauna of the Carpathians also includes such species as wild cat, wild boar, badger, marten, otter, deer, fox or squirrel.[508] Overall, there are more than 435 vertebrate animal species including 280 bird species belonging to 16 orders (using Carpathians for nesting, wintering or stopover during seasonal migrations).[509] Among examples of endemic species there is Carpathian triton (newt) belonging to the order *Anura*.[510] According to the Green Data Book of Ukraine, the cenofund of the Ukrainian Carpathians is represented by 801 associations.[511] More than 2000 species of plants are found in the Carpathian Mountains, with about 2 per cent of them being endemic ones found only in the Eastern Carpathians and with some of the species belonging to the category of rare relict plant species.[512]

It is reported that the Carpathian Biosphere Reserve, well representing the landscape and biogeographical diversity of the Ukrainian part of the Carpathian Mountains, protects over 1300 species of vascular plants, 314 species of vertebrate animals, and nearly 3200 species of invertebrates.[513] Out of them, 201 plant and fungi species and 108 animal species are listed

---

505 Smaliychuk and Grabener, *Natural forests of Ukrainian Carpathians*, 15.

506 Smaliychuk and Grabener, *Natural forests of Ukrainian Carpathians*, 17; For the description of clusters of natural forests identified within these units see ibid., 40–97.

507 Robin Webster, Suzie H. Holt and Charlie A. Avis, "The status of the Carpathians : a report developed as a part of the Carpathian Ecoregion Initiative" (2001) cited in Król et al., *Carpathian List of Endangered Species*, v-vi.

508 Ukraine Biodiversity Analysis (Assessment) Team, *Ukraine Biodiversity Analysis, prepared by* ECODIT for USAID/ Ukraine (June, 2017), 7.

509 *National Report of Ukraine on the Implementation of the Biodiversity Protocol*, 6.

510 *National Report of Ukraine on the Implementation of the Biodiversity Protocol*, 6.

511 Yurii Sheliah-Sosonko et al., eds, *Green Book of Ukraine. Forests* (Kyiv: Naukova dumka, 2002), https://nature.land.kiev.ua/green-book-02.pdf.

512 Ukraine Biodiversity Analysis (Assessment) Team, *Ukraine Biodiversity Analysis, prepared by* ECODIT for USAID/ Ukraine (June, 2017), 6.

513 "Carpathian Biosphere Reserve," Bern Convention, accessed September 20, 2024, https://www.coe.int/en/web/bern-convention/-/carpathian-biosphere-reserve.

in the Red Data Book of Ukraine (2009).[514] When it comes to the protection granted by international legal instruments, the Carpathian Biosphere Reserve hosts 284 species protected by the Bern Convention (and since 2016, it has been considered to form a part of the Emerald Network), 86 species protected by the CMS and 67 species protected by the CITES.[515]

The employees of the National Natural Park "Hutsulshchyna" mentioned among the rare bird species found on the territory of this park black stork (*Ciconia nigra*), red-backed shrike (*Lanius collurio*), three-toed woodpecker (*Picoides tridactylus*), capercaillie (*Tetrao urogallus*), and hazel grouse (*Tetrastes bonasia*). It was also reported that approximately 60 plant species enlisted in the Red Data Book of Ukraine are found on its territory, among which there are 30 species of orchids.[516]

As of October 2022, there were 185 protected areas in the Ukrainian Carpathians.[517] The wider network of the NRF sites in the four oblasts within which the Ukrainian Carpathians are located was estimated in 2017 to comprise 1670 territories and objects amounting to over 657 thousand ha.[518] Moreover, as of 2021, 30 sites within the Ukrainian Carpathians were officially granted the status of Areas of Special Conservation Interest, forming the Emerald Network in accordance with the Bern Convention. They mostly overlap with the protected areas, and their total area is slightly over 654 thousand ha.[519]

The share of primeval, quasi-primeval and natural forests within the Ukrainian Carpathians amounts to nearly 94 thousand ha. Out of them, ap-

514 "Carpathian Biosphere Reserve," Bern Convention, accessed September 20, 2024, https://www.coe.int/en/web/bern-convention/-/carpathian-biosphere-reserve.

515 "Carpathian Biosphere Reserve," Bern Convention, accessed September 20, 2024, https://www.coe.int/en/web/bern-convention/-/carpathian-biosphere-reserve.

516 Scientific employee, NNP "Hutsulshchyna" L11 (N), personal communication, September 6, 2022.

517 Department of Nature Conservation of the Ministry of Climate and Environment of Poland, *Impact of war on natural environment of the Carpathians in Ukraine*, report prepared by Zbigniew Niewiadomski (October, 2022), 22, https://www.gov.pl/attachment/9ed63b69-87d8-4c52-a74a-1c88385f5508.

518 Department of Nature Conservation, *Impact of war on natural environment of the Carpathians in Ukraine*, 21; *National Report of Ukraine on the Implementation of the Biodiversity Protocol*, 19.

519 Department of Nature Conservation, *Impact of war on natural environment of the Carpathians in Ukraine*, 23; See Standing Committee, *Updated list of officially adopted Emerald Network sites (December 2021)*, T-PVS/PA(2021)11, (Strasbourg, 2021), https://rm.coe.int/pa11e-2021-updated-list-officially-adopted-emerald-sites-final/1680a4be3d, 26–33.

proximately 45 thousand ha grow in protected areas, among which almost 29 thousand ha are designated as World Heritage Property "Ancient and Primeval Beech Forests of the Carpathians and Other Regions of Europe" and almost 10 thousand ha grow in special primeval forest natural monuments.[520]

Historically, the Carpathian region within Ukraine and its forests have experienced significant anthropogenic pressure. The timber was harvested, and the forest cover was reduced for the purposes of cattle grazing. In addition, from the middle of the 19th century until World War I, the oil mining and refining industry was active in the Carpathian region, shaping the landscapes and requiring timber for building the infrastructure of this industry. During this period, the areas of clear-cuts of natural beech and fir-beech forests were often replaced with artificially planted spruce monocultures.[521] At the same time, within the broader Carpathian region, the forests of the eastern part of the Carpathians, including Ukrainian Carpathians, are considered to be better preserved than in other parts of this ecoregion.[522]

Currently, the economic development of the Carpathian region in Ukraine is described as "relatively low".[523] Forests play a crucial role in the subsistence needs of the local population, and human settlements in the Carpathian regions have been characterised by sociologists as "forest-dependent communities".[524] In addition, 715 settlements in the Ukrainian Carpathians have been granted the status of mountain settlements. This status means that the altitude of such settlements exceeds 400 metres above sea level, and other criteria defined by the Law "On the status of mountain settlements in Ukraine", such as the size of arable land and climatic condi-

520 Department of Nature Conservation, *Impact of war on natural environment of the Carpathians in Ukraine*, 19.

521 Department of Nature Conservation, *Impact of war on natural environment of the Carpathians in Ukraine*, 18.

522 Jerzy A. Kondracki, "Carpathian Mountains," *Encyclopedia Britannica*, last updated September 13, 2024, https://www.britannica.com/place/Carpathian-Mountains.

523 Volodymyr Khymynets, "Carpathian region in the context of sustainable development of Ukraine," *Scientific Bulletin of Uzhhorod National University*, Series 'Economics' No.3 (Part3) (2012): 42, https://dspace.uzhnu.edu.ua/jspui/handle/lib/23763.

524 Nataliia Pohorila and Ihor Soloviy, eds, *Carpathian forests as a resource and common good* (Lviv: UCU, 2022), 9–10.

tions, are taken into account. 279 out of these settlements are located above 600 metres above sea level and are considered to be difficult to reach.[525]

In the course of the research interviews, it was noted by the majority of respondents from several villages in the Carpathian region (Ivano-Frankivsk oblast, in the vicinity of Kolomyia) that the forests around their villages have been cut in recent 10–20 years with greater intensity than before, and the condition of the forests is 'poorer' than it used to be.[526] The residents noted that there are almost no enterprises that could create jobs in the region, therefore forestry continues to be an important source of profit. Except for logging and processing of the wood (both of which may be undertaken 'officially' or 'unofficially' that is semi-lawfully or unlawfully), there are not many profitable activities in the region. The older generations in a village sustain their livelihoods by raising cattle and selling milk and meat, while younger generations usually migrate abroad (mostly to Poland, Italy and Germany) for seasonal or permanent jobs.[527] It was also reported that some people combine jobs at state enterprises and government institutions with agricultural activities. Some people also own private businesses, mostly shops. Still others engage in traditional crafts, such as making blankets and rugs called *'lizhnyk'* but this activity is engaged in less frequently than before.[528] Some people also continue to produce certain local cheese-like dairy products specialities, including *'budz'* and *'brynza'*, that have been traditionally manufactured at Carpathian *'polonynas'* (the meadows used for cattle grazing). It was also noted that previously orcharding was profitable (including growing apples for sale), but not anymore due to the shrinking market, including because of the Russian war against Ukraine.[529]

While characterising other forest uses than logging, local residents noted that until recently, when there was no gas in the village, the firewood was collected and used, and presently some people still take wood for fuel, but

525 Department of Nature Conservation, *Impact of war on natural environment of the Carpathians in Ukraine*, 16.

526 Local resident L1, personal communication, September 5, 2022; Local resident – local councillor L3 (A), personal communication, September 5, 2022; Local resident – settlement mayor L4 (A), personal communication, September 5, 2022; Local resident – sawmill owner L5 (B), personal communication, September 5, 2022; Local resident L8, personal communication, September 5, 2022; Local resident L9, personal communication, September 6, 2022.

527 L1, personal communication, September 5, 2022; L3 (A), personal communication, September 5, 2022.

528 L2, personal communication, September 5, 2022.

529 L3 (A), personal communication, September 5, 2022.

this occurs at a lower scale than before.[530] Non-timber products gathered in the Carpathian forests include mushrooms and berries, especially bilberry and lingonberry, that could be gathered in small amounts for private use or on a larger scale for commercial purposes.[531]

The Ukrainian Carpathians belong to the famous tourist destinations in Ukraine, including hiking in warmer months and skiing in winter. There is a perspective of further development of sustainable tourism in the region, including ecotourism, nature-based tourism and culture tourism, contributing to the economic development and preservation of biodiversity.[532] At the same time, tourism in the Ukrainian Carpathians often leads to nature degradation through the deterioration of the soil and vegetation cover and pollution. For instance, the rapid development of such ski resorts as "Bukovel" in the Ivano-Frankivsk region or "Play" in the Lviv region were reported to constitute significant anthropogenic pressure by earthwork and deforestation. Other manifestations of the impact of tourism in the Ukrainian Carpathians include degradation of tourist trails due to excessive tourist load, littering in the most visited places in national parks and 'jeeping' – a tourist attraction practised in recent years in various parts of the Carpathian Mountains, which consists in transporting people from the bottom to the top of the mountain by jeeps.[533] The tourist infrastructure and pressure are unevenly distributed within the region, as are the profits associated with the hospitality sphere in the Ukrainian Carpathians, where large resorts generate profits rather for the benefit of oligarchic circles than for the local residents.[534]

---

530 L1, personal communication, September 5, 2022; L2, personal communication, September 5, 2022; Local resident L14, personal communication, September 6, 2022.

531 L2, personal communication, September 5, 2022; Press secretary of the forest enterprise F20, personal communication, September 21, 2022.

532 Natalia Pankiv and Oksana Roik, "Sustainable Development of Tourism in The Carpathian Region," in *Modern Aspects of Science,* 21- th volume of the international collective monograph, (Czech Republic: Mezinárodní Ekonomický Institut, 2022), http://perspectives.pp.ua/public/site/mono/monography-21.pdf, 286–287.

533 Pankiv and Roik, "Sustainable Development of Tourism in The Carpathian Region," 289–291; See also Y. Zinko, M. Malska, M. Ivanyk, S. Blagodyr, "Tourism in the Carpathian Region:Threat to the Environment and Ways of Sustainable development," *Visnyk of the Lviv University*, Series Geography 45 (2014): 443–451; L11 (N), personal communication, September 6, 2022.

534 An infamous example is "Bukovel" resort, currently associated with the Palytsia family from the circle close to oligarch Ihor Kolomoiskyi, see "'There is no Kolomoyskyi in Bukovel at all'. Who currently owns the most famous Ukrainian resort,"

The population of the Carpathian region within Ukraine (as of time before the full-scale invasion in February 2022) constitutes approximately 6,4 million, amounting to a 12.3 per cent share of the total population of Ukraine.[535] According to the sociological data, the overall level of religiosity and trust in the Church in Ukraine is quite high (68 per cent at the end of 2021, 74 per cent in November 2022 and 70.5 per cent at the end of 2023). In the Western regions of Ukraine (7 oblasts, including 4 of those within which the Ukrainian Carpathians are located and the additional 3 oblasts), the level of religiosity is higher than the average, and in 2023, it was reported to constitute 84.1 per cent. In terms of confessional affiliation, the two dominant Christian confessions in the Western regions are Orthodoxy (45 per cent) and Greek-Catholic Church (39.6 per cent). The share of Roman Catholic Church is slightly lower than 3 per cent.[536]

The interviews with residents of several villages in the Carpathians in the Ivano-Frankivsk region confirmed the generally high level of religiosity and importance of Church authority, with the two dominant confessions being the Ukrainian Greek-Catholic Church and the Orthodox Church of Ukraine.[537] The residents who identify as active members of the Church in their village were asked additional questions on their opinion of the Church authority in environmental matters, that is whether environmental themes feature in Church communities known to them, whether any practical steps on care for the environment are undertaken and whether in their opinion Church teaching on creation can serve as an impetus in behaviour changes with respect to environment, in the first instance with respect to forest ecosystems of the Carpathians. The results show that care for the environment is usually not included in faith-related matters (as one resident noted, "our people have not simply traced any ties between their faith and care for the environment").[538] At the same time, the majority of respondents

NV, June 27, 2023, https://biz.nv.ua/ukr/markets/bukovel-komu-naspravdi-nalezhit-nayvidomishiy-kurort-ukrajini-rozsliduvannya-nv-50334936.html.

535 Khymynets, "Carpathian region in the context of sustainable development of Ukraine," 40.

536 "Religiosity, trust in the Church, confessional affiliation and inter-church relations in Ukrainian society (November, 2023)," *Razumkov Centre*, December 28, 2023, https://razumkov.org.ua/en/research-areas/surveys/religiosity-trust-in-the-church-confessional-affiliation-and-inter-church-relations-in-ukrainian-society-november-2023.

537 Settlement mayor L12 (A), personal communication, September 6, 2022; L14, personal communication, September 6, 2022.

538 F20, personal communication, September 21, 2022.

mentioned an example of the Church initiative on the reduction of the use of plastic flowers and wreaths at the cemeteries, and some mentioned the clean-up campaigns on the riverbanks, organised by the village council and supported by the Church.[539] The practice of bringing plastic flowers to cemeteries, which became widespread in the region in the 1990s, has been gradually replaced over the last 5–10 years by the practice of planting real flowers or bringing decorations made of natural materials.[540] When asked whether this success story could potentially be repeated if the Church was actively supporting forest protection, such as the reduction of illegal logging, the respondents provided diverse answers. Some respondents voiced doubts, explaining them by the extreme dependency of the population on forest exploitation and the high profits that it generates.[541] However, there were also suggestions as to the possible reduction of illegal logging. The possibility of change was explained by the respect awarded to the Church in society.[542] It was also noted, that as a general rule, no logging is undertaken on Sundays or on important religious feasts.

2.2. Legal landscape of the biodiversity protection of forest ecosystems in the Ukrainian Carpathians

The legal landscape of the biodiversity protection in forest ecosystems in the Ukrainian Carpathians is fragmented and complex. Given the absence of strategies and laws focused on regulating biodiversity protection in Ukraine directly, the norms from several areas have to be considered, such as general legislation on nature protection and forestry. This subchapter begins by exploring strategic documents in this sphere and continues by analysing laws and regulations on nature protection and forestry.

539 L1, personal communication, September 5, 2022; L2, personal communication, September 5, 2022; L5 (B), personal communication, September 5, 2022; L14, personal communication, September 6, 2022.

540 Local resident L8, personal communication, September 5, 2022.

541 L4 (A), personal communication, September 5, 2022; L11 (N), personal communication, September 6, 2022.

542 L12 (A), personal communication, September 6, 2022; L14, personal communication, September 6, 2022.

2.2.1. The strategic documents in Ukraine relevant to the biodiversity protection

Despite early attempts to create strategic documents on biodiversity, as of 2024, the comprehensive national strategy on biodiversity, as well as any alternatives to it on subregional or regional levels, are absent.

The initial steps to develop a relevant national strategy were undertaken in 1997, when, shortly after the ratification of the CBD by Ukraine, the Cabinet of Ministers of Ukraine adopted the Concept of the Conservation of Biological Diversity of Ukraine.[543] The resolution on its adoption envisioned the subsequent development of the national programme on protection of biodiversity for the period of 1998 – 2015, which was, however, never adopted as a standalone document. Instead, it was decided by the Verkhovna Rada of Ukraine in 1999 that the legislative draft of the national programme on the protection of biodiversity shall be incorporated into the draft Law on the Programme for the Formation of the National Ecological Network of Ukraine for 2000 – 2015.[544] Both the 1997 Concept and the Programme make references to the CBD and the non-binding Pan-European Biological and Landscape Diversity Strategy.[545]

The biodiversity is characterised in the 1997 Concept as the "national wealth of Ukraine, which provides ecosystem and biosphere functions of living organisms, their communities, and shapes the human environment".[546] It is noted with regret that biodiversity is in decline due to various types of economic activities, such as the construction or development of transport infrastructure. The Concept also expresses the moral duty of passing the biological diversity to future generations "in the most preserved condition".[547] The definition of objects of protection by this Concept notes

543 Concept of the Conservation of Biological Diversity of Ukraine, approved by the Resolution of the Cabinet of Ministers of Ukraine No. 439, Document 439–97-p (May 12, 1997), https://zakon.rada.gov.ua/laws/show/439-97-%D0%BF#Text.

544 "On the merging of the draft laws of Ukraine: On the Program for the Formation of the National Ecological Network of Ukraine for 2000–2015 and On the National Program for the Conservation of Biological Diversity for 2000–2015," Resolution of the Verkhovna Rada of Ukraine, No. 1289-XIV, Document 1289-XIV (December 14, 1999), https://zakon.rada.gov.ua/laws/show/1289-14#Text.

545 "Pan-European Biological and Landscape Diversity Strategy," approved by the Ministers of the Environment of the 55 states present at the Ministerial Conference "Environment for Europe" (Sofia, Bulgaria, 23–25 October 1995), https://www.cbd.int/doc/nbsap/rbsap/peblds-rbsap.pdf.

546 Concept of the Conservation of Biological Diversity of Ukraine, 1997.

that the conservation of biodiversity involves the protection of both individual organisms and their groups along with the habitats within specific territories, as well as ecosystems as a whole. The range of legal, financial, organisational, scientific, and educational tools are mentioned among the means for implementing this Concept.

The Concept listed subject areas of biodiversity protection, among which of particular relevance to the Ukrainian Carpathians are forest ecosystems, mountain ecosystems, conservation of species and populations and the creation of a national ecological network. When it comes specifically to the forest ecosystems, the Concept accentuates the need for special protection of the riparian forests and old-growth forests, restoration of forests in their natural growth areas and afforestation of the new territories, rational use of the forest resources coupled with preservation of their flora and fauna, including the gene pool of hunting species, preservation in the certain areas of hollow trees and rotten trunks serving as habitats for species, optimisation of recreational pressure on forests and implementation of the monitoring system for forest ecosystems that would take into account the biodiversity protection. With respect to mountain ecosystems, it was additionally suggested to take measures to restore mountain forests and organize ecological networks of mountain forest areas in the Carpathians as one of the key systems for biodiversity conservation and the "unique centre of endemism" in Ukraine. The protection of the species, including rare ones and those which are threatened with extinction, was supposed to entail development of the programmes and measures for the conservation of individual plant and animal species or their groups, including those listed in the Red Data Book of Ukraine and international lists of rare and endangered species; creation of the centres for artificial breeding and reacclimatisation of rare and endangered plant and animal species; organisation of continuous monitoring of the species and populations; development of the geoinformation systems, particularly for plant and animal species listed in the Red Data Book of Ukraine and plant groups listed in the Green Data Book of Ukraine; conducting the inventory of genetic diversity of animals and plants; and publications of various handbooks, encyclopaedias and other materials on the biodiversity of Ukraine. Lastly, according to the Concept, the creation of the national ecological network entailed the development of the criteria for its designation, ensuring its compatibility with the international requirements and analogous networks of the neigh-

547 Concept of the Conservation of Biological Diversity of Ukraine, 1997.

bouring countries, optimisation of the network of territories and sites of the Nature Reserve Fund (NRF) as its central elements and creation of the regional ecological networks, including one in the Ukrainian Carpathians.[548]

Another short concept on biodiversity protection (or concept of the future programme) was adopted in 2004 and covers the period of 2005 – 2025.[549] Similarly to the 1997 Concept, the resolution on its adoption presupposed the development of the draft of the nationwide programme on biodiversity protection, which, however, was not adopted (as of 2024). The 2004 Concept provides an overview of the numbers of various groups of species in Ukraine and highlights some of the sources of environmental degradation and threats to biodiversity. In the section on ways and means for solving the problem, it, however, simply states that the future programme will envisage the measures for the preservation of the flora and fauna species, their groups and communities, ecosystems (including mountain and forest ecosystems) and structural elements of the ecological network, and lists without any further elaboration the types of the means, such as legal, institutional, economic and other types. More precision may, however, be found in the section on the expected results of the programme, where apart from the aim of avoiding the irrevocable loss of biodiversity, a number of tangible results in other areas are mentioned in light of the sustainability, such as reduction of unemployment and social tension. It also contains provisions on legal and institutional dimensions. In particular, the need to systematise laws and regulations and to harmonise them with international legal instruments is mentioned. Furthermore, it accentuates the need to coordinate activities of the executive authorities, local authorities, business entities and non-governmental organizations on the protection of biodiversity and mentions the need to activate international cooperation in this area and ensure the fulfilment of Ukraine's obligations in this sphere. The 2004 Concept lists three stages of the programme's implementation, suggesting possible directions of action under each of them and talking of continuous monitoring throughout this process. The first stage of the programme (the implementation of which was planned until 2010) presupposed the alignment of Ukrainian legislation with the

548 Concept of the Conservation of Biological Diversity of Ukraine, 1997.

549 Concept of the National Program for Biodiversity Conservation for 2005–2025, approved by the Resolution of the Cabinet of Ministers of Ukraine No. 675-r, Document No. 675–2004-r, (September 22, 2004), https://zakon.rada.gov.ua/laws/show/675-2004-%D1%80#Text.

requirements of international law.[550] Unfortunately, it was not possible to identify any official publication tracking the progress of the implementation of this concept. Moreover, its relevance and significance for the day-to-day activities of the governmental bodies in Ukraine are difficult to assess given the fact that the subsequent programme, which was supposed to become a main document in this sphere, and was to be created based on this Concept, was not adopted.

The document adopted in lieu of the proper biodiversity programme is the Programme for the Formation of the National Ecological Network of Ukraine for 2000 - 2015.[551] This Programme was adopted in 2000, and in 2004 the creation of the ecological network of Ukraine was further fortified by the Law "On Ecological Network of Ukraine".[552] After a decade, in 2015, the Procedure for including territories and objects in the lists of territories and objects of the ecological network was adopted by the resolution of the Cabinet of Ministers.[553] The 2000 Programme aimed *inter alia* at creating "a territorially unified system that ensures the possibility of natural migration routes and the spread of plant and animal species, thereby preserving natural ecosystems, species of flora and fauna, and their populations".[554] The network was to "perform leading functions in preserving biodiversity" and additionally was to be conducive to the sustainable use of biological resources in economic activities.[555] Some of the general tasks of the programme included the gradual granting of protected status to areas rich in biodiversity, including, among others, the old-growth natural formations, mountainous forests, and rare and endangered species; and the resolution of questions related to the transboundary combination of the ecological networks of the neighbouring countries with the view of form-

550 Concept of the National Program for Biodiversity Conservation for 2005–2025.

551 Programme for the Formation of the National Ecological Network of Ukraine for 2000–2015, approved by the Law of Ukraine No. 1989-III, Document 1989-III, (September 21, 2000), https://zakon.rada.gov.ua/laws/show/1989-14#Text.

552 "On Ecological Network of Ukraine," Law of Ukraine, Document 1864-IV, Bulletin of the Verkhovna Rada of Ukraine, No. 45, p. 502 (2004), https://zakon.rada.gov.ua/laws/show/1864-15#Text.

553 Procedure for including territories and objects in the lists of territories and objects of the ecological network, approved by the Resolution of the Cabinet of Ministers of Ukraine No. 1196, Document 1196–2015-p (December 16, 2015), https://zakon.rada.gov.ua/laws/show/1196-2015-%D0%BF#Text.

554 Programme for the Formation of the National Ecological Network of Ukraine for 2000 - 2015.

555 Programme for the Formation of the National Ecological Network of Ukraine for 2000 - 2015, § 3 (Goals and tasks).

ing the Pan-European ecological network. The particular tasks pertaining to biodiversity comprised *inter alia* conservation and restoration of key ecosystems and habitats for plant and animal species; taking account of the aims of biodiversity conservation and sustainable use of biodiversity in all of the spheres that utilise biodiversity or influence it; and implementation of the targeted measures, corresponding to the needs of protection of the various types of ecosystems, including mountainous and forest ecosystems, however with the reservation that these are to be based on the legal and financial opportunities of nature users and governmental bodies.[556]

The ecological network, according to the 2000 Programme, comprises several functionally differing elements: the natural regions, the natural corridors and the buffer zones. In addition, these elements could be of various levels of significance: local, national or international, depending on several factors, such as their area and species composition.[557]

The types of units that may be included within the ecological network elements were also listed in the 2000 Programme. Such units include, for instance, nature reserves, biosphere reserves, national parks and other types of reserves (landscape, forest, botanical, general zoological, ornithological, entomological, ichthyological, hydrological, general geological, paleontological, and karst-speleological reserves), natural landmarks, as well as their protective zones, botanical gardens, forests, plots on which natural plant communities listed in the Green Data Book of Ukraine grow or plots that are habitats or growth areas of species of animals and plants listed in the Red Data Book of Ukraine.[558]

It was planned to take into account the international commitments of Ukraine, in particular those under the Bern Convention, during the planning of the ecological network. In this regard, it was planned to identify areas of special conservation interest both within the areas included in the NRF of Ukraine and areas of special conservation interest beyond the NRF. The implementation of these tasks was planned for 2001 – 2005.[559]

---

556 Programme for the Formation of the National Ecological Network of Ukraine for 2000 – 2015.

557 Programme for the Formation of the National Ecological Network of Ukraine for 2000 – 2015.

558 Programme for the Formation of the National Ecological Network of Ukraine for 2000 – 2015.

559 Programme for the Formation of the National Ecological Network of Ukraine for 2000 – 2015, Annex 7, Measures on creation of the national ecological network.

Furthermore, scientific support of the implementation of this Programme included several measures on monitoring, entailing studying species diversity, and cenotic diversity, conducting mapping of natural complexes and their components for comprehensive monitoring, as well as creating geoinformation systems, development of the concept and strategy for the conservation and management of ecosystems in national parks and development of the model for monitoring of the biodiversity within the territories of the NRF. All of these measures were to be implemented during 2000 – 2015.[560]

The current strategic document of relevance to biodiversity protection is the general strategy in the field of environmental protection, adopted by the 2019 Law on the Fundamental Principles (Strategy) of the State Environmental Policy of Ukraine for the Period until 2030.[561] It was preceded by the Strategy of State Environmental Policy of Ukraine until 2020, adopted in 2010, which was characterised in Ukraine's national report to the CBD as the NBSAP.[562]

The description of the status quo and environmental issues in the Strategy until 2030 includes a section on biological and landscape diversity, outlining the key problems in this sphere. The key goal of this document is "achievement of a good quality of environment by means of implementing an ecosystem approach towards all directions of socio-economic development of Ukraine with a view to guarantee the constitutional right of every citizen of Ukraine to clean and safe environment, implementation of balanced use of natural resources as well as preservation and restoration of natural ecosystems".[563] This wording is interesting in several aspects. Firstly,

560 Programme for the Formation of the National Ecological Network of Ukraine for 2000 – 2015, Annex 7, Measures on creation of the national ecological network.

561 "On the Fundamental Principles (Strategy) of the State Environmental Policy of Ukraine for the Period until 2030," Law of Ukraine, Document 2697-VIII, Bulletin of the Verkhovna Rada of Ukraine, No. 16, p. 70 (2019), https://zakon.rada.gov.ua/laws/show/2697-19#Text.

562 "On the Fundamentals (Strategy) of the State Environmental Policy of Ukraine until 2020," Law of Ukraine, Document 2818-VI, Bulletin of the Verkhovna Rada of Ukraine, No. 26, p. 218 (2010), https://zakon.rada.gov.ua/laws/show/2818-17#Text; I. I. Schmalhausen Institute of Zoology and WWF Ukraine, *Sixth National Report of Ukraine on the Implementation of the Convention on Biological Diversity: English version* (Kyiv, 2018) https://www.cbd.int/doc/nr/nr-06/ua-nr-06-en.pdf, 115 [*Sixth National Report of Ukraine on the Implementation of the Convention on Biological Diversity*].

563 The Fundamental Principles (Strategy) of the State Environmental Policy of Ukraine for the Period until 2030.

the use of the notion of 'ecosystem approach', which was developed within the CBD and described in Chapter I of this thesis, seems to be extended here from the narrower field of biodiversity protection to the protection of the environment as such (as are the closing phrases on preservation and restoration of the ecosystems). Secondly, it ties nature protection to the substantial constitutional right to an environment of a certain quality, that is, the human right to a healthy environment. The foundations of the state policy for environmental protection, include, for example, the achievement by Ukraine of the Sustainable Development Goals, the integration of ecological considerations into the development of the state planning documents, sectoral, regional, and local development plans, and in the decision-making process regarding planned activities of projects that may have a significant impact on the environment, that is the principle of integration. Some other principles of international environmental law and EU law mentioned here include precaution, prevention, rectifying pollution at source, and 'polluter pays'.[564]

This document further includes the set of strategic goals and tasks. The first among them is the 'formation' of environmental values and principles of sustainable consumption and production in society. This goal is to be achieved, among other things, through ecological education and upbringing, awareness-raising activities, and public participation in decision-making in the fields of environmental protection and the use of natural resources. Importantly, the evaluation of attitudes towards an increase of awareness about the 'values of biodiversity' and measures that are necessary for its preservation, restoration and sustainable use are mentioned here directly.[565]

The second goal deals with ensuring the sustainable development of Ukraine's natural resource potential and includes several tasks that directly address biodiversity loss. They include the reduction of the loss of biological and landscape diversity, in particular through enhancement of the principles of the formation of the ecological network, its expansion and sustainable use, as well as preservation of the unique natural landscapes; preservation and restoration of the populations of species of natural flora and fauna, including migratory species, their habitats, rare and endangered

564 The Fundamental Principles (Strategy) of the State Environmental Policy of Ukraine for the Period until 2030.

565 The Fundamental Principles (Strategy) of the State Environmental Policy of Ukraine for the Period until 2030, Goal 1.

species of animals and plants, and typical natural plant communities; combating illegal circulation and trade of wild fauna and flora; increasing and expanding the territories of the NRF, ensuring the preservation and functioning of a representative and effectively managed system of territories and objects of the NRF including transboundary ones and those of European and international significance. In addition, balanced forest management is included among the tasks.[566]

The third goal deals with the integration of environmental policy into the decision-making process on the socio-economic development of Ukraine. With respect to biodiversity, it mentions the need to develop a sectoral strategy for the preservation of biodiversity and landscapes and the inclusion of biodiversity value considerations in national, local, strategic, and programmatic documents and plans for economic development.[567]

Within the fourth goal, the one on reduction of environmental risks and minimisation of their impact, the most relevant (for biodiversity) tasks include the prevention of the spread of invasive species, especially in natural ecosystems and the prevention of the uncontrolled release of genetically modified organisms into the natural environment.[568]

The last goal, the improvement and development of the state system of environmental management, deals with the implementation of good governance principles and capacity building that are relevant throughout all spheres of environmental policy and all aspects of environmental governance in Ukraine. For instance, it suggests splitting the powers of nature protection and use of natural resources for economic purposes (the dimension that is highly relevant for the forestry sector in Ukraine[569]) and

566 The Fundamental Principles (Strategy) of the State Environmental Policy of Ukraine for the Period until 2030, Goal 2.

567 The Fundamental Principles (Strategy) of the State Environmental Policy of Ukraine for the Period until 2030, Goal 3.

568 The Fundamental Principles (Strategy) of the State Environmental Policy of Ukraine for the Period until 2030, Goal 4.

569 See State Strategy for Forest Management of Ukraine until 2035, approved by the Order of the Cabinet of Ministers of Ukraine No. 1777-r, Document 1777–2021-r (December 29, 2021), https://zakon.rada.gov.ua/laws/show/1777-2021-%D1%80#Text, Chapter 3; [Forest Management Strategy] National Action Plan for Environmental Protection until 2025, approved by the Order of the Cabinet of Ministers of Ukraine No. 443-r, Document 443–2021-p (December 21, 2021), https://zakon.rada.gov.ua/laws/show/443-2021-%D1%80#n12, § 187 [National Action Plan].

ensuring a clear division of responsibilities on environmental protection at nationwide, regional, and local levels.[570]

The section on the expected results also mentions biodiversity directly, albeit tying it to the notion of ecosystem services in a somewhat ambiguous way. In particular, the "development of ecosystem services" (whatever this phrase may mean) is expected to create opportunities for sustainable development. Then, the following sentence is used: "Ukraine's biodiversity, which provides ecosystem services, should be conserved, assessed, and appropriately restored by 2030". This sentence is ambiguous because it seems to suggest that the conservation of biodiversity depends on the extent to which it provides ecosystem services, sounding thus in a purely utilitarian way. In addition, however, there is a separate expected outcome of the implementation of this strategy – the reduction of the loss of biological and landscape diversity and the creation of a comprehensive and representative ecological network.[571]

In accordance with the Strategy of the State Environmental Policy of Ukraine until 2030, a more detailed National Action Plan covering a period until 2025 was adopted in 2021.[572] Actions related to biodiversity protection include a range of measures starting with designing, renewing and implementing regional and local programmes on the formation of the ecological network, as well as setting priorities on the formation of the national ecological network[573], continuing with various systems for gathering information on biodiversity including keeping the Red Data Book records and state cadastres of animal and plant species,[574] updating or creating norms regulating construction that will concern wildlife crossings on roads and railway,[575] creating a plan for protection of migratory species,[576] enhancing control over international trade in endangered species,[577] and ending with various action on expansion of the territories of the protected areas, including the Emerald network sites, and advancing their management, moni-

570 The Fundamental Principles (Strategy) of the State Environmental Policy of Ukraine for the Period until 2030, Goal 5.

571 The Fundamental Principles (Strategy) of the State Environmental Policy of Ukraine for the Period until 2030, VI. Expected results.

572 See National Action Plan.

573 National Action Plan, § 34–35.

574 National Action Plan, § 36–40.

575 National Action Plan, § 41–42.

576 National Action Plan, § 43.

577 National Action Plan, § 44–45.

toring, governance, financing and promotion among the population.[578] It is worth noting that a separate action unit is dedicated to the development of a strategic document for biodiversity protection in Ukraine in accordance with the post-2021 global biodiversity framework.[579] In addition, various legislative acts on biosafety, genetic diversity, access to genetic resources, and invasive alien species are to be adopted.[580] Moreover, the integration of biodiversity protection, the value of biodiversity and ecosystem services into national and local development strategies, planning processes, and the national accounting and reporting system is required.[581]

The previous Strategy on environmental policy that covered the period 2010 – 2020 also envisaged action on biodiversity by including the Goal "Halting the loss of biological and landscape diversity and forming an ecological network", the objectives of which generally corresponded to the Aichi targets.[582]

The National Strategy on Forest Management until 2035, which was adopted in 2021, also contains provisions that are highly relevant for biodiversity protection in the forest ecosystems of the Ukrainian Carpathians. Remarkably, 'biodiversity preservation' is, in general, mentioned among the rationales behind the creation of this document.[583] The lack of design and implementation of the system for the monitoring of biodiversity in forests, the general forest degradation, and the lack of measures for the prevention of biodiversity degradation in forests are mentioned in the description of the current situation and issues that need to be resolved.[584] Strategic goals identified by this document include environmental resilience, which includes the preservation of biodiversity in forests; reproduction of genetic diversity in forests; protection of the old or remarkable trees and their groups; formation, preservation and rational use of the ecological network; reduction of introduced tree and plant species capable of invasions; and adaptation of forests to climate change in particular through the transition

578 National Action Plan, § 46–64.

579 National Action Plan, § 131.

580 National Action Plan, § 132–136, 162.

581 National Action Plan, § 143.

582 "On the Fundamentals (Strategy) of the State Environmental Policy of Ukraine until 2020," Law of Ukraine, Document 2818-VI, Bulletin of the Verkhovna Rada of Ukraine, No. 26, p. 218 (2010), https://zakon.rada.gov.ua/laws/show/2818-17#Text, Goal 5.

583 Forest Management Strategy, Chapter 1.

584 Forest Management Strategy, Chapter 2.

to the close-to-nature forestry.[585] While conducting economic activities in forestry, the relevant state entity or state forestry joint-stock company has to take measures for the preservation of biodiversity in forests as part of the main tasks that such entity or company is exercising.[586] The tasks aimed at the achievement of the strategic goals relevant to biodiversity protection also include the use of environmentally friendly logging technologies, especially in the mountainous areas; protection of all identified primeval forests, quasi-primeval forests and natural forests among the natural monuments, nature reserves, protected areas of the national parks of biosphere reserves, which entails the application of regime of complete non-intervention in natural processes, including the establishment of necessary protective zones around them in accordance with the law; monitoring of identified primeval forests as reference areas to track long-term changes in the forest cover; or establishment of protective zones for the conservation of biodiversity in forests. It is further mentioned that the network of designated particularly valuable areas should encompass the full diversity of forests, and the management of individual sites should be aimed at maintaining their values.[587]

Within this strategy, the set of measures under the subheading of preservation of biodiversity in forests begins by stating that preservation of biodiversity is undertaken by means of the network of the objects of the NRF, primeval, quasi-primeval forests and natural forests, objects of the Emerald network, especially valuable areas as well as by taking account of the specific requirements on protection of particular species and habitats both within and outside the protected areas. The network of these various types of protected areas has to include habitats or growth areas of rare plant and animal species, areas of animal concentration, connecting territories, and other forest areas significant for biodiversity. It is further stated that the monitoring of forest biodiversity has to be undertaken in accordance with the adopted methodology (the entities responsible for undertaking it are, however, not specified). Moreover, the habitats falling under the scope of the Emerald network have to be identified, and special materials on forest management that include requirements for the protection of rare species and habitats have to be designed. The need to preserve certain elements important for biodiversity, such as old forests, hollow trees, standing and

585 Forest Management Strategy, Chapter 3.

586 Forest Management Strategy, Chapter 4.

587 Forest Management Strategy, Chapter 4.

fallen deadwood and non-intervention in natural processes as one of the options of forest management is also mentioned. On the ecosystem level, the preservation of biodiversity is planned to be ensured by "supporting and restoring the mosaic of species and age diversity in forests according to local natural conditions".[588] A wide range of results is expected to be achieved through the implementation of this strategy, including the identification of areas of growth of rare plant species and habitats of rare animal species and ensuring their protection, as well as monitoring of biodiversity in forests and monitoring of introduced species capable of invasions.[589] The national strategy is accompanied by a brief operational plan, covering the period of three years (currently valid for the period of 2022 – 2024). This timeframe, however, does not encompass measures that would be directly aimed at the preservation of biodiversity.[590]

When it comes to the Carpathian region specifically, the Strategy for the Implementation of the Framework Convention on the Protection and Sustainable Development of the Carpathians until 2020 was adopted in 2007.[591] It referred to both obligations under the Carpathian Convention as such and the implementation of measures defined by other international treaties, to which Ukraine is a party, in the Carpathians. The requirements on the basis of international agreements explicitly mentioned in this document include the designation of wetlands of international importance, the development of the Emerald network, the listing of the beech primeval forests among the UNESCO heritage sites, and participation in the development of the network of biosphere reserves by creating Ukrainian-Romanian biosphere reserve in Transcarpathia and Marmarosh mountain range. Interestingly enough, the directions of its implementation included not only the implementation of the treaty provisions but also a wider scope of the related soft-law norms. For instance, recommendations of the COP of the CBD are mentioned, including those on the Programme of Work

588 Forest Management Strategy, Chapter 4.

589 Forest Management Strategy, Chapter 5.

590 Forest Management Strategy, Operational plan for 2022 – 2024.

591 Strategy for the implementation of the Framework Convention on the Protection and Sustainable Development of the Carpathians, approved by the Order of the Cabinet of Ministers of Ukraine No. 11-r, Document 11–2007-r (January 16, 2007), https://zakon.rada.gov.ua/laws/show/11-2007-%D1%80#Text.

on Mountain Biological Diversity.[592] Based on this Strategy, regional action plans were adopted for its implementation.[593]

In addition, there is a separate Action Plan on the preservation of the Ukrainian part within the UNESCO heritage site "Ancient and Primeval Beech Forests of the Carpathians and Other Regions of Europe" and the sustainable development of the adjacent areas.[594] This Action Plan envisages the creation of favourable conditions for the development of the biosphere reserves and natural reserves within which there are forests belonging to the UNESCO heritage, in particular, by the adoption of the methodological recommendations for managing the sites and their buffer zones, as well as by cooperation with local executive authorities and local self-government bodies. The necessary actions further include ensuring the proper protection regime of the sites and creating a monitoring system for them and their buffer zones; conducting scientific research on the biotic and landscape diversity of the sites; and developing territorial organisation projects and the effective management of the sites. These measures were to be implemented during 2018 – 2023 by the Ministry of Environmental Protection and Natural Resources of Ukraine (Ministry of Environmental Protection), the Ministry of Education and Science of Ukraine and the State Forest Resources Agency of Ukraine (State Forestry Agency).[595]

Historically, the state programme "Forests of Ukraine", in its edition before 2009, afforded special status to the Carpathian forests and included

592 Strategy for the implementation of the Framework Convention on the Protection and Sustainable Development of the Carpathians; See also: "Programme of Work on Mountain Biological Diversity," CBD, April 9, 2007, https://www.cbd.int/mountain/pow.shtml.

593 See Action Plan for the Implementation of the Strategy for the Framework Convention on the Protection and Sustainable Development of the Carpathians for 2008–2020 in the Zakarpattia Region (February 5, 2008), https://view.officeapps.live.com/op/view.aspx?src=https%3A%2F%2Fecozakarpat.gov.ua%2Fwp-content%2Fpzf_ekomereja%2Fplan_strat.doc&wdOrigin=BROWSELINK.

594 Action Plan for the Conservation of the Ukrainian Part of the UNESCO World Heritage Site "Ancient and Primeval Beech Forests of the Carpathians and Other Regions of Europe" and the Sustainable Development of Adjacent Territories, approved by the Order of the Cabinet of Ministers of Ukraine No. 892-r, Document 892–2018-r (November 21, 2018), https://zakon.rada.gov.ua/laws/show/892-2018-%D1%80#Text [Action Plan for the Conservation of the UNESCO World Heritage Site 2018].

595 Action Plan for the Conservation of the UNESCO World Heritage Site 2018, § 2.

such measures as replacing derivative spruce forests in the beech and oak forest belts with native types of forest stands.[596]

Furthermore, there is a separate Concept of the development of mountainous territories of the Ukrainian Carpathians that covers the period of 2019 – 2027 and mentions "conservation, sustainable use, and restoration of biological and landscape diversity in the Carpathian region" among the suggested measures.[597]

There was also a separate State Programme for the Development of the Ukrainian Carpathian Region for 2020 – 2022, accompanied by the Action Plan.[598] This programme takes a balanced approach in line with sustainable development, seeking "to combine the interests of economic growth with the preservation of the unique landscape and biological diversity, as well as the distinct culture and traditions of the local population".[599] The action plan, accompanying this programme contains the following actions on biodiversity restoration: reforestation of the areas of clear-cuts from the previous year; reduction of the number of clear-cut harvests by conducting selective, gradual, and combined harvests; and construction of an international educational and research centre for the conservation of beech primeval forests, ecological education, and sustainable development in the Carpathian Biosphere Reserve.[600] This State Programme, covering rather short period of time, states that the long-term development priorities of mountainous areas in Ukraine should be defined in the State Regional Development Strategy for the period until 2027, regional development strategies for 2021 – 2027 and the action plans for their implementation. It also mentions the plans for the creation of the new EU macro-regional

596 Sofiia Shutiak, *Analysis of Ukraine's Implementation of the Framework Convention on the Protection and Sustainable Development of the Carpathians* (Committee of the National Association of Advocates of Ukraine on Agrarian, Land, and Environmental Law, 2024), https://shorturl.at/g63qw, 25.

597 Concept of the Development of Mountainous Areas of the Ukrainian Carpathians, approved by the Order of the Cabinet of Ministers of Ukraine No. 232-r, Document No. 232–2019-r (April 3, 2019), https://zakon.rada.gov.ua/laws/show/232-2019-%D1%80#Text.

598 State Programme for the Development of the Ukrainian Carpathian Region for 2020 – 2022, approved by the Resolution of the Cabinet of Ministers of Ukraine No. 880, Document 880–2019-p (October 20, 2019), https://zakon.rada.gov.ua/laws/show/880-2019-%D0%BF#Text.

599 State Programme for the Development of the Ukrainian Carpathian Region for 2020 – 2022, General Part.

600 State Programme for the Development of the Ukrainian Carpathian Region for 2020 – 2022, Annex I.

strategy for the Carpathian region based on the joint declaration of intent signed in 2018 by the governments of Ukraine, Poland, Hungary and Slovakia within the cooperation on the implementation of the Carpathian Convention.[601]

On the regional level within Ukraine, implementation of the Carpathian Convention is mentioned among the opportunities of the Transcarpathian region in its 2021 – 2027 strategy, and it seeks to increase the area of the territories and objects of the NRF, integrate the environmental component into the spatial development plans, implement sustainable approaches and renew region's forest and hunting resources.[602]

The strategy of development of the Ivano-Frankivsk region for 2021 – 2027 includes an operational goal of environmental safety, which involves the protection of biotic and landscape diversity. For this purpose, the creation of new protected areas, "improvement" of the existing protected areas, and formation of the ecological network are to be implemented. Better connectivity of the territories and objects of the NRF is expected to assist species migration and preservation of the habitats. Halting biodiversity and landscape diversity loss are among the expected results of the strategy. The indicators of results, however, list only limited parameters on the number and size of the NRF sites. The possible areas for implementation of the projects include development of land management projects for the organisation and demarcation of the boundaries for nature reserve areas, preparing documentation for the state cadastre of the NRF sites in Ivano-Frankivsk region, ensuring environmentally sustainable natural resource management and protecting ecosystems from anthropogenic impact.[603]

The strategy for the development of the Lviv region for 2021–2027 also pays attention to biodiversity, mentioning that ecosystems have "scientific, ecological, social, health, and landscape-aesthetic value".[604] Biodiversity protection and development of the NRF sites constitute a separate opera-

601 State Programme for the Development of the Ukrainian Carpathian Region for 2020–2022, General Part.

602 Regional Development Strategy of the Zakarpattia Region for the Period 2021–2027, approved by the decision of the regional council No. 1630 (December 20, 2019) with the changes based on the decision No. 1840 (October 1, 2020), https://carpathia.gov.ua/storage/app/sites/21/Economics/201001-1840p.pdf, 65, 77, 79, 83, 89.

603 Development Strategy of the Ivano-Frankivsk Region for 2021–2027, approved by the decision of the regional council No. 1381–34/2020 (February 21, 2020), https://www.if.gov.ua/storage/app/sites/24/documentu-2021/10-06-2021-strategiya-rozvitku-ivano-frankivskoi-oblasti-na-2021-2027-roki.pdf, 77–78.

tional goal, which is similar to the one in the Ivano-Frankivsk region, but also pays special attention to the "principle of sufficient object and functional representativeness" of the protected areas in the region.[605] In addition, Carpathian biodiversity was mentioned in the 2018 – 2022 Strategy for the Development of Mountainous Areas of the Lviv Region.[606] In this document, the value of the forest massifs is acknowledged, and it is noted that almost 30 per cent of Carpathian forests are excluded from main-use forestry. It is noted that the forest shall be understood not only as a source of timber but also as a "habitat for the flora and fauna of the unique Carpathian region", whose "numerous recreational and conservation functions play an important environmental role in preserving mountain ecosystems as a whole".[607] It is stated that, for the biodiversity protection and prevention of negative anthropogenic impacts, it is necessary to implement principles of close-to-nature forestry, cultivate "elite planting material", ensure afforestation and enhancement of forest productivity, develop a network of forest roads and conduct aerial timber skidding, as well as regularly conduct forest inventories and monitoring of biological conditions.[608] For the protection of mountainous biodiversity in the NRF sites in the Lviv region, it is planned to carry out scientific research on the natural complexes of the protected areas, secure the demarcation of the boundaries of the NRF sites, transfer the lands from the Skole Military Forestry to the permanent management of the National Nature Park "Skolivski Beskydy", and complete the establishment of the national natural park "Boikivshchyna".[609] The latter measure was implemented in 2019.[610]

604 Development Strategy of the Lviv Region for the Period of 2021–2027, approved by the decision of the regional council No. 948 (December 24, 2019), https://loda.gov.ua/documents/49999, 67.

605 Development Strategy of the Lviv Region for the Period of 2021 – 2027, 119–120.

606 Development Strategy of the Mountainous Areas of the Lviv Region for 2018 – 2022, Lviv Regional State Administration, Lviv Regional Council (Lviv, 2017), https://old.loda.gov.ua/upload/users_files/22/upload/Strategy_Lviv_region_mountians%20terytories%20565_str.pdf.

607 Development Strategy of the Mountainous Areas of the Lviv Region for 2018 – 2022, 80.

608 Development Strategy of the Mountainous Areas of the Lviv Region for 2018 – 2022, 80.

609 Development Strategy of the Mountainous Areas of the Lviv Region for 2018 – 2022, 81.

610 "The National Nature Park "Boikivshchyna,"" Boikivshchyna National Nature Park, accessed September 20, 2024, https://boikivshchyna-park.in.ua/.

The strategy for the development of the Chernivtsi region until 2027 accentuates the need to create an ecological corridor for the migration of animal species of the Ukrainian Carpathians, such as European bison (*Bison bonasus)*, bear, lynx, wild cat (*Felis silvestris*), deer (*Cervus elaphus*) or wild boar (*Sus scrofa*). In this regard, the reference to the scheme of the Bukovinian Ecological Corridor that was developed within the framework of the project "Implementation of Transboundary Ecological Connectivity in the Ukrainian Carpathians" (2008 - 2010), funded by the Government of the Netherlands, is made and the possibility of creating transboundary protected areas in cooperation with Romania is mentioned.[611] An important example of biodiversity protection in the Chernivtsi region is the measures on conservation of the Bukovinian subpopulation of the European bison, consisting of the enlargement of the zoological nature reserve of local significance, "Zubrovytsia".[612] The measures that need to be taken include the formation of a regional ecological network and eco-educational centres; passportization and better organization of the locally designated NRF sites; restoration of forests on clear-cut areas; reduction of the number of clear-cuttings by switching to selective, gradual, and combined main-use cuttings; and development of the national nature parks "Vyzhnytskyi", "Cheremoskyi", and "Khotynskyi".[613]

In addition, various regional programs on environmental protection or the formation of ecological networks were adopted in the Carpathian regions of Ukraine.[614]

Besides the regional strategies within Ukraine, the Carpathians are also a focus of regional cooperation between Ukraine and neighbouring states. In particular, the State program for the development of cross-border cooperation for 2021–2027 pays special attention to the mountainous border areas of the Carpathians. The task of "deepening cooperation on the preservation of primeval and ancient forests of the Carpathian region and combating environmental crimes" is included among the tasks in this area.[615]

---

611 Development Strategy of the Chernivtsi Region for the Period until 2027, approved by the decision of the session of the Chernivtsi Regional Council No. 2-31/20 (February 4, 2020), https://bukoda.gov.ua/storage/app/sites/23/uploaded-files/strategia-chernivetska-2027.pdf, 79.

612 Development Strategy of the Chernivtsi Region for the Period until 2027, 80.

613 Development Strategy of the Chernivtsi Region for the Period until 2027, 116–117.

614 Department of Nature Conservation, *Impact of war on natural environment of the Carpathians in Ukraine*, 19.

615 State Programme for the Development of Cross-Border Cooperation for 2021–2027, approved by the Resolution of the Cabinet of Ministers of Ukraine No. 408, Docu-

Furthermore, Ukraine has expressed its voluntary contributions in the framework of the implementation of the United Nations Strategic Plan for Forests for 2017 – 2030, acknowledging its recognition of the importance of the goals outlined in this Plan and support of the concept of sustainable forest management. In this document, Ukraine refers to the measures suggested in the 2017 Presidential Decree "On additional measures for the development of forestry, rational use of nature and conservation of objects of the nature reserve fund", which will contribute to the implementation of certain components of the Global Forest goals 4 and 5.[616] The contribution to the Global Forest goals 1 and 3 is planned by increasing the nationwide forest cover to 16.3 per cent and by increasing "the percentage of different types of nature protected heritage in forests" – which probably means forests designated as protected areas or also protected areas within forests – to 18 per cent. In addition, the suggestion to develop a medium-term action plan for the adaptation of forestry in Ukraine to climate change, which contributes to the achievement of Global Forest Goal 1 and which was envisioned in the 2017 Order of the Cabinet of Ministers, is mentioned.[617]

Apart from general strategic documents on environmental protection or forestry, some other sectoral strategies are crucial for the protection of biodiversity of the forest ecosystems of the Ukrainian Carpathians, including such areas as climate change, transportation, urban planning and tourism.

When it comes to climate change, two strategies were adopted in recent years: the Strategy for Environmental Safety and Climate Change Adaptation for the Period until 2030 (hereinafter the Strategy for climate change

---

ment 408–2021-p, (April 14, 2021), https://zakon.rada.gov.ua/laws/show/408-2021-%D0%BF#Text, Annex 1.

616 Permanent Mission of Ukraine to the United Nations, *Communication by the State Forest Resources Agency of Ukraine on voluntary national contributions in the framework of implementation of the United Nations Strategic Plan for Forests for the period 2017 – 2030*, No. 4132/28–199–700 (May 4, 2018), https://www.un.org/esa/forests/wp-content/uploads/2018/10/Ukraine.pdf; "On additional measures for the development of forestry, rational use of nature and conservation of objects of the nature reserve fund" Decree of the President of Ukraine, No. 381, Document 381/2017, (November 21, 2017), https://zakon.rada.gov.ua/laws/show/381/2017#Text.

617 Permanent Mission of Ukraine to the United Nations, *Communication by the State Forest Resources Agency of Ukraine on voluntary national contributions in the framework of implementation of the United Nations Strategic Plan for Forests for the period 2017 – 2030*; "On approval of the action plan for the implementation of the Concept of implementation of state policy in the area of climate change until 2030", Order of the Cabinet of Ministers of Ukraine No. 878-r, Document 878–2017-r (December 6, 2017), https://zakon.rada.gov.ua/laws/show/878-2017-%D1%80#Text.

adaptation) adopted in 2021 and the Strategy for the Formation and Implementation of State Policy in the Sphere of Climate Change for the Period until 2035 (hereinafter the Strategy of state policy in the sphere of climate change) adopted in 2024.[618]

The Strategy on climate change adaptation until 2030 mentions biodiversity and forests among the socio-economic sectors that are vulnerable to climate change, also stating that the Carpathians might be among the most vulnerable ecosystems.[619] It is mentioned that the issue of the adaptive capacity of forest ecosystems to climate change and anthropogenic impact requires immediate attention and that forests need increased care and the implementation of measures based on ecologically oriented and close-to-nature forestry practices.[620] The suggested actions in this Strategy include reduction of the clear-cutting in the Carpathian region.[621] The Strategy of state policy in the sphere of climate change until 2035 includes a strategic goal of "climate change adaptation, enhancing resilience, and reducing climate-related risks", which involves an indicator of sectoral research on the vulnerability of biodiversity and forest resources and the result of biodiversity conservation.[622] In addition, in the accompanying operational action plan, there is a task of "conducting risk and vulnerability assessments of biodiversity to climate change", planned for 2024, and that has to be publicly accessible on the webpage of the Ministry of Environmental Protection.[623]

---

618 Strategy for Environmental Safety and Climate Change Adaptation for the Period until 2030, approved by the Order of the Cabinet of Ministers of Ukraine No. 1363-r, Document 1363–2021-r (October 20, 2021), https://zakon.rada.gov.ua/laws/show/1363-2021-%D1%80#Text; The Strategy for the Formation and Implementation of State Policy in the Sphere of Climate Change for the Period until 2035, approved by the Order of the Cabinet of Ministers of Ukraine No. 483-r, Document 483–2024-r, (May 30, 2024), https://zakon.rada.gov.ua/laws/show/483-2024-%D1%80#Text.

619 Strategy for Environmental Safety and Climate Change Adaptation for the Period until 2030, Chapter II.

620 Strategy for Environmental Safety and Climate Change Adaptation for the Period until 2030, Chapter II.

621 Strategy for Environmental Safety and Climate Change Adaptation for the Period until 2030, Chapter IV.

622 The Strategy for the Formation and Implementation of State Policy in the Sphere of Climate Change for the Period until 2035, Strategic Goal 3, tasks for the achievement of the Strategic Goal 3.

623 Operational Action Plan for the Implementation in 2024 – 2026 of the Strategy for the Formation and Implementation of State Policy in the Sphere of Climate Change for the Period until 2035, approved by the Order of the Cabinet of Ministers of

The National Transport Strategy of Ukraine mentions the strategic environmental assessment (SEA) during the development of plans and programmes in the transport sector among the tasks that have to be implemented.[624] It states that such assessment requires exploration of alternative options to prevent or minimise the negative impact on the environment, forests and protected areas, including the possibility of constructing special crossings and protective barriers in the areas of animal migration.[625] The Action plan for implementation of the National transport strategy elaborates on this point, mentioning the actions on preparing recommendations and finding alternatives to preserve biological and landscape diversity, conducting research on existing road and railway networks to study animal migration routes and identify areas where migration and transport routes intersect, and on preparing proposals for organizational and technical solutions to reduce animal mortality related to transport.[626]

The Strategy for the development of tourism and resorts for the period until 2026 states that the sphere tourism contributes to the "preservation of an environmentally safe natural environment" and aims to utilise tourism and resort-recreational potential to this end. "Environmental (green)" tourism is mentioned among the key types of tourism and is the field where the implementation of an international service quality system is planned. Moreover, this Strategy mentions the need to monitor the state of the environment at resorts, tourist areas, and recreational sites.[627] There are, however, no norms aimed specifically at biodiversity or Carpathians in this Strategy.

In the field of urban planning, methodological recommendations on strategic environmental assessment, adopted in 2023, require an assessment

Ukraine No. 483-r, Document 483–2024-r, (May 30, 2024), https://zakon.rada.gov.ua/laws/show/483-2024-%D1%80#Text.

624 National Transport Strategy of Ukraine for the Period until 2030, approved by the Order of the Cabinet of Ministers of Ukraine No. 430-r, Document 430–2018-r (May 30, 2018), https://zakon.rada.gov.ua/laws/show/430-2018-%D1%80#Text.

625 National Transport Strategy of Ukraine for the Period until 2030.

626 Action Plan for the Implementation of the National Transport Strategy of Ukraine for the Period until 2030, approved by the Order of the Cabinet of Ministers of Ukraine No. 321-r, Document 321–2021-r, (April 7, 2021), https://zakon.rada.gov.ua/laws/show/321-2021-%D1%80#Text.

627 Strategy for the Development of Tourism and Resorts for the Period until 2026, approved by the Order of the Cabinet of Ministers of Ukraine No. 168-r, Document 168–2017-r, (March 16, 2017), https://zakon.rada.gov.ua/laws/show/168-2017-%D1%80#Text.

of the impacts on biodiversity.[628] Before evaluating the impacts, it is recommended to include information on the NRF sites and their functional zones, sites of the ecological network and Emerald network, wetlands of international importance, UNESCO "Man and biosphere" biosphere reserves, UNESCO heritage sites and sites of the forest fund into the characteristics of the territory.[629] It is also recommended to evaluate the impact of planned decisions and measures on the implementation of action plans or measures necessary for the preservation of reproduction of animals and plants listed in the Red Data Book of Ukraine or that are subject to special protection on a regional, national or international level; and for the protection of natural ecosystems from degradation, protection of forests from fires and protection from the spread of invasive plant or animal species.[630]

2.2.2. Nature protection laws and regulations in Ukraine relevant for the biodiversity protection in the forest ecosystems of the Ukrainian Carpathians

Out of the laws on nature protection, the key general norms are contained in the 1991 Law "On Environmental Protection", which sets the "legal, economic and social" foundations for the protection of the environment in Ukraine.[631] It was adopted before the CBD, which may explain the lack of direct attention to the issue of biodiversity or even the initial lack of mention of this term altogether.[632] From the very beginning, however, it

---

628 Methodical Recommendations on Conducting Strategic Environmental Assessment of Urban Planning Documentation, approved by the Order of the Ministry of Environmental Protection and Natural Resources of Ukraine No. 705, Document v0705926–23 (October 18, 2023), https://zakon.rada.gov.ua/rada/show/v0705926-23#Text, Chapter II, Sections 3.2; 3.4; 3.5, 3.6; 3.7; 3.9.

629 Methodical Recommendations on Conducting Strategic Environmental Assessment of Urban Planning Documentation, Chapter III, Section 3.2.

630 Methodical Recommendations on Conducting Strategic Environmental Assessment of Urban Planning Documentation, Chapter III, Section 3.9.

631 "On Environmental Protection," Law of Ukraine, Document 1264-XII, Bulletin of the Verkhovna Rada of Ukraine, No.41, p. 546 (1991) https://zakon.rada.gov.ua/laws/show/1264-12#Text, Preamble.

632 Subsequently, the term 'biological diversity' appeared in its provisions as a result of amendments in the context of public access to environmental information and in context of genetically modified organisms (based on the Cartagena Protocol on Biosafety to the CBD). See "On Environmental Protection," Law of Ukraine, Articles 20, 25, 40.

contained a synonymous wording of "preservation of spatial and species diversity and integrity of natural objects and complexes" used while describing the principles of environmental protection in Ukraine.[633] For instance, the terms "natural diversity" and "gene pool of animal and plant species" are used among characteristics of plots and objects that may be included in the NRF of Ukraine,[634] and granting special protection to the "rare and endangered species of flora and fauna".[635] In the preambular provisions, this Law, similarly to some of the international law instruments, mentions the interests of the present and future generations, as well as refers to the sustainable economic and social development.[636] Environmental policy, according to this Law is aimed at "preserving a safe environment for both living and non-living nature, protecting the lives and health of the population from the negative impacts caused by environmental pollution, achieving harmonious interaction between society and nature, and conservation, rational use, and replenishment of natural resources".[637] Among the basic principles of environmental protection that could be equated with the relevant principles of international law, the principle of preventive action or precaution, sustainable development and public participation in the decision-making are mentioned (albeit with some variation of wording compared to the international instruments).[638] Citizens are guaranteed a set of environmental rights, including the substantive human right to a healthy environment,[639] and they also have the right to the general use of natural resources to satisfy their aesthetic, health-improving, recreational, material and other vital needs.[640]

It is also specified which resources are of "national importance", and this category includes forest resources, natural resources within the territories and objects of the nationwide NRF, wild animals in a state of natural freedom and some other objects of the animal world.[641] The use of natural resources is subject to environmental requirements such as rational and efficient use or preservation of the territories enjoying special protection.[642]

633 "On Environmental Protection," Law of Ukraine, Article 3.
634 "On Environmental Protection," Law of Ukraine, Article 61.
635 "On Environmental Protection," Law of Ukraine, Article 64.
636 "On Environmental Protection," Law of Ukraine, Preamble.
637 "On Environmental Protection," Law of Ukraine, Preamble.
638 "On Environmental Protection," Law of Ukraine, Article 3, (в), (е), (ж).
639 "On Environmental Protection," Law of Ukraine, Article 9.
640 "On Environmental Protection," Law of Ukraine, Article 38.
641 "On Environmental Protection," Law of Ukraine, Article 39.
642 "On Environmental Protection," Law of Ukraine, Article 40.

Special protection, in turn, is afforded to the "natural territories and objects of great ecological value, such as unique and typical natural complexes", including in the first instance territories and objects of the NRF of Ukraine, but also other types, such as recreational areas, water protection areas, land protection areas and other categories defined by Ukrainian legislation.[643] The plots and areas included in the NRF are objects of special "ecological, scientific, aesthetic, and economic value" and are partially or completely withdrawn from economic use. There is a variety of their types, including: "state reserves, natural national parks, nature reserves, nature monuments, botanical gardens, dendrological and zoological parks, parks-monuments of garden and park art, and protected tracts."[644]

The 1992 Law "On Nature Reserve Fund" elaborates on these provisions and forms the basis for the organisation, protection and use of the territories and objects of the NRF and management in this area.[645] Among other provisions, it defines the main measures for the protection of the territories and objects of the NRF, including the establishment of a reserve regime; organization of systematic monitoring of the state of the natural complexes and objects of the NRF; conducting research activities; consideration of the protection requirements while carrying out economic and other activities, such as forestry management; introducing the economic incentives to stimulate the protection of objects and territories of the NRF; exercise of state and public control over compliance with the regime of their protection and use; ensuring responsibility for violations of the regime of their protection and use; and conducting international cooperation in this field.[646] It lists all of the possible types of the NRF objects and provides distinct norms on each type's status and protective regime.[647] In addition, particular functions, activities and regimes of the territories and objects of the NRF are defined in the regulations that are adopted by different governmental bodies at the national and regional levels.[648]

Article 7 sets the restrictions as to the land use of the territories belonging to the NRF, prohibiting activities that may adversely affect the state of the

643 "On Environmental Protection," Law of Ukraine, Article 5, Article 60, Article 61.
644 "On Environmental Protection," Law of Ukraine, Article 61.
645 "On Nature Reserve Fund," Law of Ukraine, Document 2456-XII, Bulletin of the Verkhovna Rada of Ukraine, No. 34, p. 502 (1992), https://zakon.rada.gov.ua/laws/show/2456-12/conv#n12, Article 1.
646 "On Nature Reserve Fund," Law of Ukraine, Article 8.
647 "On Nature Reserve Fund," Law of Ukraine, Article 3, Articles 14–40.
648 "On Nature Reserve Fund," Law of Ukraine, Article 5.

natural or historical and cultural objects or which hinder their use for their intended purposes.[649] The purposes for which the territories and objects of the NRF could be used include conservation, scientific research, environmental monitoring, recreational and educational purposes, as well as some additional purposes (harvesting of timber, medicinal and other valuable plants, their fruits, haymaking, grazing of livestock, hunting and fishing) which shall, however, not contradict the purposes of the relevant territories or objects and requirements as to their protection.[650] The so-called 'special use' of natural resources within the territories of the NRF is also possible, subject to certain limits, permits and other restrictions. For instance, forest formation and health improvement felling, as well as other types of felling, could be carried out within the framework of approved plans and based on the decisions of the scientific and technical councils of the NRF institutions in accordance with the limit on the use of natural resources and based on permits.[651]

Different types of the NRF sites might have different territorial structures and functional zones, which define the categories of activities that are allowed or prohibited in the respective zones. For instance, for biosphere reserves, these are: protected zone (and zone of regulated protective regime), buffer zone, and anthropogenic landscape zone.[652] In a natural national park, a protected zone, a regulated recreation zone, a stationary recreation zone, and an economic zone can be created.[653] Protected zone of both biosphere reserves and national natural parks enjoys the highest possible protection, which for their forest ecosystems means the prohibition of main-use logging, all types of gradual and clear-cutting, as well as felling of hollow trees.[654] The territorial planning of the NRF sites is defined in the project on their creation and in the regulations created for each object individually.[655]

---

649 "On Nature Reserve Fund," Law of Ukraine, Article 7.
650 "On Nature Reserve Fund," Law of Ukraine, Article 9.
651 "On Nature Reserve Fund," Law of Ukraine, Article 9–1.
652 "On Nature Reserve Fund," Law of Ukraine, Article 18.
653 "On Nature Reserve Fund," Law of Ukraine, Article 21.
654 "On Nature Reserve Fund," Law of Ukraine, Article 18, Article 21.
655 See Methodical Recommendations for Developing Projects for the Creation of Natural Areas and Objects of the Nature Reserve Fund of Ukraine, approved by the Order of the Ministry of Environmental Protection and Natural Resources of Ukraine No. 306, Document v0306737–18 (August 21, 2018) https://zakon.rada.gov.ua/rada/show/v0306737-18#Text; See for example "On Approval of the Regulations on the Carpathian Biosphere Reserve in a New Edition,"

Since 2017, a new category of the NRF highly important for biodiversity protection was added to the Law "On Nature Reserve Fund" – the 'primeval forest nature monuments'. In these nature monuments, all types of felling are prohibited, "including the sanitary felling, forest formation and health improvement felling, and removal of clutter (except for maintenance of linear objects and cutting of individual trees during fire suppression)".[656]

The main basis for assessing the state and changes in natural complexes in nature reserves and for developing appropriate measures for protection, resource use and ecological safety in biosphere reserves and national natural parks is the Chronicles of Nature kept by these institutions and updated on a yearly basis.[657] The Chronicles of Nature require a detailed assessment and description of a wide range of parameters, including the composition of flora, that is, all plant species that grow on the territory of the relevant NRF and are identified during inventory. In this process, special attention shall be paid to the rare, endangered, relict and endemic species. In addition to assessing the presence of individual plant species, the composition and structure of cenoses must be studied and described in this document.[658] Similarly, for fauna species, "collection, accumulation, and generalisation of data on species diversity of animals, the dynamics of their population numbers, territorial distribution, reproduction, migration, interactions with other species, and ecological-faunal complexes" is undertaken, and some methods for identifying numbers of certain species are recommended.[659] Moreover, rare and endangered species of both flora and fauna that are listed in the Red Data Book of Ukraine, regional list on protection of species, and international lists of protection relevant for Ukraine, including Bern Convention, CMS, CITES, and European Red List have to be separately described in the special tables and on the maps. A similar description is required for habitats in accordance with Resolution

---

Order of the the Ministry of Environmental Protection and Natural Resources of Ukraine No. 336, Document v0336737–11 (September 23, 2011) https://zakon.rada.gov.ua/rada/show/v0336737-11#Text.

656 "On Nature Reserve Fund," Law of Ukraine, Article 28.

657 "On Nature Reserve Fund," Law of Ukraine, Article 43.

658 Programme of the Chronicles of Nature in Reserves and National Nature Parks, approved by the Order of the Ministry of Environmental Protection and Natural Resources of Ukraine and National Academy of Sciences of Ukraine No. 465/430, Document v465_737–02, (November 25, 2002) https://zakon.rada.gov.ua/rada/show/v465_737-02#Text, Chapter 4, Plant World.

659 Programme of the Chronicles of Nature in Reserves and National Nature Parks, Chapter 5, Animal World.

№ 4 (1996) of the Bern Convention Committee.[660] Furthermore, a separate Chapter is dedicated to the participation of the NRF sites in the implementation of the biodiversity treaties, to which Ukraine is a party.[661]

Another dimension of the legal mechanism of biodiversity protection in Ukraine concerns the protection of plant and animal species, and in addition to the aforementioned laws, is regulated by the laws "On Plant World", "On Animal World" and "On the Red Data Book of Ukraine".

The 'plant world' in the relevant Law means the "entirety of all plant species, as well as fungi and the communities they form in a given area".[662] Attention to the plant world is required while carrying out economic activities that may affect it. In particular, the preservation of the natural spatial, species, population, and community diversity of plant life and of the habitats of wild plants and natural plant communities must be considered.[663] There are two modes of the use of plant resources: the general and the special ones. The former one is aimed at meeting the private needs of individuals as well as recreational, health, cultural, educational and upbringing purposes, while the latter one may be undertaken by natural or legal persons for the purposes of production and research, and for gaining profit from sale or processing of these resources and requires permits.[664] The set of measures for the protection of the plant world that are aimed at preserving the spatial, species, population, and cenotic diversity and integrity of plant objects, protection of their habitats, prevention of destruction and damage and safeguarding against fires, pests, and diseases, as well as ensuring sustainable use are described in Articles 25–32.[665] The monitoring of the plant world forms a part of the monitoring of the natural environment and is undertaken according to the regulation that has to be adopted by the Cabinet of Ministers of Ukraine.[666] Currently in force is a

660 Programme of the Chronicles of Nature in Reserves and National Nature Parks, Chapter 6, Conservation of Plant and Animal Species, and Natural Habitats Listed in International Registries that are Binding for Ukraine.

661 Programme of the Chronicles of Nature in Reserves and National Nature Parks, Chapter 10, Participation of Reserves and Parks in the Implementation of International Conventions applicable in Ukraine.

662 "On the Plant World," Law of Ukraine, Document 591-XIV, Bulletin of the Verkhovna Rada of Ukraine, No. 22–23, p. 198 (1999), https://zakon.rada.gov.ua/laws/show/591-14#Text, Article 3.

663 "On the Plant World," Law of Ukraine, Article 5.

664 "On the Plant World," Law of Ukraine, Article 10.

665 "On the Plant World," Law of Ukraine, Articles 25–32.

666 "On the Plant World," Law of Ukraine, Article 33.

Regulation adopted in 1998, which should have been amended by another Regulation, adopted in 2024, which is not in force yet due to the war.[667]

The Law on the Animal World, before defining the components forming its subject matter, includes preambular points where some of the ethical rationales for the protection of the 'animal world' are presented. Namely, it is called "national treasure of Ukraine, a source of spiritual and aesthetic enrichment and education for people, an object of scientific research, and an important basis for obtaining industrial and medicinal raw materials, food products, and other material values", and has to be protected and used sustainably in the interests of present and future generations.[668] One of the tasks of this Law includes "ensuring the conditions for preserving the entire species and population diversity of animals".[669] The objects of the 'animal world' include wild animals in all their species and populations diversity in all stages of their development, their parts, products of their life activity and their habitats.[670] This Law also sets out requirement and principles that have to be taken into account during implementation of measures on conservation, rational use and reproduction of wild animals, including preservation of conditions of existence of species and populations diversity in a state of natural freedom, unacceptability of the deterioration of habitats, migration routes and breeding conditions and preservation of the integrity of the natural groupings of wild animals.[671] Article 36 provides a non-exhaustive list of measures that are to be taken for the purpose of

667 Regulation on the State Environmental Monitoring System, approved by the Resolution of the Cabinet of Ministers of Ukraine No. 391, Document 391–98-p, (March 30, 1998), https://zakon.rada.gov.ua/laws/show/391-98-%D0%BF#Text; "Certain Issues of the Functioning of the State Environmental Monitoring System and Its Subsystems," Resolution of the Cabinet of Ministers of Ukraine No. 684, Document 684–2024-p (June 13, 2024), https://zakon.rada.gov.ua/laws/show/684-2024-%D0%BF#Text; "On Amendments to Certain Legislative Acts of Ukraine Regarding the State Environmental Monitoring System, Environmental Condition Information (Environmental Information), and Information Support for Environmental Management," Law of Ukraine, Document 2973-IX, Bulletin of the Verkhovna Rada of Ukraine, No. 63, p. 208 (2023), https://zakon.rada.gov.ua/laws/show/2973-20#Text, Closing Provisions, 1.

668 "On the Animal World," Law of Ukraine, Document 2894-III, Bulletin of the Verkhovna Rada of Ukraine, No. 14, p. 97 (2002), https://zakon.rada.gov.ua/laws/show/2894-14#Text.

669 "On the Animal World," Law of Ukraine, Article 2.

670 "On the Animal World," Law of Ukraine, Article 3.

671 "On the Animal World," Law of Ukraine, Article 9.

protecting the 'animal world'.[672] The subsequent articles clarify and build upon some of these measures, such as the provision on limitations as to the activities that are the source of the increased noise and disturbance for the animals during the reproductive season within the time limits from the 1st of April until the 15th of June. With respect to forests, this provision means prohibition as to carrying out of all types of the main-use logging, forest formation and health-improving logging on all forest plots belonging to the regeneration areas according to the management of hunting grounds, high mountain forests, subalpine forests, within the NRF sites and some other categories of forests.[673]

For the territories that are characterised as habitats of rare and endangered animal species and are recognised as such, there is a possibility to set more stringent environmental standards than the general norms valid for the whole of Ukraine.[674] The animal world within the territories and objects of the NRF is also additionally regulated by the Law "On Nature Reserve Fund of Ukraine".[675]

Importantly, in recent years, action plans on the protection of particular species have been adopted, including such species found in the Ukrainian Carpathians as lynx and brown bear.[676]

In addition to the norms of protection of the 'animal world' there are also provisions on regulation of populations of wild animals, which could be invoked for a non-exhaustive list of reasons, including human health and safety, prevention of decease among the domesticated animals, prevention of damage to the natural environment and to economic activities.[677] There is also a provision on the regulation of the populations of "predatory and

672 "On the Animal World," Law of Ukraine, Article 36.

673 "On the Animal World," Law of Ukraine, Article 39.

674 "On the Animal World," Law of Ukraine, Article 39.

675 "On the Animal World," Law of Ukraine, Article 43.

676 "On Approval of the Action Plan for the Conservation of the Eurasian lynx (*Lynx lynx* L.) in Ukraine," Order of the Ministry of Environmental Protection No. 595, (September 16, 2021), https://mepr.gov.ua/documents/pro-zatverdzhennya-planu-dij-shhodo-zberezhennya-rysi-yevrazijskoyi-lynx-lynx-l-v-ukrayini/; "On Approval of the Action Plan for the Conservation of the Brown Bear (*Ursus arctos* L.) in Ukraine," Order of the Ministry of Environmental Protection No. 679, (October 20, 2021), https://mepr.gov.ua/documents/pro-zatverdzhennya-planu-dij-shhodo-zberezhennya-vedmedya-burogo-ursus-arctos-l-v-ukrayini/; "On Approval of the Action Plan for the Conservation and restoration of the European bison (*Bison bonasus* L.) in Ukraine," Order of the Ministry of Environmental Protection No. 557, (December 28, 2022), https://mepr.gov.ua/nakaz-mindovkillya-557-vid-28-12-2022/.

677 "On the Animal World," Law of Ukraine, Article 32.

harmful animals", which is regulated by the Law "On Hunting Economy and Hunting". The notion of 'harmful animals' is itself questionable, and these, according to the said law, include, for instance, wolves.[678]

Rare and endangered animal species are subject to special protection, and they are listed in the Red Data Book of Ukraine.[679] In addition, species not included in the Red Data Book, but that have special scientific, nature-protection or other value, may be inscribed into the list of animals under special protection.[680] Breeding of endangered and rare species in captivity may be allowed under certain conditions, including when their conservation, protection and reproduction in the natural conditions is not possible, as well as for scientific purposes.[681] In addition, the creation of "gene banks" for storing genetic materials of rare and endangered species is possible.[682]

The rare and endangered species of flora and fauna in Ukraine are, in general, protected by listing them in the Red Data Book of Ukraine.[683] The Red Data Book is an official document listing such species along with the information on the current situation of their populations and measures on their preservation and restoration, forming a basis for the creation and implementation of the programmes on the protection of these species.[684] The protection of the species listed in the Red Data Book is ensured through the systematic work on the identification of their habitats and monitoring of their populations; creation of the territories and objects of the NRF and ecological network in the territories where they are found, including the migration routes of the rare and endangered animal species; and taking the needs of special protection into account during planning of

678 "On Hunting Economy and Hunting," Law of Ukraine, Document 1478-III, Bulletin of the Verkhovna Rada of Ukraine, No. 18, p. 132 (2000), https://zakon.rada.gov.ua/laws/show/1478-14#Text, Article 33.

679 "On the Animal World," Law of Ukraine, Article 44.

680 "On the Animal World," Law of Ukraine, Article 44; See, for instance, "On Approval of the List of Animal Species Subject to Special Protection in the Territory of Volyn Region," Order of the Ministry of Environmental Protection No. 140, (September 14, 2020), https://mepr.gov.ua/documents/pro-zatverdzhennya-pereliku-vydiv-tvaryn-shho-pidlyagayut-osoblyvij-ohoroni-na-terytoriyi-volynskoyi-oblasti/.

681 "On the Animal World," Law of Ukraine, Article 45.

682 "On the Animal World," Law of Ukraine, Article 45.

683 "On Environmental Protection," Law of Ukraine, Article 64.

684 "On the Red Data Book of Ukraine," Law of Ukraine, Document 3055-III, Bulletin of the Verkhovna Rada of Ukraine, No. 30, p. 20 (2002), https://zakon.rada.gov.ua/laws/show/3055-14#Text, Article 3.

economic activities, including by means of the EIA.[685] Natural regeneration of the populations of rare and endangered species, as well as keeping and breeding the species in captivity, are recognised as means of reproduction of the species. In addition, research, educational activities and increased accountability for destruction or damage caused to the species listed in the Red Data Book and their habitats belong to the ways of ensuring protection and reproduction of the Red Data Book objects.[686]

The presence of the species listed in the Red Data Book on a certain territory counts as a ground for founding there an object of the NRF. Furthermore, protective zones of a certain size and shape could be established for the long-term preservation of the species. In lands belonging to the forestry, protection of the Red List species is undertaken by means of creating "protected areas to preserve biodiversity in forests".[687] The governmental regulations on the procedures for the creation of these special protected areas of the Red Data Book species have been adopted quite recently.[688]

Species listed in the Red Data Book are subject to the 'state accounting', which entails recording various types of information about them and is undertaken in accordance with a separate regulation.[689] Special use (extraction, collection) of the Red Data Book species is possible only for scientific and breeding purposes and is subject to a special permit.[690]

The new editions of the Red Data Book are to be published every 10 years, however, the last official version was issued in 2009, while the preparation and publication of the most recent edition was delayed, slightly mitigated by the orders of the Ministry of Environmental Protection on this topic, which, however, cannot substitute the full version of the Red Data Book.[691]

---

685 "On the Red Data Book of Ukraine," Law of Ukraine, Article 11.

686 "On the Red Data Book of Ukraine," Law of Ukraine, Article 11.

687 "On the Red Data Book of Ukraine," Law of Ukraine, Article 11.

688 Procedure for Establishing Protective Zones for the Preservation of Objects Listed in the Red Data Book of Ukraine, approved by the Resolution of the Cabinet of Ministers of Ukraine No. 499, Document 499–2023-p, (May 12, 2023), https://zakon.rada.gov.ua/laws/show/499-2023-%D0%BF#n89.

689 "On the Red Data Book of Ukraine," Law of Ukraine, Article 12; "On Approval of the Procedure for State Accounting of Rare and Endangered Species of Fauna and Flora Listed in the Red Data Book of Ukraine," Order of the Ministry of Environmental Protection No. 486, (October 9, 2012), https://zakon.rada.gov.ua/laws/show/z2031-12#n16.

690 "On the Red Data Book of Ukraine," Law of Ukraine, Article 19.

691 "On Approval of the Lists of Animal Species Included in the Red Data Book of Ukraine (Animal World) and Animal Species Excluded from the Red Data Book of

Apart from the Red Data Book, there exists the Green Data Book. The Green Data Book, unlike the Red Data Book, which protects certain species of flora and fauna, is aimed at protecting rare, endangered, and typical natural plant communities.[692] It was conceptualised by the Ukrainian scientists in the 1980s and later became an official state document, mentioned as an instrument of protection in the Law on the Plant World.[693] The most recent list of plant communities enlisted in the Green Data Book was adopted in 2020.[694]

In addition to the nationwide Red Data Book, regional councils are entitled to adopt lists of the plant and animal species that are subject to protection on a regional level, and such lists were adopted in all four Ukrainian regions, where the Carpathians are located.[695]

The Law "On Environmental Impact Assessment" (EIA), adopted in 2017, is another legislative act directly relevant to biodiversity protection in the Ukrainian Carpathians. The definition of the impact on the environment according to this Law includes the consequences of the planned activity for biodiversity.[696] Likewise, the report on the EIA has to include information about the natural resources or materials that are expected to

---

Ukraine (Animal World)," Order of the Ministry of Environmental Protection No. 29, (January 19, 2021), https://zakon.rada.gov.ua/laws/show/z0260-21#Text; "On Approval of the Lists of Plant and Fungi Species Included in the Red Data Book of Ukraine (Plant World) and Plant and Fungi Species Excluded from the Red Data Book of Ukraine (Plant World)," Order of the Ministry of Environmental Protection No. 111 (February 2, 2021), https://zakon.rada.gov.ua/laws/show/z0370-21#Text; "Is the Red Data Book of Ukraine stuck in a deadlock again?," Ukrainian Nature Conservation Group, February 10, 2022, https://uncg.org.ua/chervona-knyha-ukraìny-znov-u-hlukhomu-kuti/.

692 Regulations on the Green Data Book of Ukraine, approved by the Resolution of the Cabinet of Ministers of Ukraine No.1286, Document 1286–2002-p, (August 29, 2002), https://zakon.rada.gov.ua/laws/show/1286-2002-%D0%BF#Text, § 1–2.

693 Yakiv Didukh et al., ed, *Green Book of Ukraine* (Kyiv, Alterpres, 2009), https://komekolog.rada.gov.ua/uploads/documents/36467.pdf, 6; "On the Plant World," Law of Ukraine, Articles 26, 31.

694 List of Rare, Endangered, and Typical Natural Plant Communities Subject to Protection and Included in the Green Data Book of Ukraine, approved by the Order of the Ministry of Environmental Protection No. 368, Document z0130–21, (December 17, 2020), https://zakon.rada.gov.ua/laws/show/z0130-21#n17.

695 Department of Nature Conservation, *Impact of war on natural environment of the Carpathians in Ukraine*, 20; *National Report of Ukraine on the Implementation of the Biodiversity Protocol*, 12–15.

696 "On Environmental Impact Assessment," Law of Ukraine, Document 2059-VIII, Bulletin of the Verkhovna Rada of Ukraine, No. 29, p. 315 (2017), https://zakon.rada.gov.ua/laws/show/2059-19#Text, Article 1.

be used for the purposes of the planned activity, among which biodiversity is mentioned. Furthermore, the description of the influence of planned activity on biodiversity and evaluation of the scale of the impact form a part of the report on the EIA.[697] Forestry belongs to the fields of economic activities that are subject to the EIA, including "all clear-cutting and gradual cutting for main use, as well as all clear sanitary cutting on areas exceeding 1 hectare; all clear sanitary cutting in the territories and objects of the nature reserve fund" and "forest planting (excluding reforestation works) on areas exceeding 20 hectares or in the territories and objects of the nature reserve fund or in their protective zones on areas of 5 hectares or more" or "forest development" on the lands with analogous parameters.[698] The reports on the EIA have to be considered in the forest management planning process.[699] The EIA is also mentioned across the norms of the laws "On the Animal World" and "On the Plant World," stating that the impact on the flora and fauna has to be duly considered.[700]

In addition to the EIA, in furtherance of the idea of sustainable development and integration of environmental considerations in various sectoral policies, the law "On Strategic Environmental Assessment" (SEA) was adopted in 2018.[701] The SEA concerns the documents of state planning and requires assessment of their impact on the environment, including flora, fauna, biodiversity, natural territories and objects, other factors, as well as interaction among these factors.[702] The central elements of the SEA include the preparation of a report, holding public discussions and consultations, and monitoring of the consequences of the implementation of the state planning document.[703] The report on SEA has to include certain categories of information, including characteristics of the state of the natural environment and human health as well as forecasted changes to their state without

697 "On Environmental Impact Assessment," Law of Ukraine, Article 6.

698 "On Environmental Impact Assessment," Law of Ukraine, Article 3.

699 Procedure for Conducting Forest Management Planning, approved by the Resolution of the Cabinet of Ministers of Ukraine No. 112, Document 112–2023-p, (February 7, 2023), https://zakon.rada.gov.ua/laws/show/112-2023-%D0%BF#Text, § 16, 21, 25–29, 114.

700 See "On the Animal World," Law of Ukraine, Articles 9, 41; "On the Plant World," Law of Ukraine, Articles 26, 28.

701 "On Strategic Environmental Assessment," Law of Ukraine, Document 2354-VIII, Bulletin of the Verkhovna Rada of Ukraine, No. 16, p. 138 (2018), https://zakon.rada.gov.ua/laws/show/2354-19#Text, Article 2.

702 "On Strategic Environmental Assessment," Law of Ukraine, Article 1.

703 "On Strategic Environmental Assessment," Law of Ukraine, Article 9.

adoption of the document that is subject to this procedure; 'environmental problems' related to the document of state planning, including those that concern territories with the protected status; obligations on environmental protection, including on international, national and other levels, which are related to the document of state planning and ways to take these obligations into account; environmental impacts of various nature and temporal dimension, including transboundary impacts; or measures on mitigation and minimisation of negative impacts.[704] For the purposes of this procedure, the category of civil society is restricted to those individuals and legal entities that are registered in the territory covered by the strategic planning document.[705] In 2023, the Unified Register of Strategic Environmental Assessment was launched, and the information that it contains is supposed to be public and openly accessible. However, it requires registration and authorisation.[706]

2.2.3. Legislation on forestry in Ukraine and biodiversity protection

The Forest Code of Ukraine is a central legislative source regulating 'forest relations' in Ukraine.[707] According to this document, forests are understood in the first place as ecosystems and are considered to be "national wealth of Ukraine", contributing to various functions, such as protective, sanitary, health, recreational, aesthetic or educational ones, but also "serve as a source for meeting society's needs for forest resources".[708] The 'forest resources', in turn, include two categories, the first one comprising products

704 "On Strategic Environmental Assessment," Law of Ukraine, Article 1.
"On Strategic Environmental Assessment," Law of Ukraine, Article 11.

705 "On Strategic Environmental Assessment," Law of Ukraine, Article 1.

706 "On Strategic Environmental Assessment," Law of Ukraine, Article 9–1; Procedure for Maintaining the Unified Register of Strategic Environmental Assessments, approved by the Resolution of the Cabinet of Ministers of Ukraine No. 430, Document 430–2023-p, (May 2, 2023) https://zakon.rada.gov.ua/laws/show/430-2023-%D0%BF#n10; "The Ministry of Environmental Protection is Launching a Test Version of the Unified Register of Strategic Environmental Assessments," The Ministry of Environmental Protection of Ukraine, May 23, 2023, https://mepr.gov.ua/mindovkillya-zapuskaye-testuvannya-novoyi-poslugy-strategichnu-ekologichnu-otsinku-mozhna-zamovyty-na-ekosystemi/.

707 See Forest Code of Ukraine, Document 3852-XII, Bulletin of the Verkhovna Rada of Ukraine, No. 17, p. 99 (1994), https://zakon.rada.gov.ua/laws/show/3852-12#Text, Article 2, Article 3.

708 Forest Code of Ukraine, Article 1.

(such as wood, technical, medicinal and other products) and the second one involving properties of forests (such as ability to mitigate negative impacts of the natural phenomena, protection of soil from erosion, purification of the environment, contribution to the improvement of the human health and aesthetic education).[709] The categories of use of resources and functions of forests are somewhat blurred conceptually in the joint reading of Article 1 and Article 6 of the Forest Code. Theoretically, forests in Ukraine can be in three modes of ownership: state, communal, or private one.[710] In practice, however, the private possession of forests (less than 0.1 per cent of all forested areas in Ukraine) is so low that it can almost be disregarded statistically.[711] The use of forests is possible in two modes: permanent and temporary one with the latter being subdivided into the long-term use (from 1 to 50 years) and short-term use (up until 1 year).[712] These modes of use define rights and obligations of the users.[713] With the slight difference of the wording, regardless of the type of the user, all of them are obliged "to conduct activities in ways that ensure the preservation of the health and protective properties of forests, as well as create favourable conditions for the protection, safeguarding, and reproduction of typical and unique natural complexes and objects, rare and endangered species of animal and plant life, and promote the formation of an ecological network".[714] Moreover, the use of forest resources by means that are detrimental to the natural environment and do not ensure preservation of the protective, health and other beneficial properties of the forests is mentioned among the grounds for termination of the right of permanent use of forests.[715]

Based on their ecological and socio-economic role, the forests in Ukraine are divided into 4 categories: protective forests; recreational and health improving forests; forests of nature protection, research, historical and cultural purposes; and exploitation forests.[716] The characteristics of these

709 Forest Code of Ukraine, Article 6.
710 Forest Code of Ukraine, Article 7.
711 "Public Report of the Head of the State Forest Resources Agency of Ukraine for 2022," State Forest Resources Agency of Ukraine, accessed September 20, 2024, https://forest.gov.ua/storage/app/sites/8/publich_zvit/publichnii-zvit-za-2022.pdf, 5.
712 Forest Code of Ukraine, Articles 16–18.
713 Forest Code of Ukraine, Articles 19–24.
714 Forest Code of Ukraine, quoted from Article 20, compare Articles 19 and 21.
715 Forest Code of Ukraine, Article 22.
716 Forest Code of Ukraine, Article 39.

forests are defined in the relevant procedure.[717] The 'exploitation forests' are defined as forests that do not belong to any other category and serve the purpose of "meeting the needs of the national economy for timber".[718] In addition, there are two special groups of categories of forests or some parts of them that are crucial for biodiversity protection: the first one comprising primeval forests, quasi-primeval forests, and natural forests and the second one comprising specially protected forest areas.[719] The primeval, quasi-primeval and natural forests are recognised as the natural national heritage of Ukraine. They belong to the nature protection category of forests and are designated as specially protected forest areas. Primeval, quasi-primeval and natural forests are exempt from all kinds of logging, but for the maintenance of linear objects and the cutting of individual trees during fire extinguishing.[720] Additionally, protective zones are created around them, where clear-cutting and gradual cutting are prohibited.[721] Identification of the primeval, quasi-primeval and natural forests is undertaken in accordance with the special methodological guidelines that describe a range of factors such as the structure, documented uses of these forests, and minimal size or shape.[722] The introduction of the category of "primeval, quasi-primeval and natural forests" and provisions ensuring their protection was undertaken in the recent past by means of the Law "On Amending Certain Legislative Acts of Ukraine Regarding the Protection of Primeval Forests in Accordance with the Framework Convention on Conservation and Sustainable Development of the Carpathians".[723] The

717 Procedure for Classifying Forests into Categories and Designating Specially Protected Forest Areas, approved by the Resolution of the Cabinet of Ministers of Ukraine No. 733, Document 733–2007-p, (May 16, 2007), https://zakon.rada.gov.ua/laws/show/733-2007-%D0%BF#n10.

718 Procedure for Classifying Forests into Categories and Designating Specially Protected Forest Areas (2007), § 8.

719 Forest Code of Ukraine, Articles 39–1 and 41 respectively.

720 Forest Code of Ukraine, Articles 39–1, Article 70.

721 Forest Code of Ukraine, Article 39–1.

722 Methodology for Determining the Classification of Forest Areas as Primeval Forests, Quasi-Primeval Forests, and Natural Forests, approved by the Order of the Ministry of Environmental Protection No. 161, Document z0707–18, (May 18, 2018), https://zakon.rada.gov.ua/laws/show/z0707-18#n14.

723 "On Amending Certain Legislative Acts of Ukraine Regarding the Protection of Primeval Forests in Accordance with the Framework Convention on Conservation and Sustainable Development of the Carpathians," Law of Ukraine, Document 2063-VIII, Bulletin of the Verkhovna Rada of Ukraine, No. 37, p. 379 (2017), https://zakon.rada.gov.ua/laws/show/2063-19#n26, § 3.

explanatory note to the relevant legislative draft acknowledged that the adoption of this law was necessary to ensure compliance of Ukraine with its obligations under the Carpathian Convention and the Protocol on Sustainable Forestry in light of the troublesome practice of destruction of primeval forests in the exploitation forests and forests within the NRF sites alike.[724]

The category of specially protected forest areas entails the possibility to introduce a restricted forest use regime to certain areas, such as prohibiting certain types of cutting.[725] Designation of such areas is undertaken in accordance with the set of standards and local conditions.[726] The features, presence of which entails designation of specially protected forest areas, include, for instance, the forest areas around capercaillie leks, in which case the forest plots with a radius of 300 metres are to be designated. It is, however, also stated that "no more than three such plots are allocated per 10,000 hectares of forest land."[727] Other features that could be protected by means of the specially protected forest areas include forest plots in protected areas around territories and objects of the NRF and forest plots in protected zones around primeval forests, quasi-primeval forests, and natural forests not designated as objects of the NRF.[728]

One of the most crucial procedures of the forestry sector that in many aspects is definitive for the preservation of biodiversity is the process of "forest organisation" or "forest management planning" (*'лісовпорядкування'* – *'lisovporyadkuvannya'* in Ukrainian). It entails a range of measures aimed at obtaining an accurate picture and effectively organising forestry in Ukraine.[729] In particular, it includes identifying the species and age composition of tree stands, their condition, and the qualitative and quantitative characteristics of forest resources, calculating the allowable cut and the vol-

724 "The Committee Proposes to Adopt as a Basis Draft Law No. 4480 on Amendments to Certain Legislative Acts of Ukraine Regarding the Protection of Primeval Forests in Accordance with the Framework Convention on the Protection and Sustainable Development of the Carpathians," The Committee of the Verkhovna Rada of Ukraine on Environmental Policy and Nature Management, October 26, 2016, https://komekolog.rada.gov.ua/news/main_news/73942.html.

725 Forest Code of Ukraine, Article 41.

726 Procedure for Classifying Forests into Categories and Designating Specially Protected Forest Areas (2007), § 9–10.

727 Procedure for Classifying Forests into Categories and Designating Specially Protected Forest Areas (2007), Annex V.

728 Procedure for Classifying Forests into Categories and Designating Specially Protected Forest Areas (2007), Annex V.

729 Forest Code of Ukraine, Article 45 and the whole Chapter 8.

umes of utilization of other types of forest resources, identifying primeval forests, quasi-primeval forests, natural forests, typical and unique natural complexes, habitats of rare and endangered species of flora and fauna, which are subject to protection and inclusion in the ecological network and various other research activities.[730] This process is supposed to be undertaken every 10 years for the plots over 100 ha and every 20 years for the plots smaller than 100 ha, and is based on the detailed procedure, which has been renewed recently.[731] The main method of forest organisation is the "age-class method" which means grouping forest stands into management units and sections based on their age.[732] There is, however, also a possibility to use another method – the "compartment" or "plot" method, entailing the formation of permanent management compartments. This method is to be applied in "particularly valuable forests, in nature reserves, and in forests where a multi-aged stand structure has been formed, with the aim of preserving and enhancing the protective and conservation functions of the forests", and it is used in the tree stands where selective logging is planned, primarily in mountain forests, that is in the forests of the Ukrainian Carpathians. The decision on applying this method is taken by the territorial bodies of the State Forestry Agency.[733]

Apart from the information intended to be used for economic purposes, such as planning of the allowable cut and 'logging funds', the documents and materials prepared during the basic forest management process include some general environmental data, such as forest inventory descriptions and data directly related to the biodiversity, such as conclusions regarding the classification of specific forest plots or their parts as primeval forests, quasi-primeval forests, or natural forests; information on the results of zoological, botanical, and geobotanical research (with the reservation that this information has to be included when such research is available) and data on the location of flora and fauna species and their natural habitats, which are protected in accordance with the Bern Convention (with the reservation that this data has to be obtained from the Ministry of Environmental Protection rather than collected during the process of forest organization itself).[734] Some categories of information, such as data on the presence

730 Forest Code of Ukraine, Article 46.
731 Forest Code of Ukraine, Article 47, Procedure for Conducting Forest Management Planning (2023).
732 Procedure for Conducting Forest Management Planning (2023), § 11.
733 Procedure for Conducting Forest Management Planning (2023), § 12.
734 Procedure for Conducting Forest Management Planning (2023), § 30.

of the Red Data Book species in the area, the presence of the regionally rare species and information on territories of the ecological network or territories and objects of the NRF, have to be collected proactively during the stage of preparation for the forest organization.[735] Moreover, if rare and endangered species or typical and unique natural complexes are identified during the forest organisation, these territories are to be included in the NRF or ecological network.[736] In addition, special protective zones for biodiversity preservation shall be created, and the designation of primeval, quasi-primeval and natural forests and protective zones around them shall be undertaken with the inclusion of the relevant cartographical materials into the materials on forest organization.[737]

The procedure of forest organization also entails decision-making as to the economic use of the forests, including the planning of the annual logging volume.[738] Based on the forest organization, the yearly allowable cut, that is the rate for timber harvesting under main use (*'розрахункова лісосіка'* – *'rozrakhunkova lisosika'* in Ukrainian) is approved.[739]

One of the sections of the regulation on forest organisation deals with the nature-protection measures, stating that the materials on forest organisation shall contain measures aimed at conservation, protection and restoration of rare and endangered species designated as such in the Red Data Book of Ukraine, regional lists of species that need special protection.[740] Importantly, this section also contains a general clause which integrates biodiversity protection into all activities of forestry, stating that "all planned forestry activities should contribute to the conservation of biodiversity and the enhancement of the protective role of forests".[741]

The procedure for forest organisation, accordingly, plays a crucial role in the consideration of biodiversity in the economic and all other activities of the forest sector in Ukraine. Other procedures, processes and measures that directly or indirectly contribute to the gathering of accurate information about forests as such and their biodiversity, include the State Forest

735 Procedure for Conducting Forest Management Planning (2023), § 39.
736 Procedure for Conducting Forest Management Planning (2023), § 64.
737 Procedure for Conducting Forest Management Planning (2023), § 65.
738 Procedure for Conducting Forest Management Planning (2023), § 74–76.
739 Procedure for Conducting Forest Management Planning (2023), § 120–124; Forest Code, Article 43, 44, 71.
740 Procedure for Conducting Forest Management Planning (2023), § 101.
741 Procedure for Conducting Forest Management Planning (2023), § 102.

Cadastre and forest accounting,[742] forest monitoring as part of the national system of environmental monitoring, and forest inventory.[743]

Apart from the indirect provisions on forestry, which, however, influence biodiversity, there are also norms directly addressing it. "Preservation of biotic and other natural diversity in forests" is mentioned among the six main requirements for economic activities and management in forestry.[744] Article 85 clarifies this provision by listing ways for preserving biodiversity in the forests. According to it, owners and permanent users take measures on protecting biodiversity at the level of genes, species, populations and ecosystems through: creation of territories and objects of the NRF and development of the ecological network, creation and preservation of the valuable gene fund, prevention of genetic contamination of the gene pools of indigenous species and prevention of invasions of introduced species into natural ecosystems, the use of ecologically-oriented ways of forest regeneration and the use of forest resources, and creation of protective zones to preserve biodiversity in forests.[745] The latter is undertaken on the basis of the separate regulation, which states that the categories of the protected objects within such protective zones include: objects of the Red Data Book of Ukraine; objects enlisted in the lists of rare species, endangered species and species that have special scientific, nature-protection or other value that are protected on a certain territory, including species listed in the biodiversity-related international treaties ratified by Ukraine, plant communities listed in the Green Data Book of Ukraine and species subject to special protection on the level of regions within Ukraine; typical and unique natural complexes and objects; breeding grounds of wild animals; and the oldest or notable trees and their groups.[746] The regime of protection, along with

742 Forest Code of Ukraine, Chapter 9; Procedure for Maintaining the State Forest Cadastre and Forest Inventory, approved by the Resolution of the Cabinet of Ministers of Ukraine No. 848, Document 848–2007-p, (June 20, 2007), https://zakon.rada.gov.ua/laws/show/848-2007-%D0%BF#Text.

743 Forest Code of Ukraine, Chapter 10; Procedure for Conducting the National Forest Inventory, approved by the Resolution of the Cabinet of Ministers of Ukraine No. 392, Document 392–2021-p, (April 21, 2021), https://zakon.rada.gov.ua/laws/show/392-2021-%D0%BF#n10.

744 Forest Code of Ukraine, Article 64.

745 Forest Code of Ukraine, Article 85.

746 Procedure for Establishing Protective Zones for Biodiversity Conservation in Forests, approved by the Resolution of the Cabinet of Ministers of Ukraine No. 499, Document 499–2023-p, (May 12, 2023) https://zakon.rada.gov.ua/laws/show/499-2023-%D0%BF#n10, § 3.

the configuration of the shape and size of the protective zone, is established on a case-by-case basis and is recorded in the "passport of the protective zone".[747] When such zones are created with a view to protecting the Red Data Book species in the forest ecosystems, the minimum requirements of the protective regime include prohibition of the clear-cutting and final stage of cutting under a gradual felling system, extraction of minerals, and alteration of the hydrological regime.[748] In addition, Annex I contains a set of the minimal requirements as to the size of protected areas, regime of protection and grounds for annulment of protected areas for some of the Red Data Book species.[749]

The Forest Code of Ukraine in addition contains norms on the "protection and defence" of forests from "fires, illegal logging, damage, weakening, and other harmful impacts, as well as protecting them from pests and diseases", that is undertaken mostly by the units for forest protection operating within the State Forest Agency.[750]

There are two types of the use of forest resources: the general (that is collection of wild herbaceous plants, flowers, berries, nuts, mushrooms, etc., for personal consumption not exceeding certain limits) and the special one (such as timber harvesting, collection of resin and other materials, grazing of livestock, haymaking and other similar forest uses or use of beneficial properties of forests for cultural, health, recreational or educational purposes, sports, tourism, hunting, and for conducting scientific research).[751] The special use of forests is subject to detailed regulation, and all the logging undertaken in the forest and commercial use of other resources and properties of forests fall under the scope of this category.[752] According to this regulation, four types of the main-use logging are possible: selective

747 Procedure for Establishing Protective Zones for Biodiversity Conservation in Forests (2023), § 6–7.

748 Procedure for Establishing Protective Zones for Biodiversity Conservation in Forests (2023), § 9.

749 Procedure for Establishing Protective Zones for Biodiversity Conservation in Forests (2023), Annex II.

750 Forest Code of Ukraine, Chapter 16; Regulations on the State Forest Protection Service, Forest Protection of Other Permanent Forest Users, and Forest Owners, approved by the Resolution of the Cabinet of Ministers of Ukraine No. 976, Document 976–2009-p, (16 September 2009) https://zakon.rada.gov.ua/laws/show/976-2009-%D0%BF#Text.

751 Forest Code of Ukraine, Articles 65–67.

752 "On Regulating Issues Related to the Special Use of Forest Resources," Resolution of the Cabinet of Ministers of Ukraine No. 761, Document 761–2007-p, (May 23, 2007), https://zakon.rada.gov.ua/laws/show/761-2007-%D0%BF#Text.

(where overmature and mature trees are periodically felled, while the forest plot remains continuously covered with forest vegetation), gradual (felling of the stand is planned over several stages), clear-cutting (the entire tree stand is harvested, except for the seed trees, viable undergrowth and young trees, valuable and rare species of trees and shrubs) and combined (the one combining elements of selective and gradual logging).[753] Regardless of the type, during the logging of the main use the preservation of viable undergrowth and young growth of the economically valuable species has to be ensured and the felling and damage of valuable and rare species of trees and shrubs listed in the Red Data Book of Ukraine, as well as seed trees and plus trees, are not permitted.[754] The volumes of timber harvesting within the main use in combination with clear sanitary felling have to stay within the limits of the rate for timber harvesting. However, the volume of the rate for timber harvesting that was not used in the past may be harvested additionally.[755] Furthermore, a mechanism of control of the special uses of forests is established, namely the inspection (examination) of forest resource use areas after the use of the resources.[756] The rules on the organisation of this inspection, however, have to be established additionally by the Ministry of Environmental Protection on the basis of a suggestion by the State Forestry Agency. An attempt to adopt such rules (that have been valid for less than a year) was undertaken in 2013, and it was not possible to find the current document in force regulating this procedure.[757] On this basis, it could be concluded that this control mechanism is not being used in practice.

The Forest Code further clarifies norms on timber harvesting (based on the amendments made later than the adoption of Regulation on the special use of forests) that require consideration of rare and endangered

753 "On Regulating Issues Related to the Special Use of Forest Resources" (2007), § 5.

754 "On Regulating Issues Related to the Special Use of Forest Resources" (2007), § 11.

755 "On Regulating Issues Related to the Special Use of Forest Resources" (2007), § 10.

756 "On Regulating Issues Related to the Special Use of Forest Resources" (2007), § 56–65.

757 "On Approval of Methodological Guidelines for the Allocation and Assessment of Logging Areas, Issuance of Logging Tickets, and Inspection of Timber Harvesting Sites in the Forests of the State Forest Resources Agency of Ukraine," Order of the State Forest Resources Agency of Ukraine No. 9, Document v0009820-13, (January 1, 2013), https://zakon.rada.gov.ua/rada/show/v0009820-13#Text; "On Revocation of the Order of the State Forest Resources Agency from 21.01.2013 No. 9," Order of the State Forest Resources Agency of Ukraine No. 272, Document v0272820-13, (September 25, 2013), https://zakon.rada.gov.ua/rada/show/v0272820-13#Text.

species, stating that during the timber harvesting felling or damaging of the following trees and shrubs is not permitted: rare and endangered species of trees and shrubs listed in the Red Data Book of Ukraine, of seed and plus trees, of hollow and oldest trees, and of trees with the nests of the rare bird species enlisted in the Red Data Book of Ukraine, providing examples of black stork, osprey (*Pandion haliaetus*) and white-tailed eagle (*Haliaeetus albicilla*).[758]

Besides the general rules, there are also special rules on the main-use logging undertaken in the mountainous forests of the Carpathians.[759] These rules mention 'ecosystem approach' (applied in this document to protect water catchments from deforestation[760] and to protect soil[761]) and close-to-nature forestry as a basis for logging in the mountainous forests in the Carpathians.[762] Interestingly, preservation of biodiversity is mentioned among the 'purposes of logging', which, if read separately, sounds somewhat controversial.[763] Among the prohibitions on harvesting or damaging, along with the Red Data Book species, seed and plus trees, a category of "other trees that have exceptional meaning for the protection of biodiversity" is mentioned.[764] It is also not allowed to carry out the final stage of selective logging in beech forests from May 1 to September 30.[765] Furthermore, the main-use logging in the Carpathian forests has to be carried out in accordance with restrictions set in the Law of Ukraine "On the prohibition of clear-cutting in the mountain fir-beech forests of the Carpathian

758 Forest Code of Ukraine, Article 70.

759 Regulations for Main-Use Logging in the Mountain Forests of the Carpathians, approved by the Resolution of the Cabinet of Ministers of Ukraine No. 929, Document 929–2008-p, (October 22, 2008), https://zakon.rada.gov.ua/laws/show/929-2008-%D0%BF#Text.

760 Regulations for Main-Use Logging in the Mountain Forests of the Carpathians (2008), § 13.

761 Regulations for Main-Use Logging in the Mountain Forests of the Carpathians (2008), § 41–43.

762 Regulations for Main-Use Logging in the Mountain Forests of the Carpathians (2008), § 1.

763 Regulations for Main-Use Logging in the Mountain Forests of the Carpathians (2008), § 2.

764 Regulations for Main-Use Logging in the Mountain Forests of the Carpathians (2008), § 5.

765 Regulations for Main-Use Logging in the Mountain Forests of the Carpathians (2008), § 11.

region".[766] It concerns the tree stands composed of beech and a minimum of 25 per cent of fir, where it is prohibited to undertake any main-use clear-cutting, as well as clear-cutting for the formation and revitalisation of forests.[767]

The types of logging in the Carpathian forests depend on the category of forests (exploitation forests or forests with a special regime) and differ based on the tree species. The rules for the oak, hornbeam, ash, maple, beech, fir, spruce and a category of 'soft-leaf deciduous trees' are prescribed.[768] It is also required that the complex logging operations, including the preparation of logging areas, be carried out using methods that exclude or limit the negative impact on the condition of forests and their regeneration.[769] In particular, the preservation of undergrowth and the second layer of tree species has to be ensured.[770]

In addition to the main-use logging, there is also the so-called logging undertaken within the 'sanitary measures', that is, measures aimed at improving the sanitary conditions of the forests and implementing sanitary requirements set to protect forests during forestry activities.[771] There are four types of sanitary measures: selective sanitary felling, clear-cut sanitary felling, elimination of clutter and pests and forest disease control.[772] Special rules on approval of the sanitary logging apply to the forests in the territories and objects of the NRF generally, while in some types of them or areas within them, including the protected zones of biosphere reserves, national nature and regional landscape parks, on the territory of nature reserves, natural monuments, primeval forest natural monuments and their

---

766 Regulations for Main-Use Logging in the Mountain Forests of the Carpathians (2008), § 11–1; "On the prohibition of clear-cutting in the mountain fir-beech forests of the Carpathian region", Law of Ukraine, Document 1436-III, Bulletin of the Verkhovna Rada of Ukraine, No. 13, p. 99 (2000), https://zakon.rada.gov.ua/laws/show/1436-14#Text.

767 "On the prohibition of clear-cutting in the mountain fir-beech forests of the Carpathian region", Law of Ukraine, Article 2.

768 Regulations for Main-Use Logging in the Mountain Forests of the Carpathians (2008), §§ 21–30.

769 Regulations for Main-Use Logging in the Mountain Forests of the Carpathians (2008), § 31.

770 Regulations for Main-Use Logging in the Mountain Forests of the Carpathians (2008), § 53.

771 Sanitary Rules in the Forests of Ukraine, approved by the Resolution of the Cabinet of Ministers of Ukraine No. 555, Document 555–95-p, (July 27, 1995), https://zakon.rada.gov.ua/laws/show/555-95-%D0%BF#Text, § 1.

772 Sanitary Rules in the Forests of Ukraine (2005), § 4.

protective zones, any types of sanitary logging and elimination of clutter are prohibited. It is also not allowed to undertake sanitary measures around the nesting sites of the birds of prey listed in the Red Data Book of Ukraine, black stork, lekking grounds of capercaillie and black grouse.[773]

Moreover, even during the clear-cut sanitary felling, old hollow trees, viable trees of the main forest-forming species, and other valuable species with significant biocenotic value shall be spared from logging. In the high-mountain forests located above 1100 meters above sea level and in protective forest areas of the Carpathian region, clear-cut sanitary felling is carried out only in artificial forests. In addition, clear-cut sanitary felling is not conducted on steep slopes in fir-beech mountain forests of the Carpathian region and all of the clear-cut sanitary felling on areas exceeding 1 hectare, as well as on the territories and objects of the NRF are carried out in accordance with the Law of Ukraine "On Environmental Impact Assessment".[774]

During the elimination of clutter, individual fallen dead trees, which serve as habitats and protection for other living organisms, are to be preserved. Furthermore, in forests within the NRF, it is necessary to leave at least 30 cubic meters of non commercial timber per hectare, while in the deciduous forests within the NRF, decluttering is not conducted altogether.[775]

Most of the abovementioned norms on restrictions of sanitary logging are relatively new and were added in 2020 with the adoption of the relevant resolution of the Cabinet of Ministers.[776] The same resolution introduced the analogous restrictions on logging in the Carpathians with respect to the types of logging, regulated by the Rules for Improving the Quality Composition of Forests.[777]

The Rules for Improving the Quality Composition of Forests concern types of logging that are aimed at "increasing the resilience and productivity of tree stands, preserving forest biodiversity, improving their health, and enhancing protective, sanitary-hygienic, recreational, and other func-

773 Sanitary Rules in the Forests of Ukraine (2005), § 5.
774 Sanitary Rules in the Forests of Ukraine (2005), § 27.
775 Sanitary Rules in the Forests of Ukraine (2005), § 36.
776 "On Amending Certain Resolutions of the Cabinet of Ministers of Ukraine," Resolution of the Cabinet of Ministers of Ukraine No. 1224, Document 1224–2020-p, (December 9, 2020), https://zakon.rada.gov.ua/laws/show/1224-2020-%D0%BF#Text.
777 "On Amending Certain Resolutions of the Cabinet of Ministers of Ukraine" (2020).

tions".[778] They comprise the following types of felling that can be undertaken for forest formation and health improvement: tending, sanitary, reforestation, restructuring, reconstruction-related, and landscape felling.[779] These rules also include specific restrictions concerning the Carpathian forests. Namely, they prohibit clear-cutting for forest formation and health improvement in the Carpathians with a few exceptions. These comprise clearing of windfalls and breakages, as well as stands completely affected by pests and diseases, in high-mountain forests that grow above 1100 meters above sea level, forests in avalanche-prone and mudflow-prone basins and forest protection areas along riverbanks.[780] The same provision also clarifies that forest formation and health improvement felling in the Carpathians has to take into account restrictions set by the Law "On the Prohibition of Clear-Cutting in the Mountain Fir-Beech Forests of the Carpathian Region". Moreover, 'reforestation logging' cannot be performed in the mountainous forests of the Carpathians.[781] In addition, 'reconstruction-related logging' can be conducted only in those Carpathian mountainous forests where the main-use logging is allowed.[782]

Apart from logging, one of the dimensions of the use of the beneficial properties of forests is hunting. This type of use is regulated by the Law "On the Animal World" and the Law "On Hunting Economy and Hunting".[783] The Forest Code, however, also requires that the use of forest resources

---

778 "On Approval of the Rules for Improving the Qualitative Composition of Forests, Conducting Other Logging Operations, and Performing Works Related and Unrelated to Forestry Management," Resolution of the Cabinet of Ministers of Ukraine No. 724, Document 724–2007-p, (May 12, 2007), https://zakon.rada.gov.ua/laws/show/724-2007-%D0%BF#Text, § 1.

779 "On Approval of the Rules for Improving the Qualitative Composition of Forests, Conducting Other Logging Operations, and Performing Works Related and Unrelated to Forestry Management" (2007), § 2.

780 "On Approval of the Rules for Improving the Qualitative Composition of Forests, Conducting Other Logging Operations, and Performing Works Related and Unrelated to Forestry Management" (2007), § 6.

781 "On Approval of the Rules for Improving the Qualitative Composition of Forests, Conducting Other Logging Operations, and Performing Works Related and Unrelated to Forestry Management" (2007), § 26.

782 "On Approval of the Rules for Improving the Qualitative Composition of Forests, Conducting Other Logging Operations, and Performing Works Related and Unrelated to Forestry Management" (2007), § 39.

783 Forest Code of Ukraine, Article 75, See "On the Animal World," Law of Ukraine; "On Hunting Economy and Hunting," Law of Ukraine.

be conducted with consideration for the preservation of the favourable conditions for the wild animals.[784]

Besides the rules on forest use, including tree felling, there are provisions on forest regeneration, which can take place either in the form of reforestation or afforestation.[785] Notably, the need to preserve natural ecosystems has to be considered during forest regeneration. The manner in which it is conducted has to ensure the creation of forests resilient to climate change and prevent invasions of alien species into natural ecosystems.[786] In the rules on forest organization the term 'natural regeneration' is used, where the preservation and maintenance of the undergrowth during logging activities is recognized as the main way to promote natural regeneration of forests, and this type of regeneration is used when there is a sufficient amount of the viable undergrowth, as defined in the logging rules.[787]

The compliance with forest legislation is ensured through a combination of state and public control.[788] Violation of forest legislation may entail disciplinary, administrative, civil, or criminal liability.[789]

2.3. Institutions and actors influencing biodiversity protection of the forest ecosystems of the Ukrainian Carpathians

Similarly to the complexities of the normative framework on forest biodiversity protection in the Ukrainian Carpathians, the institutions and actors involved in this sphere form a varied landscape. Governmental bodies, state-owned enterprises and entities are empowered to implement measures on biodiversity in both commercially used forests, protected areas and other categories of forests. In addition, the role of non-governmental organisations and voluntary initiatives on forest certification is crucial for ensuring the integration of biodiversity protection interests into the forestry sector. In general, the following groups of actors could be said to shape biodiversity protection in the region: state bodies and local self-government, non-governmental organisations, the business sector and individuals.

784 Forest Code of Ukraine, Article 76.
785 Forest Code of Ukraine, Chapter 14.
786 Forest Code of Ukraine, Article 82.
787 Procedure for Conducting Forest Management Planning (2023), § 91.
788 Forest Code of Ukraine, Chapter 17.
789 Forest Code of Ukraine, Chapter 22.

Out of state bodies, the leading role is played by the Ministry of Environmental Protection and Natural Resources of Ukraine. It is responsible for the formation and implementation of the state policy on environmental protection, including biodiversity protection and forests, namely "the conservation, restoration, and sustainable use of biological and landscape diversity; the protection, defence, use, and regeneration of forests; and the formation, conservation, and utilization of the ecological network; organization of the protection and use of the natural reserve fund".[790] It is also responsible for forming and implementing state policy on forestry and the hunting economy.[791]

The Ministry's powers on biodiversity protection are exercised by the Department of Nature Reserve Fund and Biodiversity of the Ministry of Environmental Protection.[792] The biodiversity protection is exercised mainly by means of a network of territories and objects belonging to the NRF. The NRF of the Ukrainian Carpathians are represented by various types of areas, including the nature reserve, the biosphere reserve, national nature parks, regional landscape parks, natural monuments and other forms of territories and objects of the NRF of various organisational and legal forms and different significance (either national or local). The majority of areas of the NRF in the Ukrainian Carpathians are governed by the institutions of the NRF subordinate to the Ministry of Environmental Protection. Some territories and objects of the NRF are governed by the State Forestry Agency, the state enterprise "Forests of Ukraine" and its branches, territorial communities, local councils or enterprises. The list of the territories and objects of the NRF is updated on a yearly basis and is publicly available among the open data published by the Ministry of Environmental Protection.[793] The territories of the NRF in the Carpathian region have been gradually extended over the years. After the legislative amendments on primeval forests have been introduced, a significant number of new

790 Regulations on the Ministry of Environmental Protection and Natural Resources of Ukraine, approved by the Resolution of the Cabinet of Ministers of Ukraine No. 614, Document 614–2020-p, (June 25, 2020), https://zakon.rada.gov.ua/laws/show/614-2020-%D0%BF#n13, § 3.

791 Regulations on the Ministry of Environmental Protection and Natural Resources of Ukraine (2020), § 3.

792 "Department of Nature Reserve Fund and Biodiversity", Ministry of Environmental Protection of Ukraine, accessed September 20, 2024, https://mepr.gov.ua/pro-nas/struktura/departament-pryrodno-zapovidnogo-fondu-ta-bioriznomanittya/.

793 "Open Data," Ministry of Environmental Protection of Ukraine, accessed September 20, 2024, https://mepr.gov.ua/diyalnist/vidkryti-dani/.

objects of the NRF have been created. For instance, in Ivano-Frankivsk oblast, 54 plots with a total area of 9976,5 ha have been designated as primeval and quasi-primeval or natural forests during 2020 – 2023, while in Transcarpathia, 34 new plots of this category of protected areas with the total area of 5463,6 ha have been designated.[794] In addition, in 2024, it was announced that the enterprise "Forests of Ukraine" approved of the creation of a new protected area in the Carpathians – the forest reserve of national significance "Arshytsia" with an area of 200 ha. This area is located in Gorgany, and it represents a plot of well-preserved high-mountain old-growth forests of natural origin, identified by the WWF-Ukraine. To be fully established, however, some further steps are needed.[795]

Given a variety of possible constellations on subordination, the governance of the NRF sites is quite complex. Moreover, sometimes territories overlap and one NRF site could comprise other objects. A bright example of such a situation is National Nature Park "Hutsulshchyna", which, as of January 2024, comprises 17 objects of the NRF.[796] Therefore, the intricacies of the governance of the precise biodiversity-rich territory of the NRF and its particular conditions shall be assessed on a case-by-case basis.

The territories and objects of the NRF, especially those that have their own administrations, play an important role in biodiversity monitoring and conservation. For instance, in the National Nature Park "Hutsulshchyna", the programmes for the renaturalisation of yew tree (*Taxus baccata*) and the reproduction of stone pine (*Pinus cembra*) were launched.[797]

There is an ongoing reform of the management of the protected areas in Ukraine undertaken to modernise the system and make it more efficient. Some of the central goals of this reform include, for instance, division of functions of formation and realisation of policies on nature protection, 'new philosophy' of control and protection of the territories and objects

794 "State Cadastre of Territories and Objects of the Nature Reserve Fund of Ukraine. Boundaries of the territories and objects of the Nature Reserve Fund of Ukraine (Dataset for 2023)," Diia, accessed September 20, 2024, https://data.gov.ua/dataset/mepr_05.

795 "Over 200 hectares of forests in the "Arshytsia" mountain range are to be granted protected status at the national level," WWF, March 28, 2024, https://www.wwf.mg/?13339891/More-than-200-hectares-of-forests-in-the-Arshytsia-mountain-range-are-to-be-granted-protected-status-at-the-national-level.

796 "State Cadastre of Territories and Objects of the Nature Reserve Fund of Ukraine. Boundaries of the territories and objects of the Nature Reserve Fund of Ukraine (Dataset for 2023)".

797 *National Report of Ukraine on the Implementation of the Biodiversity Protocol*, 14.

of the NRF and integration of the ecosystem approach into sectoral policies. It is undertaken by the state institutions, including the Verkhovna Rada of Ukraine Committee on Environmental Policy and Nature Management, Ministry of Environmental Protection, State Service of Ukraine for Geodesy, Cartography, and Cadastre, National Academy of Sciences of Ukraine in cooperation with the project "Support to Nature Reserves in Ukraine" co-financed by the German government through the public-sector financial institution KfW, UNDP in Ukraine and non-governmental organisations, such as "Ecology-Law-People", Ukrainian Nature Conservation Group, All-Ukrainian Ecological League, Frankfurt Zoological Society and other organizations.[798]

In the forestry and hunting economy field, the key state body is the State Forest Resources Agency of Ukraine, which is subordinate to the Minister of Environmental Protection and Natural Resources of Ukraine.[799] The State Forestry Agency is the single largest forest user in Ukraine, and it is responsible for managing 73 per cent of the forests in Ukraine.[800] There is a lack of detailed data on the percentage of forests managed by the State Forestry Agency, precisely in the territory belonging to the Ukrainian Carpathians. Until recently, the structure of subordinate units of the State Forestry Agency comprised 24 regional departments created based on administrative-territorial units of Ukraine and a number of state-owned forest management enterprises subordinate to these regional departments (158 enterprises as of 2022 before the reform).[801] Since September 2022, it was decided by the Cabinet of Ministers of Ukraine to create a single state enterprise "Forests of Ukraine" (instead of 158 enterprises) and to reorgan-

798 "Management of Protected Areas," Ministry of Environmental Protection of Ukraine, accessed September 20, 2024, https://mepr.gov.ua/diyalnist/reformy/upravlinnya-pryrodoohoronnymy-terytoriyamy/.

799 Regulations on the State Forest Resources Agency of Ukraine, approved by the Resolution of the Cabinet of Ministers of Ukraine No. 521, Document 521–2014-p, (October 8, 2014), https://zakon.rada.gov.ua/laws/show/521-2014-%D0%BF#n8, § 3.

800 "National Report on the State of the Environment in Ukraine in 2021," Ministry of Environmental Protection of Ukraine, https://mepr.gov.ua/wp-content/uploads/2023/01/Natsdopovid-2021-n.pdf, 85.

801 "Forestry reform: what does the creation of a single SE "Forests of Ukraine" provide for?" State Forest Resources Agency of Ukraine, September 7, 2022, https://forest.gov.ua/en/news/reforma-lisovoho-hospodarstva-shcho-peredbachaie-stvorennia-iedynoho-dp-lisy-ukrainy.

ise 24 regional departments into 9 regional offices.[802] The rationale behind such a transformation included "better economic results", attracting investments, introduction of new technologies, transparency and standardization of business processes, and more efficient management.[803] This reform, rapidly undertaken during the time of war with little public participation, naturally became subject to criticism on behalf of the civil society that voiced their concerns as to the integral danger of the monopolisation of forestry sector leading to the increases in volume of logging, domination of economic interests over nature protection (evidenced, for instance, by slowing down of the creation of the new protected areas), and potential increase of corruption risks.[804]

After reorganization of the regional departments, the majority of the Carpathian forests are within the competence of the Western Interregional Administration of Forestry and Hunting comprising Transcarpathia, Lviv, Ivano-Frankivsk oblast, which includes special "Carpathian forest office". The Carpathian forests located within Chernivtsi oblast belong to the Southwestern Interregional Administration of Forestry and Hunting.[805] Biodiversity protection is explicitly mentioned among the directions of activities of the Western Interregional Administration of Forestry and Hunting. Unfortunately, however, the relevant page on biodiversity protection provides solely the information on the numbers of the NRF sites within the three oblasts, without any information as to how exactly biodiversity is taken into account and safeguarded in the course of the economic activities within the forestry in the region.[806]

The interviews with the high-ranking officials from the Lviv Regional Forestry and Hunting Economy Authority and Ivano-Frankivsk Regional

---

802 "Certain Issues of Reforming Forest Industry Management," Resolution of the Cabinet of Ministers of Ukraine No. 1003, Document 1003–2022-p, (September 7, 2022), https://zakon.rada.gov.ua/laws/show/1003-2022-%D0%BF#Text.

803 "Forestry reform: what does the creation of a single SE "Forests of Ukraine" provide for?" State Forest Resources Agency of Ukraine, September 7, 2022.

804 Volodymyr Boreiko, "'Forest Reform' – A Road to Nowhere," Interfax-Ukraine, August 30, 2023, https://interfax.com.ua/news/blog/931888.html.

805 "Certain Issues of Reforming Forest Industry Management" (2002); Regulations on the Western Interregional Administration of Forestry and Hunting Economy, approved by the Order of the State Forest Resources Agency of Ukraine No. 1006 (November 9, 2022), https://w.forest.gov.ua/upload/users_files/1/upload/traven%202023/Polozhennya%20pro%20ZMULMG.PDF.

806 "Conservation of Biological Diversity," Western Interregional Administration of Forestry and Hunting Economy, accessed September 20, 2024, https://w.forest.gov.ua/activities_recreation.

Forestry and Hunting Economy Authority, conducted for the purpose of the present doctoral project in September 2022 (that is shortly before the reorganisation), demonstrate that the biodiversity protection is partially or only marginally considered in the day-to-day work of such organisations. Statistically, within the Lviv region, Carpathian forests constitute a small numerical share of the region's forests, and within the Ivano-Frankivsk region, Carpathian forests constitute the majority of the forests. This difference in share might provide an explanation for the differences in the attitudes voiced during the interviews – for the Lviv region, the focus was on protecting Carpathian forests as valuable ecosystems, and for the Ivano-Frankivsk region, the narrative of dissatisfaction with 'too many' protected areas and the need for a 'pragmatic approach to forests' was voiced.[807]

Answering the question of "How is biodiversity considered in the activities of your organisation and what measures are implemented?", the representative of the Lviv Regional Forestry and Hunting Economy Authority named a shift towards selective logging in the region, which was initiated in 2003. This change was implemented in cooperation with the National Forestry University of Ukraine. It was reported that as of 2022, 80 per cent of logging in the Carpathians within the Lviv region belongs to the category of selective logging. It was also explained how, by moving to a selective logging system, both the ecological significance of the forest (as the forest exists continuously) and the economic advantages of it are increased. The economic benefits are namely related to the increase in forest growth in comparison to the single-layered forest, which became possible due to the increase in light feeding. For example, in the Morshyn Reserve, the growth rate in the sample area, where selective logging was conducted, amounts to 12 cubic meters per year, while in areas where no logging was undertaken, it is close to just 4.5 cubic meters per year. Moreover, since 2007, the legislative changes allowed for the 'transformation cutting', which was implemented in the Lviv region since 2008 as a scientific experiment, at first with the close scientific supervision and later also without it, based only on notification of the Department of Ecology of the Lviv region State Administration. It was explained that implementing this type of logging under such a procedure is a peculiarity of the Lviv region. This was allowed

807 High-ranking civil servant F18 (A), Lviv Regional Forestry and Hunting Economy Authority, personal communication, September 12, 2022; High-ranking civil servant F16 (A), Ivano-Frankivsk Regional Forestry and Hunting Economy Authority, personal communication, September 7, 2022.

by the State Forestry Agency based on site visits and conclusions of a collegial body. In addition, the fact that FSC certification, which requires attention to some elements of biodiversity, has been awarded since 2005 for the forests in the Lviv region, was mentioned. Within this process, the plots of special importance (hosting rare and endangered species) are monitored on a yearly basis. In the national park "Skolivsky Beskydy", which is subordinate to this institution, the study of local biodiversity is undertaken. The importance of cooperation with NGOs on the identification and protection of primeval forests was also acknowledged.[808]

The representative of the Ivano-Frankivsk Regional Forestry and Hunting Economy Authority stated that biodiversity is taken into account in forestry only indirectly and only to the extent that the felling equipment allows. The documents on forest management, updated every 10 years, were mentioned as the main instrument for the consideration of biodiversity. It was stated that based on them, one can infer from indirect indicators to what extent biodiversity is affected by economic activities. In the opinion of this civil servant, biodiversity has to be protected in the NRF sites, while the foresters working in the commercial forestry "have no obligations to identify habitats of rare species or distinguish between different species of woodpeckers on the fly". He stated that the creation of special protective zones, like the ones around the nests of the black stork, has to be undertaken by someone else, not the forest sector employees themselves. If such information is present and enters materials on forest management, then there is a possibility of creating protective zones. Moreover, in his view, there are too many categories of forests where logging is restricted, such as riverbank protection forests. Such forests are not officially included among the NRF territories, thus limiting the freedom of economic activities. In his opinion, this fact imposes unjustified restrictions and will continue to do so given the future expansion of the NRF according to a national goal to achieve 15 per cent of protected areas. Furthermore, in the opinion of this official, the projected Emerald Network is not fully legitimate, as "it was marked on a map without any research". For instance, he said that the projected Emerald network comprises 80 per cent of the "Vyhodskyi" state forestry enterprise, whereas no territories of the "Verkhovynskyi" state forestry enterprise are included. Among the factors that helped to preserve biodiversity in the Ukrainian Carpathians, the lack of road infrastructure and accessibility of such forests were named. At the same time, it was stated

808 F18 (A), personal communication, September 12, 2022.

that to switch from the clear-cutting to selective cutting, the building of forest roads and better technical capacities are needed.[809]

In the neighbouring Lviv Regional Forestry and Hunting Economy Authority, in response to the question regarding the technical capacities for selective cutting, it was replied that the philosophy of action is a primary factor, whereas technical equipment is secondary and subordinate to this philosophy. However, the planned reform on the creation of one enterprise "Forests of Ukraine" was welcomed for its potential to generate funds for securing better technical equipment that could be used for selective logging.[810]

The head of the "Forests of Ukraine" reported in 2024 some successful changes to the system, associated with the reform, such as greater transparency and division of control and operational functions. For instance, all of the timber harvesting permits ('logging tickets'), including those for sanitary logging, are issued by the State Forestry Agency's management departments and photo documentation of the wood is required.[811] Moreover, some changes occurred in the Carpathian forest office, including the change of the leadership, the work on renewing forest management plans, that was not undertaken for 15 years (where it should be undertaken every 10 years), progress in registering of the land ownership and control over timber accounting to reduce corruption risks.[812]

The reform that the field of forest management is undergoing seeks to ensure sustainable forest management. It is expected that the new model will take into account the protection of biodiversity and adaptation to climate change. To achieve the change, new requirements and standards will be introduced, and the transformation of the field towards close-to-nature forestry will be undertaken.[813]

Apart from the State Forestry Agency and the "Forests of Ukraine" enterprise, there are some other organisations subordinate to the State Forestry

809 F16 (A), personal communication, September 7, 2022.

810 F18 (A), personal communication, September 12, 2022.

811 Yurii Bolokhovets, "Branches of the State Enterprise "Forests of Ukraine" Have Received Nearly 10,000 Electronic Logging Tickets," Facebook, February 15, 2024, https://www.facebook.com/permalink.php?story_fbid=pfbid02Bpd6gMRB3r3BpcoCRbwn1rffPuq4j7VYbqWBXjC2ocQWYNcYfP9u9MnwL3M4SjFdl&id=100010028957829.

812 Yurii Bolokhovets, "The leadership of the Carpathian Forest Office has changed," Facebook, February 27, 2024, https://www.facebook.com/permalink.php?story_fbid=pfbid02kAdkVnFiaoh9fqcnWjvjsADmu43U3qWs7thjprDw3CpmxCAYPCKKzA4Ec33siY6Ul&id=100010028957829.

Agency that are entrusted with particular tasks. For example, the "Ukrainian State Project Forest Management Production Association" is responsible for forest management and forest inventory.[814]

In addition to the state bodies directly responsible for nature protection or forests, there are numerous other governmental bodies and law enforcement agencies that could be directly or indirectly involved in biodiversity protection of forest ecosystems of the Ukrainian Carpathians. The special role is played by the State Environmental Inspectorate of Ukraine (SEI), which is empowered to ensure compliance with environmental legislation.[815] The experts from the NGOs, however, note that SEI is currently very limited in its activities. A law on the reform of eco-control is expected to be adopted, which may improve the work of SEI.[816] In addition, the whole mechanism of state law enforcement bodies might be relevant for biodiversity protection, including by tackling environmental crime and corruption. These bodies include National Police, Office of the Prosecutor General, State Border Guard Service, State Customs Service of Ukraine, State Bureau of Investigation, National Anti-Corruption Bureau of Ukraine, National Agency of Ukraine for finding, tracing and management of assets derived from corruption and other crimes (ARMA), State Audit Service of Ukraine and courts of all levels.

State authorities on the regional level and local authorities also have powers over nature protection. For instance, at the regional level, departments of ecology and natural resources are in charge of implementing the state environmental policy and law enforcement.[817] Some of the powers and responsibilities of local authorities on the protection of the components of biodiversity are mentioned in all of the main laws relevant to biodiversity protection in the Ukrainian Carpathians. For instance, the Law "On Environmental Protection" states that local councils bear responsibility for the

---

813 "Sustainable Forest Management," Ministry of Environmental Protection of Ukraine, accessed September 20, 2024, https://mepr.gov.ua/diyalnist/reformy/stale-vedennya-lisovogo-gospodarstva/.

814 "About us," Ukrainian State Project Forest Management Production Association, accessed September 20, 2024, https://lisproekt.gov.ua/objednannja.

815 Regulations on the State Environmental Inspectorate of Ukraine, approved by the Resolution of the Cabinet of Ministers of Ukraine No.275, Document 275–2017-p, (April 19, 2017), https://zakon.rada.gov.ua/laws/show/275-2017-%D0%BF#Text.

816 Oksana Omelchuk, Ecodiya (Ecoaction), personal communication, September 28, 2022.

817 Department of Nature Conservation, *Impact of war on natural environment of the Carpathians in Ukraine*, 8.

state of environment on their territory and to the extent of their competencies permit location of enterprises, institutions and organisations on their territories, organise environmental research, take decisions on organisation of the territories and objects of the NRF and other territories that require special protection, and control compliance with the legislation on nature protection.[818] In practice, however, it is unclear whether such powers are exercised, as the interviews with the representatives of the local self-government demonstrated avoidance in answering the question on their powers on biodiversity protection or ability to control the establishment and functioning of the private sawmills operating on their territory.[819]

Given the variety of institutions and overlap in their powers that leads to inaction, it is understandable why, among the strategic changes in the field of environmental protection, the clear division of powers between authorities of different levels is mentioned.[820] Moreover, there is a common-sense perception of biodiversity protection in Ukraine as almost exclusively within the competence of the Ministry of Environmental Protection, while the role of other executive bodies or local self-governance remains marginal.[821]

There are also certain working groups contributing to Ukraine's integration into the EU or the implementation of Ukrainian international obligations in the biodiversity-related areas. For instance, in the field of coordination of international technical assistance, there is a Sectoral Working Group on environmental protection that includes thematic subgroups "nature reserve fund and biodiversity" and "forestry sector reform".[822] There also existed a Coordinating Council on the implementation of the Carpathian Convention that was created in 2004. The documents establishing it remain valid, however, as noted by Sofiia Shutiak, due to reorganisations of different ministries, this body does not function.[823]

---

818 "On Environmental Protection," Law of Ukraine, Article 15.

819 L12 (A), personal communication, September 6, 2022.

820 The Fundamental Principles (Strategy) of the State Environmental Policy of Ukraine for the Period until 2030, Goal 5.

821 Oleksiy Vasyliuk, *The Status of Reflection in Ukraine's Programmatic Documents and the Implementation of the Provisions of the UN Convention on Biological Diversity*, Analytical Report, (Kyiv, October 2017), https://www.undp.org/ukraine/publications/implementing-un-convention-biological-diversity-ukraine, 25.

822 "Environmental Protection," Government Portal, accessed September 20, 2024, https://www.kmu.gov.ua/en/yevropejska-integraciya/coordination/environmental-protection.

823 Shutiak, *Analysis of Ukraine's Implementation of the Framework Convention on the Protection and Sustainable Development of the Carpathians*, 9.

In addition to the bodies, institutions, and organisations mentioned above, state-owned universities and research institutions contribute to the protection of biodiversity in the Ukrainian Carpathians. For instance, the following institutions undertake relevant research: National Forestry University of Ukraine, Ivan Franko National University of Lviv, Institute of Ecology of the Carpathians of the National Academy of Sciences of Ukraine, and the Ukrainian Research Institute of Mountain Forestry named after P.S. Pasternak.

In addition to governmental institutions, a leading role in voicing concerns as to the protection of biodiversity in the Ukrainian Carpathians and undertaking action or encouraging state policies to this end is played by the non-governmental organisations, both Ukrainian and international ones. The examples of the prominent NGOs in this field include the Ukrainian Nature Conservation Group (UNCG), WWF-Ukraine, Ecodiya, "Environment-People-Law" (EPL), and Frankfurt Zoological Society. For instance, among the main directions of activities of the UNCG, there are biodiversity, the Emerald Network, the protection of forests and the establishment of new protected areas[824]. Members of the UNCG collect data on biodiversity in Ukraine and integrate it into the Global Biodiversity Information Facility (GBIF) database; work on the creation of the new objects of the NRF; identify instances of illegal logging and take actions to counteract it; and advocate for nature-friendly legislative amendments.[825] Another important NGO is WWF-Ukraine, which includes 'rare species' and 'forests' among its areas of work.[826] Within the species conservation activities, WWF-Ukraine, for instance, works on the conservation of large carnivores, including bear and lynx, by means of mapping their habitats, carrying out awareness-raising campaigns to prevent conflicts between large carnivores and humans, advocating creation of ecological corridors or improving the nature-protection legislation.[827] In particular, upon the initiative of experts from the WWF-Ukraine, the plans for conserving the Eurasian lynx and brown bear

824 "What We Do," Ukrainian Nature Conservation Group (UNCG), accessed September 20, 2024, https://uncg.org.ua/en/activities/.

825 Yehor Hrynyk, UNCG, personal communication, September 27, 2022.

826 "What We Do," WWF-Ukraine, accessed September 20, 2024, https://wwf.ua/.

827 "Rare Species," WWF-Ukraine, accessed September 20, 2024, https://wwf.ua/our-work/wildlife/; "Hurry up to save the lynx," WWF-Ukraine, accessed September 20, 2024, https://specials.wwf.ua/lynx?fbclid=IwZXh0bgNhZW0CMTAAAR2GCSDA0ss5fmDsFy6b4vMRpnl7_NUv7GGHSrp4Lv8Vr6tmixTXxiTvyGA_aem_AaqTGGx0LF6CnkpKfMmjK08Ej0mjeq-GQrgNPpAxuade8wc-Lhn48-_EBExBGEbR3MZRKTO99sQvWqatxrphCuiR.

have been developed. The work of WWF-Ukraine on forests includes the identification and protection of old-growth forests, ensuring sustainable forestry, and contributing to the modernisation of forest policy in Ukraine by initiating dialogue among various actors in this sphere and counteracting illegal logging.[828] In the direction on old-growth forests, for instance, thanks to the work of this organisation, the territory of the UNESCO-protected primeval forests in the Ukrainian Carpathians has been extended, the legislative framework for the protection of primeval, quasi-primeval and natural forests has been created and some of the forests corresponding to these legislative criteria were designated as natural monuments.[829] Within the counteraction of illegal logging, the WWF-Ukraine created an interactive process chart for the main-use logging and for sanitary logging, both inside and outside the protected areas.[830] An expert from the EPL reported that this organisation is active in the identification of illegal logging and participating in the process of development of laws and regulations, such as the one on restricting sanitary logging within the NRF sites, helping to preserve especially valuable trees with hollows, fungi or nests.[831] Moreover, the Ukrainian NGOs are active in creating petitions and participating in the court proceedings, exemplified by the Borzhava and Svydovets cases described below.[832] From the NGOs outside Ukraine, Frankfurt Zoological Society has been active in supporting protected areas in the Ukrainian Carpathians by helping with equipment, infrastructure and training.[833]

The business entities can also influence the situation with biodiversity protection in the forest ecosystems of the Ukrainian Carpathians. Such an influence could be both beneficial and detrimental one. For instance, the interest of wood processing enterprises in the origins of wood could enhance compliance with the environmental legislation on behalf of the timber harvesting enterprises. One of the tools in this regard is the FCS certification system. Even though the latter was criticised as ineffective in

828 "Forests," WWF-Ukraine, accessed September 20, 2024, https://wwf.ua/our-work/forest/.

829 "Preservation of Primeval Forests," WWF-Ukraine, accessed September 20, 2024, https://wwf.ua/our-work/forest/unique-forests/.

830 "Countering Illegal Logging," WWF-Ukraine, accessed September 20, 2024, https://wwf.ua/our-work/forest/fight-illegal-logging/#stages-t2-l1.

831 Bohdan Kuchenko, EPL, personal communication, September 29, 2022.

832 See subchapter 2.5.

833 "Support for protected areas in the Carpathians," Frankfurt Zoological Society, accessed September 20, 2024, https://fzs.org/en/support/support-for-protected-areas-in-the-carpathians/.

Ukrainian conditions, it creates at least some motivation for compliance.[834] A new impetus of the business community's interest in sustainable forestry that considers biodiversity might be generated in Ukraine by the EU's recent adoption of the Regulation on deforestation-free products (EUDR).[835]

On the contrary, turning a blind eye to the origins of wood in pursuance of the sole aim of maximising profits motivates an increase in illegal and unsustainable logging, resulting in the degradation of the ecosystems. The danger of such a negative impact on the Ukrainian Carpathians is quite real and can involve large companies across Europe.[836] Locally, the network of illegal or semi-legal sawmills present in numerous sites in the Carpathian region within Ukraine might also contribute to the degradation of forest ecosystems and the decline of biodiversity.[837] Moreover, businesses might be interested in modifying the land use or initiating activities that are potentially harmful to biodiversity, as the examples of developmental plans on Borzhava and Svydovets described below demonstrate.

Both state-owned and non-governmental organisations of various types ("scientific institutions, environmental public organisations, or other interested enterprises, institutions, or organisations") can contribute to biodiversity protection by initiating the creation of protected areas in the forests.[838]

The role of individuals, including local residents of the Carpathian area in the first place, might vary from engaging in or tolerating illegal logging and wood processing practices in their villages to taking an active stance in identifying and counteracting these developments. The local populations might also participate in the EIA or SEA procedures for projects affecting

834 See Serhii Rozvod, "Prospects and Risks of Voluntary Forest Certification in the Context of the Ongoing Reform of Ukraine's Forestry Sector," Presentation for the Ukrainian Forest Platform, February 2023, https://cdn.prod.website-files.com/62b33cda52fedd6ad62d4c22/63f3db3c82cd3bdabbb773a6_Sergey%20%20%20Rozvod.ppt.pdf; "Illegal Sanitary Logging in the Carpathians! Now – Vyhodsky Forest Enterprise," UNCG, December 7, 2020, https://uncg.org.ua/vyhodskyj-lishosp/.

835 See materials of the 2024 EUDR Forum available at "EUDR Forum in Ukraine: results and prospects," Forest Stewardship Council (FSC), March 27, 2024, https://www.ua.fsc.org/ua-en/newsfeed/eudr-forum-in-ukraine-results-and-prospects; "Regulation on Deforestation-free Products," European Commission, accessed September 20, 2024, https://environment.ec.europa.eu/topics/forests/deforestation/regulation-deforestation-free-products_en.

836 Earthsight, *Complicit In Corruption: How billion-dollar firms and EU governments are failing Ukraine's forests*, Report (July 2018) https://fe8a03e2-1131-44e7-a06a-fb468c2a30d4.filesusr.com/ugd/624187_673e3aa69ed84129bdfeb91b6aa9ec17.pdf.

837 L11 (N), personal communication, September 6, 2022.

838 Procedure for Establishing Protective Zones for Biodiversity Conservation in Forests (2023), § 10.

the biodiversity of the Carpathians. Tourists may also influence biodiversity protection in the Carpathians by their preference for either sustainable or unsustainable options.

2.4. *The selected specific issues on biodiversity protection in the forest ecosystems of the Ukrainian Carpathians*

2.4.1. Monitoring of biodiversity

The monitoring of the natural environment, as such, biodiversity or certain elements of it, is mentioned in a number of laws of Ukraine, starting with the 1991 Law "On Environmental Protection" adopted around the time of the regaining of Ukraine's independence. It is also mentioned in the accompanying 1998 Regulation on the state system of monitoring of the environment adopted by the Cabinet of Ministers of Ukraine.[839] Each of the specialised laws related to biodiversity protection contains some norms on monitoring, yet the relevant subordinate regulatory acts in most cases were not adopted.[840] For instance, the Forest Code of Ukraine, Law of Ukraine "On the Plant World", Law of Ukraine "On the Animal World", Law of Ukraine "On the Natural Reserve Fund of Ukraine" and the Law of Ukraine "On the Ecological Network of Ukraine" entail monitoring and adoption of the relevant procedures. The monitoring suggested in these laws concerns forest monitoring, monitoring of the plant world, monitoring of the animal world, background environmental monitoring, and state monitoring of the ecological network, respectively. Owing to the lack of regulations on procedure, the implementation of the norms for monitoring various components of biodiversity faces significant obstacles.

The relevant provisions of the Law "On Environmental Protection" include Article 22, which entails monitoring of the environment, and Articles 25 and 25–1 on information on the state of the natural environment (ecological information).[841] According to Article 22, the state system of monitoring has to be created, and the central governmental body that imple-

839 Regulation on the State Environmental Monitoring System (1998).

840 Reform Support Team of the Ministry of Environmental Protection of Ukraine, *Environmental Monitoring: Analytical Note on the State and Prospects for the Development of the State Environmental Monitoring System*, (Kyiv, 2023), https://mepr.gov.ua/wp-content/uploads/2023/02/Monitoring-Green-Paper_15_02_2022.pdf, 9–10.

841 "On Environmental Protection," Law of Ukraine.

ments state policy in the field of environmental protection (that is the Ministry of Environmental Protection) carries out observations as to the state of the environment together with other governmental bodies, enterprises and organisations whose activities may adversely affect the environment. Based on this data, state bodies together with relevant research institutions ensure forecasting of changes in the natural environment, which have to be considered during the design and implementation of the programmes of economic and social development.[842] Accordingly, monitoring of the natural environment is one of the clear linkages between the components of sustainable development. In situations where it is not undertaken, the very source of information for the decision-making process is absent, putting the consideration of the environment in the developmental policies at risk. Article 25 of the Law "On Environmental Protection" defines categories of ecological information, among which "biological diversity and its components", as well as "flora and fauna", are explicitly mentioned.[843]

Article 25–1 on environmental information support mentions a yearly national report on the state of the environment and free access to the environmental information that is not classified as a state secret.[844] The national reports on the state of the environment usually contain a separate chapter on the state of biodiversity.[845] In recent years, additional information systems and platforms were created to gather and present environmental information in Ukraine, including information on biodiversity. These include the platform "EcoSystem", which provides information and enables access to certain digital administrative services related to the environment. For instance, it includes information on forests and data related to the NRF, such as the list of NRF entities subordinate to the Ministry of Environmental Protection, limits on the special use of natural resources within the territories and objects of the NRF of national significance, lists of permits for the export (re-export) and import of wild fauna and flora species in accordance with the CITES or hunting quotas for game animals. Some of the

842 "On Environmental Protection," Law of Ukraine, Article 22.
843 "On Environmental Protection," Law of Ukraine, Article 25.
844 "On Environmental Protection," Law of Ukraine, Article 25–1.
845 The reports from 2009 to 2021 are publicly available at the webpage of the Ministry of Environmental Protection, see "National Reports on the State of the Environment in Ukraine," Ministry of Environmental Protection of Ukraine, https://mepr.gov.ua/diyalnist/napryamky/ekologichnyj-monitoryng/natsionalni-dopovidi-pro-stan-navkolyshnogo-pryrodnogo-seredovyshha-v-ukrayini/.

categories of information are, however, currently inactive, and moreover, certain authorisation is needed to access the contained information.[846]

According to the 1998 Regulation on state system of monitoring of the environment, which is called to define procedure of monitoring in accordance with the Article 22 of the Law "On Environmental Protection" the Ministry of Environmental Protection is responsible for monitoring of the land ecosystems, endangered plant and animal species or the species under special protection and for the "environmental mapping" of the territory of Ukraine for the purposes of evaluation of the environment and its changes due to economic activities.[847] The State Forestry Agency is responsible for monitoring forest vegetation (including its biodiversity, conditions and damage from biotic and abiotic factors) and game fauna (its species, quantity and special characteristics).[848]

In 2024, the new Regulation, which is supposed to substitute the mentioned 1998 Regulation, was provisionally adopted; however, its entry into force depends on the cancellation or termination of martial law.[849]

Some information on the state of biodiversity is also available in the State Cadastre of Animal World, in the reports on maintaining the State Cadastre of Ukraine's Plant World, which include information on medicinal plants in the Carpathians and some information on invasive alien species, and species listed in the Red Data Book of Ukraine.[850]

Environmental monitoring in Ukraine, including biodiversity monitoring, has been subject to scholarly attention, with various proposals being

---

846 "EcoSystem," Ministry of Environmental Protection of Ukraine, https://eco.gov.ua/.

847 Regulation on the State Environmental Monitoring System (1998), § 8.

848 Regulation on the State Environmental Monitoring System (1998), § 8.

849 See "Certain Issues of the Functioning of the State Environmental Monitoring System and Its Subsystems," (2024); "On Amendments to Certain Legislative Acts of Ukraine Regarding the State Environmental Monitoring System, Environmental Condition Information (Environmental Information), and Information Support for Environmental Management," Law of Ukraine (2023).

850 "State Cadastre of Animal World," Diia, accessed September 20, 2024, https://data.gov.ua/dataset/mepr_04; "Maintenance of the State Cadastre of Plant World of Ukraine," Ministry of Environmental Protection of Ukraine, accessed September 20, 2024, https://mepr.gov.ua/diyalnist/napryamky/bioriznomanittya/chervona-knyga-ukrayiny/vedennya-derzhavnogo-kadastru-roslynnogo-svitu-ukrayiny/; Valentyna Minarchenko, "Maintenance of the State Cadastre of Plant World of Ukraine," Report on Scientific Research Work, accessed September 20, 2024, https://mepr.gov.ua/wp-content/uploads/2023/05/Cadastr2018.pdf; "Red Data Book of Ukraine," Diia, accessed September 20, 2024, https://data.gov.ua/dataset/b5cdb316-6074-4ef3-a0c5-463ff3a72e68.

voiced over time on the improvement of both its legal basis and practical operation.[851] It has been noted that the monitoring of biodiversity is problematic given the lack of both established principles for monitoring and actual biodiversity monitoring (except for game species and some species considered pests in forestry or agriculture, as well as a small percentage of objects within the NRF).[852]

The need to establish a system for monitoring the natural habitats and rare and endangered species of flora and fauna in Europe featured, for instance, in one of the President's decrees (2017). However, it is unclear whether it resulted in any measures being taken towards that end.[853] The unsatisfactory condition of the system of state monitoring of the natural environment was acknowledged in the Strategy on Environmental Policy until 2030.[854] Some other recent governmental publications mention the lasting problems in this sphere, such as a lack of coordination between the state system for environmental monitoring and decision-making bodies that are supposed to use this information in their decisions, lack of coordination of data collection by various central executive authorities, disallowing comparison and a comprehensive analysis of the state of the environment, and raising questions as to the completeness and quality of such information.[855] The reform is still needed to ensure adequate monitoring of biodiversity, meaning at least the designation of the responsible entities.[856]

The lack of comprehensive monitoring of biodiversity in the forest ecosystems of the Ukrainian Carpathians does not, however, mean the complete absence of data. The leading role in data collection is played

---

851 See for example: Vasiliy Kostiushyn, Serhii Gubar, and Volodymyr Domashlinets, *Strategy for Developing the Monitoring of Biodiversity in Ukraine* (Kyiv: ECNC-European Centre for Nature Conservation, National Ecological Centre of Ukraine, 2009).

852 Vasyliuk, *The Status of Reflection in Ukraine's Programmatic Documents and the Implementation of the Provisions of the UN Convention on Biological Diversity*, 14–16, 26.

853 "On additional measures for the development of forestry, rational use of nature and conservation of objects of the nature reserve fund" Decree of the President of Ukraine (2017).

854 The Fundamental Principles (Strategy) of the State Environmental Policy of Ukraine for the Period until 2030, Chapter I. Existing Problems and the Current State of the Environment in Ukraine.

855 Reform Support Team of the Ministry of Environmental Protection of Ukraine, *Environmental Monitoring*, 111–116.

856 Reform Support Team of the Ministry of Environmental Protection of Ukraine, *Environmental Monitoring*, 119.

by the NRF institutions, even though the quality and completeness of monitoring undertaken by these institutions is limited, being dependent on the availability of staff and resources, in particular, technical equipment for monitoring.[857]

The activities undertaken by the NRF institutions may be exemplified based on the interviews conducted for the purposes of the present work with the employees of the National Natural Park "Hutsulshchyna". It was reported that some activities on biodiversity monitoring have been undertaken since the foundation of this institution. Certain territories have been designated as monitoring sites, where botanical monitoring is being undertaken three times a year, and where forest specialists undertake a complete inventory of trees, dead wood and undergrowth once every five years. Furthermore, the book Chronicles of Nature, which notes the monitoring work throughout the year, is kept on a yearly basis. The cartography of species is undertaken with a view to identifying whether certain species were present before or are newly discovered in the territory of the park.[858] Regarding the staff, the employee of the National Natural Park "Hutsulshchyna" reported that as of 2022, the team undertaking biodiversity monitoring comprised a climatologist, a mycologist, a geographer and several forest specialists. It was also noted that recently, a zoologist joined the team, planning to monitor birds' populations and possibly large mammals. In the past, there was an ornithologist and certain monitoring of insects.[859]

The National Natural Park "Hutsulshchyna" features all altitudinal forest belts within the Carpathian mid-mountains and hosts some of the rare species. On its territory, the plant and mushroom species listed in the Red Data Book of Ukraine are closely monitored. There has also been close cooperation with the Ukrainian Society for the Protection of Birds and Frankfurt Zoological Society, which provided camera traps to monitor the animals. Thanks to this equipment, badgers, wolves, and bears have been recorded on the National Natural Park "Hutsulshchyna" territory.[860]

---

857 Yaroslav Dovhanych and V. Y. Dovhanych, "The monitoring system of mammals in the Carpathian Biosphere Reserve," *Monitoring and conservation of biodiversity in Ukraine: Applied aspects of biodiversity monitoring and conservation, Series* "Conservation Biology in Ukraine" Issue 16, Vol. 3 (2020): 68–69, https://uncg.org.ua/wp-content/uploads/2020/05/T3_WEB_MonOchBioriz_Konference_2.pdf.

858 L11 (N), personal communication, September 6, 2022.

859 L11 (N), personal communication, September 6, 2022.

860 L11 (N), personal communication, September 6, 2022.

It was reported that in the Lviv region, the "Skolivski Beskydy" is one of the parks where biodiversity research is conducted.[861] In addition, it was reported that within the framework of the FSC certification, some monitoring is undertaken in the form of yearly monitoring of certain plots of commercially used forests, where rare or endangered species of plants and animals are found. In the Lviv region, among these species, there are black stork, bear, lynx, saffron, and many other species."[862]

The experts from the environmental NGOs voice concerns about the wide knowledge gap on the state of biodiversity in Ukraine. It was reported that the usual approach taken by those interested in the status quo of biodiversity in Ukraine is to look at the data from other central European states and try to apply it to Ukraine, given some similarity of natural parameters. They acknowledge the fact that some kind of monitoring is indeed exercised in the sites of the NRF or regarding game species, but the general monitoring system is lacking, and consequently, there is no "comprehensive picture".[863] Furthermore, they draw attention to the fact that the quality of the Chronicles of Nature kept by the NRF depends on the experience and expertise of the employees, and the very model of keeping reports on biodiversity in this format is criticised.[864] Moreover, they note that the monitoring of biodiversity remains incomplete if it is undertaken only by the NRF sites. In theory, according to the Ukrainian legislation, the state forestry enterprises are also obliged to identify protected species, which is, however, almost never implemented in practice.[865] Another problem with the knowledge on the state of biodiversity in the Ukrainian Carpathians or Ukraine in general is the fact that the collected data is rarely further analysed and relied on during decision-making.[866]

The reform in this sphere is ongoing. In 2023, the Working group tasked specifically with preparing suggestions on reform of the state system of

861 F18 (A), personal communication, September 12, 2022.

862 F18 (A), personal communication, September 12, 2022.

863 Yehor Hrynyk, UNCG, personal communication, September 27, 2022.

864 Yurii Moskalenko, "The "Chronicle of Nature" program for reserves and national parks of Ukraine – what is wrong with it?" *Monitoring and conservation of biodiversity in Ukraine: Applied aspects of biodiversity monitoring and conservation, Series* "Conservation Biology in Ukraine" Issue 16, Vol. 3 (2020): 91–106, https://uncg.org.ua/wp-content/uploads/2020/05/T3_WEB_MonOchBioriz_Konference_2.pdf.

865 Bohdan Kuchenko, EPL, personal communication, September 29, 2022.

866 Yehor Hrynyk, UNCG, personal communication, September 27, 2022.

environmental monitoring in the direction of "biodiversity" was created.[867] The creation of this Working group is based on the amendments to the Law "On Environmental Protection", including Article 64–1 on biodiversity, made earlier that year.[868]

2.4.2. Ecological network

As was mentioned above, in the early 2000s, the creation of an ecological network became a policy alternative to the creation of a separate programme on biodiversity protection in Ukraine.

The Law "On Ecological Network" elaborates on the Programme for the Formation of the National Ecological Network of Ukraine for 2000 – 2015 described above. There are, however, some differences between these documents, starting with the very definition of 'ecological network' or its elements. According to the Law "On Ecological Network", there are four categories of components: core areas, buffer zones, transition areas and restorative areas, whereas according to the Programme, there are natural regions, natural corridors and buffer zones.[869]

The Law "On Ecological Network" outlines the principles of creation, protection and utilisation of the ecological network, such as ensuring the integrity of the ecosystem functions of the components of the ecological network; halting the loss of natural or semi-natural territories; public participation in the decision making; or systematic consideration of the ecological, social, and economic interests of society, that is sustainable development.[870] The creation of the nationwide ecological network is based on the designation of regional and local ecological networks, which is un-

---

867 "On the establishment of the Working Group for preparing proposals on reforming the state environmental monitoring system in Ukraine in the area of "Biodiversity"," Order of the Ministry of Environmental Protection No. 527 (July 24, 2023) https://mepr.gov.ua/diyalnist/napryamky/bioriznomanittya/monitoryng-bioriznomanittya/.

868 "On Amendments to Certain Legislative Acts of Ukraine Regarding the State Environmental Monitoring System, Environmental Condition Information (Environmental Information), and Information Support for Environmental Management," Law of Ukraine.

869 "On Ecological Network of Ukraine," Law of Ukraine, Article 16; Programme for the Formation of the National Ecological Network of Ukraine for 2000 – 2015, Section 4.

870 "On Ecological Network of Ukraine," Law of Ukraine, Article 4.

dertaken by the relevant councils after approval by the corresponding state administrations. The consolidated scheme for the formation of Ukraine's ecological network is adopted by the Verkhovna Rada of Ukraine.[871] In the Carpathians within Ukraine, the formation of the ecological network is facilitated by the programmes of Transcarpathia, Lviv, Ivano-Frankivsk and Chernivtsi regional councils that are either directly dedicated to the ecological network or include it among general programmes of environmental protection.[872]

The designation of the areas and objects is based on their significance from the viewpoint of ecology, botany, zoology and landscape studies, whereby in the first place, the areas and objects of nationwide significance in terms of landscape- and biodiversity are included in the ecological network.[873] The Procedure for including objects into the ecological network was adopted by the Cabinet of Ministers in 2015.[874] Importantly, the inclusion of the areas and objects into the ecological network is undertaken without prejudice to the rights of the owners of these territories. The owners and users of these territories, however, are obliged to preserve natural resources and use them in an ecologically balanced and rational way.[875]

Furthermore, the Law "On the Ecological Network" envisages the monitoring that entails observations aimed at evaluating coherence of the network, conditions of the natural complexes and objects, identification of the adverse developments as well as the creation of forecasts and recommendations on formation, preservation and use of the ecological network.[876] The

871 "On Ecological Network of Ukraine," Law of Ukraine, Article 15.

872 *National Report of Ukraine on the Implementation of the Biodiversity Protocol*, 9–10 [Mentioning Programs of perspective development of nature conservation and ecological network in the Zacarpattia oblast for 2006–2020 (from January 12, 2006, No. 695); Regional program of formation of the ecological network of the Lviv oblast for 2007–2015 (from 03.06.2007 № 340); Programs of environmental protection of Ivano-Frankivsk oblast (subprogram "Protection of nature reserve fund, formation of ecological network") (from 06.06.2011 № 161-6 / 2011 and from 25.12.2015, № 59-2 / 2015); Integrated Environmental Protection Program of the Chernivtsi oblast "Ecology" for 2016–2018 (from 10.03.2011 № 10-4 / 11 and from 15.03.2016 № 19-4 / 16)].

873 "On Ecological Network of Ukraine," Law of Ukraine, Article 17.

874 Procedure for including territories and objects in the lists of territories and objects of the ecological network (2015).

875 "On Ecological Network of Ukraine," Law of Ukraine, Article 16.

876 "On Ecological Network of Ukraine," Law of Ukraine, Article 20.

procedure for such monitoring shall be adopted by the Cabinet of Ministers of Ukraine, but has not been adopted as of September 2024.[877]

The increase in the area of the ecological network belongs to the strategic tasks of the environmental policy in Ukraine. Such an increase is supposed to primarily occur through the enlargement of existing and the creation of new territories and objects of the NRF.[878]

A separate sub-issue within the creation of the ecological network in Ukraine is the creation of the Emerald network, based on the Bern Convention and Resolutions to it, as described in Chapter I. The Ukrainian legislation on the ecological network forms a general basis for including in it the areas of special conservation interest in accordance with the Bern Convention. This is illustrated by the wording used in the relevant Programme and Law. For instance, while describing the ecological network concept, it is noted that the territory of the national ecological network comprises elements of international, national and local importance. In addition, the legal basis for the ecological network includes international treaties, to which Ukraine is a party, where all of the biodiversity treaties ratified by Ukraine are mentioned, including the Bern Convention. The 'natural territories' within the ecological network include territories that correspond to the conditions set in the international treaties and which serve the purpose of protecting biological and landscape diversity, especially those that include habitats of rare and endangered species.[879] According to the Law "On Ecological Network", the very definition of 'ecological network' includes territories of particular value for protecting the natural environment and, in accordance with Ukraine's international obligations, are subject to special protection.[880] It follows from the logic of these documents that the ecological network in Ukraine shall include the territories serving the protection of species and habitats of special conservation interest based on the Bern Convention. This means that the Emerald network within Ukraine shall be included in the ecological network and has the same legal basis.

The work on the creation of the Emerald network was undertaken in Ukraine since 2009 by numerous scientific institutions. During 2009 –

877 See Reform Support Team of the Ministry of Environmental Protection of Ukraine, *Environmental Monitoring*, 9.

878 The Fundamental Principles (Strategy) of the State Environmental Policy of Ukraine for the Period until 2030.

879 Programme for the Formation of the National Ecological Network of Ukraine for 2000 – 2015, Section 4.

880 "On Ecological Network of Ukraine," Law of Ukraine, Article 3.

2015, 194 potential objects with a total area of 53 613.2 square kilometres, amounting to 8.9 per cent of Ukraine's territory were identified.[881] As of 2023, there are 377 Emerald sites in Ukraine, officially adopted by the Standing Committee of the Bern Convention. The total terrestrial area of adopted Emerald sites within Ukraine constitutes 68 916.5 square kilometres, which amounts to 11.4 per cent of Ukraine's territory.[882]

Apart from the legal basis of its creation, there are, however, not many norms defining the legal status of the Emerald network in Ukraine. Therefore, in recent years, the expert circles voiced the need to adopt a separate legal regulation, and the corresponding legislative draft was created in 2020.[883] The attention to the Emerald network in Ukraine was to a large extent reinvigorated by the conclusion of the Association Agreement between the EU and Ukraine, where the cooperation on nature protection comprises biodiversity and landscape diversity, including "eco-networks".[884] Such cooperation means the need for Ukraine to approximate its legislation in environmental matters, as defined in the Annex XXX.[885] The Annex XXX includes requirements on the approximation of nature protection obligations under the Birds and Habitats Directives, including "completion of the inventory of potential Emerald sites and establishment of protection and management measures for these sites" necessary for the approximation of the Habitats Directive.[886] The rationale of the EU integration was also men-

881 Leonid Protsenko, "The current state of the development of the Emerald Network in Ukraine 2009 -2015," Presentation, accessed September 20, 2024, https://wwfcu.awsassets.panda.org/downloads/emerald_network_protsenko.pdf, 11.

882 "Barometer statistics per country: Ukraine", Emerald Barometer Dashboard, accessed September 20, 2024, https://tableau-public.discomap.eea.europa.eu/views/EmeraldBarometerdashboard/Barometerstatisticspercountry?%3AshowAppBanner=false&%3Adisplay_count=n&%3AshowVizHome=n&%3Aorigin=viz_share_link&%3AisGuestRedirectFromVizportal=y&%3Aembed=y; For the full list of the adopted Emerald sited within Ukraine see: Standing Committee, *Updated list of officially adopted Emerald Network sites (December 2023)*, T-PVS/PA(2023)08, (Strasbourg, 2023) https://rm.coe.int/draft-list-of-adopted-emerald-network-sites/1680ad54a1.

883 "Emerald Network," UNCG, accessed September 20, 2024, https://uncg.org.ua/emerald/; "What is the Emerald Network and why is it important for Ukrainians?" Ecodiya (Ecoaction), June 24, 2022, https://ecoaction.org.ua/emerald-ua.html; "The Progress in Creation of the Emerald Network in Ukraine: Policy Brief" EPL, October 18, 2023, https://epl.org.ua/eco-analytics/stan-stvorennya-smaragdovoyi-merezhi-v-ukrayini/#.

884 Association Agreement between the EU and Ukraine, Article 361 (f).

885 Association Agreement between the EU and Ukraine, Article 363.

886 Association Agreement between the EU and Ukraine, Annex XXX to Chapter 6, Environment, Nature Protection.

tioned in the explanatory note to the draft law on the Emerald network. Despite the importance of this legislative draft in light of the obligations under the Bern Convention and the Association Agreement between the EU and Ukraine, it was not adopted in the first reading and was sent in 2021 for a repeated first reading.[887] As of 2024, there has been little progress on its adoption, and there is no clarity as to the timing of revitalising the efforts to this end. The experts from the Ukrainian NGOs explain such a status quo by "a strong opposition to the Emerald Network in some business circles in Ukraine, mainly based on myths and manipulations".[888]

2.4.3. Old-growth forests

The protection of the old-growth forests in Ukraine in recent years has witnessed a dramatic increase in attention and action. Tremendous work on the identification of such forests was undertaken by the NGOs, and the change of the Ukrainian legislation towards enhanced protection of the old-growth forests was motivated by the adoption of the "Criteria and Indicators for identification of virgin forests in the Carpathians" by the Parties to the Carpathian Convention in 2014.[889]

As mentioned above, the legislative developments of 2017 added to the Ukrainian legislation previously non-existent categories of 'primeval', 'quasi-primeval' and 'natural' forests as well as methodology of their identification. The Forest Code was amended respectively, and the new category of natural monuments was added to the Law "On Nature Reserve Fund".[890]

---

887 "The Draft Law On the Territories of the Emerald Network (4461 from 04.12.2020)," Verkhovna Rada of Ukraine, https://itd.rada.gov.ua/billInfo/Bills/Card/4847.

888 Bohdan Kuchenko, EPL, personal communication, September 29, 2022.

889 Department of Nature Conservation, *Impact of war on natural environment of the Carpathians in Ukraine*, 26; See Subchapter 2.3.

890 "On Amending Certain Legislative Acts of Ukraine Regarding the Protection of Primeval Forests in Accordance with the Framework Convention on Conservation and Sustainable Development of the Carpathians," Law of Ukraine; Methodology for Determining the Classification of Forest Areas as Primeval Forests, Quasi-Primeval Forests, and Natural Forests (2018); Methodology for Determining the Classification of Territories as Primeval Forest Nature Monuments, approved by the Order of the Ministry of Environmental Protection No. 162, Document z0707–18, (May 18, 2018) https://zakon.rada.gov.ua/laws/show/z0708-18#n14; Forest Code of Ukraine, Articles 1, 37, 39–1, 46, 70, 79, 84, 105; "On Nature Reserve Fund," Law of Ukraine, Articles 3, 28.

Before these developments, the important role in the protection of old-growth forests in Ukraine was played by the large NRF sites, some of which were founded as early as 1968 (the Carpathian biosphere reserve), 1974 (nature park "Synevyr"), 1980 (Carpathian nature park) or 1996 (nature reserve "Gorgany").[891]

The work on identifying such categories of forests has been carried out by the NGO WWF-Ukraine in cooperation with partner organisations for over a decade. The successful identification bore fruit of enlarging the area of the UNESCO heritage site of beech primeval forests within Ukraine and ensuring protection of other primeval forests by granting them a protective status either within the NRF site or within other categories of forests.[892] The work that led to the identification of primeval forests in the Ukrainian Carpathians began in 2006 – 2010 with the pilot identification of the high conservation value forests and inventory of primeval forests in 2008 – 2012.[893]

The employees of the NRF sites have also contributed to the identification of the primeval forests. As was explained during the interview, the employees of the national natural park "Hutsulshchyna" identified such forests, for instance, at the Kabanystyi ridge. It was further explained that these and other old-growth forests were preserved mostly because they are located in the hard-to-reach areas with no road infrastructure in the vicinity, and partly because the trees there are crooked.[894]

It is, however, noted that during 2014 – 2017, about 10.000 hectares of plots with characteristics of old-growth forests were cut, and even after the temporary moratorium on cutting such forests was introduced by the State Forestry Agency in 2018, logging of old-growth forests on some plots continued.[895] In a study exploring the disturbance of old-growth forests in the Ukrainian Carpathians by means of analysing summertime satellite images, it was reported that between 2010 and 2019, a total area of 1334.9 ha of old-growth forests was disturbed, with particularly severe disturbance

891 Smaliychuk and Grabener, *Natural forests of Ukrainian Carpathians*, 29.

892 "Preservation of Primeval Forests," WWF-Ukraine, accessed September 20, 2024, https://wwf.ua/our-work/forest/unique-forests/.

893 Department of Nature Conservation, *Impact of war on natural environment of the Carpathians in Ukraine*, 26.

894 L11 (N), personal communication, September 6, 2022.

895 Department of Nature Conservation, *Impact of war on natural environment of the Carpathians in Ukraine*, 26; Ministry of Ecology and Natural Resources of Ukraine, *Sixth National Report of Ukraine on the Implementation of the Convention on Biological Diversity* (Kyiv, 2018), https://www.cbd.int/doc/nr/nr-06/ua-nr-06-en.pdf, 115.

in the North-West Marmarosh.[896] It is suggested that during 2015 – 2018, the rate of disturbance was almost constant, while in 2019, it decreased to 0.19 per cent a year, which is twice as low as in the previous four years, suggesting that legislative amendments might have positively affected the rate of disturbance.[897]

2.5. Risks, threats, and challenges to biodiversity protection in the forest ecosystems of the Ukrainian Carpathians

The biodiversity of the forests of the Ukrainian Carpathians faces a whole range of threats. These may be related to both global trends on factors driving biodiversity loss, and to peculiar local conditions.

Globally, the following factors are recognised to constitute the main threats to biodiversity (in the order of relevance for the region of Europe and Central Asia): changes in land use, including habitat loss and degradation; species overexploitation; invasive species and disease; pollution; and climate change.[898] In the Millennium Ecosystem Assessment, the following factors have been assessed as drivers of biodiversity loss: habitat change, climate change, invasive species, overexploitation and pollution. For temperate forests, to which the Carpathian forests belong, the habitat loss, overexploitation and pollution were named as key drivers of change during the last century; and the climate change and invasive species were named among the factors that are on the rise.[899]

In the Strategy of the State Environmental Policy of Ukraine for the Period until 2030, it is noted that the main threat to the biodiversity in Ukraine is posed by the human activities and destruction of habitats, including decline in natural forests, deforestation and subsequent change of the land use, and the spread of non-native species in natural ecosystems. Regarding

896 Benedict D. Spracklen and Dominick V. Spracklen, "Identifying European Old-Growth Forests Using Remote Sensing: A Study in the Ukrainian Carpathians," *Forests* 10, no. 2 (5 February 2019): 9–10, https://doi.org/10.3390/f10020127.

897 Benedict D. Spracklen and Dominick V. Spracklen, "Identifying European Old-Growth Forests Using Remote Sensing: A Study in the Ukrainian Carpathians," 11.

898 *Living Planet Report 2020 – Bending the Curve of Biodiversity Loss*, ed. R.E.A. Almond, M. Grooten and T. Petersen (Gland: WWF, 2020) https://f.hubspotuserco ntent20.net/hubfs/4783129/LPR/PDFs/ENGLISH-FULL.pdf, 20–21.

899 Ecosystems and Human Well-being: Biodiversity Synthesis, *Millennium Ecosystem Assessment* (Washington, DC: World Resources Institute, 2005) https://www.millen niumassessment.org/documents/document.354.aspx.pdf, 9.

the problems in the forestry sector, the factors mentioned in the Strategy include the inadequacies in the management, the absence of incentives for the introduction of nature-conserving technologies, and the imperfection of the tax system.[900] The major risks for protected areas in the Carpathians voiced by the Ukrainian government in the international conference in 2021, included climate change, manifesting itself in mass drying of trees, but also massive floods; disposal of household waste including littering of rivers; increased number of cars and recreational load; and risks related to the construction of ski resorts, wind farms, small hydropower plants and other objects.[901]

The Strategy of the State Environmental Policy of Ukraine further notes that since regaining independence in 1991, Ukraine has doubled the area belonging to the NRF sites. However, it is not sufficient for the preservation of rare and endangered species of fauna and flora and their habitats. The problems are explained by the imperfection of the existing legislative framework, lack of the clearly defined strategy of nature conservation activities, inadequate system of management, low level of financial and material-technical support for the organization and functioning of the NRF sites as well as lack of social guarantees for its employees, and low level of general environmental education and public awareness. It is noted that the risk of losing reserved and potentially valuable natural complexes for future conservation has significantly increased.[902]

The Ukrainian experts on forest policy named the following threats and risks as the most relevant for the forest ecosystems of the Ukrainian Carpathians: forest management in its current form, uncontrolled tourism including building of resorts and jeeping, climate change;[903] or in different words: illegal and unsustainable logging, construction, poaching, and jeeping.[904] Other notable problems include the ineffectiveness of the SEI, lack of financing of forest protection, lack of state system of monitoring of the biodiversity, lack of awareness on biodiversity among the local residents,

---

900 The Fundamental Principles (Strategy) of the State Environmental Policy of Ukraine for the Period until 2030, Section I.

901 Eduard Arustamian, "Protected Areas System in the Ukrainian Carpathians," *Protected Areas – Cornerstones of Ecological Connectivity in the Carpathians and Beyond International Conference*, (Visegrád, Hungary, 28–30 September 2021) https://keep.eu/api/project-attachment/49664/get_file/, 9–10.

902 The Fundamental Principles (Strategy) of the State Environmental Policy of Ukraine for the Period until 2030, Section I.

903 Yehor Hrynyk, UNCG, personal communication, September 27, 2022.

904 Bohdan Kuchenko, EPL, personal communication, September 29, 2022.

including forest sector employees and local authorities, general problems with corruption, judiciary and law enforcement, and the Russian war of aggression that exacerbates the situation in forestry and nature protection across the country.[905]

The threat of illegal or unsustainable logging, accompanied also by the way in which felling is exercised by state enterprises and put into a wider context of forest management, is manifold and complex. Often, it is related to other governance problems, including corruption, the operation of law enforcement agencies or the bankruptcy of municipal enterprises. Illegal logging in a narrow sense in Ukraine usually means logging undertaken without proper authorisation or in violation of some legislative norms. However, a related broader notion of unsustainable logging is used by the experts to denote a logging that complies with formal requirements and for which permit has been granted, but which contradicts the concept of sustainability or international obligations of Ukraine, such as the clear-cutting of the natural forest, for which the permits have been granted. The experts suggest a typology comprising three categories of illegal logging in Ukraine: logging by private actors such as local residents and various criminal groups; logging by forest management officials (undertaken with or without permits); and illegal forest conversion.[906] Another analytical study earlier identified the following main *modi operandi* for forest crimes in Ukraine: logging outside the boundaries of officially permitted areas; logging of trees that are not designated for cutting on plots with issued logging permits; and logging of trees in protected zones and transporting illegally harvested timber without a waybill.[907] On the question of unsustainable logging, an expert noted that there is an 'ideological struggle' from the environmentalists' side to have unsustainable or inappropriate logging activities recognised on a legislative level as illegal ones.[908]

---

905 Yehor Hrynyk, UNCG, personal communication, September 27, 2022.

906 Yehor Hrynyk, Andrii Biletskyi and Amanda Cabrejo le Roux, "How corruption threatens the forests of Ukraine: Typology and case studies on corruption and illegal logging," *Environmental Corruption Deep Dive Series*, Working Paper 43 (Basel: Basel Institute on Governance, 2023) baselgovernance. org/publications/deepdive1-ukraine, 20.

907 "Gap Analysis: Ukraine," *EU Forest Crime Initiative*, (Brussels: WWF, August 2020) https://wwfeu.awsassets.panda.org/downloads/____1_1_1_1_1.pdf?2432466/forest-crime-analysis-ua, 6.

908 Oksana Omelchuk, Ecodiya (Ecoaction), personal communication, September 28, 2022.

One of the most common factors making the logging illegal is the violation of the rules on logging, including the rules on main-use logging (in particular the rules on main-use logging in the Carpathians), the rules on improvement of the quality composition of forests and the sanitary rules. In addition, the norms on especially valuable trees or rare species are often neglected. There are also violations of the law on the EIA, mainly the lack of it in cases when it should be conducted according to legislation, of the Red Data Book requirements and the legislation on the NRF.[909]

There is also a possibility of circumventing the law and conducting sanitary logging in forests that do not require it from an ecological viewpoint. The tragedy of such sanitary logging lies in the fact that oftentimes when such initial unnecessary sanitary logging (clear-cut) is undertaken arbitrarily, it may lead to the drying out of neighbouring trees in that area, which opens the room for the next sanitary logging that became justified by these circumstances (initially caused by that unnecessary first logging). Out of the Carpathian oblasts within Ukraine, such practice is especially common in Transcarpathia.[910]

Unauthorised logging by private actors also belongs to this category of threats. The cases of unauthorised felling occur in sites where there is a lack of control, such as in sites that formerly belonged to collective farm forests and are currently governed by the bankrupt municipal forest enterprises. Such enterprises (called *'райагроліс'* – *'rayagrolis'* in Ukrainian) continue to exist on paper but are not in a position to continue operations due to their bankruptcy. These forests are not included in the state forestry fund, and there is no possibility of guarding them. Moreover, many of them comprise territories that were in private ownership before the Soviet annexation of the Western part of Ukraine, which was formerly governed by the Austro-Hungarian Empire and Poland, in 1939. The descendants of the owners and, in general, local residents of these areas preserve the knowledge of the family ownership over these forests, and they continue to feel moral entitlement to use such forests (including logging) in case they need, grounding such entitlement on some sort of local custom rather than on any official documents. The quality of such forests differs: while some of them experience degradation, others are surprisingly well-preserved.

909 Bohdan Kuchenko, EPL, personal communication, September 29, 2022; Yehor Hrynyk, UNCG, personal communication, September 27, 2022.

910 Bohdan Kuchenko, EPL, personal communication, September 29, 2022.

Overall, the (dis)functioning of these structures constitutes a huge problem on a local level, for instance, in Ivano-Frankivsk oblast.[911]

Among the reasons behind the violation of the rules on logging is often ignorance or negligence on behalf of the forest sector employees, who may not wish to make an effort to track legislative changes and instead prefer to continue 'business as usual'. More common reason is, however, a deliberate violation or circumvention of the norms to maximise profit. Employees are used to performing the 'easiest' types of logging, which generate the largest sums of immediate financial profit. At the same time, in the view of experts, there is a potential to use more advanced types and techniques of logging, which would allow conducting profitable forest management and at the same time to take care of biodiversity, such as transition to transformation cutting. These measures have to be implemented, however, in a prudent way, as the latter type of logging would be meaningful only in the monoculture forests.[912]

The illegal logging in the Ukrainian Carpathians is often closely tied to corrupt practices. In forestry, corruption manifests itself on various levels and in numerous 'schemes' that continue to emerge. The experts characterise some of the schemes as 'classical ones' (such as the 'sanitary' logging, under which guise the healthy trees are cut to generate profits that can be divided among participants of the scheme), while other schemes continue to emerge as the legislation changes (for instance, the legislation on timber sales that changed from direct contracts to public procurement system "Prozorro" and then to commodity exchange, 'prompting' creation of new corrupt schemes to circumvent the legislation). It is unclear how the profits generated through corrupt schemes are divided. According to the expert opinion, it is presumed that some portion stays locally, while a certain amount is 'sent' to the higher hierarchical levels, as "were these schemes not centralised, they would not have existed". In addition, however, there are situations where a forester on-site decides to cut 'a bit more' for themselves.[913] The situation with illegal logging is also exacerbated by the 'general' corruption, not the one peculiar to the forestry, but affecting the law enforcement bodies and judiciary, helping perpetrators to escape justice.[914] Another expert identified the lack of punishment for corruption or

---

911 L11 (N), personal communication, September 6, 2022.

912 Bohdan Kuchenko, EPL, personal communication, September 29, 2022.

913 Yehor Hrynyk, UNCG, personal communication, September 27, 2022; Civil servant, F24 (A), State Forestry Agency, personal communication, September 19, 2022.

914 Yehor Hrynyk, UNCG, personal communication, September 27, 2022.

'weak punishment' among the key factors enabling corruption in forestry. It was noted that in cases when someone does bear the punishment for the corruption in forestry, these are mostly the forest workers, rather than the officials of the State Forest Agency or other high-ranking officials of governmental institutions.[915]

The investigative research, undertaken several years ago by the non-profit organisation Earthsight, reveals some of the intricacies of the corruption in forestry in Ukraine, including the Carpathian region, and the fact that the EU is the largest destination of the wood from Ukraine that has been harvested or traded illegally.[916] In particular, according to this report, the majority of the illegal timber harvesting in Ukraine is being undertaken by the governmental forestry enterprises in deliberate and systematic violation of legislative regulations. Moreover, nearly 60 per cent of logging (and mostly in the form of sanitary felling) occurs outside the limits established during the process of forest management. It is also noted that corruption accompanies various stages of forestry: harvesting, sale, processing and export of wood.[917] Importantly, this report attests to the fact that the EU Timber Regulation did not prevent the illegally-harvested wood in Ukraine from being exported to the EU and suggests several reasons for this, including the fact that this law concerns only companies appearing on the import documents (and not the 'middleman firms' that are used in practice), and the due diligence is reduced to the reliance on the FSC certification system, which itself has fundamental flows letting the forests where violations occur remain to be 'certified' and thus not being in a position to ensure legality. In fact, 90 per cent of forests in the Ukrainian Carpathians that are subordinate to the State Forest Agency are FSC-certified.[918]

In another study, it was suggested that the main obstacle to combating illegal logging (and wildlife crime) in the broader Danube-Carpathian region, including the Ukrainian Carpathians, is the implementation and enforcement of national legislation.[919]

915 Oksana Omelchuk, Ecodiya (Ecoaction), personal communication, September 28, 2022.
916 Earthsight, *Complicit In Corruption.*
917 Earthsight, *Complicit In Corruption*, 4–5.
918 Earthsight, *Complicit In Corruption*, 8.
919 Lynn Schlingemann et al., ed, *Combating Wildlife and Forest Crime in the Danube-Carpathian Region*
(UN Environment – Eurac Research – WWF, 2017) https://wwfint.awsassets.panda.org/downloads/combating_wildlife_and_forest_crime_in_the_danube_carpathian_region_report_2017_1.pdf, 7.

As ecologists acknowledge, the impact of deforestation in the Ukrainian Carpathians is immense, as it causes both habitat loss and disturbance of species. For instance, due to deforestation, lynx lose their habitat and have to move to different areas. Owls prefer to settle in the old forests, the logging of which, accordingly, destroys their habitat. Logging in the mid-mountain areas of the Carpathians may lead to a decline in the population of bird species such as hazel grouse and capercaillie. Deer are currently more prevalent in the higher altitudes of the Carpathians because the disturbance at lower levels, in particular, through logging, is significant.[920]

The illegal and unsustainable logging in the Ukrainian Carpathians at a present stage is particularly damaging for nature, as historically the region has already fallen prey to unsustainable logging and forest management: "Over the last three hundred years, most of the old Carpathian forests have been lost, and instead, the majority of forests have been artificially created; these forests resemble plantations, and consequently, a large number of living organisms that require an old forest for their existence are simply losing their habitat. Almost no virgin forests are left, and what remains of these is in the mountainous areas that are difficult to reach."[921]

Another major reason for the disturbance of species and the threat to the ecosystems is associated with the construction works (often related to the development of tourist infrastructure). The are two notorious cases of the plans on undertaking huge building projects in the biodiversity-rich areas of the Ukrainian Carpathians, and a legal battle on their protection. The first is the case of the Borzhava ridge, which is related to the plans on building the wind farm, and the second is the case of the Svydovets ridge, which is related to the plans on building a ski resort.

The crux of the Borzhava case is the attempt of a foreign investor to build a wind farm with a total capacity of 120 MW on a Carpathian ridge located in Transcarpathia, which is important for biodiversity and was designated as an Emerald Network site UA0000263 "Polonyna Borzhava". The environmental NGOs voiced their concern about such a project, especially after the EIA on this project was made publicly available. The case ended up in the courts, where NGOs have been asking to declare the Conclusion on the EIA (based on which the Transcarpathia State Administration considered implementation of the planned activity as feasible) as illegal and revoke

920 L11 (N), personal communication, September 6, 2022.
921 Yehor Hrynyk, UNCG, personal communication, September 27, 2022.

it.[922] In addition, two other series of cases emerged – the one on construction permits and another one on the change of land use designation and the leasing of land plots, as well as the annulment of lease agreements, both of which were decided in 2024 in a way favourable for the preservation of Borzhava's nature.[923]

Moreover, after the land plots for the construction of a wind power plant were allocated, the NGO "Ukrainian Nature Conservation Group" has used a complaint mechanism within the Bern Convention to make Standing Committee aware of the situation, which might constitute a threat to this Emerald site, important for bat and bird species, many of which are listed in the Annex II of the Bern Convention.[924]

In 2021, the report of the online advisory mission, commissioned by the Standing Committee, was prepared, based on which the Standing Committee adopted Recommendation No. 213 (2021). In the report, the experts found out that the development of this scale within the Emerald Network Site would "conflict with the requirements and spirit of the Bern Convention".[925] They analysed the numerous flaws of the EIA, suggested by the Ukrainian civil society, primarily related to the fact that the EIA failed to pay attention to these territories as the Emerald Network site and the necessary assessment of its features was not undertaken. The experts recognised among the most significant flows the impacts of the lack of attention to the avifauna resident within and nearby the site, and migratory

922 Olha Sushyk, "Legal Framework of Wildlife Protection on the Area of Natura 2000 (Emerald Network) on Wind Energy Site: Case of Ukraine," *Studia Iuridica Lublinensia* 30, no. 3 (16 September 2021): 219, https://doi.org/10.17951/sil.2021.30.3.207-225; Case №260/771/19, Case file number: К/990/26571/22; Date of entry into force: 10.08.2023 https://reyestr.court.gov.ua/Review/112757712.

923 Case №260/1058/19, Case file number: К/9901/25888/20, Date of entry into force: 24.04.2024 https://reyestr.court.gov.ua/Review/118599491; Case №907/801/20 Date of entry into force: 10.07.2024 https://reyestr.court.gov.ua/Review/120623796.

924 "Presumed threat to Emerald site "Polonina Borzhava" (UA0000263) from wind energy development," Case page, Bern Convention, accessed September 20, 2024, https://www.coe.int/en/web/bern-convention/-/presumed-threat-to-emerald-site-polonina-borzhava-ua0000263-from-wind-energy-development.

925 Lawrence Jones-Walters and Bernard Fleming, *Presumed threat to Emerald Network site "Polonina Borzhava" from wind energy development (UA0000263) (Ukraine)*, Report of the Online Advisory Mission, Complaint on stand-by No. 2018/01, T-PVS/Files(2021)77, (Strasbourg, 2021) https://rm.coe.int/0900001680a460ce, 4.

species, including raptors, cranes and storks, that are protected by the Bonn Convention.[926]

Based on this report, the Standing Committee of the Bern Convention issued a Recommendation addressed to the government of Ukraine. In this document, having considered Borzhava ridge and its surroundings as territories that "contain rare and endemic species and habitats as well as migratory species of European importance that are conservation priorities and which Ukraine has undertaken to protect under, among others, the Bern and Bonn Conventions", the Standing Committee recommended to cancel the plans on this windfarm or to repeat the EIA under different methodology; to initiate the creation of the nature reserve on this site; suggested nation-wide improvements to the practice of the EIA; and recommended steps to improve overall implementation of the Emerald Network in Ukraine.[927]

Another infamous case – the one on Svydovets massif and surrounding areas, concerns the threat of the construction of a massive ski resort. The plans for the construction of the large resort in the Svydovets massif became known to the public in 2016. The environmental activists fighting for the preservation of Svydovets massif have founded the Free Svydovets initiative, that has published numerous analytical materials explaining the value of this site, possible dangers for environment and local population arising from implementation of this project, and the intricacies of possible corrupt practices that drive action on this project, linked to the notorious oligarchical circles. It is also explained how, in addition to the plans for the future building of roads and development of ski resort infrastructure, the forests in this area have already been suffering for years from illegal and unsustainable logging, involving the destruction of the old-growth forests.[928]

---

926 Lawrence Jones-Walters and Bernard Fleming, *Presumed threat to Emerald Network site "Polonina Borzhava"*, 6, 9–10.

927 Standing Committee, *Recommendation No. 213 (2021) of the Standing Committee, adopted on 3rd December 2021, on the presumed threat to Emerald Network site "Polonina Borzhava" from wind energy development (UA0000263) (Ukraine)*, (Strasbourg, 2021) https://rm.coe.int/2021-rec-213e-polonina-borzhava/1680a4c2c4.

928 See "Svydovets," Initiative group "Free Svydovets", https://freesvydovets.org/en/; "Trees cannot scream: How unsustainability and illegality are destroying the forests of the Ukrainian Carpathians," Free Svydovets Group, 2021, Bruno Manser Fonds and European Cooperative Longo Maï, https://freesvydovets.org/en/; "The Great Carpathian Land Grab: How oligarchs are using Ukraine's war economy to get hold of one of Europe's last great wilderness areas," Bruno Manser Fonds, European

Some of the main concerns from the nature-protection and sustainability perspectives consist in the location, scale and operation of the Svydovets resort and two additional resorts: Bystrytsia and Turbat (the plans for which became known in 2021 and 2022). Together, this network of ski resorts will cover approximately 3.000 hectares of forests, meadows and rivers, out of which at least 1.270 hectares are forests, among which there are primeval, quasi-primeval and natural forests (with confirmed or pending protection status or without protection status). It will threaten at least 169 species of plants, invertebrates and vertebrates listed in the Red Data Book of Ukraine.[929] Svydovets is a part of the Emerald Network and covers 17 habitat types listed in Annex 1 of the Habitat Directive. It is noted that the "central part of the Svydovets mountain range and the upper part of the Chorna Tysa river are particularly important as biodiversity hotspots and wildlife corridors for the whole region". Interestingly, it was also noted that in this area, no single invasive alien species occurs.[930] Moreover, the planned development is located in close proximity to the UNESCO heritage site of ancient and primeval beech forests within the Ukrainian Carpathians.[931] The project will also encroach upon the community-owned agricultural lands used as pastures and hayfields that will be partly or fully privatised by the investors, depriving local communities of their livelihoods.[932] What is more, the jobs potentially generated by the ski resorts in this area, as the experience of Bukovel shows, will not necessarily be held by local people.[933] The example of Bukovel also illustrates the problems with water management, leading to water shortages and pollution resulting from a lack of wastewater treatment by the ski resort.[934]

The European Parliament, within the framework of implementation of the Association Agreement between the EU and Ukraine, drew Ukraine's attention to the detrimental plans on building the Svydovets resort, linked to illegal logging in the primeval forests, and urged Ukraine to fight these and invest in sustainable tourist infrastructure instead. In addition,

Cooperative Longo Maï and the Free Svydovets Group, April 2024, https://freesvydovets.org/wp-content/uploads/2024/04/Great_Carpathian_Land_Grab_Eng_web-1.pdf.

929 "The Great Carpathian Land Grab," Bruno Manser Fonds, 19.

930 "The Great Carpathian Land Grab," Bruno Manser Fonds, 12–13.

931 "The Great Carpathian Land Grab," Bruno Manser Fonds, 8 (map).

932 "The Great Carpathian Land Grab," Bruno Manser Fonds, 17.

933 "The Great Carpathian Land Grab," Bruno Manser Fonds, 21.

934 "The Great Carpathian Land Grab," Bruno Manser Fonds, 16.

it called on Ukraine to halt future environmental damage by enhancing transparency, due diligence, procedures like the EIA, and access to environmental information.[935] Unfortunately, no adequate reaction on behalf of the Ukrainian authorities followed.[936] The petition for creation of the protected area in Svydovets, namely, the landscape reserve of national importance, that was launched by several leading environmental NGOs in Ukraine in March 2023, and that quickly reached the necessary number of signatures to be reviewed by the authorities (25 thousand), also did not result in any governmental action on protection of this biodiversity-rich area.[937]

When it comes to the court proceedings related to the protection of Svydovets, in 2017, local residents filed a lawsuit against Tyachiv and Rakhiv District State Administrations concerning annulment of their decisions on the detailed territorial plan on the grounds of violation of the legal requirements on transparency and public participation. Since that time, the case has been heard in all instances, returned by the Supreme Court to the first instance, and then returned back to the Supreme Court. The appellate court supported the position of the District State Administrations. Ultimately, the Cassation Administrative Court within the Supreme Court, in the decision announced on October 9, 2024, annulled this decision and upheld the decision of the court of first instance (annulling the decisions of the Rakhiv and Tyachiv District State Administrations regarding the approval of the detailed plan for the Svydovets resort).[938] The key issues that had to be resolved by the Supreme Court concerned Articles 12 and 19 of the Law of Ukraine "On Regulation of Urban Planning Activities".[939]

Similarly to the Borzhava case, the case of Svydovets was also brought by the Ukrainian NGO to the attention of the Standing Committee of the

935 European Parliament resolution of 11 February 2021 on the implementation of the EU Association Agreement with Ukraine (2019/2202(INI)), European Parliament, https://www.europarl.europa.eu/doceo/document/TA-9-2021-0050_EN.html.

936 "The Great Carpathian Land Grab," Bruno Manser Fonds, 28.

937 "The Great Carpathian Land Grab," Bruno Manser Fonds, 50–51.

938 See "The Great Carpathian Land Grab," Bruno Manser Fonds, 48; "The Cassation Administrative Court has once again postponed the hearing of the case concerning the Svydovets resort," EPL, August 15, 2024 https://epl.org.ua/announces/kasatsijnyj-administratyvnyj-sud-znovu-vidklav-rozglyad-spravy-po-kurortu-svydovets/; "Judicial Protection of the Svydovets Particularly Valuable Massif," EPL, February 24, 2024, https://epl.org.ua/announces/sudovyj-zahyst-osoblyvo-tsinnogo-masyvu-svydovets/; "Today, the Supreme Court protected the picturesque mountain ranges from the mega-resort Svydovets," October 9, 2024, https://epl.org.ua/announces/sogodni-vs-zahystyv-malovnychi-girski-hrebty-vid-mega-kurortu-svydovets/.

939 "Judicial Protection of the Svydovets Particularly Valuable Massif".

Bern Convention as a complaint in 2019. As of 2024, this complaint remains on stand-by.[940] The most recent development of this case is the report by the government of Ukraine in August 2024, where the government asks to dismiss the case No 2018/1, explaining such a request by the fact that due to the war, "the development of a ski resort in Ukraine is not timely".[941] The Annex 1 to the governmental letter that addresses the situation with Svydovets states that the territories at issue are protected by the Laws "On the Red Data Book of Ukraine", "On Plant World", "On Animal World", and that the final documents of the EIA on the project have not been received. In addition, it is noted that SEA is not necessary for this project (as the law "On Strategic Environmental Assessment" was adopted in Ukraine after the project was initiated, and thus does not apply retrospectively).[942] Such a governmental report, however, looks at the least 'naïve' given the continued ongoing efforts of the investors to implement this project.

Experts generally note the potential risks for the biodiversity of the Ukrainian Carpathians related to uncontrolled and unsustainable tourism in various forms.[943] One category of such risks stems from the gaps in the urban planning legislation that, coupled with corruption, can lead to the building of hotels and resorts to the detriment of natural habitat.[944] Another category is related to transportation, including the building of roads and traffic load, leading to land erosion, particularly the so-called 'jeeping'.[945] Jeeping can be especially dangerous to the Carpathian newt, which lays eggs in puddles.[946]

---

940 "Alleged threats to the Emerald Network sites Skhidnyi Svydovets, Marmaroski ta Chyvchyno-Hryniavski Hory and Carpathian biosphere Reserve," Bern Convention, May 2018, https://www.coe.int/en/web/bern-convention/-/alleged-threats-to-the-emerald-network-sites-skhidnyi-svydovets-marmaroski-ta-chyvchyno-hryniavski-hory-and-carpathian-biosphere-reserve.

941 Ministry of Environmental Protection and Natural Resources of Ukraine, *Alleged threats to the Emerald Network sites Skhidnyi Svydovets, Marmaroski ta Chyvchyno Hryniavski Hory and Carpathian Biosphere Reserve 2018/05 (Ukraine)*, Report by the Government, T-PVS/Files(2024)60, (Strasbourg, 2024) https://rm.coe.int/files60-2024-ukraine-skhidnyi-svydovets-gov-report-2787-7062-5290-1/1680b15226.

942 Ministry of Environmental Protection and Natural Resources of Ukraine, *Alleged threats to the Emerald Network sites Skhidnyi Svydovets, Marmaroski ta Chyvchyno Hryniavski Hory and Carpathian Biosphere Reserve 2018/05 (Ukraine)*, Annex I.

943 Yehor Hrynyk, UNCG, personal communication, September 27, 2022.

944 Bohdan Kuchenko, EPL, personal communication, September 29, 2022.

945 L11 (N), personal communication, September 6, 2022.

946 Bohdan Kuchenko, EPL, personal communication, September 29, 2022.

Poaching is also among the threats to the biodiversity of forest ecosystems of the Ukrainian Carpathians. Poaching of large carnivores is a problem for all of the Carpathian countries.[947] According to the expert evaluations, the Ukrainian-Romanian border is one of the central poaching locations, where nearly half of the illegal killing of the brown bear in the Ukrainian Carpathians occurs (out of 15 bears that are estimated to be illegally killed on a yearly basis).[948]

In the documents accompanying plans on the conservation of lynx and brown bear of Ukraine, the assessment of the particular risks for these species is provided. For lynx, the key role is played by the availability of habitat, which is large massifs of natural forests. Moreover, their connectivity is important, not least as it is crucial for the subpopulations of lynx to be connected by the ecological corridors. The significant danger is posed by the development of road and rail infrastructure, which may lead to death by road accidents and to habitat fragmentation, creating barriers for migration. Poaching might also constitute a threat to lynx, including the use of snares and traps set to capture other species. Disturbance by mass logging in the Carpathians that generates noise, as well as frequent use of jeeps and quad bikes in the Carpathian highlands, negatively affects lynx, especially during the period of reproduction. Furthermore, the decline of populations of ungulates (roe deer and red deer), the main food base of lynx, due to climate change and hunting, is a significant factor limiting the population of lynx. The general conflict of interest between the conservation of lynx and forestry, hunting and agriculture sectors is an issue that has to be addressed with practical solutions for harmonious coexistence.[949]

Similar risks were identified for the populations of brown bear in the Ukrainian Carpathians. The intensive forest exploitation and recreational pressure lead to the transformation and degradation of the habitat of this species, in particular, by causing a decline in places suitable for den sites and a decline in the food base. Disturbance of the brown bear is also caused by massive berry and mushroom gathering in summer and noisy logging in winter. Habitat fragmentation, development of infrastructure,

947 Schlingemann, *Combating Wildlife and Forest Crime in the Danube-Carpathian Region*, 30.

948 Schlingemann, *Combating Wildlife and Forest Crime in the Danube-Carpathian Region*, 32.

949 "On Approval of the Action Plan for the Conservation of the Eurasian lynx (*Lynx lynx* L.) in Ukraine," Order of the Ministry of Environmental Protection, Annex, 14–19.

low subpopulation size, poaching, and conflict between the purposes of conservation and other economic activities similarly constitute a threat to the brown bear.[950]

Climate change can potentially constitute a significant threat to the biodiversity of forest ecosystems of the Ukrainian Carpathians. Biodiversity is recognised in the official Ukrainian documents as one of the sectors affected by climate change. Out of its components, the mountainous ecosystems and species of the Carpathians, as well as forest ecosystems (those affected by the change in hydrological regime, those damaged by the spread of pests and diseases or by windfalls) belong to the category of the most vulnerable ecosystems.[951] In part on forests and climate change, in the legislative acts, it is noted that the proportion of weakened and drying trees has increased, particularly among secondary spruce forests in the Carpathians. The main negative impact of climate change on forests in Ukraine is related to the shrinking of forest biodiversity and a decrease in the productivity of forest ecosystems and enterprises. Therefore, the objectives of assessing the risks and vulnerabilities of forestry to climate change include the protective aspect of "preserving the ecosystem functions and biodiversity of forest ecosystems" and a commercial aspect of the preservation of the value of forests as a source of timber.[952]

It was noted by the expert in 2022 that no measures on climate change adaptation of the forests of the Ukrainian Carpathians have been undertaken or planned.[953] The Methodological recommendations adopted in 2023 note that according to the assessment of the FAO, the priorities of

950 "On Approval of the Action Plan for the Conservation of the Brown Bear (*Ursus arctos* L.) in Ukraine," Order of the Ministry of Environmental Protection, Annex, 14–15.

951 Strategy for Environmental Safety and Climate Change Adaptation for the Period until 2030, approved by the Order of the Cabinet of Ministers of Ukraine (2021), Chapter II; Methodological Recommendations for Assessing Risks and Vulnerability of Socio-Economic Sectors and Natural Components to Climate Change, approved by the Order of the Ministry of Environmental Protection No. 386, Document v0386926-23, (June 3, 2023) https://zakon.rada.gov.ua/rada/show/v0386926-23#Text, 53.

952 Strategy for Environmental Safety and Climate Change Adaptation for the Period until 2030, approved by the Order of the Cabinet of Ministers of Ukraine (2021), Chapter II; Methodological Recommendations for Assessing Risks and Vulnerability of Socio-Economic Sectors and Natural Components to Climate Change, approved by the Order of the Ministry of Environmental Protection (2023), 55–56.

953 Oksana Omelchuk, Ecodiya (Ecoaction), personal communication, September 28, 2022.

the Ukrainian forest sector on adaptation to climate change shall include certification of forests, an increase in forest cover, a change in planting schedules, minimising areas of monoculture forests and creation of mixed and structurally complex forest stands.[954]

Invasive alien species constitute a rising problem for the biodiversity of the forest ecosystems of the Ukrainian Carpathians, partly due to climate change and partly due to forestry operations. For instance, the employee of the natural park "Hutsulshchyna" reported that the red oak (*Quercus rubra*) poses a threat to local ecosystems, as it completely occupies the area that it can take, and underneath it there is a dead cover — its leaves hardly decompose, as there are no local bacteria that can effectively break it down.[955] The representative of the forestry sector in Ivano-Frankivsk region stated, in contrast, that the invasive species, including the red oak, are present in the Ukrainian Carpathians, but do not constitute a problem.[956] In 2023, there was an attempt to regulate the use of invasive alien species in the process of forest regeneration, when the Ministry of Environmental Protection adopted a list of species that shall not be used during forest regeneration based on the Cabinet of Ministers of Ukraine Resolution No. 1410 of December 20, 2022, "On Amendments to the Rules of Forest Reproduction". This document was celebrated by the environmental NGOs as a milestone achievement. However, the joy was premature, as, weirdly enough, based on the notification of the State Regulatory Service of Ukraine and the letter from the Ministry of Justice in September 2023, in October 2023, the Ministry of Environmental Protection cancelled this list.[957] Such a course of action is explained by the pressure from the forestry sector. In summer 2023, the WWF-Ukraine published a material in support of the list at issue, refuting the most manipulative statements and mentioning that in the circles of the forest sector, the attempts to cancel this list continue to

954 Methodological Recommendations for Assessing Risks and Vulnerability of Socio-Economic Sectors and Natural Components to Climate Change, approved by the Order of the Ministry of Environmental Protection (2023), 59.

955 L11 (N), personal communication, September 6, 2022.

956 F16 (A), personal communication, September 7, 2022.

957 "On Approval of the List of Invasive Tree Species with a High Capacity for Uncontrolled Spread, Prohibited for Use in Forest Reproduction Processes," Order of the Ministry of Environmental Protection No. 184, Document z0641–23 (April 3, 2023), not in force since October 19, 2023, https://zakon.rada.gov.ua/laws/show/z0641-23#Text.

circulate.[958] The "Society of Foresters of Ukraine" boasted on its webpage its victory over the cancellation of the list of invasive species, based on its appeal to the State Regulatory Service of Ukraine.[959]

A separate category of risks for the biodiversity of the forest ecosystems of the Ukrainian Carpathians might be broadly named 'institutional risks'. This category is partly related to the corruption risks and the risks related to construction and tourism. However, it also includes other institutional tensions or weaknesses undermining the efforts on biodiversity conservation. For instance, during the interviews, it became clear that there is little to no communication between different national parks in the Ukrainian Carpathians. This obviously hinders the exchange of experience, such as knowledge-sharing on good practices applied in the objects of the NRF. It was noted, however, that recently the situation with communication has somewhat improved thanks to the cooperation within the project on the protection of the Carpathian primeval forests.[960]

The greater problem for natural parks lies, however, in the tensions with other forest users, including the state forestry enterprises, and is related to the forest ownership. In the interviews with the employees of the national natural park "Hutsulshchyna", for instance, it was reported that certain tensions exist between the powers of the national natural park, the forest sector, and the local territorial community. Some territories belonging to the national natural park are the 'territories without withdrawal from regular users', where forestry enterprises continue to operate. The task of forestry enterprises is to generate profits by felling the forests, which conflicts with the natural park's purpose of protecting the forests. For instance, when the natural park's employees identify the areas of old-growth forests seeking their protection, the forestry enterprises may take the position of not confirming the status of these forests, so that the forestry sector may continue 'normal' logging operations. Moreover, recently, the forestry enterprises stopped seeking the natural park's approval for the felling of

958 "We support the Ministry of Environmental Protection's order approving the list of invasive tree species prohibited in forest reproduction," WWF-Ukraine, July 27, 2023, https://www.wwf.mg/?11403791/pproval-of-a-list-of-invasive-tree-species.

959 "We are being thanked for the victory: the Ministry of Environmental Protection's order on the list of invasive tree species prohibited for use has been repealed," Society of Foresters of Ukraine, October 27, 2023, https://tlu.kiev.ua/pro-nas/novini-zakhodi/novina/article/nam-djakujut-za-peremogu-vtrativ-chinnist-nakaz-mindovkillja-pro-perelik-invaziinikh-vidiv-derev-zabo.html.

960 L11 (N), personal communication, September 6, 2022.

trees, even though this is a legislative requirement. They created their own scientific-technical council, comprising loyal employees, so that there are almost no nature protection limitations on logging. In theory, the actions of forestry enterprises could be overseen by departments of the regional administration, but in practice, there is little influence and restrictions on the activities of the forestry enterprises.[961] The experts from the NGOs note that the State Forest Agency also has competencies for taking care of the forest, however, its economic function clearly predominates.[962] In addition, there seems to be a competition for profit from tourist infrastructure, as it was also reported that the recreational facility that the natural park creates is immediately subject to encroachment attempts.[963]

The NRF sites face general issues with land ownership, as they usually do not have state acts for all the land. Accordingly, there are problems with boundaries of the natural park with both forestry enterprises and individual landowners.[964] Such a risk is acknowledged in the Strategy on nature protection until 2030, where it is stated that the "absence of legally established boundaries for protected areas and objects on the ground leads to violations of the requirements of the protected regime".[965]

In the governmental publications, the following risks related to the governance of the NRF are identified: ineffective system of state governance in this field, insufficient control over compliance with nature protection legislation and lack of inevitability of punishment for its violation, insufficient funding of measures on protection of the NRF, biological and landscape diversity, and insufficient realization of the recreational potential of the NRF.[966] Furthermore, the issues spotted during the "Support to Nature Protected Areas in Ukraine" project, include the poor quality of the management plans and poor conservation management, absence of knowledge on ecosystem services, absence or low quality of equipment and infrastructure, insufficient know-how on participatory approaches and interaction

961 L11 (N), personal communication, September 6, 2022.
962 Oksana Omelchuk, Ecodiya (Ecoaction), personal communication, September 28, 2022.
963 L11 (N), personal communication, September 6, 2022.
964 L11 (N), personal communication, September 6, 2022.
965 The Fundamental Principles (Strategy) of the State Environmental Policy of Ukraine for the Period until 2030, Section I.
966 "Management of Protected Areas," Ministry of Environmental Protection of Ukraine.

with the local stakeholders, and low awareness about cultural heritage both inside and outside the protected areas.[967]

Moreover, there are clear differences in ethical stances towards biodiversity protection among the main actors in this sphere. The interview with the employee of the national nature park demonstrates that the difference in attitudes is real, and might create obstacles for nature protection and pose a threat to activists. It was reported that the forestry sector employees perceive forests as merely 'raw material'. For example, on a question on identification of rare species, it was mentioned that the black stork was spotted on the territory of park, however no nest was identified, with addition that "even if we did find nest, we would need to keep it less publicized, as the forestry enterprise might intentionally destroy it [not to apply the restrictions of logging activities according to the legislation]". The conflict of nature protection and forestry activities was also illustrated by the following experience of the nature park employee "when we set up the camera traps and saw animals there where logging was taking place, I ran away to avoid being seen and run over [by logging equipment]".[968]

An expert from the NGO, while answering the question on perception of forests, noted problematic stance of nature protection as such in comparison with other goals, pointing out that such a situation complicates public dialogue on forestry: "unfortunately, the nature protection is currently in the opposition; when you say [to the people working in forest sector including civil servants] that you are from an environmental organization, you are immediately perceived as an opponent".[969] It was added that on the one hand, foresters claim to care about the forest, but it mostly boils down to 'plantations' and extensive logging. The NGOs try to explain the interconnectedness of factors, the fact that because the forest as a 'plantation' is weak, there are numerous fires, pest infestations, and susceptibility to temperature increases. However, such explanations are often faced with scepticism.[970]

967 "Selected PAs have the necessary planning documents for their development," Support to Nature Protected Areas in Ukraine, accessed September 20, 2024, https://snpa.in.ua/en/english-diyalnist-proektu/diyalnist-proektu-1/.

968 L11 (N), personal communication, September 6, 2022.

969 Oksana Omelchuk, Ecodiya (Ecoaction), personal communication, September 28, 2022.

970 Oksana Omelchuk, Ecodiya (Ecoaction), personal communication, September 28, 2022.

Another expert shared a similar observation, additionally noting the discrepancy between the values declared in the legislation and the real-life practice in the forestry sector. It was noted, that the Forest Code characterises forest as an ecosystem that performs numerous functions, where its role as a 'source of timber' is mentioned only towards the end, but if the legislation on forestry is taken as a whole, the fact that a forest is a source of timber is "given a top priority". The same applies to foresters, who, "when asked about their perception of forests, may say that a forest is, in the first instance, an ecosystem, but at the same time (somewhat cynically and profit-orientedly), every forester can easily evaluate any area in terms of the value of timber. There is a significant difference between what is declared and what is implemented."[971] This statement corresponds to the result from the interviews with the foresters, who, when asked about their perception of forests as either a resource or an ecosystem, chose the latter option.[972] Overall, the Carpathians are considered to constitute one of the frontlines of the fight between profit maximisation and nature protection in Ukraine. The aim of profit-making (whether legal or illegal) often outweighs all the other considerations of forest management to the detriment of biodiversity.[973]

The new major risk for the forest biodiversity of the Ukrainian Carpathians is the Russian war of aggression – the international armed conflict that started in 2014 with the occupation of Crimea and turned on 24th of February 2022 from the military action localised the eastern regions of Ukraine into the full-scale war spreading to the whole territory of Ukraine. Although the major battlefields of the war of 2014 – 2024 are located relatively far away from the Carpathian Mountains, this war nevertheless influences their forest ecosystems. On the occasion of the Carpathian Ministerial Conference in 2022, the Ministerial Declaration was issued that took account of the "Russian military aggression in Ukraine and its negative ecological, socio-economic and humanitarian consequences for the Carpathian region" based on the report on the impact of war on the natural environment of the Carpathians in Ukraine. The Ministers of the Carpathian states expressed

---

971 Yehor Hrynyk, UNCG, personal communication, September 27, 2022.

972 Forest sector employee F17, personal communication, September 8, 2022.

973 Cf. Kateryna Norenko, Petro Testov and Oleksiy Vasyliuk, *Forest territories for wild nature: new policy of forest management* (Kyiv: EPL, 2018), http://epl.org.ua/wp-content/uploads/2018/07/Green-paper_forests_ENG_cover.pdf, 6.

their willingness to assist Ukraine in addressing the direct and indirect impacts of the war on the Carpathians.[974]

The direct physical destruction in the Carpathian region associated with war has been low, limited by some instances of long-range missile shelling.[975] Nevertheless, the impact of war on the Ukrainian Carpathians has been significant and includes at least increased harvesting, pressure on the nature protecting institutions, and limitations on the actions of civil society. Namely, there is a tendency in increase of the harvesting of wood both for the needs of firewood by the local population and for building the trenches at the frontline. Even though the Carpathians are located relatively far away from the frontlines, their forests constitute an important source of wood for the trenches due to the destruction and mining of forests in the eastern part of Ukraine. Moreover, the export of Ukraine's wood to the EU continues, and given the EU sanctions against the Russian Federation, the demand for Ukraine's wood, in particular, the one coming from the Ukrainian Carpathians located directly at the border with the EU, has increased in recent years.[976]

When it comes to lifting the restrictions on logging due to war, the so-called 'silence season' – legal prohibition of logging during reproduction of wildlife – has been halted since spring 2022.[977] It is, however, explained by the authorities that the cancellation of the 'silence season' does not affect the mountain fir-beech forests of the Ukrainian Carpathians and the forests

974 Carpathian Ministerial Conference, *Ministerial Declaration of the Carpathian Convention on the impact of war on the environment in Ukraine and the need for cooperation and assistance* (Rzeszów, November 2022), http://www.carpathianconvention.org/tl_files/carpathiancon/Downloads/03%20Meetings%20and%20Events/Others/Carpathian%20Ministerial%20Conference/Carpathian%20Ministerial%20Declaration_impact%20of%20war%20on%20Ukraine%20and%20the%20need%20for%20cooperation_FINAL.pdf.

975 Department of Nature Conservation, *Impact of war on natural environment of the Carpathians in Ukraine*, 46.

976 See Department of Nature Conservation, *Impact of war on natural environment of the Carpathians in Ukraine*, 46; Valeria Kolodezhna, "Protecting the environment in times of war: An interview with environmentalist Yehor Hrynyk," *UWEC*, 14 (2023): 33–37, https://uwecworkgroup.info/protecting-the-environment-in-times-of-war-an-interview-with-environmentalist-yehor-hrynyk/.

977 "Svydovets 2023: Fighting for Wildlife Amid the War," Free Svydovets Initiative Group, 2023, https://freesvydovets.org/wp-content/uploads/2023/02/svydovets2023_en_compressed.pdf, 7.

within the NRF.[978] In 2023, the obligation to conduct biological studies when preparing forest management plans was suspended.[979] It has also become easier to convert forest lands into other land uses like agriculture or construction.[980] Moreover, there was a legislative draft on cancelling restrictions on sanitary logging, which was naturally criticised by the environmental NGOs.[981]

Furthermore, for the administrations of the NRF sites located in the Carpathians the war means decrease in funding from the central state budget, decline in revenues from paid services of these entities, accommodation of the internally displaced persons at the expense of the administrations of protected areas, donation of vehicles and equipment for the needs of the Armed Forces of Ukraine and absence of some of the employees of the NRF administration due to their drafting or voluntary military service.[982]

For the civil society activists, the war also means severe restrictions on nature-protection activities, including limited access to information, such as information on logging permits and planned sanitary logging, forest maps, cadastre maps and materials on the EIA.[983] The imposition of martial law

978 "Explanation Regarding the "Quiet Season" During Martial Law," State Forest Resources Agency of Ukraine, April 4, 2022, https://forest.gov.ua/news/rozyasnennya-shchodo-sezonu-tishi-u-period-voyennogo-stanu.

979 "The Great Carpathian Land Grab," Bruno Manser Fonds, 14; "The Cabinet of Ministers believes that biological research in the forest is not necessary!" UNCG, February 2, 2023, https://uncg.org.ua/biolohichni-doslidzhennia-v-lisi/.

980 "The Great Carpathian Land Grab," Bruno Manser Fonds, 14; Yehor Hrynyk, Kateryna Harbarchuk, and Petro Tiestov, "Biodiversity in the rear of Ukraine: What has changed in nature protection in 2022–23? (UNCG, November 2023), https://uncg.org.ua/en/wp-content/uploads/2023/11/EN_compressed.pdf.

981 Yehor Hrynyk, UNCG, personal communication, September 27, 2022; Yuliia Hordiienko "The Threat to Ukrainian Forests Amid War: Ukraine Eases Logging Rules in the Carpathians," Misto vechirne, May 22, 2022, https://mistovechirne.in.ua/zagroza-ukrayinskym-lisam-v-umovah-viyny-v-ukrayini-sproshchuyut-pravyla-rubok-v-karpatah; "WWF-Ukraine does not support draft law 9516, which contradicts Ukraine's European integration commitments," WWF-Ukraine, March 13, 2024, https://www.wwf.mg/?13182666/WWF-Ukraine-does-not-support-draft-law-9516-which-contradicts-Ukraines-European-integration-commitments.

982 Department of Nature Conservation, *Impact of war on natural environment of the Carpathians in Ukraine*, 46; and in more detail 47–58.

983 "Svydovets 2023: Fighting for Wildlife Amid the War," 7; "The Great Carpathian Land Grab," Bruno Manser Fonds, 14; "Explanation for the Public," Ministry of Environmental Protection of Ukraine, accessed September 20, 2024, https://mepr.gov.ua/diyalnist/otsinka-vplyvu-na-dovkillya/roz-yasnennya-predstavnykam-gromadskosti/.

also leads to the prohibition of all forms of protests and rallies that are important tools for manifesting the position of civil society in environmental matters. Moreover, some of the environmental activists joined the Armed Forces of Ukraine and the attention of civil society as such is focused on the war itself (overlooking other areas such as continued illegal logging or developmental projects like Svydovets that potentially violate both domestic legislation and international obligations of Ukraine).[984] Furthermore, due to the war, physical access to some of the forests, in particular in border areas, was limited for civil society.[985]

Conclusions to Chapter 2

The forests of the Carpathian ecoregion, some of which belong to the most preserved natural forests of Europe, host a wide variety of species. Ukraine's share in the Carpathian ecoregion, being relatively small numerically, is important for the forest biodiversity of this region.

Within Ukraine, the Carpathians are situated in four administrative regions, mainly in Transcarpathia and Ivano-Frankivsk regions. From the economic perspective, the settlements in the Carpathian region experience a relatively low level of economic development and are often characterised as forest-dependent communities, relying on both logging and other uses of the forest for their subsistence. The society in the Ukrainian Carpathian region is characterised by a high level of religiosity with Christianity as a dominant religion (mostly the Ukrainian Greek-Catholic Church and the Orthodox Church of Ukraine). However, the connection between caring for the environment and Christianity often remains unclear (except for the successful initiative to reduce plastic in cemeteries, promoted by the Church).

Since Ukraine's independence and ratification of the CBD, several attempts to create strategic documents on biodiversity protection have been undertaken; however, as of 2024, there is no comprehensive national biodiversity strategy or regional biodiversity strategies. Soon after adoption of the concept on biodiversity protection in 1997, based on which the relevant programme was to be adopted, the state policy on biodiversity in Ukraine

984 "The Great Carpathian Land Grab," Bruno Manser Fonds, 14.

985 "The Great Carpathian Land Grab," Bruno Manser Fonds, 15; Mariana Rusyn, "In Transcarpathia it has been forbidden to visit forests," July 21, 2023, Suspilne Uzhhorod, https://suspilne.media/534129-na-zakarpatti-zaboronili-vidviduvati-lisi-2/.

switched from the creation of a separate course of action focused on biodiversity to the subordination of the issue of biodiversity protection to the task of formation of the ecological network in Ukraine. Based on the next conceptual document focused on biodiversity and covering a significant period of 2005 – 2025, the separate programme on biodiversity also should have been created, however, this action has not been implemented yet.

In recent years, the absence of a biodiversity strategy was somewhat mitigated by the adoption of the general strategy on environmental protection and accompanying action plan, both of which contain strategic points on biodiversity. For the forests specifically, there is a separate strategic document that elaborates on the protection of biodiversity within all categories of forests, which covers commercially exploited forests. Furthermore, for the Carpathian region within Ukraine specifically, there are further specific strategic documents, concepts, or action plans on the implementation of the Carpathian convention, on the development of the Carpathian region, on the development of mountainous territories, and on the protection of the beech forest ecosystems within the relevant UNESCO heritage sites. Each of the four Carpathian regions within Ukraine has adopted regional strategies that concern the implementation of certain aspects of the nationwide legislation on environmental protection. Cross-border cooperation of Ukraine with the neighbouring states also includes preservation of the Carpathian forests. In addition, sectoral strategies in the areas of climate change, transport, tourism, and urban planning directly or indirectly aim to enhance biodiversity protection of the forest ecosystems of the Ukrainian Carpathians.

The need for the creation of the comprehensive national biodiversity strategy, however, remains, as is the need for further integration of biodiversity protection into all spheres of economic activity in line with the principle of integration.

The legislative norms on biodiversity protection that either explicitly or implicitly incorporate this notion are fragmented and complex. The general framework of nature protection in Ukraine is outlined in the Law "On Environmental Protection" adopted before the CBD. The protection of biodiversity by means of the creation of protected areas in their varied forms and legal regimes is regulated mainly by the Law "On Nature Reserve Fund". Protection of the flora is addressed by the Law "On Plant World" and the Green Data Book of Ukraine. The fauna species enjoy the protection based on the Law "On Animal World," and for some Carpathian species, particularly lynx, brown bear, and bison, separate action plans have been adopted. The endangered species of both flora and fauna are also protected by listing them in the Red Data Book of Ukraine. These laws often overlap, complement one another and apply cumulatively. For instance, the protection of the animal world within the NRF sites is regulated by both the law "On Animal World" and "On Nature Reserve Fund of Ukraine". Some of them also express the principle of integration, such as the Law "On Plant World," which requires attention to the plant world in the course of economic activities. Even greater role of integration of biodiversity protection in economic activities is played by the relatively recently adopted laws on the EIA and the SEA, requiring assessment of impact on biodiversity concerning planning of some developmental activities or documents of state planning. For the forest biodiversity, particularly promising recent legislative changes include the possibility of designation of the "protected areas to preserve biodiversity in forests" based on the Red Data Book.

The legislation on forestry is, on the one hand, supposed to be codified by the Forest Code of Ukraine, but on the other hand, comprises many more laws and regulations, some of which establish a particular regime for the forest ecosystems in the Ukrainian Carpathians. In recent years, norms on forestry were amended to incorporate the concern of biodiversity protection.

The main procedure for taking biodiversity into account in commercial forestry activities is the procedure for forest organisation (management), undertaken every 10 or 20 years. For particularly valuable forests, the compartment method of this procedure is used. The inclusion of nature protection into this procedure partly relies on information on the location of flora and fauna species that has to be obtained from the Ministry of Environmental Protection, and partly has to be collected proactively. The identification of the Red Data Book species during this procedure may lead to the designation of new NRF sites or the enlargement of the environmental network. Importantly, it is stated that not only actions directly aimed at nature protection, but all planned forestry activities shall contribute to biodiversity conservation.

The seemingly important tool for biodiversity protection in forests is creation of protective zones to preserve biodiversity in forests serving the aim of protecting rare and endangered species including those listed in local lists, Red Data Book of Ukraine and protected by international treaties, breeding grounds of wild animals, and the oldest or notable trees and their groups. Creation of such zones limits logging, such as by exempting these areas from clear-cutting and the final stage of the gradual felling. Other tools for protecting biodiversity in forestry include the creation and preservation of the valuable gene fund, the prevention of genetic contamination of the gene pools of indigenous species and the prevention of invasions of introduced species into natural ecosystems, including during forest regeneration activities.

Moreover, during all types of timber harvesting, felling or damaging of the rare and endangered species of trees and shrubs listed in the Red Data Book of Ukraine, of seed and plus trees, of hollow and oldest trees, and of trees with the nests of the rare bird species enlisted in the Red Data Book of Ukraine are not permitted.

The special norms for Carpathian forests include separate rules on the main-use logging, referring to the ecosystem approach and close-to-nature forestry, the norms on prohibition of clear-cutting in the mountain fir-beech forests of the Carpathian region, and special provisions in the Rules for Improving the Quality Composition of Forests.

The following groups of actors shape biodiversity protection in the region: state bodies and local self-government, non-governmental organisations, the business sector and individuals. Two primary state bodies are the Ministry of Environmental Protection and the State Forestry Agency. The administrations of the NRF sites, subordinate to the Ministry of Environmental Protection, undertake a wide range of actions on biodiversity protection, including keeping the comprehensive Chronicles of Nature book. The State Forestry Agency is the single largest forest user in Ukraine. According to the recent reorganisation, the enterprise "Forests of Ukraine" was created in place of numerous smaller forestry enterprises, and most of the Carpathian forests are governed by the Western Interregional Administration of Forestry and Hunting. Regional departments of ecology and natural resources and local self-governing bodies also have certain powers on biodiversity protection, and greater clarity in their delimitation is required. The main governmental body in charge of ensuring compliance with the environmental legislation is SEI, but other law enforcement agencies may also be important. The national and international NGOs in Ukraine are one of the leading driving forces of the development of the biodiversity-protection legislation in Ukraine and monitoring compliance with it. The businesses and individuals may both encourage or hinder biodiversity protection.

Some of the specific issues that are particularly important for protecting forest biodiversity of the Ukrainian Carpathians include monitoring, creation of the ecological network and preservation of the old-growth forests.

Even though the attempts to create a system of environmental monitoring, including biodiversity monitoring, have been undertaken in Ukraine for over 25 years, and some data is being collected, the reform is still needed to ensure adequate comprehensive monitoring, which can serve as a basis for decision-making. The creation of the ecological network in Ukraine is a similarly lengthy process, where 15 years have passed between the adoption of the program for the formation of this network and the procedure for the inclusion of territories into it. The additional important issue is the creation of the Emerald network in Ukraine, which, on the one hand, could be created based on the general Ukrainian legislation on ecological network, but the functioning of which will benefit from the specific law that was developed several years ago but has not been adopted yet. Despite the absence of such a law, the Emerald network sites were nominated by Ukraine and officially adopted by the Standing Committee of the Bern Convention. The creation and operation of the Emerald network in Ukraine also serve the purpose of implementing obligations stipulated in the Association Agreement between the EU and Ukraine. The identification, designation, and special protection of the old-growth forests (primeval, quasi-primeval and natural forests) in the Ukrainian Carpathians was invigorated by the implementation of the Carpathian Convention and the action of the NGOs. The protection of these forests from logging is crucial for biodiversity conservation.

The category of risks, threats, and challenges to the biodiversity protection of the Ukrainian Carpathians is varied. It is formed by the globally-identified risks, such as habitat loss, overexploitation, climate change, and invasive species, which have clear local manifestations in the Ukrainian Carpathians, as well as by the peculiarities of functioning of the forestry sector and the NRF sites in Ukraine, and the Russian war of aggression, which significantly affects protection of biodiversity in the Ukrainian Carpathians (even though Carpathian region is located relatively far away from the battlefield and have been almost spared from the direct hitting of the missiles). Some of the most acute direct threats to biodiversity in the forest ecosystems of the Ukrainian Carpathians include illegal or unsustainable logging, often linked to corruption, and unsustainable developmental plans, such as plans on building ski resorts or wind farms in biodiversity-rich areas. In addition, climate change and the spread of invasive alien species belong to the rising threats. Moreover, there are tensions and differences in the perception of forests among the key actors responsible for biodiversity protection. All these factors taken together lead to the conclusion that the biodiversity of the forest ecosystems of the Ukrainian Carpathians is under acute threat.

CHAPTER 3. THE OPPORTUNITIES FOR THE BIODIVERSITY PROTECTION IN THE FOREST ECOSYSTEMS OF THE UKRAINIAN CARPATHIANS AT THE INTERSECTION OF LAW, ETHICS, AND POLICY

3.1. Implementation of the international obligations of Ukraine according to the key biodiversity treaties

Implementation of the biodiversity treaties, ratified by Ukraine, is an ongoing process. As shown in Chapter 2, the process of the development of the nature protection legislation and norms on forestry that would incorporate concern for biodiversity was often significantly delayed. For instance, the identification of the areas of special conservation interest for the purpose of creation of the ecological network *inter alia* based on the Bern Convention was initially planned for the period of 2001 – 2005, and while the latest list of the Emerald network sites in Ukraine was adopted in 2021, the laws making this network fully operational were not adopted.[986]

In recent years, especially after the 2013 – 2014 Revolution of Dignity, Ukraine witnessed some milestone developments on the incorporation of biodiversity concerns into its legislation. Most of the biodiversity protection tools and mechanisms described in Chapter 2 were not known to Ukrainian legislation before 2013, and their introduction is to a large extent directly motivated by the requirements of the Association Agreement between the EU and Ukraine. Some of the key latest achievements serving the purpose of implementation of the international obligations on biodiversity protection include the procedures of the EIA and SEA, the provisions on primeval, quasi-primeval and natural forests as well as general development of the legislation on forestry with a view to allow for the integration of biodiversity protection into all types of forestry activities.

986 The latest list of the Emerald network sites nominated by Ukraine was adopted by the Standing committee of the Bern Convention in the end of 2021, while the law that would directly regulate legal status of the Emerald network in Ukraine has not been adopted yet (as of December 2024), see subchapter 2.4.2.

The full spectrum of implementation of the international obligations of Ukraine with respect to biodiversity of the forest ecosystem of the Ukrainian Carpathians over the years since the ratification of relevant international conventions described in Chapter 1 could be assessed by means of analysing national reports submitted to the institutional mechanisms of these biodiversity treaties. Based on the analysis of the provisions of the biodiversity treaties undertaken in Chapter 1, it is suggested that the current state of the implementation of international obligations of Ukraine with respect to biodiversity of the Carpathian forests could be evaluated by assessing the implementation of the norms of the CBD as an 'umbrella convention' as well as of the Bern Convention, and Carpathian Convention along with the Protocol on Biodiversity, addressing regional and subregional levels.

Within the CBD mechanism, Ukraine submitted six national reports, the latest of which was prepared in 2018.[987] The implementation of the CBD by Ukraine as of 2017 was also assessed by non-governmental Ukrainian experts.[988] The progress on implementation of the CBD during 2013 – 2017 described in the sixth national report of Ukraine, is explained through the implementation of the "The Strategy of State Environmental Policy of Ukraine until 2020" (2010), which is regarded as the "officially adopted NBSAP" incorporating directly or indirectly all of the Aichi Biodiversity Targets, and which precedes the current Strategy until 2030.[989] The achievements in advancing implementation of the Strategy and hence the CBD, include an increase in the square of protected areas generally, and an increase in the number of sites within the UNESCO World Heritage property "Ancient and Primeval Beech Forests of the Carpathians and Other Regions of Europe", adoption by the Standing Committee of the Bern Convention of 271 sites of the Emerald Network in 2017 (extended in 2021), an increase in area of forests certified by the FSC, ongoing work on identifying the primeval forests, enaction of the programme on monitoring of the black stork, support of the projects on summarizing data on rare species and priority species identified by the Bern Convention, creation of centres for environmental education as well as a gradual increase of state budget

987 *Sixth National Report of Ukraine on the Implementation of the Convention on Biological Diversity.*

988 See Vasyliuk, *The Status of Reflection in Ukraine's Programmatic Documents and the Implementation of the Provisions of the UN Convention on Biological Diversity.*

989 *Sixth National Report of Ukraine on the Implementation of the Convention on Biological Diversity*, 115.

funding for environment. One of the main problems with the assessment of the situation of biodiversity protection, identified in this report, is the weakness of the monitoring mechanisms.[990]

The scholarly assessment of the implementation of the CBD in Ukraine mentions three issues among the key problems with its implementation. One of them, noted also in the national report described above, is the lack of monitoring of biodiversity. Another issue is the lack of integration of the CBD into all areas of life, which accordingly leads to a lack of action on biodiversity protection. The third issue is the fact that the legislation and actions on biodiversity in Ukraine often target consequences and not the root causes of the problems.[991]

What is additionally suggested by the Ukrainian experts as an effective tool for increasing attention to biodiversity and enhancing its protection is the monetary evaluation of the ecosystem services. In particular, it is suggested to develop a methodology for the valuation of biodiversity, based on the market assessment of the value of ecosystem services and potential damages from losses, as well as to develop the rates of fees for calculating the amount of compensation for damages, taking into account the ecosystem effect of the disturbance of biotic territories and the ecosystem integrity of objects.[992]

One of the basic obligations under the CBD, closely linked to the implementation of all other obligations, is the one under Article 6 concerning national strategies and plans as well as cross-sectoral integration of biodiversity conservation and sustainable use. In Ukraine, in terms of the nationwide strategic documents dedicated specifically to biodiversity, there is currently only the 1998 Concept of the Conservation of Biological Diversity. In recent years, this situation was mitigated by the adoption of the general Strategy of the State Environmental Policy of Ukraine for the Period until 2030 and the accompanying Action Plan. These documents might serve as a provisional substitution of the separate strategic document on biodiversity, but they also envisage the creation of the strategic document on biodiversity in line with the post-2021 global biodiversity framework.[993] The implementation

990 *Sixth National Report of Ukraine on the Implementation of the Convention on Biological Diversity*, 116–117.

991 Vasyliuk, *The Status of Reflection in Ukraine's Programmatic Documents and the Implementation of the Provisions of the UN Convention on Biological Diversity*, 26

992 Vasyliuk, *The Status of Reflection in Ukraine's Programmatic Documents and the Implementation of the Provisions of the UN Convention on Biological Diversity*, 73.

993 National Action Plan, § 131.

of the measures outlined in the Action Plan has the potential to contribute to the greater integration of biodiversity protection concerns across the various spheres of life. Some progress on the key obligations under the CBD, including Articles 7 (identification and monitoring), 8 (*in-situ* conservation), 10 (sustainable use) and 14 (impact assessment) was achieved in the recent years, as illustrated in Chapter 2, however, there remains room for improvement with respect to implementation of all of the key obligations under the CBD.[994]

The implementation of the Bern Convention might be assessed on the basis of voluntary general reports on implementation, biennial national reports presenting information on exceptions according to Article 9, and recommendations given by the Standing Committee with regard to the cases concerning the Carpathians within Ukraine. The latest biennial report submitted by Ukraine (2015–2016) notes without specifying the region (potentially covering also Ukrainian Carpathians) the authorisation of deliberate capture and keeping and deliberate killing of wolves, stating that in 2015 982 individuals out of 2051 and in 2016 1083 individuals out of 2212 were removed, amounting to 49,5 per cent of the population.[995] Such taking corresponds, however, to Ukraine's reservation accompanying ratification of the Bern Convention.[996] It is worth noting that in September 2024, based on the two assessments of the situation of the wolf in Europe developed by the Large Carnivores Initiative for Europe for the Bern Convention in 2022 and the analysis developed by the European Commission's DG Environment in 2023, pointing out to the increase in population numbers over the last decade and the need to ensure sustainable human-large carnivores coexistence, the European Union suggested to consider at the 44th meeting of the Standing Committee of the Bern Convention a proposal to move wolf from Appendix II to Appendix III.[997]

---

994 See Natalia Subbotina "Ukraine's Implementation of the Key Obligations Under the Convention on Biological Diversity: Challenges and Prospects for the Forest Ecosystems", *Journal of the Ukrainian Free University: Academia Iuniora*, 3 (2023).

995 Ministry of Ecology and Natural Resources of Ukraine, "Biennial Report 2015–2016," https://rm.coe.int/biennial-report-ua-2015-2016/1680a86331, 8.

996 "Reservations and Declarations for Treaty No.104 – Convention on the Conservation of European Wildlife and Natural Habitats (ETS No. 104)," Council of Europe Treaty Office, accessed December 30, 2024, https://www.coe.int/en/web/conventions/full-list?module=declarations-by-treaty&numSte=104&codeNature=0.

997 Secretariat of the Bern Convention, *Proposal to amend Appendices II and III of the Bern Convention of the Conservation of European Wildlife and Natural Habitats by moving the wolf (Canis lupus) from Appendix II to Appendix III*, Proposal by the

Out of the voluntary general reports, there is only one Ukraine's report, which covers the period of 1999 – 2003 and contains notes current as of 2005.[998] This report lists the species protected by the Bern Convention that are found in Ukraine, mentioning several species found in the Carpathians and some of the negative factors affecting their populations. For instance, for bat species, out of which *Eptesicus nikssoni* is distributed within Ukraine only in the Carpathian region, the causes of decline include "degradation and destruction of caves as a result of speleo-tourism". Forest cat, European lynx and brown bear are affected by the cases of illegal hunting.[999] The latter was included in the Red Data Book of Ukraine in 2004, and at the time of Ukraine's ratification of the Bern Convention, was subject to the same reservation as a wolf. Among the most vulnerable rodents are the European gopher or ground squirrel (*Citellus citellus)* and Bukovyna blind mole-rat (*Spalax graecus*), negatively affected by the transformation of natural biotopes due to human activities. The capercaillie found in the Carpathians and Polissya requires special protection, in particular against poaching. The order of Strigiformes is represented by 6 species included in Appendix II of the Bern Convention, which are found mostly in the Carpathians (with isolated spots in Polissya), of which the barn owl (*Ty-to alba)* is a rare and almost extinct species in Ukraine. The species of Carpathian triton (*Triturus montandoni*), yellow-bellied toad (*Bombina va-riegata*) and Dalmatian toad (*Rana dalmatina*) are considered vulnerable, but their populations remain stable, not requiring any special measures other than those needed for all the amphibians. The deforestation of hardwoods, in particular old oak trees, is among the main causes of the decline in numbers of the rare capricorn beetle (*Cerambyx cerdo*). Another species dependent on mature hardwoods, in particular, drying trees in the Carpathian highland beechwoods is the Alpine longhorn beetle (*Rosalia alpina*).[1000]

The same report also notes the steps needed to establish the Emerald network in Ukraine based on Recommendations 16 and 25 of the Standing

European Union, T-PVS/Inf(2024)15, (Strasbourg, 2024) https://rm.coe.int/inf15e-2024-submission-on-behalf-of-the-european-union-of-a-proposal-f/1680b1e94e.

998 "General Reports (2001–2004)," Convention on the conservation of European wildlife and natural habitats – 29th meeting of the Standing Committee (Bern, 23–26 November 2009), https://search.coe.int/democracy/eng?i=0900001680746c04.

999 "General Reports (2001–2004)," 29th meeting of the Standing Committee (2009).

1000 "General Reports (2001–2004)," 29th meeting of the Standing Committee (2009).

Committee of the Bern Convention. It is mentioned that Ukraine does not have an Action plan on the implementation of the Bern Convention. However, some other documents, as well as participation in thematic seminars and workshops, lay the foundations for the coordination of the implementation activities. It is also stated that the European Commission developed a special document for the purposes of the 5th Ministerial Conference "Environment for Europe", which describes the conditions and circumstances creating obstacles for the implementation of Bern Convention and other international agreement in environmental domain, which were relevant for the beginning of 2000s, and which are seemingly still relevant for Ukraine. These include, for example, insufficient political support and inadequate understanding of the obligations among executive power officials, limited technical, administrative and financial capacities, lack of coordination between institutions, incomplete mechanisms of implementation, inaccurate data and other issues.[1001] In the national report, it was also acknowledged that in Ukraine, economic priorities dominate over other goals and impede the strengthening of the sectoral co-operation and integration of biodiversity protection and ecosystem approach into the areas of transport, agriculture, tourism and other spheres.[1002] Interestingly, however, as of 2005, Ukraine was proud of its leadership in adopting legislation on the ecological network for the purposes of implementation of the Bern Convention, celebrating it as a 'real accomplishment' and suggesting it as a model for other countries in transition.[1003]

The Standing Committee of the Bern Convention recommended, in the context of the "Polonyna Borzhava" Case described in Chapter 2, several actions concerning the overall progress on the implementation of the Emerald Network. Namely, the recommendations concerned the adoption of legislation on environmental protection and, in particular, the prompt adoption of the Law on the Emerald Network. Likewise, it was recommended to initiate a multi-stakeholder process with a view to identify key issues that constrain progress, key organisations responsible for these, mechanisms which would allow for the effective and timely detection, reporting, assessment and resolution of potential conflicts before they put at risk international obligations of biodiversity as well as identification of a timeline to secure and monitor the process. It was further recommended to

1001 "General Reports (2001–2004)," 29th meeting of the Standing Committee (2009).
1002 "General Reports (2001–2004)," 29th meeting of the Standing Committee (2009).
1003 "General Reports (2001–2004)," 29th meeting of the Standing Committee (2009).

undertake the quantitative assessment of the contribution of the Emerald Network to carbon sequestration and storage.[1004] A Ukrainian expert noted in the 2022 interview that the Bern Convention will remain underimplemented in Ukraine as long as there is no Law on the Emerald Network.[1005]

In the context of the Svydovets Case and implementation of the Association Agreement between the EU and Ukraine, the European Parliament urged Ukraine to fight illegal logging in the primeval forests in the Carpathians and to invest in environmentally safe and sustainable tourist infrastructure. It was further recommended to improve transparency, due diligence and access to environmental information, as well as the implementation of the relevant procedures, such as the EIA, to prevent future environmental damage.[1006]

When it comes to implementation of the Carpathian Convention, the state of the implementation of the key biodiversity-related obligations based on the convention and the protocols to it might be assessed on the basis of the 2017 National Report of Ukraine on the Implementation of the Biodiversity Protocol and the recent non-governmental Analysis of Ukraine's Implementation of the Framework Convention on the Protection and Sustainable Development of the Carpathians.[1007] The former outlines key achievements in the recent years, to which the legislative ammendments, such as those to the Rules of cutting of the main use in the mountain forests of the Carpathians, ammendments related to the protection of the primeval, quasi-primeval and natural forests or introduction of the 'season of silence' as well as other ammendments undertaken in the recent years (and described in Chapter 2) belong. In the latter, it is recommended to define the concept of the mountain areas in the Carpathians and to take action to maintain ecological balance threatened by the increased anthropogenic pressures. In particular, it is suggested to encourage preservation of the local communities and generation of income that does not lead to the destruction of natural ecosystems, by encouraging the development

1004 Standing Committee, *Recommendation No. 213 (2021)*, § 10–12.
1005 Bohdan Kuchenko, EPL, personal communication, September 29, 2022.
1006 "The Great Carpathian Land Grab," Bruno Manser Fonds, 28; European Parliament resolution of 11 February 2021 on the implementation of the EU Association Agreement with Ukraine (2019/2202(INI)).
1007 See *National Report of Ukraine on the Implementation of the Biodiversity Protocol*; Shutiak, *Analysis of Ukraine's Implementation of the Framework Convention on the Protection and Sustainable Development of the Carpathians.*

of tourism, fish farming, or eco-friendly mineral extraction.[1008] In the same Analysis, it is also stated that the Forest Protocol to the Carpathian Convention has, to a large extent, been implemented by the introduction of foundations of sustainable forestry and close-to-nature forestry to the Forest Code of Ukraine.[1009] Some of the important recent achievements also include the development of the Regulation on the identification of specially protected forest areas.[1010] Other achievements in the context of implementation of the Carpathian Convention include the extension of the existing and designation of the new NRF sites and the gradual integration of the EU environmental acquis into the Ukrainian legislation.[1011]

The implementation of the Association Agreement between the EU and Ukraine as such is important for the implementation of Ukraine's international biodiversity obligations. In the recent report on the implementation of the Association Agreement between the EU and Ukraine, certain improvements of the EIA and SEA procedures are mentioned. In particular, it is stated that the consultations on the EIA report with other executive authorities and local self-government bodies were introduced in 2023 based on the Law "On amendments to certain laws of Ukraine regarding the improvement and digitalisation of the environmental impact assessment procedure",[1012] and that the Cabinet of Ministers adopted resolution "On approval of the Procedure for maintaining the Unified Register of Strategic Environmental Assessment"[1013] aimed at digitalisation of the SEA procedure.[1014] The need to implement recent EU Regulation on deforestation-free

1008 Shutiak, *Analysis of Ukraine's Implementation of the Framework Convention on the Protection and Sustainable Development of the Carpathians*, 4.

1009 Shutiak, *Analysis of Ukraine's Implementation of the Framework Convention on the Protection and Sustainable Development of the Carpathians*, 14.

1010 Shutiak, *Analysis of Ukraine's Implementation of the Framework Convention on the Protection and Sustainable Development of the Carpathians*, 15.

1011 Department of Nature Conservation, *Impact of war on natural environment of the Carpathians in Ukraine*, 57.

1012 "On Amendments to certain laws of Ukraine regarding the improvement and digitalisation of the environmental impact assessment procedure," Law of Ukraine, Document 3227-IX, Bulletin of the Verkhovna Rada of Ukraine, No. 84, p. 305 (2023) https://zakon.rada.gov.ua/laws/show/3227-20#Text.

1013 "On approval of the Procedure for maintaining the Unified Register of Strategic Environmental Assessment," Resolution of the Cabinet of Ministers of Ukraine No. 430, Document 430–2023-p, (May 2, 2023) https://zakon.rada.gov.ua/laws/show/430-2023-%D0%BF#Text.

1014 "The Report on Implementation of the Association Agreement between Ukraine and the European Union for 2023," Government Office for Coordination of Eurosupply chains 2023/1115 (EUDR) in Ukraine for the purposes of preventing illegal logging and corruption in forestry is acknowledged in the literature as crucial for Carpathian forests, particularly, as this regulation, unlike its predecessor EU Timber Regulation (EUTR), aims to counteract logging which is legal under national legislation but which results in the deforestation or forest degradation.[1015] Furthermore, Ukraine needs to continue working on the implementation of the Birds and Habitats Directives.[1016] It has been noted in the literature that in Ukraine, unlike the EU, where the designation of the ecological network is based on habitat characteristics, which corresponds to the Emerald network formation criteria, the designation of the ecological network is based rather on the existing nature reserve fund areas with occasional addition of other special categories such as water-protective or recreational areas.[1017] Therefore, the approach to the formation of the ecological network in Ukraine has to be changed to correspond to the EU practices of designation and functioning of the Natura 2000 network.[1018]

When it comes to the implementation of Ukraine's current National Action Plan on the environment based on the 2030 Strategy, several achievements have been noted in the 2023 Report on its implementation. In particular, with respect to the Red Data Book and Green Data Book, it is noted that the measures are being taken with a view to implement the activities envisaged in the action plans on the preservation of particular species, including black stork, brown bear, European bison, and lynx; and that the regulations on protective zones for the preservation of biodiversity and protective zones for the preservation of the objects

---

pean and Euro-Atlantic Integration of the Secretariat of the Cabinet of Ministers of Ukraine (Kyiv, 2024), https://www.kmu.gov.ua/storage/app/sites/1/18%20-%20Department/18%20-%20PDF/2024/03.2024/AA%20implementation%20report%20for%202023.pdf.

1015 "The Great Carpathian Land Grab," Bruno Manser Fonds, 28; EUDR.

1016 "The Great Carpathian Land Grab," Bruno Manser Fonds, 28.

1017 G. Bondaruk et al., *Legal Framework of Biodiversity Protection in Forest Sector of Ukraine: Analysis and Prospects* (Lviv: WWF, 2013), 201–202; Bevz, "Legal Regulation of the Emerald Network: National and Global Aspects," 92.

1018 Bondaruk et al., *Legal Framework of Biodiversity Protection in Forest Sector of Ukraine: Analysis and Prospects*, 201–202; "Ostap Semerak: The Association Agreement requires the swift implementation of the Birds and Habitats Directives in Ukraine," Government Portal, March 13, 2018, https://www.kmu.gov.ua/news/ostap-semerak-ugoda-pro-asociaciyu-vimagaye-yaknajshvidshogo-vprovadzhennya-v-ukrayini-ptashinoyi-ta-oselishnoyi-direktivi.

of the Red Data Book were adopted.[1019] On the creation of the strategic document on biodiversity protection, it is stated that the implementation of this action is in progress by means of the project "Global Biodiversity Framework Early Action Support" implemented by the UNDP, according to which the drafting of the national strategy and action plan based on the Kunming-Montreal Global Biodiversity Framework is taking place in the framework of international technical assistance.[1020] On the measure of integration of the issues of biodiversity protection, value of biodiversity and ecosystem services to the national and local strategies of development, it is stated that the SEA is undertaken for these purposes.[1021] When it comes to the actions on invasive alien species, the major achievements include the establishment of the cross-departmental working group on invasive alien plant and animal species under the Ministry of Environmental Protection (established in 2023) and the ongoing process on the creation of criteria for the classification of plant and animal species as invasive alien species. Particularly important in this regard are developments in Lviv region, where the Institute of Ecology of the Carpathians of the National Academy of Sciences of Ukraine has developed a concise methodological guidelines for preparing a list of invasive species for Lviv Oblast and criteria for identifying these species and in cooperation with the group of scientists from various institutions in Lviv compiled a list of invasive plant and animal species specific to Lviv Oblast, which has been submitted to the Lviv Regional State Administration for approval. It is further stated that the measures for the eradication of the invasive alien species are undertaken on the local level.[1022]

1019 "Report on the Implementation Status as of 2023 of the National Action Plan for Environmental Protection until 2025, approved by the Order of the Cabinet of Ministers of Ukraine from April 21, 2021 No. 443," Ministry of Environmental Protection and Natural Resources of Ukraine https://mepr.gov.ua/wp-content/uploads/2024/03/Rozmishhennya-Zvit-po-vykonannyu-NPD-za-2023.pdf, § 36.

1020 "Report on the Implementation Status as of 2023 of the National Action Plan for Environmental Protection until 2025," Ministry of Environmental Protection and Natural Resources of Ukraine, § 131.

1021 "Report on the Implementation Status as of 2023 of the National Action Plan for Environmental Protection until 2025," Ministry of Environmental Protection and Natural Resources of Ukraine, § 143.

1022 "Report on the Implementation Status as of 2023 of the National Action Plan for Environmental Protection until 2025," Ministry of Environmental Protection and Natural Resources of Ukraine, § 162.

3.2. Best practices and recommendations on biodiversity protection in the forest and mountainous ecosystems

Among the best practices on biodiversity protection identified at the international level, those explicitly concerning mountain biological diversity and forest biological diversity are the most relevant for the forest ecosystems of the Ukrainian Carpathians. In addition, best practices in related thematic areas, such as protected areas, ecological connectivity or sustainable tourism, are also applicable and significant for ensuring biodiversity protection. The selected best practices will be presented largely based on the CBD, the Bern Convention and the Carpathian Convention. In addition to thematic areas, sustainable development as such is considered a general framework for biodiversity-related action.

3.2.1. Mountain and forest biodiversity recommendations

In the field of mountain biodiversity, the recommendations on action at the national level informed by a global perspective could be found, for instance, within the programme of work under the CBD.[1023] In the decision on its adoption, the parties were invited to identify priorities among the recommended actions and urged to include these in their national biodiversity strategies and action plans, as well as in plans on the implementation of the regional mountain conventions, which implies the Carpathian Convention for the region of the Ukrainian Carpathians. It is simultaneously suggested that the ecosystem approach be taken into account, and that the contribution towards reducing biodiversity loss should coincide with the contribution to poverty reduction, benefiting local communities dependent on the mountains.[1024] This programme of work further takes account of the studies conducted by the SBSTTA on the trends of and threats to mountain biological diversity,[1025] and on the measures taken for the conservation and

1023 The Programme of Work on Mountain Biological Diversity under the CBD was agreed upon during the seventh meeting of the COP. See Conference of the Parties, *Mountain biological diversity,* CBD COP Decision VII/27 (2004), Annex; "Programme of Work on Mountain Biological Diversity," CBD, September 4, 2007, https://www.cbd.int/mountain/pow.shtml.

1024 CBD COP Decision VII/27, § 3.

1025 SBSTTA, *Status and trends of, and threats to, mountain biological diversity,* UNEP/CBD/SBSTTA/8/5, CBD (2002), https://www.cbd.int/doc/meetings/sbstta/sbstta-08/official/sbstta-08-05-en.pdf.

sustainable use of mountain biological diversity[1026] as a basis for deciding on the early action.[1027] The category of measures taken ranges from the application of the ecosystem approach, undertaking management of the protected areas, restoration and rehabilitation of degraded ecosystems and recovery of threatened or endangered species, and management of invasive alien species to applying traditional knowledge of local and indigenous communities and exploring options for sustainable tourism and sustainable use, all of which need appropriate institutional and socio-economic enabling environment.[1028] In addition, there is a set of recommendations suggested by the SBSTTA for the purposes of creating a programme of work, which potentially also might be useful for national governments.[1029]

The programme of work itself includes three elements: "direct actions for conservation, sustainable use and benefit-sharing", "means of implementation for conservation, sustainable use and benefit-sharing", and "supporting actions for conservation, sustainable use and benefit-sharing".[1030] These elements comprising goals and actions were to be implemented until 2010, however, given the threats to the Ukrainian Carpathians described in Chapter 2, this set of measures remains highly relevant and may be used as a policy framework for creating national or regional biodiversity strategy aimed at preservation of the mountain forest ecosystems of the Ukrainian Carpathians.

Similarly, in the area of forest biodiversity, the Forest Biodiversity Programme of Work has been created within the CBD. It was developed by the SBSTTA and adopted at the sixth meeting of the CBD COP in 2002. This programme comprises three elements: "conservation, sustainable use and benefit-sharing", "institutional and socio-economic enabling environment", and "knowledge, assessment and monitoring", further subdivided into 12

1026 SBSTTA, *Measures taken for the conservation and sustainable use of mountain biological diversity*, UNEP/CBD/SBSTTA/8/6, CBD (2002), https://www.cbd.int/doc/meetings/sbstta/sbstta-08/official/sbstta-08-06-en.pdf.

1027 CBD COP Decision VII/27, § 12.

1028 *Measures taken for the conservation and sustainable use of mountain biological diversity*, UNEP/CBD/SBSTTA/8/6.

1029 SBSTTA, *Proposed elements for a programme of work on mountain biological diversity*, UNEP/CBD/SBSTTA/8/7, CBD (2002), https://www.cbd.int/doc/meetings/sbstta/sbstta-08/official/sbstta-08-07-en.pdf.

1030 CBD COP Decision VII/27, Annex.

goals and 27 objectives.[1031] The elements of the work programme on forests within the CBD initially included "holistic and inter-sectoral ecosystem approaches that integrate the conservation and sustainable use of biological diversity, taking account of social, cultural and economic considerations" and "comprehensive analysis of the ways in which human activities, in particular forest-management practices, influence biological diversity and assessment of ways to minimize or mitigate negative influences".[1032]

Apart from the programmes of work on mountain and forest biodiversity, the related areas of work within the CBD mechanism include (among others) protected areas,[1033] ecosystem approach,[1034] climate change,[1035] invasive alien species[1036] and sustainable use.[1037]

Regional agreements on mountains, such as the Carpathian Convention, are considered to be valuable tools for ensuring adaptability to specific situations.[1038] Furthermore, one of the governance solutions for enhancing mountain biodiversity is international cooperation at the subnational level, such as between regions or districts belonging to different states. Such an approach is supposed to ensure necessary attention to the interests of local communities and peculiarities of the mountain areas.[1039]

It is also underscored in the literature that for mountain ecosystems, control of invasive alien species is particularly critical.[1040] The IUCN has created guidance for national law and policy makers on strengthening legal and institutional frameworks on invasive alien species, which, among others, builds on prevention, precaution and ecosystem approach and suggets

1031 Conference of the Parties, *Forest biological diversity*, CBD COP Decision VI/22 (2002); "Forest Biodiversity Programme of Work," CBD, July 27, 2012, https://www.cbd.int/forest/pow.shtml.

1032 Secretariat, *Handbook of the Convention on Biological Diversity*, 231–232.

1033 "Protected Areas – an overview," CBD, accessed November 11, 2024, https://www.cbd.int/protected/overview.

1034 "Ecosystem Approach," CBD, accessed November 11, 2024, https://www.cbd.int/forest/ecosystem.shtml.

1035 "Climate Change," CBD, accessed November 11, 2024, https://www.cbd.int/forest/CC.shtml.

1036 "Invasive Alien Species," CBD, accessed November 11, 2024, https://www.cbd.int/invasive.

1037 "Sustainable Use of Biodiversity," CBD, accessed November 11, 2024, https://www.cbd.int/sustainable; "Programmatic Links," CBD, accessed November 11, 2024, https://www.cbd.int/forest/plinks.shtml.

1038 Fodella, "Mountain biodiversity," 171.

1039 Fodella, "Mountain biodiversity," 169.

1040 Fodella, "Mountain biodiversity," 171.

ways of integrating alien species into the strategic planning process as well as suggests a range of legal tools and techniques for regulating invasive alien species.[1041]

In the light of sustainability, special attention is paid to the intersection of nature protection and social dimension while conserving biodiversity. In particular, it is necessary to guarantee the participation of mountain communities in the processes of biodiversity management with a view to safeguarding their interests and ensuring biodiversity conservation.[1042] One of the strategies to this extent, aimed at preservation of biodiversity and poverty reduction, includes providing compensation to mountain communities for biodiversity conservation or other ecosystem services provided by them to 'downstream users' within the 'upland-lowland holistic approach to mountain biodiversity issues'. Such compensation might take various forms and include engagement of various actors (governments, international organisations and the private sector). Some of the known forms include, for instance, contract-based direct payments by the beneficiaries of services, subsidies or incentives, and compensation in non-monetary form, such as by implementing projects benefiting such communities. The application of such an approach is also regarded as coherent with other key priorities related to mountain biodiversity, such as connectivity conservation and ecosystem-based adaptation to climate change in mountains.[1043]

The need for attention to all three components of sustainability (economic, social and environmental) in the context of mountain regions is clearly reflected in the General Assembly resolution 75/271 "Nature knows no borders: transboundary cooperation – a key factor for biodiversity conservation, restoration and sustainable use". In particular, the General Assembly encourages "the use of economic models in the context of sustainable development and poverty eradication that are aimed at accelerating inclusive and sustainable economic growth and improving human well-being and social equity, while significantly reducing environmental degradation".[1044] In addition, the efforts of the International Partnership for

1041 See Clare Shine, Nattley Williams, and Lothar Gündling, *A Guide to Designing Legal and Institutional Frameworks on Alien Invasive Species*, IUCN Environmental Policy and Law Paper 40 (Gland Cambridge: IUCN, 2000), especially 31–84.

1042 Fodella, "Mountain biodiversity," 172.

1043 Fodella, "Mountain biodiversity," 171–172.

1044 *Nature knows no borders: transboundary cooperation – a key factor for biodiversity conservation, restoration and sustainable use*, General Assembly Resolution 75/271, A/RES/75/271, April 20, 2021, § 5.

Sustainable Development in Mountain Regions (Mountain Partnership), launched during the World Summit on Sustainable Development, are noted in this regard.[1045] Moreover, the Kunming-Montreal Global Biodiversity Framework speaks of its interrelatedness with the 2030 Agenda for Sustainable Development, including its contribution to the fulfilment of the SDGs and the need to achieve sustainable development in all its three dimensions to create conditions necessary for implementing the goals and targets of this Framework.[1046]

3.2.2. The scope of obligations on the creation and functioning of the Emerald Network

When it comes to the Bern Convention and the creation of the Emerald Network, the nature and scope of the related obligations deserve particular attention for the purpose of their better implementation in Ukraine. In describing the scope of obligations, we attempt to summarise some of the key points of the intricate analysis undertaken by Arie Trouwborst.[1047]

Initially, it is observed that the provisions of the Bern Convention, forming the basis for the creation of the Emerald Network, along with numerous resolutions and recommendations, establish an obligation of result.[1048] The result at stake is conservation of habitats, defined as the "maintenance and, where appropriate, the restoration or improvement of the abiotic and

1045 *Nature knows no borders: transboundary cooperation – a key factor for biodiversity conservation, restoration and sustainable use*, General Assembly Resolution 75/271, Preamble; See "International Partnership for Sustainable Development in Mountain Regions (Mountain Partnership)," United Nations Department of Economic and Social Affairs, accessed November 11, 2024, https://sdgs.un.org/partnerships/international-partnership-sustainable-development-mountain-regions-mountain.

1046 *Kunming-Montreal Global Biodiversity Framework*, Annex, Section D, 8; For explanation of the SDGs and biodiversity see also *Global Biodiversity Outlook 5*, 9.

1047 Arie Trouwborst, *Obligations of Bern Convention Parties Regarding the Conservation of Candidate and Adopted Emerald Network Sites: A Legal Analysis*, Document prepared on behalf of the Bern Convention, T-PVS/PA(2020)07, (Strasbourg, 2020) https://pure.uvt.nl/ws/portalfiles/portal/58698518/Emerald_Network_obligations_2020.pdf.

1048 Arie Trouwborst, *Obligations of Bern Convention Parties Regarding the Conservation of Candidate and Adopted Emerald Network Sites: A Legal Analysis*, 4–6.

biotic features which form the habitat of a species or a natural habitat."[1049] The wording "abiotic and biotic features" used here might well encompass ecological processes and connections, which is supported by the use of the notion of the "integrity" of habitats and sites, used in documents of the Standing Committee.[1050] Other key notions include the maintenance and restoration of the "ecological character" or "ecological characteristics" of sites.[1051] Importantly, according to Trouwborst, the obligation of result at issue applies similarly to both the candidate and adopted Emerald Network sites.[1052] A part of this obligation is the prevention of deterioration of the conservation status of species and habitats within the candidate and adopted Emerald Network sites, and in cases when the current status is unfavourable or unsatisfactory, restoration of it to a favourable or satisfactory status.[1053] Such observations might be particularly crucial for protecting biodiversity in the Ukrainian Carpathians, for instance, as an additional argument of the environmental NGOs for the protection of candidate sites, as well as generally for raising awareness of the need for protecting the Emerald Network sites adopted on an international level by the Standing Committee of the Bern Convention, but not officially protected on a national level within Ukraine, given the lack of national legislation on the Emerald Network.

Regarding the temporal perspective, it is the long-term survival of the species and habitats that is expected to be reached by the Emerald Network

1049 Trouwborst, *Obligations of Bern Convention Parties Regarding the Conservation of Candidate and Adopted Emerald Network Sites: A Legal Analysis*, 7; Standing Committee, *Resolution No. 1 (1989)*, § 2 (c).

1050 Trouwborst, *Obligations of Bern Convention Parties Regarding the Conservation of Candidate and Adopted Emerald Network Sites: A Legal Analysis*, 8.

1051 Trouwborst, *Obligations of Bern Convention Parties Regarding the Conservation of Candidate and Adopted Emerald Network Sites: A Legal Analysis*, 8; See also Dave Pritchard, *The Concept of the 'Ecological Character' of Sites in the Bern Convention/Emerald Network Context, and Options for Addressing Changes in Ecological Character*, Bern Convention Document T-PVS/PA(2017)8 (Strasbourg, 2017) https://rm.coe.int/the-concept-of-the-ecological-character-of-sites-in-the-bern-conventio/168073f68d and Dave Pritchard, *Proposal for Guidance on Detecting, Assessing, Reporting and Responding to Changes and Likely Changes in the Ecological Character of Emerald Network Sites*, Bern Convention Document T-PVS/PA(2018)13, (Strasbourg, 2018) https://rm.coe.int/proposal-for-guidance-on-detecting-assessing-reporting-and-responding-/16808db4e0.

1052 Trouwborst, *Obligations of Bern Convention Parties Regarding the Conservation of Candidate and Adopted Emerald Network Sites: A Legal Analysis*, 26–27.

1053 Trouwborst, *Obligations of Bern Convention Parties Regarding the Conservation of Candidate and Adopted Emerald Network Sites: A Legal Analysis*, 11–12.

sites, although it is less clear whether there is any timeframe for the performance of obligations (for instance, on the restoration of habitats to a favourable status).[1054] Concerning the level at which the achievement of the favourable or satisfactory conservation status is expected (such as site, population, national territory, biogeographical region or Europe), there is no definitive clarity, which might mean that it is expected to be achieved separately or in parallel at multiple levels.[1055]

The components of the obligation of result under Article 4 of the Bern Convention in the context of the Emerald Network include at least "setting in place a protection regime" and "taking practical management measures".[1056] A good practice in this regard is the development and implementation of protected area management plans or their equivalents.[1057] Another good practice regarding protected areas is the performance of research with a view to enhancing understanding of the critical elements in the management.[1058] Still other recommended action is stakeholder involvement in the planning and management of the sites, as well as in the implementation and monitoring of the management measures.[1059] It is also recommended that adequate personnel, training, equipment and resources are provided by the state to enable proper management and conservation. In addition, adequate monitoring is crucial as it serves the purposes of planning management measures and enables meaningful assessment of compliance.[1060]

1054 Trouwborst, *Obligations of Bern Convention Parties Regarding the Conservation of Candidate and Adopted Emerald Network Sites: A Legal Analysis*, 1–8, 12; Standing Committee, *Resolution No. 8 (2012) of the Standing Committee, adopted on 30 November 2012 on the national designation of adopted Emerald sites and the implementation of management, monitoring and reporting measures*, (November 30, 2012), https://rm.coe.int/1680746515, § 3 (3).

1055 Trouwborst, *Obligations of Bern Convention Parties Regarding the Conservation of Candidate and Adopted Emerald Network Sites: A Legal Analysis*, 11.

1056 Trouwborst, *Obligations of Bern Convention Parties Regarding the Conservation of Candidate and Adopted Emerald Network Sites: A Legal Analysis*, 13.

1057 Trouwborst, *Obligations of Bern Convention Parties Regarding the Conservation of Candidate and Adopted Emerald Network Sites: A Legal Analysis*, 16.

1058 Trouwborst, *Obligations of Bern Convention Parties Regarding the Conservation of Candidate and Adopted Emerald Network Sites: A Legal Analysis*, 17; Standing Committee, *Recommendation No. 16 (1989)*, § 3 (c).

1059 Trouwborst, *Obligations of Bern Convention Parties Regarding the Conservation of Candidate and Adopted Emerald Network Sites: A Legal Analysis*, 17; Standing Committee, *Resolution No. 8 (2012)*, § 2 (4).

1060 Trouwborst, *Obligations of Bern Convention Parties Regarding the Conservation of Candidate and Adopted Emerald Network Sites: A Legal Analysis*, 17.

In addition, the obligations on conservation of the habitats are not limited to the territories designated as Emerald Network sites as such, but also include control over the activities beyond site's boundaries that may result in the deterioration of protected habitats or in other words, protection from external threats that may affect species or habitats within the site.[1061] In this regard, comprehensive impact assessments that take into account cumulative impacts are critically important for identifying the incompatibility of the planned projects with the conservation requirements.[1062] It is, however, noted that some minor degree of damage to the site might be allowed, given that its avoidance is 'impossible' and that it does not undermine the favourable or satisfactory conservation status of species, habitats or the site's ecological character.[1063]

For Ukraine, the formation and functioning of the Emerald Network remains a task in progress. As Olena Bevz justly observes, the Ukrainian legislation is in need of a set of amendments to reconcile current approach to the ecological network formation with the criteria established by documents on formation of the Emerald Network within Bern Convention and analogous EU legislation, including Directive 92/43/EC and Directive 97/62/EC, which Ukraine undertook to implement based on the Association Agreement between the EU and Ukraine.[1064]

3.2.3. Key action plans, projects and recommendations on biodiversity within the Carpathian Convention

Within the Carpathian Convention, the key current framework for actions to be implemented by States Parties and at the same time an example of a proactive regional initiative towards implementation of the Kunming-Montreal Global Biodiversity Framework is the Carpathian Biodiversity Frame-

1061 Trouwborst, *Obligations of Bern Convention Parties Regarding the Conservation of Candidate and Adopted Emerald Network Sites: A Legal Analysis*, 18; Standing Committee, *Resolution No. 8 (2012)*, § 2(1).

1062 Trouwborst, *Obligations of Bern Convention Parties Regarding the Conservation of Candidate and Adopted Emerald Network Sites: A Legal Analysis*, 19–21.

1063 Trouwborst, *Obligations of Bern Convention Parties Regarding the Conservation of Candidate and Adopted Emerald Network Sites: A Legal Analysis*, 21–22.

1064 Bevz, "Legal Regulation of the Emerald Network: National and Global Aspects," 96.

work (CBF).[1065] Apart from the CBF as such, there is a recently created Guidance Document for Streamlining the Carpathian Biodiversity Framework into National Biodiversity Strategies and Action Plans, the Annex I to which contains examples of policy measures and actions derived from the CBF, and additionally there is a useful background note highlighting key information on the CBF.[1066]

Futhermore, there are various general and thematic recommendations on the implementation of the Carpathian Convention, such as the (draft) Carpathian strategy for enhancing biodiversity and landscape conservation outside and inside the protected areas.[1067] This document contains a number of recommended practices, such as with respect to protection, management or restoration of the target priority habitats, where for forests it is recommended to include relevant provisions to the forest management plans such as "banning or limiting the clear-cuts, maintaining part of

1065 Conference of the Parties, *Carpathian Biodiversity Framework, including a Carpathian Vision 2050*, CC/COP7/DOC7/ADOPTED, (Belgrade, 2023) http://www.carpathianconvention.org/cop7/docs/officialdocuments/CC%20COP7%20DOC7_Carpathian%20Biodiversity%20Framework_ADOPTED.pdf.

1066 "Carpathian Convention Guidance Document for Streamlining the Carpathian Biodiversity Framework into National Biodiversity Strategies and Action Plans (NBSAPs)", Secretariat of the Carpathian Convention, (2024) http://www.carpathianconvention.org/wp-content/uploads/2024/02/Guidance-Document_Streamlining-CBF-into-NBSAPs_FINAL-DRAFT-0702-.pdf; Annex I to the "Carpathian Convention Guidance Document for Streamlining the Carpathian Biodiversity Framework into National Biodiversity Strategies and Action Plans (NBSAPs)", Secretariat of the Carpathian Convention, (2024) http://www.carpathianconvention.org/wp-content/uploads/2024/02/Annex I_Streamlining-CBF-into-NBSAPs_0702.pdf; "Background note for the moderated discussion on the implementation of the Carpathian Biodiversity Framework (CBF), to be held at the 15th meeting of the CC Working Group on Biodiversity on 17 June 2024," (2024) http://www.carpathianconvention.org/wp-content/uploads/2024/06/Background-note-for-the-moderated-discussion_CBF-implementation_WG-Biodiversity_17-June-.pdf.

1067 "(Draft) Carpathian strategy for enhancing biodiversity and landscape conservation outside and inside protected areas," Centralparks, Deliverable D.T1.1.3, (2021) http://www.carpathianconvention.org/tl_files/carpathiancon/Downloads/03%20Meetings%20and%20Events/Implementation%20Committee/CCIC2021/1510C2FDCentralparks_DT1.1.3_draft%20Strategy%20biodiversity%20and%20landscape%20FULL%20Document.pdf; See also "Centralparks: draft Carpathian strategy for enhancing biodiversity and landscape conservation outside and inside protected areas," Centralparks (2021) http://www.carpathianconvention.org/tl_files/carpathiancon/Downloads/03%20Meetings%20and%20Events/Implementation%20Committee/CCIC2021/1510C1FCentralparks%20WPT1%20draft%20Biodiversity%20strategy_factsheet.pdf.

the overmatured tree stands, preserving the natural forest edge and shape gentle ecotone transition zones between forest and non-forest ecosystems (with a loose top layer of tree crowns and a dense layer of shrubs)".[1068]

The good practices from the Carpathian region in the key economic areas are presented on the Mountain Biodiversity Platform, which, with regard to biodiversity, describes the BioREGIO, Alps – Carpathian Corridor, Danube parks, and Wolflife projects.[1069] The guidelines produced at the end of the BioREGIO project include insightful observations and recommendations. For instance, a trend towards shifting from protectionist to participatory nature conservation is observed at the European scale based on the literature and policy review, and the spread of the concept of ecosystem services, which is useful in communicating benefits and needs to protect biodiversity, is noted.[1070] It is, however, also observed that countries like Romania, Serbia and Ukraine are considered to be 'laggards' when it comes to using their potential in terms of natural assets in comparison with Western European countries, which might be explained by historic developments. In these countries, including Ukraine, hardly any good examples were named at stakeholder meetings and questionnaires, in contrast with plenty of examples of conflicts and problems. Such a situation resulted in a conclusion as to the need to assist the local population in finding opportunities for sustainable business, which could be addressed by policymakers, NGOs or the local entrepreneurs themselves.[1071]

The recent advancements in the field of conservation and sustainable use of biodiversity and key current projects and initiatives in this field are compiled in Decision 7/9 of the recent COP of the Carpathian Convention (2023).[1072] These include Action Plan on Conservation of Large

1068 "(Draft) Carpathian strategy for enhancing biodiversity and landscape conservation outside and inside protected areas," Centralparks, 38.

1069 "Good practices in the Carpathian countries," Secretariat of the Carpathian Convention, accessed November 11, 2024, http://www.carpathianconvention.org/mountain-biodiversity/.

1070 Mathilde Köck et al., *Integrated management of biological and landscape diversity for sustainable regional development and ecological connectivity in the Carpathians*, BioREGIO Carpathians project, (Sarajevo: ProPrint, 2014) BioREGIOCarpathians_FINALPublication.compressed.pdf, 22.

1071 Köck, *Integrated management of biological and landscape diversity for sustainable regional development and ecological connectivity in the Carpathians*, 22–23.

1072 Conference of the Parties, *Conservation and sustainable use of biological and landscape diversity, Article 4 of the Carpathian Convention*, Decision COP7/9 (Belgrade, 2023), http://www.carpathianconvention.org/cop7/docs/officialdocuments/CC_COP7_DOC3_COP7%20DECISIONS_ADOPTED.pdf.

Carnivores and Ensuring Ecological Connectivity in the Carpathians 2021 – 2026;[1073] new project LECA (Interreg Central Europe) led by the Mendel University in Brno, Czech Republic, on supporting the coexistence and conservation of the Carpathian large carnivores;[1074] the results of the SaveGREEN project, including the methodology for monitoring of ecological connectivity that Parties are encouraged to use;[1075] the results of the ConnectGREEN project, including a set of guidelines and methodologies on ecological corridors;[1076] and the Joint Declaration "Achieving functional biodiversity in the Danube-Carpathian Region by mainstreaming ecological connectivity"[1077] that may serve as a basis for the work on connectiv-

1073 Papp et al., *International Action Plan on Conservation of Large Carnivores and Ensuring Ecological Connectivity in the Carpathians.*

1074 "LECA," Interreg Central Europe, accessed November 11, 2024, https://www.interreg-central.eu/projects/leca/#.

1075 "SaveGREEN: Safeguarding the functionality of transnationally important ecological corridors in the Danube basin," Interreg Danube Transnationl Programme, accessed November 11, 2024, https://dtp.interreg-danube.eu/approved-projects/savegreen; Katrin Sedy, Christoph Plutzar, Florian Borgwardt et al., *A Methodology for Standardised Monitoring of Ecological Connectivity: Guidelines for the Analysis of Structural and Functional Connectivity*, Danube Transnational Programme DTP3–314–2.3 SaveGREEN project, (Vienna: Environment Agency Austria, 2022) https://dtp.interreg-danube.eu/uploads/media/approved_project_output/0001/56/dc86e1c6e3dac3299b3b411262b93dcd0210f85f.pdf.

1076 Gabriella Nagy, Sergio Rejado Albaina, Valentina Delconte and Nella Sergejeva, *Guidelines for the Identification, Conservation, Restoration, and Management of Ecological Corridors in the Carpathian Ecoregion*, Danube Transnational Programme ConnectGREEN Project, (Budapest: CEEweb for Biodiversity, 2021), https://dtp.interreg-danube.eu/uploads/media/approved_project_output/0001/18/8970ccbfce8e1efb26e6d89be922dca9285d973e.pdf; Zuzana Okániková, Dušan Romportl, Adéla Kluchová et al., *Methodology for Identification of Ecological Corridors in the Carpathian Countries by Using Large Carnivores as Umbrella Species*, Danube Transnational Programme ConnectGREEN Project "Restoring and managing ecological corridors in mountains as the green infrastructure in the Danube basin" (Banská Bystrica: State Nature Conservancy of the Slovak Republic, 2021), https://dtp.interreg-danube.eu/uploads/media/approved_project_output/0001/46/b06b6e925fd510bee8d1ca23fff5b03424c513fa.pdf; Maroš Finka, Vladimír Ondrejička, Milan Husár et al., *Guidelines on How to Use Spatial Planning Tools in Integrative Management of Ecological Corridors*, Danube Transnational Programme ConnectGREEN Project "Restoring and managing ecological corridors in mountains as the green infrastructure in the Danube basin," (Banská Bystrica: State Nature Conservancy of the Slovak Republic, 2021) https://dtp.interreg-danube.eu/uploads/media/approved_project_output/0001/46/4bf6e34e0cc88332516e33e95333685adf014665.pdf.

1077 *Achieving functional biodiversity in the Danube-Carpathian Region by mainstreaming ecological connectivity*, Declaration by EUSDR PA 4, EUSDR PA 5, EUSDR PA ity in the region.[1078] The Parties and relevant stakeholders are further encouraged to utilise the learnings from the NaturaConnect project (EU Horizon Europe).[1079] In the field of protected areas and harmonisation of biodiversity protection with local socio-economic development, instrumental are the results of the Centralparks project (Interreg Central Europe Programme) led by Eurac Research and including support given to the Carpathian Network of Protected Areas (CNPA) activities, involving (apart from the Carpathian strategy for enhancing biodiversity and landscape conservation outside and inside protected areas mentioned above), the Guidelines on communication between protected areas and local communities in the Carpathians,[1080] Carpathian Ecosystem Services Toolkit,[1081] and Strategy for local sustainable tourism development based on natural and cultural heritage of the Carpathians,[1082] that are endorsed by the COP of the Carpathian Convention.[1083] The note is also taken of the proposal on Concerted Action for the Eurasian Lynx under the CMS.[1084] The key

---

6, Carpathian Convention, ICPDR, (2021) http://www.carpathianconvention.org/tl_files/carpathiancon/Downloads/02%20Activities/Biodiveristy/Connectivity%20Declaration_Final_with%20logos_f.pdf.

1078 Conference of the Parties, Decision COP7/9, § 1–7, 9.

1079 Conference of the Parties, Decision COP7/9, § 7–8.

1080 "Guidelines on communication between protected areas and local communities in the Carpathians," Centralparks, Deliverable D.T1.3.3, (2021), http://www.carpathianconvention.org/tl_files/carpathiancon/Downloads/03%20Meetings%20and%20Events/Implementation%20Committee/CCIC2021/1510C3FDCentralparks_WPT1_Guidelines%20on%20communication_2021_04_26.pdf.

1081 Radoslav Považan and Ján Kadlečík, eds., *The Carpathian Ecosystem Services Toolkit*, Interreg CENTRAL EUROPE project Centralparks "Building management capacities of Carpathian protected areas for the integration and harmonisation of biodiversity protection and local socio-economic development", Deliverable D.T3.1.3. (Banská Bystrica: State Nature Conservancy of the Slovak Republic, 2021), https://programme2014-20.interreg-central.eu/Content.Node/Centralparks/D.T3.1.3-Carpathian-Ecosystem-Services-Toolkit-EN.pdf.

1082 "(Draft) Strategy for local sustainable tourism development based on natural and cultural heritage of the Carpathians," Centralparks, Deliverable D.T1.2.3 (2021), https://programme2014-20.interreg-central.eu/Content.Node/Centralparks/D.T1.2.3-Strategy-for-local-sustainable-tourism-development.pdf.

1083 Conference of the Parties, Decision COP7/9, § 10.

1084 Conference of the Parties, Decision COP7/9, § 19; IUCN SSC and Secretariat of the Carpathian Convention, *Proposal for a Concerted Action for the Eurasian Lynx (Lynx Lynx) Proposed for Listing on Appendix II (and I for L. l. balcanicus) of the Convention*, CMS, 14th Meeting of the Conference of the Parties, Samarkand, 12–17 February 2024, UNEP/CMS/COP14/Doc.32.3.4, https://www.cms.int/sites/default/files/document/cms_cop14_doc.32.3.4_proposal-ca-lynx-lynx_e_0.pdf.

materials on the recent developments are presented on the webpage of the 15th Meeting of the Working Group on Biodiversity.[1085] In addition, roughly a decade ago, the Carpathian Red List of Forest Habitats and Species and the Carpathian List of Invasive Alien Species were created within the framework of the BioREGIO Carpathians project with the aim to assist conservation, including planning of conservation action, decision-making and monitoring.[1086]

The actions on biodiversity for the period of 2024 – 2026 within the institutional mechanism of the Carpathian Convention largely involve support of the work and implementation of the abovementioned projects and initiatives, using the results of the projects undertaken in the past and additionally include such measures as revision of the Working Group on Biodiversity Work Plan (the new plan for 2024 – 2026 has already been adopted[1087]) and exchange with the other regions on relevant topics.[1088]

The recent decision on sustainable forest management draws Parties' attention to the need for implementation of the Forest Protocol and welcomes the development of the Inventory of Virgin Forests of the Carpathians, inviting the Parties to consider extending this inventory to other degrees of naturalness, such as quasi-virgin forests.[1089] Special attention is

---

1085 "15th Meeting of the Working Group on Biodiversity: 17–18 June 2024, Vienna, Austria," Carpathian Convention, accessed November 11, 2024, http://www.carpathianconvention.org/2024/03/19/15th-meeting-of-the-working-group-on-biodiversity/.

1086 Ján Kadlečík, ed., *Carpathian Red List of Forest Habitats and Species and Carpathian List of Invasive Alien Species (draft)*, BioREGIO Carpathians project, (Banská Bystrica: State Nature Conservancy of the Slovak Republic, 2014), http://www.carpathianconvention.org/tl_files/carpathiancon/Downloads/02%20Activities/RedListofSpecies_Habitats_AlienSpecies.pdf.

1087 Klaudia Kuraś, *WG Biodiversity Work Plan: COP7 Mandate, Review of the Progress in Implementation of the WG Biodiversity Work Plan 2021 – 2023 and Preparation Work Plan 2024 – 2026*, Secretariat of the Carpathian Convention (2024), http://www.carpathianconvention.org/wp-content/uploads/2024/06/2_-WG-Biodiversity-Work-Plan-2024-2026_Mandate_-15-WG-Biodiversity_K.Kuras_SCC.pdf.

1088 Conference of the Parties, *Programme of Work of the Carpathian Convention by sectors, 1 January 2024 – 31 December 2026,* Annex 1 to DECISION COP7/20, CC/COP7/DOC3/ADOPTED, (Belgrade, 2023), http://www.carpathianconvention.org/wp-content/uploads/2024/09/CC_COP7_Programme-of-Work.pdf, 35.

1089 Conference of the Parties, *Sustainable forest management, Article 7 of the Carpathian Convention,* Decision COP7/13, (Belgrade, 2023), http://www.carpathianconvention.org/cop7/docs/officialdocuments/CC_COP7_DOC3_COP7%20DECISIONS_ADOPTED.pdf, § 1–3, See also Conference of the Parties, Annex 1 to DECISION COP7/20, 36.

paid to the questions of climate change adaptation and support for Ukraine. In particular, the Parties are encouraged to act on policy recommendations (applying them in accordance with specific circumstances in the country at issue) proposed in the Assessment of climate change risks and adaptation options for the Carpathian forests and their ecosystem services, which was jointly developed by the Working Group on Climate Change and the Working Group on Sustainable Forest Management.[1090] Furthermore, the development of the project proposal ForestConnect "Towards a Climate-smart Forest Connectivity for Large Carnivores in the Balkan-Carpathian Region" (Interreg Danube Region Programme) is acknowledged and the support of the development of a Strategic Action Plan with adaptation actions and resilience-enhancing forest management practices for protected areas by several working groups is encouraged.[1091] On climate change as such, it is further suggested among the actions for 2024 – 2026 to implement the "Long-term Vision 2030 towards combating climate change in the Carpathians" and its corresponding Implementation Framework 2030, and to promote nature-based solutions in the Carpathians with a special focus on ecosystem-based adaptation.[1092]

In the context of sustainable forest management, the support to Ukraine as regards recovery and sustainable management of the Ukrainian forests and the forest sector is encouraged in cooperation with Forest Europe and on the basis of the Ministerial Declaration "Supporting the recovery and sustainable management of Ukrainian forests and its forest sector".[1093] Furthermore, the cooperation with FAO on forest-related activities and support to Ukraine is welcomed.[1094] In addition, the decision on the implementation of the Carpathian Convention recognises challenges posed by the war, mentioning the Ministerial Declaration on the impact of war

1090 Conference of the Parties, Decision COP7/13, § 5; William S. Keeton, Sabine McCallum, Klaudia Kuras, and Harald Egerer, *Assessment of climate change risks and adaptation options for the Carpathian forests and their ecosystem services*, (Nairobi: United Nations Environment Programme, 2023), http://www.carpathianconvention.org/cop7/docs/officialdocuments/CC_COP7_DOC10_Assessment%20of%20climate%20change%20risks%20Carpathian%20forests%20FINAL.pdf.

1091 Conference of the Parties, Decision COP7/13, § 7.

1092 Conference of the Parties, Annex 1 to DECISION COP7/20, 37.

1093 Conference of the Parties, Decision COP7/13, § 8.

1094 Conference of the Parties, Decision COP7/13, § 9.

on the environment and the need for cooperation and assistance[1095] as well as the set of measures to address the environmental consequences of the direct and indirect impacts of the war on the Carpathians, and encouraging Parties and stakeholders to cooperate on their implementation.[1096] Moreover, the project proposal "Support for transboundary cooperation of nature protection services in Polish and Ukrainian parts of the Carpathian region" within the Interreg NEXT Poland–Ukraine 2021 – 2027 Programme is regarded as an example of concrete action on assistance to Ukraine under the aforementioned Ministerial Declaration, while other voluntary contributions and bilateral support measures are encouraged.[1097] The implementation of these declarations, measures and relevant projects is included among the actions for 2024 – 2026.[1098]

Moreover, one of the priorities in the implementation of the Forest Protocol and Strategic Action Plan on it is the promotion of close-to-nature forest management. This is especially important as the Carpathian forests have suffered historically from the clear-cutting, massive timber extraction and in general, even-aged, plantation-style forest management approaches.[1099] To facilitate the exchange of knowledge regarding close-to-nature practices, a documentary film was prepared in the initiative led by the Czech Republic.[1100]

The advancement of sustainable forest management in the Carpathians is also included in the wider European context. To this end, the importance of cooperation with the European Environmental Agency (EEA), including on the development of the Virgin Forests Inventory in the Carpathians, is recognised. Furthermore, the collaboration is important to align implementation of the Carpathian Convention with the "objectives of the EU

1095 Carpathian Ministerial Conference, *Ministerial Declaration of the Carpathian Convention on the impact of war on the environment in Ukraine and the need for cooperation and assistance.*

1096 Conference of the Parties, *Implementation of the Carpathian Convention*, Decision COP7/1, http://www.carpathianconvention.org/cop7/docs/officialdocuments/CC_COP7_DOC3_COP7%20DECISIONS_ADOPTED.pdf, § 2–4.

1097 Conference of the Parties, Decision COP7/1, § 5–6.

1098 Conference of the Parties, Annex 1 to DECISION COP7/20, 33.

1099 "Sustainable Forest Management," Carpathian Convention, accessed November 11, 2024, http://www.carpathianconvention.org/topics/sustainable-forest-management-2/.

1100 "Sustainable Forest Management," Carpathian Convention; See Informace o Lesích, "Close to Nature Management in Carpathian Forests – as viewed by Czech foresters," video, YouTube, May 26, 2023, https://www.youtube.com/watch?v=U8Y3gS-ZZZI&ab_channel=Informaceoles%C3%ADch.

Biodiversity Strategy for 2030, the EU Forest Strategy for 2030, the imminent Nature Restoration Law, and the guiding principles of the UN Decade on Ecosystem Restoration".[1101] The Strategic Action Plan for the Implementation of the Forest Protocol also mentions the need for consideration of the Forest Protocol during the development of the Legally Binding Agreement on Forests in Europe.[1102]

The objectives of the Strategic Action Plan for the Implementation of the Forest Protocol are useful as a reference in planning national policies on forest management and include, for instance, such categories as maintaining and enlarging forest cover (Objective 4), ensuring the productive functions of the forests and their role in rural development (Objective 5), and identification and protection of natural and especially virgin forests (Objective 6). The expected results on forest cover enlargement include identification of the areas in need of afforestation and exchange of information on best practices and silvicultural measures.[1103] The actions within Objective 5 are essential for managing forests in line with the sustainable development paradigm that bridges the economic and developmental needs of the local rural communities with the environmental goals. In particular, such components as sound use of wood and systems for payment for ecosystem services and the aim of counteracting illegal logging and promoting sustainable harvesting of non-wood products are included within this objective.[1104] Another objective that clearly bridges environmental and social components is Objective 12 – social functions of the forests, which includes such expected results as taking into account job creation and employment measures in the sustainable forest management, consideration of sustainable tourism policies in forest management plans, or preservation of cultural heritage of the Carpathian forests and consideration of the fundamental needs of local populations.[1105] Conservation of biodiversity as such is mentioned among the expected results of Objective 7 – improvement of

1101 "Sustainable Forest Management," Carpathian Convention.

1102 *Strategic Action Plan for the Implementation of the Protocol on Sustainable Forest Management*, 7.

1103 *Strategic Action Plan for the Implementation of the Protocol on Sustainable Forest Management*, 8.

1104 *Strategic Action Plan for the Implementation of the Protocol on Sustainable Forest Management*, 9–10.

1105 *Strategic Action Plan for the Implementation of the Protocol on Sustainable Forest Management*, 17.

the protective forest functions.[1106] However, other objectives not mentioning the word 'biodiversity' explicitly are also crucial for its conservation and preservation, such as Objective 8 on close-to-nature forestry, which includes such results as establishment of the programmes on protection and reintroduction of rare native forest tree species in their natural ecosystems and sharing of best practices related to close-to-nature forestry among the Carpathian countries.[1107] In the same vein, Objective 10 – linking forestry, wildlife and ecological network needs in the Carpathian region, seeks to harmonise forest management and wildlife management in the Carpathian region.[1108] Similarly, Objective 6 aims at coherence between the protected areas management plans and the forest management plans in the forest protected areas of the Carpathian region, including proper zonation of the protected areas according to forest conservation needs, and pays special attention to the natural and endangered forests. The results within this measure also include better cooperation among the administrations of the protected areas in the Carpathians.[1109] Further key objectives concern mitigation of and adaptation to climate change (Objective 11), harmonising of monitoring systems (Objective 13), coordination of research and exchange of information (Objective 14), education and public awareness (Objective 17) and the action on a national level serving the implementation of the Strategic Action Plan (Objective 18), including financial possibilities and action on schemes for payment for ecosystem services provided by forests.[1110] What is crucial about this Strategic Action Plan is the integration of biodiversity protection concerns throughout various directions of work, in line with the aim "to remind meeting participants that the Forest Protocol is focused on forestry as a whole".[1111] In the current Work Plan of the Working Group on Sustainable Forest Management (for 2023 – 2026), the

1106 *Strategic Action Plan for the Implementation of the Protocol on Sustainable Forest Management*, 13.

1107 *Strategic Action Plan for the Implementation of the Protocol on Sustainable Forest Management*, 14.

1108 *Strategic Action Plan for the Implementation of the Protocol on Sustainable Forest Management*, 15.

1109 *Strategic Action Plan for the Implementation of the Protocol on Sustainable Forest Management*, 11–12.

1110 *Strategic Action Plan for the Implementation of the Protocol on Sustainable Forest Management*, 16, 18–19, 21–23.

1111 Carpathian Convention Working Group on Sustainable Forest Management, *Strategic Action Plan for the Implementation of the Protocol on SFM to the Carpathian Convention*, 2.

priority topics include natural and virgin forests, close-to-nature forestry and forestry and climate change.[1112]

3.2.4. The practices concerning protected areas, ecological connectivity, forest restoration, and other policy tools for forest biodiversity protection

One of the key directions of work with respect to protected areas is their management and monitoring of biodiversity. According to the IUCN Framework, the management of protected areas is a cyclical process with six stages: context, planning, inputs, process, outputs, and outcomes.[1113] Furthermore, there are numerous guidelines on recommended practices for Carpathian region collected within the Carpathian Countries Integrated Biodiversity Information System including: Carpathian Countries Protected Areas Management Effectiveness Tracking Tool (accompanied by the guidelines on its use), Guidelines for participatory management of protected areas, Guidelines on the assessment of goods and services for protected area managers, Studies "Common Integrated Management Measures for Key Natural Assets in the Carpathians" and "Regional Development Opportunities of Protected Areas and Natural Assets in the Carpathians" as well as report "An Assessment of the Contribution of Ecosystems in Protected Areas to Sector Growth and Human Well Being in Romania".[1114] The poor quality of management plans remains a problem in the Ukrainian Carpathians. Therefore, renewal of the management plans in the selected

1112 8th WG Forest meeting, *Carpathian Convention Working Group on Sustainable Forest Management – Work Plan 2023 – 2026 implementing the Forest Protocol and its Strategic Action Plan*, CC/COP7/DOC13 (2022), http://www.carpathianconvention.org/cop7/docs/officialdocuments/CC_COP7_DOC13_%20WG%20Forest%20Work%20Plan%202023_2026%20FINAL.pdf, 1.

1113 "Protected Areas in the Carpathians," Carpathian Integrated Biodiversity Information System, accessed November 11, 2024, https://ccibis.org/protected-areas-in-the-carpathians/; See Marc Hockings, Sue Stolton, Fiona Leverington et al., *Evaluating Effectiveness: A Framework for Assessing Management Effectiveness of Protected Areas*, 2nd ed., (Gland and Cambridge: IUCN, 2006), https://portals.iucn.org/library/efiles/documents/pag-014.pdf.

1114 "Protected Areas in the Carpathians," Carpathian Integrated Biodiversity Information System.

key NRF objects in the Ukrainian Carpathians was planned within the SNPA Project, but unfortunately, it has been halted because of the war.[1115]

In addition, what is suggested in the recent literature, currently only a negligible number of protected areas worldwide function as genetic reserves and have preservation of genetic diversity as their conservation goal. Genetic diversity is, however, essential for the preservation of biodiversity, especially in the times of climate change. It is accordingly recommended for the governments to strive to "set aside areas where natural selection can occur without human intervention", even if such a change of approach might conflict with the dominant management objectives on increased production, recreation or aesthetics. Creation of "spaces where natural selection is allowed free rein" is seen as a step further from viewing nature and biodiversity through the lenses of their service to people to a broader perspective, where "nature has an intrinsic right to exist".[1116]

For biodiversity monitoring in protected areas, there is also a recently published IUCN Framework, namely "A Framework for Monitoring Biodiversity in Protected Areas and Other Effective Area-Based Conservation Measures", introducing a new paradigm of monitoring in line with the Kunming-Montreal Global Biodiversity Framework and suggesting the best possible utilisation of the available resources.[1117]

As argued by Sarkar, the designation of national parks is not the only strategy for biodiversity conservation, as this goal is more inclusive than wilderness preservation. In fact, the creation of protected areas might be counterproductive under certain circumstances, such as where there is local political opposition to the expansion of protected areas on territories that have been traditionally used by humans. It is suggested that the creation of land management plans allowing for certain human activities but aiming to spare biodiversity from harm is a useful strategy (provided that there is

1115 "Selected PAs have the necessary planning documents for their development," Support to Nature Protected Areas in Ukraine; "The project is on pause but is helping parks," Support to Nature Protected Areas in Ukraine, accessed November 11, 2024, https://snpa.in.ua/en/english-diyalnist-proektu/diyalnist-proektu-1/.

1116 Bruno Fady and Magda Bou Dagher Kharrat, "To conserve biodiversity, create spaces where natural selection is allowed free rein," *Nature* 633, 36 (September 2024), *doi:* https://doi.org/10.1038/d41586-024-02854-z.

1117 Daniel Dalton, Vanessa Berger, Hanns Kirchmeir et al., *A Framework For Monitoring Biodiversity In Protected Areas And Other Effective Area-Based Conservation Measures: Concepts, Methods And Technologies*, IUCN WCPA Technical Report Series No. 7, (Gland: IUCN, 2024), https://portals.iucn.org/library/sites/library/files/documents/PATRS-007-En.pdf, 69.

an empirical investigation of the impact of human presence on biodiversity conservation). In some situations, human intervention, such as the use of land for grazing, might be favourable to biodiversity, as the example of Keoladeo National Park in India suggests, where the prohibition of grazing resulted in devastation of the land as a bird habitat, and the reintroduction of grazing was subsequently promoted.[1118]

There is also a recent trend in designating another area-based category for *in-situ* biodiversity conservation apart from the protected areas, namely the 'other effective area-based conservation measures' (OECMs), the definition of which was adopted by the Parties to the CBD in 2018. Such areas might be managed primarily not for the reasons of long-term conservation of nature, but they must contribute to the conservation outcomes.[1119]

One of the useful strategies for biodiversity conservation, which is particularly vital for migratory species, is the ecological connectivity. The notion of 'ecological connectivity' was developed in 2019 in the context of identifying CMS priorities for the post-2020 Global Biodiversity Framework, and is understood as "the unimpeded movement of species and the flow of natural processes that sustain life on Earth".[1120] Ecological connectivity has been actively promoted within the CMS mechanism in recent years, informing the development of the Kunming-Montreal Global Biodiversity Framework.[1121] The need for ecological connectivity is considered by the CMS COP to be a key factor in the definition of appropriate conservation management units, and it is further recommended that the parties consider preserving the "functioning of the migration process itself, as opposed to

1118 Sarkar, *Biodiversity and Environmental Philosophy*, 41–43.

1119 United Nations Environment Programme, *Environmental Rule of Law: Tracking Progress and Charting Future Directions*, (Nairobi: UNEP, 2023), https://doi.org/10.59117/20.500.11822/43943, 35.

1120 "Ecological Connectivity," CMS, accessed November 11, 2024, https://www.cms.int/en/topics/ecological-connectivity; Conference of the Parties, *Improving Ways of Addressing Connectivity in the Conservation of Migratory Species*, UNEP/CMS/Resolution 12.26 (Rev.COP13) (2020), https://www.cms.int/sites/default/files/document/cms_cop13_res.12.26_rev.cop13_e.pdf, Preamble.

1121 *Kunming-Montreal Global Biodiversity Framework*, Targets 2, 3, 12; UNEP/CMS Secretariat, *Connectivity and the Post-2020 Biodiversity Framework: An Introduction*, Fact Sheet (June 2019) https://www.cms.int/sites/default/files/publication/fact_sheet_connectivity_new.pdf; UNEP/CMS Secretariat, *Connectivity and the Post-2020 Biodiversity Framework: Elements for New Goals and Targets*, Fact Sheet (August 2019) https://www.cms.int/sites/default/files/publication/fact_sheet_connectivity_2.pdf.

merely the status of populations or habitats".[1122] The importance of ecological connectivity within the CMS is further enhanced by the Samarkand Strategic Plan for Migratory Species 2024 – 2032, adopted at the CMS COP 14. In addition, within the framework of this COP in February 2024, the new initiative on ecological connectivity was launched – the Global Partnership on Ecological Connectivity (GPEC).[1123]

Moreover, the ecological connectivity is important for the achievement of Sustainable Development Goals, and connectivity conservation is considered to be a key tool for safeguarding biodiversity and ecosystem functions, including climate resilience and disease resistance. For these reasons, in cooperation with the CMS, the connectivity conservation is also promoted by the IUCN, which issued separate Guidelines for Conserving Connectivity through Ecological Networks and Corridors.[1124] Furthermore, the importance of ecological connectivity is acknowledged in the General Assembly resolution 75/271 "Nature knows no borders: transboundary cooperation – a key factor for biodiversity conservation, restoration and sustainable use".[1125]

Ecological connectivity is also inextricably linked with ecosystem restoration, as "retaining or reinstating connectivity is crucial to securing healthy, resilient and sustainable ecosystems while restoring degraded habitat is a key management tool for improving connectivity in the landscape".[1126] Ecosystem restoration as such is a separate topic and direction of work, the global attention to which is encouraged by the proclamation of 2021 – 2030 as the United Nations Decade on Ecosystem Restoration.[1127]

1122 Conference of the Parties, UNEP/CMS/Resolution 12.26 (Rev.COP13), 1 (i), (ii).

1123 "Global Partnership on Ecological Connectivity (GPEC)," CMS, accessed November 11, 2024, https://www.cms.int/en/page/global-partnership-ecological-connecti vity-gpec.

1124 "Ecological Connectivity," CMS; IUCN World Conservation Congress 2020, *Ecological Connectivity Conservation in the Post-2020 Global Biodiversity Framework: From Local to International Levels*, WCC-2020-Res-073-EN (Marseille, 2020) https://portals.iucn.org/library/sites/library/files/resrecfiles/WCC_2020_RE S_073_EN.pdf; Jodi Hilty et al., *Guidelines for Conserving Connectivity through Ecological Networks and Corridors*, ed. Craig Groves (Gland: IUCN, 2020), https:/ /doi.org/10.2305/IUCN.CH.2020.PAG.30.en.

1125 "Ecological Connectivity," CMS; *Nature knows no borders: transboundary cooperation – a key factor for biodiversity conservation, restoration and sustainable use*, General Assembly Resolution 75/271, § 1, 2, 3, 7, 9.

1126 "Ecological Connectivity," CMS.

1127 *United Nations Decade on Ecosystem Restoration (2021–2030)*, General Assembly Resolution 73/284, A/RES/73/284 (March 1, 2019) https://documents.un.org/do

Restoration is also included among the targets of the Kunming-Montreal GBF (Target 2), contained in the already existing obligations under international law,[1128] and recently adopted EU regulation.[1129]

For forests, restoration activities include tree planting (providing that the appropriate parameters of tree species, time and place are met), assistance of natural regeneration, forest landscape restoration and rewilding.[1130] One of the legal questions on restoration is the extent to which states are obliged to undertake it. For instance, it is claimed by Arie Trouwborst and Jens-Christian Svenning that existing international law, including the Biodiversity Protocol (Article 4 and Article 8 (2)) to the Carpathian Convention, could be interpreted to require far-reaching efforts when it comes to rewilding and restoration of megafauna.[1131] In the context of the Ukrainian Carpathians, a good example of the efforts on ecosystem restoration includes the action on reintroduction of the European bison (*Bison bonasus* L.) within the Skolivsky Beskydy NRF, and the Chernivtsi region of

---

c/undoc/gen/n19/060/16/pdf/n1906016.pdf; "Preventing, Halting and Reversing Loss of Nature," United Nations Decade on Ecosystem Restoration 2021 – 2030, accessed November 11, 2024, https://www.decadeonrestoration.org/.

1128 Arie Trouwborst, *Restoring what is broken: Wildlife law in an era of ecological emergency, eye-opening science, and maturing morality*, Inaugural address (Tilburg University, 2024), 30; See Kees Bastmeijer, "Ecological restoration in international biodiversity law: a promising strategy to address our failure to prevent?" in *Research Handbook on Biodiversity and Law*, ed. Michael Bowman et al. (Cheltenham: Edward Elgar Publishing, 2016), 387.

1129 Regulation (EU) 2024/1991 of the European Parliament and of the Council of 24 June 2024 on nature restoration and amending Regulation (EU) 2022/869, *Official Journal of the European Union, L, 2024/1991, 29.7.2024,* http://data.europa.eu/eli/reg/2024/1991/oj.

1130 United Nations Decade on Ecosystem Restoration, *Ecosystem Restoration Playbook: A Practical Guide To Healing The Planet*, developed for World Environment Day 2021, https://wedocs.unep.org/bitstream/handle/20.500.11822/35858/ERP.pdf?sequence=1&isAllowed=y, 12; See also Arend De Haas, "Impact of Rewilding on Ecosystem Resilience," Rewilding Academy, accessed November 11, 2024, https://rewilding.academy/impact-of-rewilding-on-ecosystem-resilience/.

1131 Trouwborst, *Restoring what is broken*, 30; Arie Trouwborst and Jens-Christian Svenning, "Megafauna Restoration as a Legal Obligation: International Biodiversity Law and the Rehabilitation of Large Mammals in Europe," *Review of European, Comparative & International Environmental Law 31*, no. 2 (July 2022): 182, https://doi.org/10.1111/reel.12443.31; See also Arie Trouwborst, "Megafauna Restoration as an Obligation – the Role of Law in Rehabilitating Europe's Large Mammals," Rewilding symposium: people, policies, practice, video from 62:30, Wageningen University and Research Public Library, 29 September 2022, https://wur.yuja.com/V/Watch?v=260217&node=1323158&a=2135271602.

Ukraine.[1132] More efforts on the reintroduction of the European bison are expected to be undertaken in the future based on the recently adopted action plan on this species in Ukraine.[1133]

Furthermore, one of the important questions on a European level is the protection and restoration of the primary forests. A group of experts addressing this question and pointing out to the fact that less than 4 per cent of the European forests are characterised by minimal signs of human use, suggests several priority action directions. The first priority from the conservation perspective, the one relevant for the areas where primary forests still exist, is "ensuring that a sufficiently large area is adequately protected".[1134] The provisions of the EU "Biodiversity Strategy for 2030" requiring that all of the EU's extant primary and old-growth forests are mapped, monitored and strictly protected are potentially helpful in this regard.[1135] The protection of such forests shall also be strict enough to avoid degradation and preserve natural forest dynamics. Therefore, it is important to make sure that the level of protection is adequate (which constitutes the second priority). At the same time, apart from protecting primary forests, restoration of conditions and parameters close to them (such as forest structure, composition and functioning) in non-primary forests is a useful strategy for protecting forest biodiversity in Europe, which could be undertaken passively or actively. Therefore, identification of the areas where restoration of primary forests is "needed and feasible" is a third sug-

---

1132 Development Strategy of the Chernivtsi Region for the Period until 2027, 80; On bison reintroduction in Ukraine in historical perspective see Ivan Parnikoza, Volodymyr Sesin, and Volodymyr Boreiko, "History, current state and perspectives of conservation of European bison (*Bison bonasus* L.) in Ukraine," *Proceedings of the Theriological School*, Issue 10 (2010), http://www.terreco.univ.kiev.ua/_media/library/bizon/pts10-35-parnikoza-bison-3ed.pdf; [In Ukrainan: Іван Парнікоза, Володимир Сесін, та Володимир Борейко, "Історія, сьогодення та перспективи збереження популяції зубра (*Bison bonasus* L.) в Україні," Праці Теріологічної школи, Випуск 10 (2010)].

1133 Action Plan for the Conservation and restoration of the European bison (*Bison bonasus* L.) in Ukraine.

1134 Francesco M. Sabatini et al., "Protection Gaps and Restoration Opportunities for Primary Forests in Europe," *Diversity and Distributions* 26, no. 12 (December 2020): 1648, https://doi.org/10.1111/ddi.13158.

1135 Sabatini et al., "Protection Gaps and Restoration Opportunities for Primary Forests in Europe," 1648; "EU Biodiversity Strategy for 2030: Bringing nature back into our lives."

gested conservation priority.[1136] Protection of primary forests is considered to be more cost-effective than their restoration after degradation. However, restoration of existing forests "towards their ecological potential" is also crucial, especially as both a biodiversity-enhancing measure and a climate change mitigation solution.[1137]

Moreover, this European-wide study suggests that for regions where primary forests are still relatively widespread, such as in parts of Eastern Europe (which obviously includes Ukrainian Carpathians), the greater level of managers' awareness of the "uniqueness of these forests in a broader biogeographical context" is needed, especially in the light of the concerns as to the loss of such forests. Generally, forest management strategies "efficiently balancing the trade-offs between timber production and biodiversity impacts" are vital to complement protection and restoration in Europe. Attention to the management of the forests coupled with recognition of their values is the only strategy to ensure the provision of the key ecosystem services and long-term human well-being.[1138]

In another recent study on the intersection of resilience of forests and society in context of biodiversity crisis focusing on Europe, the following five main types of action capable of improving resilience have been identified: forest landscape restoration, rewilding, systematic conservation planning, reduction of pressures that interact with climate driven disturbances, and conserving functional diversity.[1139] Furthermore, the three key messages for guiding forest management and policy have been suggested, including the need for operationalisation of resilience, the need to identify and address trade-offs and win-wins, such as those between ecological and social subsystems, and the need for adaptive management for enhancing resilience in forests and society. With respect to the second message, it is clarified that enhancing resilience translates to a paradigm shift in forest management approaches, "moving from traditional practices focused on timber extrac-

1136 Sabatini et al., "Protection Gaps and Restoration Opportunities for Primary Forests in Europe," 1648.

1137 Sabatini et al., "Protection Gaps and Restoration Opportunities for Primary Forests in Europe," 1656–1657.

1138 Sabatini et al., "Protection Gaps and Restoration Opportunities for Primary Forests in Europe," 1658; See also Robin L. Chazdon, "Protecting Intact Forests Requires Holistic Approaches," *Nature Ecology & Evolution* 2, no. 6 (April 2018): 915, https://doi.org/10.1038/s41559-018-0546-y.

1139 Elena Cantarello et al., "Shaping and Enhancing Resilient Forests for a Resilient Society," *Ambio* 53, no. 8 (August 2024): 1099–1100, https://doi.org/10.1007/s13280-024-02006-7.

tion towards a more comprehensive and forward-looking approach".[1140] Within adaptive management, the increased use of mixed forests is highlighted as a response to both climate change and biodiversity loss, which is recommended, for instance, in the German and British recent silvicultural guidelines.[1141] Moreover, the mixed forests are also less vulnerable to pests compared to monoculture forests.[1142] In general, biodiversity is regarded as one of the most prominent topics in forest policy discussions in Europe, and there is a debate as to the need to renew Pan-European Criteria, Indicators and Operational Guidelines for sustainable forest management in light of the developments of the policy instruments and goals on biodiversity, including the New EU Forest Strategy for 2030.[1143]

According to the OECD, policy instruments that foster conservation, sustainable use and restoration of biodiversity could be classified as regulatory (command-and-control, including standards and prohibitions), economic (incentive-based, including fiscal instruments and payments for ecosystem services), and information and voluntary instruments (including eco-labelling and voluntary corporate standards).[1144] Recently, the OECD has conducted a study on the use of economic instruments and finance for biodiversity, which provides an overview of the use of policy instruments across the globe, helping to monitor the progress towards achieving Target 18 of the Kunming-Montreal Global Biodiversity Framework.[1145]

1140 Cantarello et al., "Shaping and Enhancing Resilient Forests for a Resilient Society," 1102–1103.

1141 Cantarello et al., "Shaping and Enhancing Resilient Forests for a Resilient Society," 1103.

1142 FAO, *Guide to Implementation of Phytosanitary Standards in Forestry*, 2nd ed., FAO Forestry Paper No. 164. (Rome: FAO, 2024) https://doi.org/10.4060/cd3046en, 26.

1143 Bernhard Wolfslehner and Stefanie Linser, *European Forest Indicators at a Glance*, Forest Europe Background Paper and Contribution to the European Forest Alliance (EFA), (November 2023) https://foresteurope.org/wp-content/uploads/2024/03/European-forest-biodiversity-indicators-at-a-glance.pdf; Markus Lier et al., "The New EU Forest Strategy for 2030: A New Understanding of Sustainable Forest Management?," *Forests* 13, no. 2 (February 2022): 245, https://doi.org/10.3390/f13020245.

1144 "Biodiversity," OECD, accessed November 11, 2024, https://www.oecd.org/en/topics/biodiversity.html.

1145 "Tracking Economic Instruments and Finance for Biodiversity 2024," OECD, October 18, 2024, https://www.oecd.org/en/data/insights/data-explainers/2024/10/Tracking-Economic-Instruments-and-Finance-for-Biodiversity-2024.html.

3.3. *The example of biodiversity protection activities in the national parks within the German federal state of Bavaria*

For the purposes of the present work, research interviews have been conducted with the employees of the two national parks in Bavaria: Berchtesgaden and the Bavarian Forest.

As an employee of the Berchtesgaden explained, this national park falls under the IUCN Management Category II,[1146] aimed at the protection of natural processes, and 75 per cent of the park's territory constitutes a core zone. Apart from the core zone, there is a management zone, comprising 25 per cent of the territory. Approximately half of the total territory is covered by forests.[1147]

No human intervention is allowed in the core zone apart from the exceptions related to the visitors' safety. In particular, there is a network of hiking trails, which has to be protected from the obvious hazards, such as a dead tree standing close to the hiking trail, which might fall on visitors. Such a dead tree may be cut without extracting it. Furthermore, no wildlife management, such as active hunting, is undertaken in the core zone. In the management zone, the protection of the processes is also undertaken, but with human intervention. The activities allowed there include those undertaken by the park management and by the third-party right holders. The management has a responsibility to restore natural forest communities in the park. Such a restoration is necessary given the intense land use history, including salt mining in the area. For instance, in terms of species composition, there are more conifers than under natural conditions. However, the trees are not actively cut down by the national park. Instead, the restoration management is undertaken, meaning that the trees are planted in the gaps caused by natural disturbances, such as a windthrow or bark beetles. When there is a lack of natural regeneration of the tree species that are important for these ecosystems, like the European beech or silver fir, the park actively plants them to achieve a more natural composition of the forests.[1148]

1146 "IUCN Category II – National Park," UNEP WCMC, last updated December 24, 2020, https://tinyurl.com/4cswa7dz.

1147 Research and monitoring employee, Berchtesgaden National Park, personal communication, December 11, 2023.

1148 Research and monitoring employee, Berchtesgaden National Park, personal communication, December 11, 2023.

When it comes to the third-party right holders, historically (and some of these rights might date back to medieval times), there have been the rights of the local farmers, such as grazing rights or rights for extracting wood. These rights continue to exist despite the creation of the national park, however, their exercise might be modified. For instance, with respect to wood used for purposes such as fuel, fencing or roofs, it is provided to these people, but not from the territory of the national park. Instead, in cooperation with the Bavarian State Forests, the wood is provided to the right holders to the extent of the right, but it is brought from areas outside the national park.[1149]

The main management tasks of the national park include visitor guidance; forest development and game population regulation in the absence of large predators and interrupted patterns of migration of the red deer; bark beetle management in the areas adjacent to commercial forests; and alpine farming. They serve the achievement of the goals of the park, "even if the actual goal is to leave nature to its own devices".[1150]

The current system of biodiversity monitoring, which "goes through the whole trophic cascade", was established in 2021. Before that, there were some spotlights on specific species, such as grouse species of birds or ungulate species, including red deer and chamois.[1151] Since 2021, biodiversity monitoring has been jointly conducted in Berchtesgaden National Park and Bavarian Forest National Park. In Berchtesgaden, a number of permanent monitoring plots representing the main habitats, including forests, were established. When it comes to forests, the different forest development phases are taken into account. The diversity of species is surveyed with the use of a broad set of methods, aiming to provide as comprehensive a picture as possible. These include mapping of the plants and determination of fungi by means of DNA sequencing from the soil and deadwood samples, use of malaise, window and ground traps to catch insects, use of audio recorders to identify birds and bats, and use of photo traps for mammal surveys.[1152]

1149 Research and monitoring employee, Berchtesgaden National Park, personal communication, December 11, 2023.

1150 "Management," Nationalparkvervaltung Berchtesgaden, accessed November 11, 2024, https://www.nationalpark-berchtesgaden.de/english/nature/national_park/management/index.htm.

1151 Research and monitoring employee, Berchtesgaden National Park, personal communication, December 11, 2023.

1152 "Biodiversity Monitoring," Nationalparkvervaltung Berchtesgaden, accessed November 11, 2024, https://www.nationalpark-berchtesgaden.de/english/research/monitoring/biodiversity/index.htm.

In total, there are 213 plots designated for obtaining baseline information on biodiversity, all of which might be revisited in 10 to 15 years. Currently, 54 of those plots are taken for monitoring and are constantly monitored in a three-year rotation of 18 of them, which are constantly monitored to allow for tracing some trends and insights of the ongoing developments. The monitoring is financed by the Ministry of the Environment.[1153]

In terms of addressing the threats to biodiversity, such as climate change, the key activities include observation and documentation, which is vital as climate change might lead to the introduction of new pests and diseases or neo-biota. There are currently hardly any management targets on protecting specific species, as the national park focuses on the processes that need to be protected rather than on individual species.[1154]

Those who violate the rules of the park are at first educated, but they may also be fined. The park is monitored by the rangers, who are in charge of law enforcement, but also education and guided excursions. Certain sites, where violations most often occur (such as an area with a waterfall that has been recently closed for visitors), are particularly closely monitored. The cases of illegal logging are rare, and if they occur, the national park informs the respective nature conservation authority, which then evaluates the situation and might fine a violator.[1155]

On the question regarding the relevance of international law instruments for the national park's activities, it was reported that, for instance, the EU regulations implemented by means of national legislation are relevant. For example, within the framework of the Natura 2000 network, the national park has to undertake certain monitoring and prepare reports.[1156]

Another national park, the Bavarian Forest, shares many similarities with the model practised in Berchtesgaden. It comprises the nature zone, operating under the motto "leave nature to its own devices", where only the trees along the trails are cut, and other zones, where human intervention is undertaken, including development zone (which might be added to nature zone in future), management (buffer) zone (where logging and hunting are

1153 Research and monitoring employee, Berchtesgaden National Park, personal communication, December 11, 2023.

1154 Research and monitoring employee, Berchtesgaden National Park, personal communication, December 11, 2023.

1155 Research and monitoring employee, Berchtesgaden National Park, personal communication, December 11, 2023.

1156 Research and monitoring employee, Berchtesgaden National Park, personal communication, December 11, 2023.

undertaken by the national park stuff) and recreation zone (hosting information centre and playgrounds). It does not, however, qualify as a national park according to the IUCN, given that its natural zone has historically been too small and only in 1997 it was enlarged to a sufficient number of 75 per cent, meaning that it will start qualifying for this category in 2027.[1157]

The park aims at the natural regeneration of forests. However, some restoration is also undertaken because the forest has been used commercially. It is normally allowed for "bark beetles to do their jobs", however, some action to control bark beetle might be taken in the development zone to accommodate the concerns of the surrounding forest owners. The national park has its own cattle, which are taken in the summer to the pastures by the park employees.[1158]

When it comes to action aimed at biodiversity protection, numerous research and monitoring activities are undertaken on a regular basis. For instance, one research project explored whether there is a contradiction between climate action and biodiversity protection when it comes to deadwood, which is said to release a sufficient amount of CO2, but which is at the same time important for biodiversity. It was, however, established that the yearly release of the CO_2 from the deadwood equates the amount of CO_2 released by the living spruce forest. A conclusion was made that the requests to remove the deadwood from the forests for the reasons of climate action are unjustified.[1159] There is also, for instance, a research project on fungi, where researchers are trying to cultivate fungi in a lab and then trying to let them grow in nature (in the management zone of the park).[1160] The invasive alien species, as of now, do not constitute a problem inside the park.[1161]

It was additionally mentioned during the interview in the context of the dead wood that the governmental incentives might be important (not

1157 Orsolya Decker (nature conservation and research employee) and Kristin Biebl (ranger), Bavarian Forest National Park, personal communication, December 18, 2023.

1158 Orsolya Decker and Kristin Biebl, Bavarian Forest National Park, personal communication, December 18, 2023.

1159 Nationalparkverwaltung Bayerischer Wald, *Forschung im Nationalpark*, (August 2022) https://www.nationalpark-bayerischer-wald.bayern.de/service/downloads/doc/broschuere/forschung_im_nationalpark_2022.pdf, 11.

1160 Orsolya Decker and Kristin Biebl, Bavarian Forest National Park, personal communication, December 18, 2023.

1161 Orsolya Decker and Kristin Biebl, Bavarian Forest National Park, personal communication, December 18, 2023.

within the park, but generally). The successful example of a forest owned by the Church, where the dead wood is left, because the government is incentivising it, was mentioned. It was explained that as long as the price is put on these things, it might assist people in undertaking these measures.[1162]

There are hiking trails and cycling areas designated for visitors. It was explained that within the core area, which is not necessarily within the nature zone, visitors are allowed to remain only within the marked area. Moreover, access to some areas is restricted during spring and winter but is allowed for four months a year. Mushroom- and berry-picking is allowed for private use, however, driving is not permitted. There are tools for digital visitor management, including the "digital ranger" and information on the webpage as to what is allowed and what is not. The national park aims to provide environmental education, for the purposes of which there are two buildings, where pupils can participate in a week-long environmental programme. There is also a format of 'junior rangers', which involves kids from the area.[1163]

If rangers identify a violation of the rules, the information is forwarded to the nature conservation authority, and a fine is possible. In cases where a violation amounts to a crime (such as fishing, hunting or arson), the matter is investigated by the police. On the question of illegal logging, it was reported that it is rather impossible, as no driving is permitted on the territory of the national park.[1164]

The Natural Park is funded by the Ministry of the Environment within the Bavarian government. However, research projects are also funded by institutions or universities. The use of all the visitor centres is free. However, some profits are generated by the parking or selling of wood, and all the profit generated by the park goes to the government. In addition to the hired staff, there is an opportunity to hire interns or rely on volunteers.[1165]

When it comes to the relevance of international legal norms, the Natura 2000 was mentioned. It was stated that there are questionnaires to be filled

1162 Orsolya Decker and Kristin Biebl, Bavarian Forest National Park, personal communication, December 18, 2023.

1163 Orsolya Decker and Kristin Biebl, Bavarian Forest National Park, personal communication, December 18, 2023.

1164 Orsolya Decker and Kristin Biebl, Bavarian Forest National Park, personal communication, December 18, 2023.

1165 Orsolya Decker and Kristin Biebl, Bavarian Forest National Park, personal communication, December 18, 2023.

out and certain restrictions on cutting the trees, including the prohibition to cut the trees during the nesting season.[1166]

3.4. The potential synergies between biodiversity protection and related legal regimes in their application to the Ukrainian Carpathians

The framework for the protection of biodiversity of the forest ecosystems of the Ukrainian Carpathians, created by various norms on the international level (global, regional and subregional) as well as by the national legislation in Ukraine (mostly on forestry and nature protection), does not exist in isolation, but is linked to many other sectors (at least by means of the principle of integration described in Chapter 1). Besides the general need for sectoral policies to include considerations of biodiversity protection, certain legal spheres are particularly closely linked to the biodiversity protection regime, being able to form synergies and affect the effectiveness of one another. Two areas that are particularly prone to such an interaction with the biodiversity protection framework are climate change and human rights. One of the bright linking components here is the ecosystem approach, which, as noted by Morgera, "creates a room for mutual supportiveness among the CBD and other international agreements, such as those on climate change or human rights."[1167] It is recognised in the literature that there is a "great potential for synergies" between biodiversity and climate change.[1168] Such synergies and awareness of them, including "the links between deforestation, the loss of biodiversity and climate change", are also of special importance for forest biodiversity, given the lack of a separate specific international agreement that would comprehensively regulate forests.[1169] Moreover, the problems of climate change, biodiversity loss and pollution, referred to in recent years as "triple planetary crisis", are interrelated.[1170] It has, for instance, been suggested that the extinction of the golden toad

1166 Orsolya Decker and Kristin Biebl, Bavarian Forest National Park, personal communication, December 18, 2023.

1167 Morgera, "The ecosystem approach and the precautionary principle," 77–78.

1168 Sandrine Maljean-Dubois and Matthieu Wemaëre, "Biodiversity and climate change," in *Biodiversity and Nature Protection Law*, ed. Elisa Morgera and Jona Razzaque (Cheltenham: Edward Elgar Publishing, 2017), 297.

1169 Savaresi, "Forest Biodiversity," 203–204.

1170 Sarkar, *Biodiversity and Environmental Philosophy*, 1; Astrid Puentes Riaño, *Overview of the implementation of the human right to a clean, healthy and sustainable environment*, Report of the Special Rapporteur on the human right to a clean,

(*Bufo periglenes*), endemic to the Monteverde cloud forest reserve of Costa Rica,[1171] and more recently extinction of Bramble Cay melomys (*Melomys rubicola*), the only mammal endemic to the Great Barrier Reef were implicated by and attributed to climate change.[1172] This subchapter focuses firstly on climate change and biodiversity followed by the human rights-based approach to biodiversity protection with the substantive human right to a healthy environment at its core, and then additionally explores links between sustainable tourism and biodiversity as well as characterises environmental rule of law as a general framework necessary for proper functioning of the biodiversity-related laws and policies.

3.4.1. Climate change and biodiversity

The Kunming–Montreal Global Biodiversity Framework names climate change among the direct drivers of change in nature.[1173] The interaction of climate change and biodiversity, according to the GBF, is twofold. On the one hand the GBF aims at the minimisation of impact of climate change on biodiversity through the mitigation, adaptation and disaster risk reduction actions (Target 8)[1174] and on the other hand, restoration, maintenance and enhancement of the nature's contributions to people, including by means of ecosystem functions and services, such as the regulation of climate, is strived for (Target 11).[1175] Furthermore, Target 19 on increasing the level of financial resources to implement national biodiversity strategies and action

---

healthy and sustainable environment, A/79/270 (August 2, 2024) https://documents.un.org/doc/undoc/gen/n24/228/44/pdf/n2422844.pdf, § 2.

1171 Sarkar, *Biodiversity and Environmental Philosophy*, 1; See J. Alan Pounds, Michael P. L. Fogden, and John H. Campbell, "Biological Response to Climate Change on a Tropical Mountain," *Nature* 398, no. 6728 (April 1999): 611–15, https://doi.org/10.1038/19297.

1172 John H. Knox, *Report of The Special Rapporteur on the Issue of Human Rights Obligations Relating to the Enjoyment of a Safe, Clean, Healthy and Sustainable Environment*, Human Rights Council, Thirty-fourth Session, A/HRC/34/49 (January 19, 2017) https://documents.un.org/doc/undoc/gen/g17/009/97/pdf/g1700997.pdf, § 38.

1173 *Kunming-Montreal Global Biodiversity Framework*, Section A.

1174 *Kunming-Montreal Global Biodiversity Framework*, Target 8; See also CEM and IUCN, *Climate Mitigation and Biodiversity Conservation*, Technical Brief, UNFCCC COP 28 (November 2023) https://iucn.org/resources/information-brief/climate-mitigation-and-biodiversity-conservation.

1175 *Kunming-Montreal Global Biodiversity Framework*, Target 11.

plans includes among the possible actions "[o]ptimizing co-benefits and synergies of finance targeting the biodiversity and climate crises".[1176]

The relationship between climate change and biodiversity regimes is, however, not as straightforward and problem-free as it might seem at first glance, given the importance of both of them and the possibilities for synergies. From the very beginning, since the emergence of the two respective framework conventions, the CBD and the United Nations Framework Convention on Climate Change (UNFCCC) in the 1992 Rio Conference, these two treaties only implicitly referred to one another.[1177] For instance, preamble of the UNFCCC mentions the fact that the increase of greenhouse effect "may adversely affect natural ecosystems" and expresses awareness as to the "role and importance in terrestrial and marine ecosystems of sinks and reservoirs of greenhouse gases" while Article 2 formulating the objective of this convention, seeks to achieve the appropriate level of the greenhouse gas concentrations "within the time-frame sufficient to allow ecosystems to adapt naturally to climate change".[1178] In addition, fragile mountain ecosystems in developing countries are mentioned among the particularly vulnerable areas to the adverse effects of climate change,[1179] which is also reflected in the commitments.[1180] Moreover, commitments include promotion of sustainable management, conservation and enhancement of "sinks and reservoirs of all greenhouse gases not controlled by the Montreal Protocol, including biomass, forests and oceans as well as other terrestrial, coastal and marine ecosystems", leading to the conclusion that protection of forest ecosystems falls under the scope of this commitment.[1181]

The Kyoto Protocol and the Paris Agreement also contain similar provisions.[1182] For instance, the planning process and implementation of the adaptation actions, including nationally determined prioritised actions,

1176 *Kunming-Montreal Global Biodiversity Framework*, Target 19 (e).
1177 Maljean-Dubois and Wemaëre, "Biodiversity and climate change," 297.
1178 Maljean-Dubois and Wemaëre, "Biodiversity and climate change," 297; UNFCCC, Preamble.
1179 UNFCCC, Preamble.
1180 UNFCCC, Article 4 (8) (g).
1181 UNFCCC, Article 4 (1) (d).
1182 Maljean-Dubois and Wemaëre, "Biodiversity and climate change," 298, 305; "Kyoto Protocol to the United Nations Framework Convention on Climate Change," opened for signature December 11, 1997, *United Nations Treaty Series* 2303, p. 162, UN Doc FCCC/CP/1997/7/Add.1, Article 2. (a)(ii); Conference of the Parties, *Paris Agreement*, UN Doc. FCCC/CP/2015/L.9/Rev/1 (December 12, 2015), Preamble, Articles 5, 7, 8 [Paris Agreement].

may include assessment of the climate change impact on vulnerable ecosystems.[1183] The Paris Agreement's key operative provisions related to biodiversity and forests is Article 5, drawing Parties' attention to "policy approaches and positive incentives for activities relating to reducing emissions from deforestation and forest degradation", "the role of conservation, sustainable management of forests and enhancement of forest carbon stocks in developing countries" as well as "alternative policy approaches, such as joint mitigation and adaptation approaches for the integral and sustainable management of forests", while also "reaffirming the importance of incentivizing, as appropriate, non-carbon benefits associated with such approaches".[1184]

In general, forests are one of the particularly obvious and important crossroads between climate change and biodiversity. This is because they clearly fall simultaneously within both of these legal regimes – as "reservoirs and sources of atmospheric carbon dioxide" when it comes to climate change and as "a component of, and a habitat for, terrestrial biological diversity".[1185] Given the lack of a separate, legally binding framework on forests, the obligations stemming from the climate change regime have to be considered in combination with those on biodiversity protection. Such a consideration, however, is not taken for granted, and some concerns on the compatibility of the climate regime with the biodiversity conservation objectives have been voiced. This could be exemplified by the enhancement of the carbon sinks in the Kyoto Protocol's Clean Development Mechanism, which did not provide any safeguards to guarantee that activities of afforestation or reforestation (counted as credits under this mechanism) protect biodiversity rather than encourage "destructive but cost-effective large-scale monoculture plantations".[1186]

One of the main problems with the achievement of synergies between the climate and biodiversity protection regimes on an international level lies in the fact that the efforts on mutual supportiveness have not been equal. As noted by Sandrine Maljean-Dubois and Matthieu Wemaëre, "there seems to be less openness to addressing biodiversity conserva-

1183 Paris Agreement, Article 7 (9) (c).

1184 Maljean-Dubois and Wemaëre, "Biodiversity and climate change," 305; Paris Agreement, Article 5.

1185 Maljean-Dubois and Wemaëre, "Biodiversity and climate change," 300.

1186 Harro Van Asselt, "Dealing with the Fragmentation of Global Climate Governance: Legal and Political Approaches in Interplay Management," *Global Covernance Working Paper* No. 30, 2007, https://doi.org/10.2139/ssrn.1335082 as cited in Maljean-Dubois and Wemaëre, "Biodiversity and climate change," 300.

tion within the UNFCCC than to addressing climate change within the CBD".[1187] Indeed, in contrast to the UNFCCC regime, the CBD COP has been active throughout the years in adopting decisions that link biodiversity and climate change, and it could be said that it acted strategically to "reframe shared understanding of biodiversity from a passive victim of climate impacts to an active part of climate change solutions".[1188] For instance, several of the Aichi Targets (5, 7, 10, 14 and 15) are considered to be "particularly relevant to addressing climate change and biodiversity in an interconnected manner".[1189] Moreover, early in 2015, the CBD Secretariat communicated a compilation of the tools, guidance and information on biodiversity and climate change to be used by the CBD Parties for the development of their Intended Nationally Determined Contributions (INDCs) in the context of the development of the Paris Agreement adopted at the end of 2015.[1190]

Apart from the CBD, the regimes under other biodiversity conventions, including the CMS and Bern Convention, also engaged with the issue of climate change.[1191] Within the Carpathian Convention, the topic of climate change has also enjoyed sufficient attention.

1187 Maljean-Dubois and Wemaëre, "Biodiversity and climate change," 298.

1188 Sikina Jinnah; Marketing Linkages: Secretariat Governance of the Climate-Biodiversity Interface. *Global Environmental Politics* 11 (3) (2011): 23–43, https://doi.org/10.1162/GLEP_a_0006 as cited in Maljean-Dubois and Wemaëre, "Biodiversity and climate change," 298–299; Conference of the Parties, *Biodiversity and climate change related issues: advice on the application of relevant safeguards for biodiversity with regard to policy approaches and positive incentives on issues relating to reducing emissions from deforestation and forest degradation in developing countries; and the role of conservation, sustainable management of forests and enhancement of forest carbon stocks in developing countries*, CBD COP Decision XI/19 (2012).

1189 Maljean-Dubois and Wemaëre, "Biodiversity and climate change," 299.

1190 Maljean-Dubois and Wemaëre, "Biodiversity and climate change," 304; See "Notification 2015–015: Tools, Guidance and Information Related to Biodiversity and Climate Change in the Context of the Expected Climate Agreement," CBD Executive Secretary, (February 2015) https://www.cbd.int/notifications/2015-015.

1191 See Arie Trouwborst, "Transboundary Wildlife Conservation in A Changing Climate: Adaptation of the Bonn Convention on Migratory Species and Its Daughter Instruments to Climate Change," *Diversity* 4, no. 3 (25 June 2012): 258–300, https://doi.org/10.3390/d4030258; Arie Trouwborst, "Conserving European Biodiversity in a Changing Climate: The Bern Convention, the European Union Birds and Habitats Directives and the Adaptation of Nature to Climate Change," *Review of European Community & International Environmental Law* 20, no. 1 (April 2011): 62–77, https://doi.org/10.1111/j.1467-9388.2011.00700.x.

What is also suggested in the literature is that despite the equal importance and significance of tackling biodiversity loss and climate change to ensure the future of planetary life, "the issue of biodiversity has in most cases been overshadowed by the issue of human-induced climate change".[1192]

The institutional mechanisms aimed at creating synergies include the Joint Liaison Group between the three Rio Conventions, acting since 2001 and which, for instance, highlighted the possibility of exploring the links between the National Biodiversity Strategy and Action Plans (NBSAPs) and National Adaptation Program Plans (NAPPs) under the UNFCCC.[1193] In addition, cooperation between the Intergovernmental Panel on Climate Change (IPCC) and the Intergovernmental Science-Policy Platform on Biodiversity and Ecosystem Services (IPBES), reinvigorated in 2014 – 2015, has the potential to better bridge climate change and biodiversity protection.[1194] Moreover, the Sustainable Development Goals 2015 – 2030 also foster new synergies between biodiversity and climate change.[1195] Finally, the concept of systemic integration emerging in the theory of international law may also contribute to a more sound interaction of the legal regimes on biodiversity and climate change.[1196]

The most crucial area for the practical application of these synergies is, however, at the national level. Indeed, the Parties themselves are primarily responsible for addressing "biodiversity and climate change in a synergetic manner, in particular through their future NDCs".[1197] The interaction between biodiversity and climate change regimes in their application on the national level is quite complex (in addition, it evolves over time and requires consideration of the particular circumstances of the state), warranting further exploration of this issue by researchers and practitioners.[1198]

1192 Maljean-Dubois and Wemaëre, "Biodiversity and climate change," 305.

1193 Maljean-Dubois and Wemaëre, "Biodiversity and climate change," 301–302; See "Joint Liaison Group," CBD, November 13, 2017, https://www.cbd.int/cooperation/liaison.shtml.

1194 Maljean-Dubois and Wemaëre, "Biodiversity and climate change," 303; See "The Lima 2014 Declaration on Biodiversity and Climate Change from Science to Policy-Makers, for Sustainable Development," delivered to the president of UNFCCC COP 20 (December 5, 2014) https://www.iai.int/admin/site/sites/default/files/THE_LIMA_2014_DECLARATION.pdf

1195 Maljean-Dubois and Wemaëre, "Biodiversity and climate change," 303.

1196 Harro Van Asselt, Francesco Sindico, and Michael A. Mehling, "Global Climate Change and the Fragmentation of International Law," *Law & Policy* 30, no. 4 (October 2008): 423–49, https://doi.org/10.1111/j.1467-9930.2008.00286.x cited in Maljean-Dubois and Wemaëre, "Biodiversity and climate change," 303.

1197 Maljean-Dubois and Wemaëre, "Biodiversity and climate change," 305–306.

3.4.2. Human rights and biodiversity

When it comes to human rights and biodiversity, the interaction between these two regimes has also been acknowledged in the Kunming–Montreal Global Biodiversity Framework. In particular, the very understanding and implementation of the GBF should be consistent with the human-rights-based approach, which includes respect, protection, promotion and fulfilment of human rights.[1199] What is more, the GBF clearly acknowledges the human right to a clean, healthy, and sustainable environment, referencing for this matter the 2022 General Assembly Resolution 76/300 recognising this right on a global level.[1200] Moreover, tools and solutions for implementation and mainstreaming of the global targets for 2030 include full, equitable and inclusive representation and participation in decision-making, access to information and justice by indigenous peoples and local communities, and protection of environmental human rights defenders.[1201]

The focused exploration of the links between the human rights and environment in general (and implicitly or explicitly including biodiversity) has been undertaken at the UN level since the creation of the mandate of the Independent Expert on human rights and the environment (later transformed into the mandate of the Special Rapporteur on the human right to a clean, healthy and sustainable environment) in 2012.[1202] Already in the first report of the mandate-holder (A/HRC/22/43), presented to the Human Rights Council in March 2013, it was highlighted that human rights and the environment are interdependent.[1203] Currently, it is recognised that on the one hand, a "safe, clean, healthy and sustainable environment is necessary for the full enjoyment of a vast range of human rights, including

1198 Maljean-Dubois and Wemaëre, "Biodiversity and climate change," 306.

1199 *Kunming-Montreal Global Biodiversity Framework*, Section C, 7 (g).

1200 *Kunming-Montreal Global Biodiversity Framework*, Section C, 7 (g); *The human right to a clean, healthy and sustainable environment*, General Assembly Resolution 76/300, A/RES/76/300 (July 28, 2022) https://digitallibrary.un.org/record/3983329?v=pdf.

1201 *Kunming-Montreal Global Biodiversity Framework*, Target 22.

1202 "Special Rapporteur on the Human Right to a Clean, Healthy and Sustainable Environment," OHCHR, accessed November 11, 2024, https://www.ohchr.org/en/special-procedures/sr-environment.

1203 John H. Knox, *Report of The Special Rapporteur on the Issue of Human Rights Obligations Relating to the Enjoyment of a Safe, Clean, Healthy and Sustainable Environment*, Human Rights Council, Thirty-seventh Session, A/HRC/37/59 (January 24, 2018) https://docs.un.org/en/A/HRC/37/59, § 2.

the rights to life, health, food, water and development" while on the other hand, "the exercise of human rights, including the rights to information, participation and remedy, is vital to the protection of the environment".[1204] Based on research and regional consultations, the Independent expert identified good practices in the use of obligations stemming from human rights law, and presented them in a separate report, as well as made them available in an online database.[1205]

The work of the Special Rapporteur resulted in the creation of the 16 Framework principles on human rights and the environment.[1206] These principles with commentary do not create new norms, however, they provide guidance on existing basic obligations of states under human rights law in relation to the enjoyment of a safe, clean, healthy and sustainable environment, found in the treaties and decisions or statements of the human rights tribunals and bodies, and in the state practice.[1207] They also constitute a basis for the further development of the obligations, expected to occur with the gradual enhancement of "our understanding of the relationship of human rights and the environment".[1208] When it comes specifically to biodiversity, for instance, the commentary to Framework principles 1 and 2 states that states should "take effective steps to ensure the conservation and sustainable use of the ecosystems and biological diversity on which the full enjoyment of human rights depends."[1209] Similarly, the commentary to Framework principle 11 mentions the need for the states to "establish, maintain and enforce effective legal and institutional frameworks for the enjoyment of a safe, clean, healthy and sustainable environment", which should include substantive standards with respect to "protected areas, conservation and biological diversity".[1210] The states are awarded some discretion in balancing between the goal of prevention of environmental harm

1204 Knox, *Report of The Special Rapporteur*, A/HRC/37/59, § 2.

1205 Knox, *Report of The Special Rapporteur*, A/HRC/37/59, § 4; John H. Knox, *Report of the Independent Expert on the Issue of Human Rights Obligations Relating to the Enjoyment of a Safe, Clean, Healthy and Sustainable Environment: Compilation of Good Practices*, Human Rights Council, Twenty-eighth Session, A/HRC/28/61 (February 3, 2015) https://docs.un.org/en/A/HRC/28/61.

1206 Knox, *Report of The Special Rapporteur*, A/HRC/37/59, Annex "Framework Principles on Human Rights and the Environment" [Framework Principles on Human Rights and the Environment].

1207 Knox, *Report of The Special Rapporteur*, A/HRC/37/59, § 8–9.

1208 Framework Principles on Human Rights and the Environment, § 2.

1209 Framework Principles on Human Rights and the Environment, § 5.

1210 Framework Principles on Human Rights and the Environment, Principle 11, § 31.

and other social goals. However, such discretion is not unlimited.[1211] Some of the other highly relevant principles include principle 6 on education and public awareness on environmental matters, which may potentially include awareness on biodiversity, and principle 7 on public access to environmental information, including information about the quality of the environment.[1212] There are also further 'procedural principles' relevant for bridging concerns for environment and human rights, such as principle 8 requiring assessment of possible environmental impacts of proposed projects and policies, including potential impacts on human rights and principle 9 on public participation in the decision-making related to the environment.[1213] Framework principle 12 concerns effective enforcement of environmental standards against public and private actors, and mentions allegedly highly relevant suggestions for the forest ecosystems of the Ukrainian Carpathians. In particular, regulation of business enterprises "to protect against human rights abuses resulting from environmental harm", implementing of training programmes for law enforcement and judiciary to enhance their understanding of environmental laws, and taking "effective steps to prevent corruption from undermining the implementation and enforcement of environmental laws" are included within this principle.[1214] Principles 14 and 15 call for special attention to the rights of the most vulnerable to environmental harm and to indigenous peoples and members of traditional communities.[1215] Finally, Framework principle 16 calls for respect of human rights in the action taken by states to address environmental challenges and pursue sustainable development as an integration of human rights perspective into environmental protection "helps to ensure that environmental and development policies improve the lives of the human beings who depend on a safe, clean, healthy and sustainable environment".[1216]

A separate report of the Special Rapporteur is dedicated to the issue of biodiversity and human rights.[1217] To be more specific, this report "ex-

1211 Framework Principles on Human Rights and the Environment, Principle 11, § 32–33.

1212 Framework Principles on Human Rights and the Environment, Principle 6, Principle 7, especially § 18.

1213 Framework Principles on Human Rights and the Environment, Principle 8, Principle 9.

1214 Framework Principles on Human Rights and the Environment, Principle 12.

1215 Framework Principles on Human Rights and the Environment, Principle 14, Principle 15.

1216 Framework Principles on Human Rights and the Environment, Principle 16, § 55.

1217 Knox, *Report of the Special Rapporteur*, A/HRC/34/49.

amines the obligations relating to the conservation and sustainable use of ecosystems and biological diversity".[1218] It explains "that biodiversity is necessary for the enjoyment of a wide range of human rights and that the loss of biodiversity threatens the enjoyment of those rights", outlining the human rights obligations relating to the protection of biodiversity and drawing the conclusions and recommendations concerning the conservation and sustainable use of biodiversity for the protection and enjoyment of human rights.[1219] Interestingly enough, in this report, the Special Rapporteur states that even though the report focuses on human rights, and accordingly, on the value of biodiversity to human beings, the intrinsic value of the components of biodiversity which may not be captured by the human rights perspective is also noted.[1220]

The link between biodiversity and human rights is explained through ecosystem services. In particular, the enjoyment of human rights such as rights to life, health, food and water depends on the services provided by ecosystems. The latter, in turn, depend on the health of ecosystems, which depends on biodiversity. Thus, the full enjoyment of human rights depends on biodiversity.[1221] The importance of a healthy and sustainable environment for the full enjoyment of human rights has also been mentioned by the Special Rapporteur before and was recognised by the Human Rights Council.[1222]

While acknowledging that the human rights law does not require that "ecosystems remain untouched by human hands" and that economic and social development depend on the use of ecosystems, the Special Rapporteur at the same time pays attention to the need for the sustainability of this development. The sustainability clearly requires healthy ecosystems, which is underlined by Goal 15 of the SDGs, by means of which the states have committed to "protect, restore and promote sustainable use of terrestrial

1218 Knox, *Report of the Special Rapporteur*, A/HRC/34/49, § 3.

1219 Knox, *Report of the Special Rapporteur*, A/HRC/34/49, § 4.

1220 Knox, *Report of the Special Rapporteur*, A/HRC/34/49, § 5 (footnote).

1221 Knox, *Report of the Special Rapporteur*, A/HRC/34/49, § 5; § 10.

1222 Knox, *Report of the Special Rapporteur*, A/HRC/34/49, § 7; See John H. Knox, *Report of the Independent Expert on the issue of human rights obligations relating to the enjoyment of a safe, clean, healthy and sustainable environment*, Human Rights Council, Twenty-second Session, A/HRC/22/43 (December 24, 2012) https://docs.un.org/en/A/HRC/22/43; and John H. Knox, *Report of the Independent Expert on the issue of human rights obligations relating to the enjoyment of a safe, clean, healthy and sustainable environment*, Human Rights Council, Twenty-fifth session, A/HRC/25/53 (December 30, 2013) https://docs.un.org/en/A/HRC/25/53.

ecosystems, sustainably manage forests, combat desertification, and halt and reverse land degradation and halt biodiversity loss".[1223]

The Special Rapporteur elaborated on the contribution of biodiversity to the rights to life and health, the right to an adequate standard of living, and the right to non-discrimination in the enjoyment of rights.[1224] The importance of biodiversity for human rights is illustrated by numerous examples. For instance, in the context of the rights to life and health, biodiversity is vital as it constitutes an irreplaceable resource for new medicines or as exposure to nature supports mental health.[1225] There is some scientific evidence suggesting that not only nature as such, but especially "contact with diverse natural habitats and many different species" is beneficial for mental health.[1226] Furthermore, forest areas significantly improve water flow regulation, thus contributing to the enjoyment of the right of access to clean and safe water.[1227] In the context of non-discrimination, the special attention is paid to indigenous peoples, forest-dwellers, fisherfolk and others who rely directly on the products of ecosystems, such as forests, for their food, fuel or medicine, and who often lack economic and political power within their countries or lack legal recognition of their rights to the territory and resources on which they depend.[1228]

The obligations of states at the intersection of human rights and biodiversity include "obligations to protect against environmental harm that interferes with the enjoyment of human rights", and these clearly "apply to biodiversity as an integral part of the environment".[1229] Both procedural

---

1223 Knox, *Report of the Special Rapporteur*, A/HRC/34/49, § 8; General Assembly Resolution 70/1.

1224 Knox, *Report of the Special Rapporteur*, A/HRC/34/49, § 10.

1225 Knox, *Report of the Special Rapporteur*, A/HRC/34/49, § 14, § 17.

1226 Knox, *Report of the Special Rapporteur*, A/HRC/34/49, § 17; See, for instance, Paul A. Sandifer, Ariana E. Sutton-Grier, and Bethney P. Ward, "Exploring Connections among Nature, Biodiversity, Ecosystem Services, and Human Health and Well-Being: Opportunities to Enhance Health and Biodiversity Conservation," *Ecosystem Services* 12 (April 2015): 1–15, https://doi.org/10.1016/j.ecoser.2014.12.007.

1227 Knox, *Report of the Special Rapporteur*, A/HRC/34/49, § 21; See Paula Harrison et al., "Linkages between Biodiversity Attributes and Ecosystem Services: A Systematic Review," *Ecosystem Services* 9 (September 2014): 195, https://doi.org/10.1016/j.ecoser.2014.05.006.

1228 Knox, *Report of the Special Rapporteur*, A/HRC/34/49, § 22, § 52 [on obligations towards those, who have close relationships to the territory that they have traditionally occupied and depend directly on nature for their material needs and cultural life].

1229 Knox, *Report of the Special Rapporteur*, A/HRC/34/49, § 26.

and substantive obligations have been identified. The procedural obligations, which are grounded in civil and political rights and clarified in environmental context, include at least the following: "to assess impacts and make environmental information public", "to facilitate public participation in environmental decision-making, including by protecting the rights of expression and association", "to provide access to remedies for harm" and to protect environmental human rights defenders.[1230] The substantive obligations include "a general obligation to safeguard biodiversity" in order to protect certain human rights from infringement, which includes a duty of the states "to protect against environmental harm from private actors" and translates to the responsibility of businesses "to respect the rights relating to biodiversity".[1231] Furthermore, the substantive obligations on biodiversity from human rights' perspectives also mean compliance with the obligations undertaken on the basis of various conservation agreements, such as the CBD. As the Special Rapporteur notes, through this convention and other agreements states "have identified the steps necessary to conserve and sustainably use biodiversity" and the implementation of these measures will "satisfy the joint obligation of States to cooperate to protect the human rights dependent upon biodiversity".[1232]

It is generally suggested that the human rights perspective is helpful for clarifying that biodiversity loss also undermines the full enjoyment of human rights, for drawing attention to the urgent need to protect biodiversity, and for promoting policy coherence and legitimacy in the conservation and sustainable use of biodiversity.[1233] It is accentuated in the conclusions and recommendations that substantively states "should establish legal and institutional frameworks for the protection of biodiversity", which would "[r]egulate harm to biodiversity from private actors as well as government" and which "respect and protect the rights of those who are particularly vulnerable to the loss of biodiversity and ecosystem services".[1234] For the implementation of the obligations with respect to biodiversity, it is also recommended that states ensure that their "national biodiversity strategies and action plans reflect the necessary scope and ambition".[1235]

1230 Knox, *Report of the Special Rapporteur*, A/HRC/34/49, § 27–32.
1231 Knox, *Report of the Special Rapporteur*, A/HRC/34/49, § 33; See John H. Knox, *Report of the Independent Expert*, A/HRC/25/53, § 58–61.
1232 Knox, *Report of the Special Rapporteur*, A/HRC/34/49, § 39.
1233 Knox, *Report of the Special Rapporteur*, A/HRC/34/49, § 66.
1234 Knox, *Report of the Special Rapporteur*, A/HRC/34/49, § 69.
1235 Knox, *Report of the Special Rapporteur*, A/HRC/34/49, § 70.

Furthermore, apart from the broad human rights perspective as such, the integration of biodiversity protection into human rights obligations is particularly clearly contained in the separate substantive human right to a healthy environment. This right has been enshrined in numerous constitutions all over the world,[1236] and in recent years (after nearly 50 years of debate as to the relevance and recognition of this right) it was recognised on a universal level by the Human Rights Council and by the General Assembly as a human right to a clean, healthy and sustainable environment.[1237]

The substantive content of this right and its recognition within the UN has been crystallising gradually, with, for instance, HRC resolution 31/8 of 2016, which Mark Limon justly held for capable of providing "the substantive content of a future international right to a clean and healthy environment".[1238] Another resolution (34/20 of 2017) contained similar wording of obligations related to the "enjoyment of a safe, clean, healthy and sustainable environment", and made a step further in drawing special attention of the states to biodiversity and ecosystems.[1239] Although universal recognition of this right as a human right has faced numerous instances of opposition, critique and scepticism, it is believed to create an important added value, such as by complementing, reinforcing and amplifying regional and national norms and jurisprudence, by leading to better understanding of interrelationship between human rights norms and environmental protection, by improving position of environmental protection among other interests that are fundamental to human dignity, equality and freedom, as well as by leading to further development of norms related to the hu-

1236 Knox, *Report of the Special Rapporteur*, A/HRC/34/49, § 13.

1237 *The human right to a clean, healthy and sustainable environment*, Human Rights Council Resolution 48/13, A/HRC/RES/48/13 (8 October 2021), undocs.org/en/A/HRC/RES/48/13; General Assembly Resolution 76/300.

1238 Marc Limon, "The Politics of Human Rights, the Environment, and Climate Change at the Human Rights Council: Toward a Universal Right to a Healthy Environment?," in *The Human Right to a Healthy Environment*, ed. by John H. Knox and Ramin Pejan (Cambridge: Cambridge University Press, 2018), 212; *Human rights and the environment*, Human Rights Council Resolution 31/8, A/HRC/RES/31/8, (March 23, 2016) https://digitallibrary.un.org/record/836906?v=pdf.

1239 *Human rights and the environment*, Human Rights Council Resolution 34/20, A/HRC/RES/34/20, (March 24, 2017) https://docs.un.org/en/A/HRC/RES/34/20.

man rights and the environment in coherent, consistent and integrated manner.[1240]

Even if the recognition of this right in the form of the HRC and GA resolutions may be enhanced in future by other forms, such as a legally binding international treaty, it is still significant in itself. One of its implications is an international consensus regarding the wording used to denote the substantive human right to an environment of a certain quality. Historically, numerous formulations were used on various fora, such as 'satisfactory', 'healthy and flourishing', 'secure, healthy and ecologically sound' environment or 'environment of a quality that permits a life of dignity and well-being'.[1241] The HRC and Special Rapporteurs in the recent years used the full wording 'safe, clean, healthy and sustainable environment', and a short version 'right to a healthy environment', and the HRC resolution 48/13 and GA resolution 76/300 uses similar wording, namely 'clean, healthy and sustainable environment'. If one tries to locate it within the discourse of anthropocentrism and ecocentrism, it would probably be close to the middle way, as it seemingly refers to both the human health and the state of the natural environment, which should be 'clean, healthy and sustainable.' The wording of this right, however, might still have many intricacies and even the very term 'healthy environment' might be problematic as "natural environment is not always healthy for humans", as other dimensions of the importance of the environment to humans, such as cultural ones are thus excluded, and as it may be "ambiguous whether the term 'healthy' extends beyond human health to include health of ecosystems".[1242]

As to the content of this right, both HRC and GA resolutions on its recognition are quite brief and have three common points (two of which are identical, and the third has some nuanced differences). First, they note the relatedness of this right to other rights and existing international law. Second, they affirm that the promotion of this right requires implementa-

1240 See John H. Knox, *Human rights obligations relating to the enjoyment of a safe, clean, healthy and sustainable environment*, Report of the Special Rapporteur on the issue of human rights obligations relating to the enjoyment of a safe, clean, healthy and sustainable environment, A/73/188 (July 19, 2018) https://docs.un.org/en/A/73/188, § 39.

1241 See Alan Boyle, "Environment and Human Rights," in *Max Planck Encyclopedia of Public International Law*, ed. Rüdiger Wolfrum (Oxford: Oxford University Press, 2012).

1242 See John H. Knox, and Ramin Pejan, "Introduction" in *The Human Right to a Healthy Environment*, ed. John H. Knox and Ramin Pejan, (Cambrige: Cambridge University Press, 2018), 12.

tion of the multilateral environmental agreements under the principles of international environmental law. Third, they call upon states (and in the case of the GA, also international organisations, business enterprises and other relevant stakeholders) to adopt policies, enhance international cooperation, strengthen capacity-building and continue to share good practices. The HRC resolution is more detailed in this regard, as it mentions the categories of entities cooperation with which should be enhanced, some modes of practice sharing, particular subject-matter regarding which the policies should be adopted and draws attention to the human rights obligations and commitments in the implementation of and follow-up to the Sustainable Development Goals. The resolutions suggest a wide scope of the human right to a healthy environment and purport to tie through it the branches of international environmental law and international human rights law. In fact, the "implementation of the multilateral environmental agreements under the principles of international environmental law" required to promote this right means that this human right directly refers to international environmental law as such. The explicit mentioning of policies with respect to biodiversity and ecosystems in the HRC resolution is also remarkable. The encouragement to adopt these policies for the enjoyment of the human right to a healthy environment may help environmental law to climb the ladder of priorities and create a level playing field between environmental protection and other societal interests.

Among the regional human rights mechanisms, the particularly clear linkage between the human right to a healthy environment and biodiversity might be seen in the Inter-American mechanism. In particular, the Inter-American Court on Human Rights took a chance in 2017 to state in its Advisory Opinion that the human right to environment "protects the components of the environment, such as forests, rivers and seas, as legal interests in themselves, even in the absence of the certainty or evidence of a risk to individuals".[1243] In 2020, the Court reaffirmed its stance on the human right to a healthy environment in its first contentious case on this matter.[1244] In addition, the progress indicators of the implementation of the Protocol of San Salvador adopted by the General Assembly of the Organi-

1243 *The Environment and Human Rights*, Advisory opinion OC-23/17 of November 15, 2017, requested by the Republic of Colombia, Inter-American Court of Human Rights (IACtHR) https://corteidh.or.cr/docs/opiniones/seriea_23_ing.pdf, § 62.

1244 *Indigenous Communities of the Lhaka Honhat (Our Land) Association v. Argentina*, February 6, 2020, IACtHR, https://www.corteidh.or.cr/docs/casos/articulos/seriec_400_ing.pdf, § 202–203.

sation of American States, among other criteria, include 'biodiversity' and 'status of forestry resources'.[1245]

In the latest report on the implementation of the human right to a healthy environment, the Special Rapporteur noted that this right is "an integral part of the effective enjoyment of all human rights, as they are interdependent, inalienable and indivisible".[1246] She also noted clarification as to the content of this right provided by her predecessors, including procedural aspects, such as "access to environmental information, participation and access to justice and effective remedy" and environmental features falling within the scope of this right, namely "clean air, a safe climate, safe and sufficient water, healthy and sustainable food, a toxic-free environment and healthy ecosystems and biodiversity".[1247] The report further provides an overview of "Healthy ecosystems and biodiversity" as one of the substantive elements of the human right to a healthy environment and states that actions towards healthy biodiversity include systemic transitions, such as a shift to a circular economy.[1248]

Similarly, among the key challenges for the implementation of this right, the economic model and unsustainable development are mentioned, such as those resulting from the "inadequate control and monitoring of business efforts to address climate change and biodiversity protection".[1249] Furthermore, a problem of weak rule of law is included among the challenges causing negative impact on biodiversity. In particular, concerns are raised as to the creation of more legal frameworks as opposed to their substantive effectiveness and as to the approach of environmental frameworks aimed at management of natural resources without attention to the planetary

---

1245 *The Environment and Human Rights,* Advisory opinion OC-23/17, IACtHR § 60; "*Progress indicators for measuring rights contemplated in the Additional Protocol to the American Convention on Human Rights in the Area of Economic, Social, and Cultural Rights, "Protocol of San Salvador"*, Working Group to examine the periodic reports of the States Parties to the Protocol of San Salvador, OAS, OEA/Ser.D/XXVI.11 (2015) https://www.oas.org/en/sedi/pub/progress_indicators.pdf, § 38.

1246 Puentes Riaño, *Overview of the implementation of the human right to a clean, healthy and sustainable environment*, A/79/270, § 14.

1247 Puentes Riaño, *Overview of the implementation of the human right to a clean, healthy and sustainable environment*, A/79/270, § 14 [referring to A/HRC/37/59, A/HRC/40/55, A/HRC/46/28, A/HRC/49/53, A/75/161 and A/76/179].

1248 Puentes Riaño, *Overview of the implementation of the human right to a clean, healthy and sustainable environment*, A/79/270, § 67–70.

1249 Puentes Riaño, *Overview of the implementation of the human right to a clean, healthy and sustainable environment*, A/79/270, § 74.

boundaries and human rights.[1250] What is necessary for the environmental rule of law is "a governance system in which all persons, including public and private individuals and institutions, are accountable to laws that are public, equally enforced, independently adjudicated and consistent with human rights" including "comprehensive control and monitoring of the drivers of the crises".[1251] Some of the important tools for ensuring environmental rule of law, including possibility of the right-holders to defend their rights include EIA and SEA.[1252] Another challenge is posed by war and conflict, as deforestation tend to increase in the presence of conflict, as is ecosystem and biodiversity loss, and violations of the human right to a healthy environment and other human rights.[1253]

On the basis of the review of the implementation of the human right to a healthy environment, its support and mainstreaming are recommended at the levels of national, subnational and international legal frameworks. Such legal frameworks should be updated to reflect the "interconnectedness between systems, humans and nature" and should address the root causes of the triple planetary crises and reduce systemic inequalities.[1254]

When it comes to further suggestions on synergies and approaches to tackling triple planetary crisis, in the recent meeting of the CBD COP, it was suggested by Inger Andersen to "focus on the country level in order to deliver an integrated package of environmental solutions".[1255] In addition, she reminded on the need of better coordination at the UN level in line

1250 Puentes Riaño, *Overview of the implementation of the human right to a clean, healthy and sustainable environment*, A/79/270, § 76.

1251 Puentes Riaño, *Overview of the implementation of the human right to a clean, healthy and sustainable environment*, A/79/270, § 76; See United Nations Environment Programme, *Environmental Rule of Law: Tracking Progress and Charting Future Directions.*

1252 Puentes Riaño, *Overview of the implementation of the human right to a clean, healthy and sustainable environment*, A/79/270, § 77.

1253 Puentes Riaño, *Overview of the implementation of the human right to a clean, healthy and sustainable environment*, A/79/270, § 77, § 84–85.

1254 Puentes Riaño, *Overview of the implementation of the human right to a clean, healthy and sustainable environment*, A/79/270, § 122.

1255 "High-Level Roundtable: Strengthening Action for Change: Synergistic Solutions to the Climate Crisis, Nature Loss, Desertification, and Pollution," IISD, October 28, 2024, https://enb.iisd.org/strengthening-action-change-synergistic-solutions?utm_medium=email&utm_campaign=ENB%20Update%20-%2031%20October%202024&utm_content=ENB%20Update%20-%2031%20October%202024+CID_35d33d96f3210bf077aded2aa5f841d2&utm_source=cm&utm_term=Strengthening%20Action.

with the UN Common Approach to Biodiversity.[1256] Similarly, the "whole-MEA" approach was mentioned by Astrid Schomaker as a "true reform agenda for the UN".[1257] The "anchoring environmental action in human rights" was also mentioned among the key suggestions.[1258]

3.4.3. Sustainable tourism and biodiversity

When it comes to sustainable tourism and biodiversity, it is recognised on a global level that "tourism sector has a complex and wide-ranging relationship with biodiversity" capable of both leading to detrimental impacts and contributing to conservation of biodiversity.[1259] The 2018 report within the CBD provides a useful overview of the developments in this area, and suggests priorities for the Parties' actions.[1260] It states that the "ecosystem-based solutions for sustainable tourism are largely available and tested" and mentions the 2004 guidelines on Biodiversity and Tourism Development as a useful reference for that matter.[1261] Relevance of these guidelines was reiterated by subsequent decisions and additional guidance on their implementation, including user's manuals "Managing Tourism and

1256 "High-Level Roundtable: Strengthening Action for Change," IISD; see "UN Common Approach to Biodiversity," CEB, accessed November 11, 2024, https://unsceb.org/un-common-approach-biodiversity.

1257 "High-Level Roundtable: Strengthening Action for Change," IISD.

1258 "High-Level Roundtable: Strengthening Action for Change," IISD.

1259 World Tourism Organization, *The Integration of Biodiversity in National Tourism Policies*, (Madrid: UN Tourism, 2024) https://doi.org/10.18111/9789284424900, 5; see Parties to the CBD, *Cancun Declaration on Mainstreaming the Conservation and Sustainable use of Biodiversity for Well-being*, COP-13 Documents (Cancun, 2016) https://www.cbd.int/cop/cop-13/hls/cancun%20declaration-en.pdf; SBSTTA, *Measures taken for the conservation and sustainable use of mountain biological diversity*, § 26.

1260 Secretariat of the CBD and World Tourism Organization, *Mainstreaming Biodiversity Into Tourism Development: Report on Status, Trends and Relevant Activities*, complement to CBD/COP/14/INF/1, (November 2018) https://www.cbd.int/tourism/doc/cop-14-tourism-background-document-en.pdf.

1261 Secretariat of the CBD and World Tourism Organization, *Mainstreaming Biodiversity Into Tourism Development*, 18; Conference of the Parties, *Guidelines on Biodiversity and Tourism Development*, CBD COP Decision VII/14 (2004).

Biodiversity"[1262] and "Tourism Supporting Biodiversity",[1263] which as of 2024 continue to serve as useful resources for planning action on sustainable tourism.[1264] The latter, for instance, includes discussion on tourism and biodiversity policy and governance as well as describes the tools and practices that could be applied to control and influence tourism impacts on biodiversity.[1265] The 2018 report also draws attention of the governments to the fact that action on biodiversity in the tourism sector has to be closely linked to adaptation and mitigation of climate change "strengthening the natural synergies related to more sustainable and lower-impact consumption and the role of ecosystems in disaster risk reduction".[1266] Despite the variety of international guidance on the matter, the recent UN Tourism Report on integration of biodiversity in national tourism policies, based on analysis of 80 national policies finds that "policies generally focus upon economic viability and social inclusion and more could be done to explicitly focus on biodiversity issues".[1267]

On the European level, to facilitate integration of biodiversity protection into tourism activities in protected areas including mountains, there exist the European Charter for Sustainable Tourism in Protected Areas, a voluntary initiative within the EUROPARC Federation, the umbrella organisation of protected areas in Europe.[1268] This Charter seeks to adapt CBD

1262 Secretariat of the CBD, *Managing Tourism and Biodiversity: User's Manual on the CBD Guidelines on Biodiversity and Tourism Development,* (Secretariat of the CBD, UNEP, 2007) https://www.cbd.int/doc/programmes/socio-eco/tourism/tourism-manual-en.pdf.

1263 Secretariat of the CBD, *Tourism Supporting Biodiversity – A Manual on Applying the CBD Guidelines on Biodiversity and Tourism Development,* (Montreal: Secretariat of the CBD, 2015) https://www.cbd.int/tourism/doc/tourism-manual-2015-en.pdf.

1264 Secretariat of the CBD and World Tourism Organization, *Mainstreaming Biodiversity Into Tourism Development,* 11–12; World Tourism Organization, *The Integration of Biodiversity in National Tourism Policies,* 7.

1265 Secretariat of the CBD, *Tourism Supporting Biodiversity,* Chapter 3 and Chapter 6.

1266 Secretariat of the CBD and World Tourism Organization, *Mainstreaming Biodiversity Into Tourism Development,* 18.

1267 World Tourism Organization, *The Integration of Biodiversity in National Tourism Policies,* 22.

1268 SBSTTA, *Measures taken for the conservation and sustainable use of mountain biological diversity,* § 27; See EUROPARC Federation, *The Charter,* European Charter for Sustainable Tourism in Protected Areas (EUROPARC Federation, 2010) https://www.europarc.org/wp-content/uploads/2015/05/2010-European-Charter-for-Sustainable-Tourism-in-Protected-Areas.pdf.

guidelines for sustainable tourism to the European level.[1269] While recognising that each protected area is different, warranting local determination of strategic priorities and action programmes, the Charter requires addressing the key issues (and sub-issues), including: protection and enhancement of natural and cultural heritage; improving the quality of the tourism experience; raising public awareness on environment and cultural heritage; development of tourism specific to the area; training of protected area staff and tourism enterprises; protection and support of the quality of life for local residents; social and economic development, including employment of the local people; and control of tourist numbers to reduce possible negative impacts on the environment.[1270]

For the Carpathian region specifically, there is a 2021 draft Strategy for local sustainable tourism development based on natural and cultural heritage of the Carpathians, suggesting a wide range of measures under the environmental, economic and social dimension of objectives.[1271]

3.4.4. Environmental rule of law as a necessary condition for biodiversity protection in the Ukrainian Carpathians

As mentioned in the subsection on human rights and biodiversity, environmental rule of law is crucial for both biodiversity and human rights. Even though it cannot be classified as a separate legal regime, environmental rule of law is placed in the section on synergies as it underpins the whole system of implementation of environmental norms ensuring their functioning in a broader social, economic and governmental contexts. The term 'environmental rule of law' was established on the international level within the UNEP in 2013 and is considered to be central for sustainable development.[1272] In particular, the preamble to the Decision 27/9 notes that "democracy, good governance and the rule of law, at the national and international levels, as well as an enabling environment, are essential for sustainable development, including sustained and inclusive economic growth, social development, environmental protection and the eradication

1269 EUROPARC Federation, *The Charter*, 3.

1270 EUROPARC Federation, *The Charter*, 7–10.

1271 "(Draft) Strategy for local sustainable tourism development based on natural and cultural heritage of the Carpathians," Centralparks.

1272 "Environmental Rule of Law," United Nations Environment Programme, accessed November 11, 2024, https://www.unep.org/explore-topics/environmental-rights-and-governance/what-we-do/promoting-environmental-rule-law-0.

of poverty and hunger", while the Executive Director is requested by this decision to lead the UN system and support national governments in the:

> development and implementation of environmental rule of law with attention at all levels to mutually supporting governance features, including information disclosure, public participation, implementable and enforceable laws, and implementation and accountability mechanisms including coordination of roles as well as environmental auditing and criminal, civil and administrative enforcement with timely, impartial and independent dispute resolution.[1273]

The importance of strong institutions and rule of law for sustainable development is also clearly acknowledged in Goal 16 of the SDGs.[1274]

The development of the environmental rule of law agenda by the UNEP include creation of the First Global Report on Environmental Rule of Law in 2019, highlighting the need to undertake such an assessment on a regular basis, and subsequent preparation of the second report Environmental Rule of Law: Tracking Progress and Charting Future Directions, published in 2023.[1275] As David Boyd wittingly observed on the occasion of preparation of the first report, it "solves the mystery of why problems such as [...] declining biodiversity [...] persist despite the proliferation of environmental laws in recent decades" adding that "[u]nless the environmental rule of law

1273 Governing Council, *Advancing justice, governance and law for environmental sustainability*, Governing Council / Global Ministerial Environment Forum at its first universal session, Decision 27/9 (2013) https://wedocs.unep.org/bitstream/handle/20.500.11822/12221/Governing%20Council%20Decision%2027-2.pdf?sequence=1, Preamble, 5.

1274 Naysa Ahuja et al., "Advancing Human Rights through Environmental Rule of Law," in *Human Rights and the Environment: Legality, Indivisibility, Dignity and Geography*, ed. James R. May and Erin Daly (Cheltenham: Edward Elgar Publishing, 2019), p. 29; See also United Nations Environment Programme, *Human Rights and Environmental Rule of Law*, Asia Pacific Issue Brief: SDG16 (March 2021) https://wedocs.unep.org/bitstream/handle/20.500.11822/35408/SDG16.pdf.

1275 "Environmental Rule of Law: First Global Report," United Nations Environment Programme, July 6, 2019, https://www.unep.org/resources/assessment/environmental-rule-law-first-global-report#:~:text=The%20UN%20Environment%20report%20found,widespread%20species%20and%20habitat%20loss; "Environmental Rule of Law: Tracking Progress and Charting Future Directions," United Nations Environment Programme, November 22, 2023, https://www.unep.org/resources/publication/environmental-rule-law-tracking-progress-and-charting-future-directions.

is strengthened, even seemingly rigorous rules are destined to fail and the fundamental human right to a healthy environment will go unfulfilled."[1276]

The 2023 report acknowledges that there is currently no intergovernmentally agreed definition of the environmental rule of law and treats this term as "the principles of rule of law applied in the environmental context" along with its seven core elements identified by UNEP.[1277] The importance of the term 'environmental rule of law' as opposed to 'rule of law' is explained by acknowledgement that there are rule of law issues particular to the environmental context and by the fact that it is capable of generating political will "among actors beyond the environmental community".[1278] The core elements of the environmental rule of law include, for instance, 'fair, clear and implementable environmental laws' (1), which means in particular that the laws have to be easily understood and unambiguous; 'accountability and integrity of institutions and decision-makers' (3), which requires demonstration of transparency and integrity to ensure public support and compliance; and 'clear and coordinated mandates and roles, across and within institutions' (4), which are crucial for effective implementation.[1279]

Other documents recognising the importance of environmental rule of law and providing guidance as to its understanding and application include the IUCN World Declaration on Environmental Rule of Law adopted in 2016 and the Political Declaration of the Special Session of the United Nations Environment Assembly to Commemorate the Fiftieth Anniversary of the Establishment of the United Nations Environment Programme, adopted in 2022.[1280] In the IUCN Declaration, the environmental rule of law

1276 "Environmental Rule of Law: First Global Report," United Nations Environment Programme.

1277 United Nations Environment Programme, *Environmental Rule of Law: Tracking Progress and Charting Future Directions*, 15, 17.

1278 United Nations Environment Programme, *Environmental Rule of Law: Tracking Progress and Charting Future Directions*, 16.

1279 United Nations Environment Programme, *Environmental Rule of Law: Tracking Progress and Charting Future Directions*, 17.

1280 United Nations Environment Programme, *Environmental Rule of Law: Tracking Progress and Charting Future Directions*, 18; *IUCN World Declaration on the Environmental Rule of Law*, IUCN World Congress on Environmental Law in Rio de Janeiro (April 2016) https://iucn.org/sites/default/files/2022-10/world_declaration_on_the_environmental_rule_of_law_final_2017-3-17.pdf; United Nations Environment Assembly of the United Nations Environment Programme, *Political Declaration of the Special Session of the United Nations Environment Assembly to Commemorate the Fiftieth Anniversary of the Establishment of the United Nations* is understood as a "legal framework of procedural and substantive rights and obligations that incorporates the principles of ecologically sustainable development in the rule of law", and thirteen principles for promoting and achieving environmental justice through the environmental rule of law are suggested.[1281]

One of the components of the environmental rule of law is the dimension of integrity and anti-corruption.[1282] As the assessment of risks and threats for the biodiversity of the forest ecosystems of the Ukrainian Carpathians presented in Chapter 2 shows, prevention and elimination of corruption on various levels and within various governmental institutions and ensuring integrity is particularly relevant for the conservation of biodiversity in the Ukrainian Carpathians. A culture of integrity and safeguards against corruption belong to the elements of the effective institutions.[1283] There is a separate resolution "Preventing and combating corruption as it relates to crimes that have an impact on the environment" within the United Nations Convention against Corruption urging the states to tackle corruption related to environment by means of legislation related to money-laundering, corruption, fraud and financial crime, to strengthen anti-corruption frameworks, to promote ethical practices, integrity and transparency, and to ensure that legal and natural persons are held accountable for corruption offences.[1284]

Tackling corruption presupposes the enhancement of transparency and accountability as well as political leadership.[1285] Some of the key techniques for tackling corruption include strengthening oversight and anti corruption authorities with adequate funding, resources, and independence; ensuring

---

Environment Programme, UNEP/EA.SS.1/4 (March 2022) https://documents.un.org/doc/undoc/gen/k22/007/72/pdf/k2200772.pdf.

1281 *IUCN World Declaration on the Environmental Rule of Law*, IUCN World Congress on Environmental Law, 2.

1282 United Nations Environment Programme, *Environmental Rule of Law: Tracking Progress and Charting Future Directions*, 40; *IUCN World Declaration on the Environmental Rule of Law*, IUCN World Congress on Environmental Law, 3–5.

1283 United Nations Environment Programme, *Environmental Rule of Law: Tracking Progress and Charting Future Directions*, 29.

1284 *Preventing and Combating Corruption as it Relates to Crimes that Have an Impact on the Environment*, Resolution 8/12, Conference of the States Parties to the United Nations Convention against Corruption, Eighth session (2019), https://www.unodc.org/corruption/en/cosp/conference/session8-resolutions.html, 2019, § 5, 6, 9.

1285 United Nations Environment Programme, *Environmental Rule of Law: Tracking Progress and Charting Future Directions*, 40.

transparent contracting, which allows citizens and institutions to identify violations; and ensuring access to information, such as spending and the distribution of resources.[1286]

It also might be set in a broader context of building the culture of compliance, which, besides fighting corruption, requires political will and leadership to implement environmental laws and to apply management techniques to inspire good performance.[1287] Moreover, institutional design that ensures clear set of functions and division of powers and thus avoids problems of both "overlap" and "underlap" is important for safeguarding integrity and promoting environmental rule of law.[1288] What is also considered to be useful in anti-corruption context is auditing conducted by independent authorities, and wistleblower-protection laws.[1289]

One of the recent trends for promoting environmental rule of law includes 'citizen science'. Defined as "scientific work undertaken by members of the general public, often in collaboration with or under the direction of professional scientists and scientific institutions,"[1290] it includes, for instance, engagement of environmental agencies with citizen volunteers to fill data gaps and to identify violations.[1291] Such data might enhance environmental rule of law by supporting decision-making processes, including through monitoring of biodiversity.[1292] Citizen science might also be important in environmental enforcement, such as by generating evidence for holding companies accountable.[1293] The greater use of citizen science has

1286 United Nations Environment Programme, *Environmental Rule of Law: Tracking Progress and Charting Future Directions*; See also ibid. Chapter 3.

1287 Ahuja et al., "Advancing Human Rights through Environmental Rule of Law," 25.

1288 Ahuja et al., "Advancing Human Rights through Environmental Rule of Law," 24–29 [Six elements important for functioning of environmental institutions include: clear and appropriate mandates, collection and use of reliable data, independent audit and review mechanisms, coordination across sectors and institutions, building a culture of compliance, and political will and leadership].

1289 Ahuja et al., "Advancing Human Rights through Environmental Rule of Law," 25, 28.

1290 United Nations Environment Programme, *Environmental Rule of Law: Tracking Progress and Charting Future Directions*, 78.

1291 Ahuja et al., "Advancing Human Rights through Environmental Rule of Law," 24.

1292 United Nations Environment Programme, *Environmental Rule of Law: Tracking Progress and Charting Future Directions*, 78.

1293 United Nations Environment Programme, *Environmental Rule of Law: Tracking Progress and Charting Future Directions*, 79; See an example from the US *San Antonio Bay Estuarine Waterkeeper v. Formosa Plastics Corp.*, No. 6:17-CV-0047 (S.D. Tex. 2019).

been advocated within the EU in the recent years. The examples of engaging with this topic include the report on Best Practices in Citizen Science for Environmental Monitoring published by the European Commission in 2020 and the research within the Sensing for Justice project.[1294] On a global scale, UNEP created the World Environment Situation Room Citizen Science Portal functioning as a knowledge platform on environmental citizen science including tools on biodiversity.[1295]

In the context of corruption-related illegal and unsustainable logging in Ukraine, it was suggested that changes in how the forestry is regulated (such as separating responsibilities for logging and monitoring of its legality) and improving transparency are important along with the protection of civil society monitors, anti-corruption activists and wistleblowers from within the forestry.[1296] Moreover, the role of the EU is important for ensuring that its member states including those hosting huge timber processing companies, comply with the regulations and do not incentivise corrupt practices harmful for the forests of the Ukrainian Carpathians.[1297] In another study on combating wildlife crime in the Carpathian region, it is recommended in the context of illegal logging, to tackle corruption and economic hardship *inter alia* by promoting integrated rural and local development, publishing reports on economic losses related to illegal logging, and by improving accessibility of public information on forest management and conservation.[1298]

3.5. The Christian environmental ethics as a moral underpinning of biodiversity protection in the Ukrainian Carpathians

The present subchapter seeks to analyse the ethical ideas on biodiversity informed by Christianity as applicable to the Ukrainian Carpathians.[1299] The policy-relevant ideas, both on the level of structures and on the level of individuals, will be in focus here.

1294 United Nations Environment Programme, *Environmental Rule of Law: Tracking Progress and Charting Future Directions*, 79.

1295 United Nations Environment Programme, *Environmental Rule of Law: Tracking Progress and Charting Future Directions*, 80.

1296 Earthsight, *Complicit In Corruption*, 8.

1297 Earthsight, *Complicit In Corruption*, 8.

1298 Schlingemann et al., ed, *Combating Wildlife and Forest Crime in the Danube-Carpathian Region*, 18.

1299 Based on the level of development of ideas on environmental ethics and relevance to the population of the Ukrainian Carpathians as described in Chapter 2, the

Before delving into the peculiarities of the Christian social teaching on environmental matters, some broader considerations regarding the relevance of morals for biodiversity protection are presented. For instance, in his 2003 article "Do Morals Matter", Christopher Stone quite critically notes that the recourse to ethics in the environmental context less frequently occurs in the documents of the US courts or Congress than, for instance, recourse to bioethics or reference to works of John Rawls.[1300] Such a situation is partly explained by the fact that environmental ethics still deals more with foundational issues, such as whether there is 'intrinsic value' and whether other species could be regarded as 'morally considerable', than provides guidance on policy-addressing level or informs coherent practical application of these concepts to real-life situations.[1301] On the other hand, Arie Trouwborst, answering a question on factors that can make public opinion more supportive towards the idea of large mammals' reintroduction in Europe (in 2022), stated that art and explaining moral obligations behind such measures may play an important role.[1302]

In addition, in a recent book on Christian environmental ethics, Michael Rosenberger discusses some of the clearly practice-oriented implications of ethics in the context of sustainability. These include, for instance, the understanding that "[g]reening forestry and agricultural policy is one of the royal roads to true sustainability".[1303] Furthermore, it is suggested that in the situations where climate protection and biodiversity conservation come into conflict and it is not possible to find solution addressing both of these concerns, "biodiversity should – ceteris paribus – be given priority over climate, for, according to the unanimous assessment of experts, its planetary boundary has already been exceeded much further than that of the climate".[1304]

The need for unprecedented transformation in decision-making that prioritises long-term sustainability over short-term profits and that treats nature as a life-support system as opposed to merely a commodity has also

---

primary focus lies on the social teaching of the Catholic Church and Orthodox Church of Ecumenical Patriarchate, developed in official documents or statements.

1300 Stone, "Do Morals Matter? The Influence of Ethics on Courts and Congress in Shaping U.S. Environmental Policies," 15.

1301 Stone, "Do Morals Matter?," 15–16.

1302 Trouwborst, "Megafauna Restoration as an Obligation," see from 84:30.

1303 Michael Rosenberger, *Christian Ethics of Creation* (Baden-Baden: Nomos, 2022), 211.

1304 Rosenberger, *Christian Ethics of Creation*, 211–212.

been voiced by the IUCN at the recent CBD COP.[1305] On the individual level, the foundation of such transformation might mean a greater awareness of the value of the natural capital of the Carpathian ecoregion, which is currently "largely absent in all the Carpathian countries" and thus impedes meaningful participation in decision-making regarding environmental policy and legislation.[1306] By analogy with the mentioned Stone's article and based on the results of the interviews presented in Chapter 2, it is on the one hand admitted that currently concern for biodiversity protection or environment in general is not perceived as part of the Christian belief in the communities in the Carpathian area within Ukraine. However, the purpose of this endeavour is to highlight the moral ideas on biodiversity embedded in Christianity, to demonstrate their potential for generating awareness of the moral dimensions of the value of the Carpathian natural heritage and biodiversity loss, as well as to look at some policy-relevant structural solutions.

The Orthodox Church of Ecumenical Patriarchate belongs to the pioneers in sensitising the attention of its faithful to the contemporary concern for the environment. Already in 1989, Patriarch Dimitrios I proclaimed September 1st, the beginning of the Church year, as a day dedicated to prayer for creation. In justifying the Church's interest in this matter and defining its approach, he noted the "centuries-long patristic tradition" combined with an "effort faithfully to interpret the eucharistic and liturgical experience of the Orthodox Church".[1307] The approach of the Orthodox Church on this matter was subsequently clarified by the yearly addresses of the Patriarch on the occasion of September 1st, as well as on numerous other occasions.[1308]

The path to the 'ecological ethic' within the Orthodox Church can be found through the prism of a personal relationship, which is based on

1305 "IUCN at UN Biodiversity Conference CBD COP16," IUCN, October 21, 2024, https://iucn.org/cbdcop16.

1306 Nagy et al., *Guidelines for the Identification, Conservation, Restoration, and Management of Ecological Corridors in the Carpathian Ecoregion*, 20–21.

1307 Ecumenical Patriarch Dimitrios, "September 1, 1989, The Church Cannot Remain Idle," as quoted in Ecumenical Patriarch Bartholomew, *On Earth as in Heaven: Ecological Vision and Initiatives of Ecumenical Patriarch Bartholomew*, ed. John Chryssavgis, Orthodox Christianity and Contemporary Thought (New York: Fordham University Press, 2012), https://doi.org/10.1515/9780823292257, 23 [*On Earth as in Heaven*, ed. Chryssavgis].

1308 See "Messages by Ecumenical Patriarch Dimitrios" in *On Earth as in Heaven*, ed. Chryssavgis.

the humanity's need to love and be loved in the context of understanding nature in its entirety as a 'creation of a personal Creator' rather than on any rationalistic codes of conduct. The human use of nature, accordingly, amounts to a genuine relationship, invoked by the beauty of creation, constituting an invitation from God to this relationship and communion with God. The contemporary ecology is understood as a practical response of humanity to this invitation.[1309]

The origin of the Church's interest in the environment is found in the faith in its Creator and love towards Him and fellow human beings. The description of all things created by God as "very good" (Gen. I.31) and the commandment to "work and keep" the earthly garden calls for the harmonious coexistence of humankind and all the creation. It allows for reasonable utilisation of the natural environment and simultaneously calls for care and responsibility so that it retains its productivity.[1310] Thus, care for creation is no more than observance of the divine command.[1311]

At least four elements of the biblical account of the relationship between humanity and the rest of creation are found in the Orthodox teaching. The first of them is the restriction regarding a certain fruit, initially imposed on humanity. It demonstrates that humanity's rule over the rest of creation is not absolute, but subject to rules set by the Creator. The second is the realisation that a gift of creation was given along with the responsibility of humanity "to keep and preserve it" (Gen. 2.15), which presupposes active behaviour rather than passivity and indifference. The third element concerns the consequences of the initial transgression, which had cosmic implications, leading to the corruption of the environment.[1312] It should not be regarded as a punishment for transgression, but rather as a new ontological interaction created because of humanity's disobedience, where initial harmony was altered.[1313] The fourth element is a special care of the Creator

1309 "Address at the Congress of the First Honorary Doctorate of the Department of Environmental Studies, University of the Aegean Mytilene, Greece, October 27, 1994" in *On Earth as in Heaven*, ed. Chryssavgis, 71.

1310 "Official Ceremony of the Binding Foundation, Vaduz, Liechtenstein December 6, 2002" in *On Earth as in Heaven*, ed. Chryssavgis, 76–77.

1311 "Official Ceremony of the Binding Foundation, Vaduz, Liechtenstein December 6, 2002" in *On Earth as in Heaven*, ed. Chryssavgis, 78.

1312 "Address at the Opening Ceremony of Symposium IV, Durres, Albania, June 6, 2002," in *On Earth as in Heaven*, ed. Chryssavgis, 93.

1313 "Address at the Opening Ceremony of Symposium III, Passau, Germany, October 17, 1999," in *On Earth as in Heaven*, ed. Chryssavgis, 88–89.

for the plants and animals (both 'useful' to humanity and 'unclean' ones) through Noah during the Great Flood, preserving them from extinction.[1314]

The relationship of humanity towards creation might therefore be characterised as the one towards the gift, not the one of possession. Certain boundaries and conditions, therefore, apply to it, including the requirement to protect it and to be self-restrained.[1315] It is noted that the 'merciful heart' that cannot tolerate harm to animals and plants and even inanimate elements of nature, and 'saintly sensitivity', making people pray for the whole of creation, is characteristic of some people (or rather of a few).[1316] It is suggested, however, that this attitude should be characteristic of every Christian.[1317]

According to the Fathers of the Church, the human person is simultaneously a partaker of the material and the spiritual world, who was entrusted with the task of helping save the creation from decay and death.[1318] Every species was created before humans, so that humankind could enter into a full kingdom to serve there as a king, priest and prophet. In the present time, it means to "constantly study, serve and pray to transform what is corruptible into what is incorruptible".[1319] The interconnectedness and interdependency of all things in the universe are also recognised, as none of the parts of the creation is self-sufficient; instead, all of them are in need of each other, a concurrence of all with each other.[1320]

Furthermore, the ecological ethos of the Orthodox Church is explained by the three dimensions: the eucharistic ethos, the ascetic ethos, and the liturgical ethos. The first of them means, among other things, using the natural resources with thankfulness, offering them back to God. The ascetic ethos, involving fasting and spiritual works, means recognising that every-

---

1314 "Address at the Opening Ceremony of Symposium IV, Durres, Albania, June 6, 2002," in *On Earth as in Heaven*, ed. Chryssavgis, 94.

1315 "Keynote Address at the International Ecological Symposium, Kathmandu, Nepal, November 2000," in *On Earth as in Heaven*, ed. Chryssavgis, 107.

1316 "September 1, 1997, Creation and Fall," in *On Earth as in Heaven*, ed. Chryssavgis, 41; "Address at the Opening Ceremony of Symposium III, Passau, Germany, October 17, 1999," *On Earth as in Heaven*, ed. Chryssavgis, 87.

1317 "September 1, 1997, Creation and Fall," in *On Earth as in Heaven*, ed. Chryssavgis, 41.

1318 Dimitrios "September 1, 1989, The Church Cannot Remain Idle," in *On Earth as in Heaven*, ed. Chryssavgis, 24.

1319 "September 1, 1995, King, Priest and Prophet," in *On Earth as in Heaven*, ed. Chryssavgis, 36.

1320 "Official Ceremony of the Binding Foundation, Vaduz, Liechtenstein, December 6, 2002," in *On Earth as in Heaven*, ed. Chryssavgis, 77.

thing is God's gift, which should not be abused and wasted. The third, liturgical ethos, includes community concern and sharing. In its context, the Church as the incarnate presence of the Lord Jesus Christ on earth looks to the salvation not only of humanity, but of the entire creation.[1321]

With regard to biodiversity, it is particularly interesting to explore the value of nature and the relationship between humanity and nature. The Orthodox Church calls its faithful to use the natural environment as nature's stewards and not owners, recognising that everything in it, "whether great or small, has importance for the life of the world, and nothing is useless or contemptible", warranting treatment of it with love and care.[1322] It is not disputed that the natural environment "has value in and of itself", which is "a relative value, given by God Himself who created it".[1323] At the same time, this value is not 'absolute'[1324] and humanity's love for nature should not seek to idolise it. Instead, it derives from our love for the Creator, who gives it to us.[1325] Humanity's place within nature is unique and should not go to extremes. Humanity should neither be demoted as to be regarded as of equal importance with all other creatures (as the 'deep ecology' proposals suggest), nor should it be misunderstood as being so superior as to use it unrestrainedly.[1326] Thus, the Orthodox Church accepts the middle stance, whereby humanity does have a superiority over the rest of creation, but as a responsible steward, seeking to preserve it for future generations;[1327] cultivating and caring for it as a 'priest of creation'.[1328]

A series of metaphors is assisting in understanding the stance of the Orthodox Church on nature. The interconnectedness and interdependence of everything are illustrated by the metaphor of a 'seamless garment'

1321 "September 1, 1994, All of creation groans," 34–35.

1322 Dimitrios, "September 1, 1990, Stewards, Not Proprietors," in *On Earth as in Heaven*, ed. Chryssavgis, 26.

1323 "September 1, 1997, Creation and Fall," in *On Earth as in Heaven*, ed. Chryssavgis, 40–41.

1324 "Address at the Opening Ceremony of Symposium II, Trabzon, Turkey, September 20, 1997," "September 1, 1997, Creation and Fall," in *On Earth as in Heaven*, ed. Chryssavgis, 80.

1325 "September 1, 1998, Creation and Idol," in *On Earth as in Heaven*, ed. Chryssavgis, 44.

1326 "Address at the Opening Ceremony of Symposium IV, Durres, Albania, June 6, 2002," in *On Earth as in Heaven*, ed. Chryssavgis, 92.

1327 "Remarks at a Reception be the Greek Ambassador to Norway, Symposium III, Oslo, June 2, 2002," in *On Earth as in Heaven*, ed. Chryssavgis, 189.

1328 "Foreword to 'Greece: Land of Diversity,' August 26, 2010," in *On Earth as in Heaven*, ed. Chryssavgis, 173.

comprised of humanity and the environment.[1329] Nature has also been described by the Church Fathers as a book: a "book that teaches us about the beauty of God's creation" (St. Anthony of Egypt) or as a "sacred book, whose letters and syllables are the universal aspects of creation" (St. Maximus the Confessor).[1330] According to St. Gregory of Nyssa, human beings can discern God's presence by gazing at and listening to creation, therefore nature is a book opened to all to learn. "Each plant, each animal, and each micro-organism tells a story, unfolds a mystery, relates an extraordinary harmony and balance, which are interdependent and complementary."[1331] The environment is also presented as an 'orchestra', where each detail is crucial, and no single element can be removed without danger to the 'entire symphony' or as a 'picture' that gets distorted or destroyed once a single tree or animal is removed.[1332]

The reason why humanity should care for the natural environment is, from the Orthodox viewpoint, at least the fact that disrespect of God's creation amounts to disrespect towards the Creator.[1333] It could be compared to the destruction of a work of an artist.[1334] Moreover, the environment is understood as home of humanity, the protection of which is crucial to prevent negative consequences of its destruction for the present and future generations.[1335]

The abuse of humanity's privileged position within the creation leads to devastating consequences, including the extinction of plant and animal species.[1336] Furthermore, the concept of sin was broadened to include tres-

1329 "Address to the Scenic Hudson, New York, November 13, 2000," in *On Earth as in Heaven*, ed. Chryssavgis, 112.

1330 "Article for Seminarium, Vatican, May 2010," in *On Earth as in Heaven*, ed. Chryssavgis, 128.

1331 "Article for Seminarium, Vatican, May 2010," in *On Earth as in Heaven*, ed. Chryssavgis, 129.

1332 "Article for Seminarium, Vatican, May 2010," in *On Earth as in Heaven*, ed. Chryssavgis, 130.

1333 "Interview with journalist Harri Saukkomaa, Finland, March 2009," in *On Earth as in Heaven*, ed. Chryssavgis, 326.

1334 "Opening Ceremony, Halki Ecological Institute, June 13, 1999," in *On Earth as in Heaven*, ed. Chryssavgis, 168.

1335 "Interview with journalist Harri Saukkomaa, Finland, March 2009," in *On Earth as in Heaven*, ed. Chryssavgis, 326.

1336 Dimitrios "September 1, 1989, The Church Cannot Remain Idle," in *On Earth as in Heaven*, ed. Chryssavgis, 24.

passes against the natural world.[1337] Biodiversity and forests are explicitly mentioned in this regard as causing the extinction of species and destroying biological diversity, as well as degrading the integrity of the earth through the destruction of natural forests, which are mentioned among the examples of sins.[1338]

When it comes to the practical dimension of environmental ethics, the Orthodox Church talks of the collective obligation "to conform to everything demanded for the sake of the protection of the environment". This obligation includes two basic elements – the active and the passive ones. The first one is to actively avoid destroying the environment and to actively restore and improve it. The second one consists of ceasing to use the products, the production of which burdens the environment or to use them rationally when this is absolutely necessary. There is also a third element of this obligation – rendering people aware of it.[1339]

Furthermore, it is considered to be crucial to reject everything that is harmful to the environment, to change the way we think and, accordingly, the way we live.[1340] The 'change of mind' about humanity's relationship with the world and with God is at the core of the effectiveness of the conservation projects, as it is through it that the tackling of the root cause of environmental sin takes place.[1341] From the viewpoint of economic activity, it is important to keep in mind that profit, especially the short-term one, should not be the only motive of humanity's actions.[1342] It is underscored that humankind's personal and collective attitudes should be harmonised with the needs of nature's ecosystems, "so that every kind of fauna and flora in the world and in the universe may live and thrive and be preserved".[1343]

1337 "Keynote Address at the Santa Barbara Symposium, California, November 8, 1997," *On Earth as in Heaven*, ed. Chryssavgis, 99; "Article for Seminarium, Vatican, May 2010," in *On Earth as in Heaven*, ed. Chryssavgis, 138.

1338 "Keynote Address at the Santa Barbara Symposium, California, November 8, 1997," in *On Earth as in Heaven*, ed. Chryssavgis, 99.

1339 "Keynote Address at the International Ecological Symposium, Katmandy, Nepal, November 2000," in *On Earth as in Heaven*, ed. Chryssavgis, 104–105.

1340 "September 1, 2009, The Global Market and the Natural Environment," in *On Earth as in Heaven*, ed. Chryssavgis, 63.

1341 "Message to the International Conference on Ethics, Religion and Environment, University of Oregon, April 5, 2009," in *On Earth as in Heaven*, ed. Chryssavgis, 171.

1342 "September 1, 2009, The Global Market and the Natural Environment," in *On Earth as in Heaven*, ed. Chryssavgis, 63.

1343 "September 1, 2010, The Financial Crisis and the Ecological Crisis," in *On Earth as in Heaven*, ed. Chryssavgis, 64.

Importantly, the Orthodox Church of the Ecumenical Patriarchate has been active in initiating ecumenical dialogue and cooperation in the field of environmental ethics. One of the examples of such cooperation is the "Common declaration on environmental ethics" by Pope John Paul II and Ecumenical Patriarch Bartholomew I, signed in 2002 in Venice (Venice Declaration).[1344] The Venice Declaration proclaims that "[r]espect for creation stems from respect for human life and dignity" and on this basis claims a specific role of Christians and other believers "in proclaiming moral values and in educating people in ecological awareness, which is none other than responsibility towards self, towards others, towards creation."[1345] It underlines that the problem of care for creation "is not simply economic and technological", but also "moral and spiritual", therefore for finding solutions a genuine conversion in Christ enabling the change of the ways we think and act, or, in other words, an inner change of heart, leading to a change in lifestyle as well as patterns of production and consumption is needed.[1346] What is advocated is a new approach and a new culture "inspired by environmentally ethical behavior stemming from our triple relationship to God, to self and to creation", relying on the principles of universal solidarity, social justice and responsibility.[1347] The declaration invites all men and women of good will to consider six ethical goals, including bearing in mind children while evaluating options for action; openness to studying true values based on the natural law sustaining every human culture; constructive use of science and technology with awareness as to the centrality of the human person, common good and the inner purpose of creation; humbleness with respect of the ownership towards creation with realisation that our power is not unlimited but the one of the stewards of the common heritage; the principle of subsidiarity, according to which all can take part in the shared effort but from the affluent societies more is demanded than from the poor ones; promotion of the peaceful approach

1344 "Common Declaration on Environmental Ethics," Common Declaration of John Paul II and the Ecumenical Patriarch His Holiness Bartholomew I, June 10, 2002, https://www.vatican.va/content/john-paul-ii/en/speeches/2002/june/documents/hf_jp-ii_spe_20020610_venice-declaration.html [Common Declaration on Environmental Ethics].

1345 Common Declaration on Environmental Ethics.

1346 Common Declaration on Environmental Ethics.

1347 Common Declaration on Environmental Ethics.

to disagreements in environmental sphere, seeking solutions through open exchange.[1348]

In the Catholic Church, the concern for the environment as such and biodiversity in particular is a comparatively recent development. Not much has been said directly about biodiversity before the 2015 encyclical letter *Laudato Si'*, which explicitly places biodiversity loss among the troubling issues that our common home is facing.[1349] At the same time, some broader passages on creation preceding this encyclical letter are found in the legacy of St. John Paul II and Benedict XVI, the Compendium of the Social Teaching of the Catholic Church (the Compendium), the Catechism, and statements of the regional conferences of bishops. Some of the central notions on addressing environment or 'creation' found in the tradition of the Catholic Church include 'gift' and 'stewardship', 'duty' (including 'duty of care' and 'common and universal duty'), 'responsibility' and 'integral ecology' while defining it and stance of humankind towards it.[1350]

For instance, the understanding of the creation and its value have been framed by St. John Paul II's as an 'ordered system',[1351] while Pope Benedict XVI talks of nature's 'grammar' and calls to view nature as something greater than a resource or a 'raw material manipulated at our pleasure', because it speaks of the Creator and His love to humanity.[1352] Pope Benedict XVI also draws attention to the responsibility that exists vis-à-vis the poor, future generations, and humanity, requiring at the same time respect towards the 'intrinsic balance of creation'.[1353] Pope Francis states that not

1348 Common Declaration on Environmental Ethics.

1349 Francis, *Laudato Si'* (2015), https://www.vatican.va/content/francesco/en/encyclicals/documents/papa-francesco_20150524_enciclica-laudato-si.html, § 32–42.

1350 See, for instance, Vogt, *Christliche Umweltethik*; Natalia Subbotina, "The Perspective of SDGs and CST on Biodiversity in the Context of the Protection of Forest Ecosystems in the Ukrainian Carpathians," *Analecta of the UCU: Theology* 9 (2022), doi: 10.47632/2075-4817-2022-9-183-199; Jame Schaefer and Tobias Winright, ed., *Environmental Justice and Climate Change: Assessing Pope Benedict XVI's Ecological Vision for the Catholic Church in the United States* (Lanham, MD: Lexington Books, 2013); Anthony Kelly, *Laudato Si: An Integral Ecology and the Catholic Vision* (Adelaide: ATF Press, 2016).

1351 John Paul II, *Solicitudo Rei Socialis* (1987), https://www.vatican.va/content/john-paul-ii/en/encyclicals/documents/hf_jp-ii_enc_30121987_sollicitudo-rei-socialis.html, §34.

1352 Benedict XVI, *Caritas in Veritate* (2009), https://www.vatican.va/content/benedict-xvi/en/encyclicals/documents/hf_ben-xvi_enc_20090629_caritas-in-veritate.html, § 48.

1353 Benedict XVI, *Caritas in Veritate*, § 48.

only are the non-human creatures more than a resource, but also they have value in themselves, grounding the basis for the recognition of such a value in a biblical perspective and citing the German bishops who speak of "priority of being over that of being useful" of the non-human creatures.[1354]

The Compendium acknowledges the environmental value of biodiversity[1355] and states that biodiversity "must be handled with a sense of responsibility and adequately protected, because it constitutes an extraordinary richness for all of humanity."[1356] Importantly, the special role of forests is underlined, as they "help maintain the essential natural balance necessary for life", justifying the appropriate action of individuals and institutions, which "must feel the commitment to protect the heritage of forests."[1357]

In terms of locating the value of creation in the environmental ethics discourse, the middle path is chosen, as both 'distorted anthropocentrism' and 'biocentrism' are criticised. The problem with the extreme anthropocentrism lies in its failure to recognise "the particular goodness of every creature",[1358] while 'biocentrism' is not welcome, as it hinders an understanding of the unique responsibility and unique capacities of knowledge, will, and freedom that human beings have.[1359]

The practical dimension of the integral ecology as understood within the Catholic Church necessitates studying the ecosystems "not only to determine how best to use them, but also because they have an intrinsic value independent of their usefulness," while the sustainable use of the creation requires attention to "each ecosystem's regenerative ability".[1360] The specialists' view on a greater protection of particularly biodiversity rich areas is also supported.[1361] The reconciliation of economic development and environmental protection is also advocated in the Catholic social teaching (CST). It is suggested that appropriate solutions "require that economic activity respect the environment to a greater degree" and that the "economy

1354 Francis, *Laudato Si'* (2015), § 33, § 69.
1355 Pontifical Council for Justice and Peace, *Compendium of the Social Doctrine of the Church* (2004), https://www.vatican.va/roman_curia/pontifical_councils/justpeace/documents/rc_pc_justpeace_doc_20060526_compendio-dott-soc_en.html, § 466.
1356 *Compendium of the Social Doctrine of the Church*, § 466.
1357 *Compendium of the Social Doctrine of the Church*, § 466.
1358 Francis, *Laudato Si',* § 69; *Catechism of the Catholic Church*, Vatican City (1997), https://www.vatican.va/archive/ENG0015/_INDEX.HTM, § 339.
1359 Francis, *Laudato Si'*, § 84.
1360 Francis, *Laudato Si'*, § 140.
1361 Francis, *Laudato Si'*, § 37.

respectful of the environment will not have the maximization of profits as its only objective."[1362] The consideration of biodiversity in this context is explicitly mentioned as the maximisation of profits blind to the ecological consequences, including "harm done to biodiversity" is criticized.[1363]

In addition to practical considerations and economic dimension, the spiritual relevance of creation for humanity is acknowledged as it "reveals the mystery of God who created and sustains it", necessitating humanity's action towards it with "gratitude and appreciation."[1364] Pope Francis further speaks of the "God's loving plan in which every creature has its own value and significance" and the understanding of creation as of "a gift from the outstretched hand of the Father of all, and as a reality illuminated by the love."[1365] Creatures are metaphorically understood as letters of the precious book written by God, leading to the conclusion that "contemplation of creation allows us to discover in each thing a teaching which God wishes to hand on to us."[1366] The spiritual relevance of creation and the idea of integral ecology led to the suggestion to add 'ecological sin' defined as "an action or omission against God, against one's neighbour, the community and the environment" to the Catechism, leading to the greater role of the duty of care for creation (including biodiversity) within the Catholic Church.[1367]

Moreover, apart from the clearly environmental passages of the CST, its general principles of solidarity, subsidiarity, common good and human dignity might inform both personal action and policy directions as related to forest biodiversity in the Ukrainian Carpathians.[1368]

In the assessment of humanity's progress in the environmental sphere by Pope Francis, the 1992 Earth Summit is praised as a real step forward,

---

1362 *Compendium of the Social Doctrine of the Church*, § 470.
1363 Francis, *Laudato Si'*, § 195.
1364 *Compendium of the Social Doctrine of the Church*, § 487.
1365 Francis, *Laudato Si'*, § 76.
1366 Francis, *Laudato Si'*, § 85 (citing Canadian and Japanese bishops).
1367 Synod of Bishops for the Pan-Amazon Region, *The Amazon: New Paths for the Church and for an Integral Ecology*, Final document, October 26, 2019, http://secretariat.synod.va/content/sinodoamazonico/en/documents/final-document-of-the-amazon-synod.html, § 82; See Nick Mayrand, "Theologians praise suggestion to add 'ecological sins' to Catholic catechism," Crux, November 20, 2019, https://cruxnow.com/church-in-the-usa/2019/11/theologians-praise-suggestion-to-add-ecological-sins-to-catholic-catechism.
1368 For instance, subsidiarity is mentioned in Kiss and Shelton, *International Environmental Law, 36.*

"prophetic for its time".[1369] At the same time, the lack of implementation of its ideas is acknowledged, which is particularly true for biodiversity, as the progress in this sphere was not as significant as desired.[1370]

In summary, one may note that the ideas of Orthodox and Catholic teaching relevant for biodiversity are consonant with the ideas of sustainable development as a policy framework and legally binding norms of biodiversity law. In fact, such ideas might complement one another in a fruitful way[1371] or even 'deeply enrich one another'.[1372] It is suggested that while policies and laws provide much more detailed guidance for practical action, the added value of the biodiversity-related ideas embedded in Christian teaching is their ability to appeal to hearts and minds, thus raising awareness of the need to integrate concern for biodiversity into personal decision-making.

3.6. The suggested lines of change in the legal, policy, and ethical components for enhanced protection of biodiversity of forest ecosystems of the Ukrainian Carpathians

The purpose of this subchapter is to provide a summary on suggested lines of change based on the status quo of the biodiversity protection in the Ukrainian Carpathians and recommendations from the global, European and Carpathian levels in the domains of law, ethics and policy.

First of all, there is a clear need to adopt a national biodiversity strategy and action plan, which would amount to a genuine fulfilment of the obligation under Article 6 of the CBD. It is apparent that the decision to protect biodiversity merely through the formation of the ecological network rather than designing a separate comprehensive strategy on biodiversity, taken by Ukraine in the early 2000s,[1373] is insufficient for ensuring biodiversity protection in line with its international obligations. This strategy has to take into account regional peculiarities of the Carpathians as a particularly biodiversity-rich area within Ukraine with precious primeval forests, repre-

1369 Cf. Francis, *Laudato Si'*, § 167.

1370 Cf. Francis, *Laudato Si'*, § 168–169.

1371 Vogt, *Christliche Umweltethik*, 516.

1372 Amanda Jaret and Frank Pasquale, "The Ethical, Legal, and Political Significance of Laudato Si'," in *Care for the World: Laudato Si' and Catholic Social Thought in an Era of Climate Crisis*, ed. Frank Pasquale (Cambrige: Cambrige University Press, 2019), 10.

1373 See Chapter 2, subchapters 2.2.1 and 2.4.2.

senting a habitat of large mammals and other endangered and rare species and constituting an important area for migratory species. Moreover, in light of sustainable development, the needs of the local residents have to be considered. Such a strategy should take into account global and regional developments, such as the most recent ones, including the Kunming-Montreal Global Biodiversity Framework and the corresponding Carpathian Biodiversity Framework, Strategies within the CMS and the CITES (and possibly also the EU Biodiversity Strategy in light of Ukraine's ambition to join the EU). It may also rely on various recommendations and guidelines on mountainous and forest biodiversity, protected areas, ecological connectivity, invasive alien species and related areas, produced over the years within the institutional mechanisms of the relevant conventions, such as the CBD, the Bern Convention, or Carpathian Convention, as well as other reputable organisations, such as the IUCN.

It is also crucial, in light of the principle of integration, to ensure that biodiversity protection is not treated in isolation from the activities directly or indirectly influencing biodiversity, such as those in the areas of forestry, transport, construction and tourism. Such an integration could be achieved both by planning relevant actions within the strategic documents on biodiversity and by integrating concern for biodiversity into sectoral policies.

Moreover, it is advisable to strive for achieving synergies between biodiversity protection and other concerns, such as climate change and human rights. For forest biodiversity, links between biodiversity protection and climate action have been thoroughly analysed on different fora, so that technical solutions and policy directions which lead to mutual reinforcement of the goals on biodiversity and climate could be identified and applied by the government. There is also a growing room for identifying links and strategies to jointly address biodiversity and human rights to the benefit of both of these areas, especially in light of the human right to a healthy environment. Framing the implementation of biodiversity treaties in Ukraine through the lenses of human rights obligations might potentially generate additional attention to the issue of biodiversity loss and broaden the array of legal tools for addressing this issue.

In addition, the work towards ensuring the rule of law generally or 'environmental rule of law' specifically, including enhancing integrity and tackling corruption as well as ensuring the inevitability of punishment for environmental crime, is of paramount importance in Ukraine. The greater transparency in forestry and efficient functioning of the law enforcement agencies in charge of supervising the implementation of the nature protection legislation and legislation on forestry are essential for the reduction of instances of illegal and unsustainable logging in the Ukrainian Carpathians. Moreover, due attention has to be paid by the government to the quality of laws, including their accessibility and clarity for the forest sector employees and civil society. Even though the legislation on forestry is supposed to be codified in the Forest Code of Ukraine, at present, the laws and regulations on forestry appear to be scattered across a number of instruments in a rather complex manner.[1374] It is commendable that numerous amendments have been made in recent years to enhance the protection of the primeval forests and biodiversity within the commercially exploited forests. However, it is unclear whether such norms are applied in good faith in practice of commercial forestry in Ukraine not in the least given the potential unawareness of the forest sector employees about the recent legislative changes, lack of political will to switch from the goal of profit maximisation to genuine concern for biodiversity protection or toleration of the instances of non-compliance with the nature protection restrictions in forestry. What is more, the clear division of powers with respect to biodiversity (including the monitoring of biodiversity in forest ecosystems and taking action on its conservation) between different levels of governance (from nation-wide to local authorities) and between different actors (such as forest enterprises and the NRF institutions) seems to be lacking, warranting action to ensure greater clarity to avoid both overlapping of powers leading to institutional tensions and underlapping, leading to inaction. Therefore, it might be advantageous to ensure the greater clarity and accessibility of the forest legislation, such as by adopting new Forest Code as well as to ensure awareness of the forest sector employees of the biodiversity-related legislative amendments, such as through attention to this topic in the academic institutions as well as through organising training and workshops.

Another basic international obligation, the one on monitoring of biodiversity, also requires action from the Ukrainian government. It is essential to create a viable system for comprehensive monitoring of biodiversity, which could inform decision-making. Such a monitoring system shall cover all of the Carpathian forests, including those under commercial forestry. For the institutions of the NRF in the Carpathians, it might be relevant to study and gradually adopt approaches to biodiversity monitoring used in the EU countries, such as the approach used by the national parks Berchtesgaden and the Bavarian Forest. The understandable financial and

1374 See Chapter 2, subchapter 2.2.3.

technical limitations of monitoring and the lack of staff might be mitigated by careful planning based on the existing resources, as well as by the involvement of volunteers or the use of 'citizen science' approaches to monitoring.

One of the important strategies for biodiversity protection includes safeguarding habitats and enhancing ecological connectivity by means of creating an ecological network. In Ukraine, such activities on the one hand could be exercised on the basis of the law "On Ecological Network", however, on the other hand, its approach to the formation of the ecological network does not correspond to the designation and functioning of the Emerald Network based on the Bern Convention (and to the analogous Natura 2000 network within the EU). The cases of Borzhava and Svydovets demonstrate the problems with understanding the nature and scope of obligations under the Bern Convention in conjunction with the formation and functioning of the Emerald Network.[1375] The Standing Committee of the Bern Convention recommended to Ukraine in light of Borzhava case to improve the implementation of the Emerald Network, suggesting some of the practical steps, such as an initiation of the multi-stakeholder process in order to identify key issues that constrain progress, assessment of the contribution of the Emerald Network to carbon sequestration and storage and adoption of the Law on the Emerald Network.[1376] The activities towards this end are also required based on the Association Agreement between the EU and Ukraine, providing for the approximation of Ukrainian legislation to the Birds and Habitats Directives. Therefore, it is highly advisable to adopt the Law on the Emerald Network (or alternatively amend existing laws) in order to fulfil these obligations. It would, however, be insufficient to simply adopt a new law, as what is needed is a genuine implementation of the obligations of result under the Bern Convention. Therefore, adoption of the legislation on the Emerald Network shall be accompanied by the broad public discussion as well as workshops and training for the actors taking part in the implementation of its provisions (including, in the first instance, forestry sector employees).

In-situ conservation of biodiversity by means of protected areas also deserves enhanced attention from the Ukrainian government. In order to achieve effective biodiversity conservation, it is oftentimes insufficient to simply designate a certain area as a protected area (that is, various types of the NRF territories and objects according to Ukrainian legislation). What

---

1375 See Chapter 2, subchapter 2.5.

1376 Standing Committee, *Recommendation No. 213 (2021).*

is necessary is the development of the management plans for the protected areas based on the circumstances and needs of a particular area and the exercise of continuous monitoring of its conditions. The designation of protected areas also has to be accompanied by solving the issues of land ownership and ensuring the necessary state acts for land, as well as boundaries of the protected area to safeguard it from encroachments by neighbouring forestry enterprises and individual landowners. What is also important in the context of the Ukrainian NRF institutions is communication and exchange of information (currently barely present), for instance, on biodiversity monitoring, developing tourist infrastructure or best practices for dealing with the risks and threats, such as invasive alien species or climate change. It might also be advisable to reduce the institutional tensions between the NRF sites and commercial forestry by clearly defining the competences and powers within certain territory (or following the example of Bavarian Forest, to completely separate areas of the NRF site, where logging could be undertaken only by the NRF institution itself, from the areas under commercial forestry).

In those areas of the Carpathians which do not belong to the primeval, quasi-primeval and natural forests, the work on the restoration of ecosystems and the application of close-to-nature forestry and sustainable forest management approaches is desirable. For instance, it is possible to switch from forming monocultural and same-age forests to mixed forests with different ages of the tree stands. In addition, programmes on renaturalisation or reintroduction of the aboriginal plant (such as yew tree) and animal species (such as European bison) that are already taking place should be supported and could be scaled in future. Simultaneously, it is important to take action on halting the distribution of the invasive alien species, at least by excluding their deliberate use during the reforestation activities. It is also advisable to use the soft methods of felling as opposed to the heavy equipment, which destroys vegetation and soil. In addition, the plans on extending road infrastructure in the Ukrainian Carpathians shall be subject to careful EIA, taking into account the location of primeval forests, habitats of rare and endangered species, and routes of migratory species.

Importantly, in light of sustainable development as the current global agenda, biodiversity protection in the Ukrainian Carpathians shall be exercised in the full awareness of the social and economic development of the Carpathian region in Ukraine. This means, in particular, ensuring decent lives for the local populations characterised as forest-dependent communities by fostering alternative employment opportunities and providing incentives or subsidies, if necessary. For instance, incentivising revitalisation of such traditional practice for Carpathian areas as sheep herding combined with the manufacturing of cheese or rugs, might be a good alternative to logging. Generation of profits from gathering berries, mushrooms and medicinal plants within the adequate limits is also a good alternative to profits from logging. Similarly, the orcharding (such as the production of apples that used to be practised in the region) might be encouraged by economic incentives. The development of sustainable tourism, which brings benefits to the local residents and contributes to biodiversity protection rather than leading to its destruction, is also desirable. The examples of the tourism-related harmful practices specific to the Ukrainian Carpathians include 'jeeping' or operation of the overpopulated resorts, and such practices should ideally be outlawed. Some of the possible strategies to enhance biodiversity preservation in part of the Carpathian forests also concern land ownership and use. For instance, to increase the preservation of some of the forests in the vicinity of the villages, which historically belonged to the local residents before the Soviet occupation, the private ownership of such forests might be reestablished (after careful planning and utilisation of participatory approaches in the decision-making). Similarly, it is important to solve the issue of the bankrupt and neglected municipal forest enterprises by assessing their status and taking the decision on, for instance, including these to the NRF, the enterprise "Forests of Ukraine", allowing for their privatisation or letting them remain within the communal ownership after certain reorganisation and enhancement of protection of such forests from unauthorised logging.

Despite the general limitations of resources available to various levels of government, it is inevitable to allocate sufficient funds for the functioning of NRF sites and nature conservation in the Ukrainian Carpathians, as far as possible, given the value of their biodiversity. One of the options for increasing the weight of biodiversity in decision-making is the monetary valuation of ecosystem services, allowing for a more eloquent representation of the invisible financial contribution of nature to well-being, which is often taken for granted. However, this is only one of the options, as apart from the monetary expression of biodiversity's value, there could be general awareness raising regarding various types of its instrumental (including medicinal, aesthetic and cultural) and intrinsic value of biodiversity. Overall, a greater awareness about the biodiversity-rich areas of the Ukrainian Carpathians and their meaning in the subregional, regional and global dimension in the context of the triple planetary crisis involving biodiversity loss is needed. It is suggested that one of the tools for raising such an awareness on the local level of the Carpathian regions within Ukraine is by increasing awareness of the ideas of Christian environmental ethics, which might serve as an inspiration for the behaviour change.

In conclusion, there is a need for a 'new philosophy' in legislative and policy approaches to protect the biodiversity of forest ecosystems of the Ukrainian Carpathians. A shift towards a greater understanding of the value of biodiversity is required, together with the integration of biodiversity considerations into various levels of decision-making and practical action.

Conclusions to Chapter 3

In recent years, especially after the 2013 – 2014 Revolution of Dignity, some progress in implementing Ukraine's international obligations on protecting the biodiversity of forest ecosystems in the Ukrainian Carpathians has been observed. Some of the milestone achievements, serving the purpose of implementation of the international biodiversity-related obligations of Ukraine as well as requirements of the Association Agreement between the EU and Ukraine include the introduction of the procedures of the EIA and SEA, the provisions on primeval, quasi-primeval and natural forests, integration of biodiversity protection into commercial forestry by introduction of categories of specially protective forest zones, introduction of foundations of sustainable forestry and close-to-nature forestry to the Forest Code of Ukraine, designation of the Emerald network sites and extension of the NRF sites.

At the same time, some of the key problems with implementation of the Ukraine's international obligations on biodiversity include lack of comprehensive biodiversity monitoring and inaccurate data, lack of integration of biodiversity protection into all of the relevant areas of life, lack of political support and understanding of the international biodiversity-related obligations among the executive power officials, limited financial, administrative and technical capacities, lack of coordination and clear division of powers on biodiversity protection between institutions as well as tackling of consequences rather than root causes of the problems. When it comes to the Bern convention, one of the clear obstacles on ensuring implementation of the obligations of the result regarding Carpathian forest ecosystems, is the absence of clear legislative norms on the status of the Emerald network in Ukraine, which warrants the adoption of the Law on the Emerald Network.

What is also needed in the context of the Emerald network, is the change of the approach as to its formation in Ukraine, that will correspond to the one recommended by the documents related to the Bern Convention and to the EU practices on designation and functioning of the Natura 2000 network.

Some of the further solutions on improvement of implementation on Ukraine's international obligations with respect to biodiversity include counteracting illegal logging in the primeval forests in the Carpathians, including by implementing the EU Regulation on deforestation-free supply chains, and investing into environmentally safe and sustainable tourist infrastructure. There is also a need for coordinated action on tackling invasive alien species, including the prevention of their introduction to the forest ecosystems of the Ukrainian Carpathians. Furthermore, one of the possible tools on generating greater public awareness and support of biodiversity-related action include introduction of the monetary evaluation of the ecosystem services.

When it comes to best practices, recommendations and examples of useful strategies on protection of biodiversity, which could be applied to enhance protection of the forest ecosystems of the Ukrainian Carpathians, there is a broad palette of possible tools and approaches, created over the years within different platforms. For instance, the materials of the programmes of work on mountain biodiversity and on forest biodiversity within the CBD, the IUCN guidance on designing institutional and legal frameworks on invasive alien species, and results of various projects in the field of conservation and sustainable use of biodiversity under the auspices of the Carpathian Convention, such as on large carnivores, ecological connectivity and ecological corridors are potentially extremely useful for the Ukrainian policy-makers. Importantly, action on biodiversity has to align with a broader sustainable development paradigm, in particular, it is recommended that the reduction of biodiversity loss and environmental degradation has to coincide with the poverty reduction in the local communities, improving human well-being and social equity.

Good practices on the obligation of the result under the Bern Convention in the context of the Emerald Network, which include maintenance, restoration or improvement of the abiotic and biotic features of habitats, and comprises at least components of 'setting in place a protection regime' and 'taking practical management measures' comprise development and implementation of management plans or their equivalents, research serving the purpose of enhancing the understanding of the critical elements in the management, stakeholder involvement in the management measures, provision of adequate personnel and resources, as well as adequate monitoring.

With respect to forests specifically, within Carpathian Convention, promotion of the close-to-nature forest management is considered one of the priorities, while key objectives of the current strategic action plan for implementation of the Forest Protocol include, for instance, maintaining and enlarging forest cover, identifying and protecting natural and especially virgin forests, ensuring productive functions of forests and their role in rural development as well as protection and reintroduction of rare native forest tree species. It is further suggested to promote nature-based solutions to addressing climate change with a special focus on ecosystem-based adaptation.

Specific thematic directions of action on biodiversity include protected areas, such as well-managed ones and those where genetic diversity is preserved by creation of spaces where natural selection occurs freely, designation of other types of areas directly or indirectly serving the purpose of biodiversity protection, promoting ecological connectivity and ecosystem restoration, including by rewilding, protecting primary forests and restoring conditions and parameters close to them in terms of forest structure, composition and functioning. What is also recommended in the context of forestry in Eastern Europe, is increasing the level of management awareness of the uniqueness of the primary forests, which are relatively widespread here, in the broader biogeographical context. What is also recommended in terms of enhancing resilience, is the need of shift of the forest management approaches from focusing on timber extraction to the broader approaches, as well as the increase of the mixed forests as opposed to monoculture forests.

The examples from the two national nature parks located in Bavaria, Germany, provide some potentially useful models of zonation of the protected areas, management goals, tourism and awareness-raising activities with the goal of 'leaving nature to its own devices', gradual and comprehensive monitoring of biodiversity, and ensuring respect of the rights of the local population and adjacent land-owners.

The interaction between climate change and biodiversity legal regimes is quite complex, as despite being implicitly intertwined since the creation of the Rio conventions on both of these matters, there is a possibility of conflict between the means used to achieve goals in both of these areas. Such a situation requires close attention from the national governments in the formulation of international commitments and national policies. One of the problematic aspects also includes the fact that despite the ample efforts on integrating climate change into biodiversity-related laws and policies on an international level, the efforts on integrating biodiversity protection into the climate change agenda have been rather marginal. There is, however, great potential for synergies given the interdependence of biodiversity and climate, as reflected in the Kunming-Montreal Global Biodiversity Framework.

There is a growing understanding of the interdependency between human rights and biodiversity as one of the components of the environment, which is also acknowledged in the Kunming-Montreal Global Biodiversity Framework and numerous documents within the UN. It is recognised that an environment of a certain quality is necessary for the full enjoyment of a number of human rights (which becomes particularly clear in the context of 'ecosystem services'), and on the other hand, certain human rights are crucial for the protection of the environment. The loss of biodiversity threatens the enjoyment of the human rights which rely on biodiversity. Therefore, the establishment and enforcement of effective legal and institutional frameworks, which shall include substantive standards regarding protected areas, conservation and biodiversity, serve the purpose of both protecting the environment and human rights. It is also said that obligations at the intersection of human rights and biodiversity include both substantive and procedural ones. The substantive obligations comprise a general obligation of states to safeguard biodiversity and protect against environmental harm from private actors, as well as include more specific obligations undertaken on the basis of international treaties on biodiversity. The procedural obligations are grounded in the civil and political rights in conjunction with the environmental context, such as to ensure access to environmental information, to facilitate public participation in environmental decision-making, to provide access to remedies for harm or to protect environmental human rights defenders. The standalone substantive human right to a healthy environment that has been recently recognised on a global level, particularly clearly ties human rights and biodiversity, as 'healthy ecosystems and biodiversity' is considered to constitute one of the elements of this right and as implementation of multilateral environmental agreements under the principles of international environmental law is required to promote this right.

Tourism and biodiversity protection have a complex relationship as tourism could be both beneficial and detrimental to biodiversity. Sustainable tourism, however, is capable of building synergies and enhancing efforts on biodiversity protection. There are numerous guidelines on the global, European and Carpathian levels to this extent, helping to direct the action of states and other actors to advance biodiversity protection through sustainable tourism.

The environmental rule of law, which partly overlaps with the human rights and biodiversity discourse, is vital for the functioning of the whole system of implementation of environmental norms in a broader social, economic and governmental context. What is required by it is a governance system where all persons are accountable to laws that are clear and precise, equally enforced and independently adjudicated. Moreover, a clear division of powers and functions of different governmental agencies is needed, along with the promotion of a culture of compliance. One of the important components of environmental rule of law is tackling corruption, which could be undertaken in numerous ways, including by increasing transparency and introducing independent auditing. The novel participatory tools for promoting environmental rule of law include 'citizen science', which could support decision-making and enforcement.

The need to prioritise long-term sustainability over short-term profits and to treat nature as a life-support system rather than a mere commodity, which has been voiced on secular international platforms, aligns well with the ideas of Christian environmental ethics. The latter might be beneficial for raising awareness of the moral dimension of value of the Carpathian natural heritage and its practical implications among the local residents and decision makers as well as for providing guidance in some of the challenging questions of environmental ethics, for instance as in both Orthodox and Catholic environmental ethics the middle stance between extreme anthropocentrism and biocentrism or deep ecology is articulated. In the CST, for instance, biodiversity is called an 'extraordinary richness for all of humanity', and the need to protect the heritage of forests by individuals and institutions is expressed. Furthermore, the maximisation of profits, blind to the ecological consequences, including "harm done to biodiversity", is criticised. In the Orthodox Church, causing the extinction of species, destruction of biodiversity and degrading the integrity of the earth through destruction of the natural forests are mentioned among the examples of sins. Some of the central ideas of Orthodox and Catholic environmental ethics alike include an understanding of creation as a gift, given along with the responsibility to take care of it, implying active behaviour of keeping and preserving it as responsible stewards, which is also coupled with humanity's self-restraint in their actions towards nature. Moreover, the notions of interconnectedness and interdependency of all things in the universe are voiced. The care for nature is considered to be not merely an economic and technological issue, but also a moral and spiritual issue, warranting the need for an inner change of heart and mind, which lies at the core of the effectiveness of the conservation projects.

On the basis of application of the good practices and recommendations to the status quo of the biodiversity protection in the Ukrainian Carpathians, including the risks and threats to biodiversity as well as problems with the implementation of Ukraine's international obligations, a set of lines of change is recommended to enhance biodiversity protection. These include adoption of the national biodiversity strategy and action plan, integration of biodiversity protection into sectoral policies, such as on transport and construction, striving for enhancing synergies with the related areas such as climate action and human rights, promoting environmental rule of law including by ensuring legislative clarity and tackling corruption, improving biodiversity monitoring, enhancing ecological connectivity and effective *in-situ* conservation of biodiversity, restoration of ecosystems and application of the close-to-nature forestry and sustainable forest management approaches, placing the issue of biodiversity protection of the forest ecosystems into a broader social and economic development of the Carpathian region, by taking into account alternative sources of income and employment opportunities, allocating (as far as possible) sufficient funds for the functioning of the NRF sites and nature conservation in the Ukrainian Carpathians, and raising awareness on the value of the biodiversity of the forest ecosystems of the Ukrainian Carpathians by various means, such as through the familiarisation with the ethical underpinning behind biodiversity protection, including the Christian environmental ethics.

CONCLUSION

In this final section, the key findings are articulated in light of the research objectives, and their broader academic and practical implications are outlined.

To begin with the ethical foundations of biodiversity protection in environmental ethics and international law, the categories of anthropocentric and non-anthropocentric arguments, as well as arguments based on instrumental and intrinsic value, have been identified as the main framework, subdivided into numerous (sometimes conflicting) facets. It was established that ethical justifications for biodiversity protection continue to be developed and reframed. The understanding of anthropocentric and instrumental value of biodiversity and their practical implications is more unanimous than that of non-anthropocentric and intrinsic value. The intrinsic (inherent) value continues to be the most controversial category among these, given the variety of approaches to define it and stipulations as to its implications. In the domain of instrumental value, the idea of 'ecosystem services' recently emerged as a practical tool to express the value of natural processes contributing to the material presence of biodiversity in the decision-making process. There is also a trend towards a search for a more holistic approach in environmental ethics, underlining human responsibility (as opposed to a focus on certain narrow aspects). Among the ideas in line with this trend, there are, for instance, 'enlightened anthropocentrism', 'anthroporelational approach' or 'retinity'.

It was found that ideas of environmental ethics from the beginning accompany international efforts on biodiversity conservation. In describing value and justifications for biodiversity protection, biodiversity treaties rely on both anthropocentric and non-anthropocentric arguments, albeit the former clearly prevails. Among the anthropocentric ideas, the special role in international environmental law is played by the concepts of concern for future generations, common concern of mankind and common heritage of humanity, reflected in the preambles of the treaties and sometimes listed among the principles of this area of law. In addition, various examples of instrumental value, such as economic, educational, cultural, recreational or aesthetic ones, are mentioned in treaty instruments. Some instruments, such as the Bern Convention and the Convention on Biological Diversity, explicitly mention intrinsic value, however, leaving the question of its definition open (and therefore leaving the space for its interpretation based on environmental ethics). The dominance of anthropocentric ideas, presumably, shall not be viewed as disadvantageous, as the anthropocentric arguments remain valid and may be applied simultaneously with the non-anthropocentric arguments, ensuring wider outreach and reception of the grounds for biodiversity protection.

The international legal framework for biodiversity protection applicable to the forest ecosystems of the Ukrainian Carpathians could be described as a robust and fragmented one. It includes (customary) principles of international environmental law, treaty provisions on a global, regional, and subregional level, as well as the EU norms (as part of the approximation of Ukraine's legislation in accordance with the Association Agreement between the EU and Ukraine).

Principles of international environmental law, whether reflected in the treaties, pertaining to the domain of customary international law or mentioned in the soft-law sources, perform an important function of linking values and rules, policy and law, international and domestic law. Some principles are enshrined in the biodiversity treaties directly, while others are implied as part of the wider area of international environmental law. Precautionary principle, intergenerational equity, no-harm principle, cooperation, public participation, environmental impact assessment, and sustainable development are among the key principles for biodiversity protection.

Among the international treaties applicable to the forest ecosystems of the Ukrainian Carpathians, the treaties with a global geographical outreach include the CBD, CITES, CMS, and the World Heritage Convention. These are complemented by the treaties on the regional (European) level, namely the Bern Convention and on the subregional level, which is the Carpathian Convention. Out of the EU norms, the Birds and Habitats Directives belong to the core provisions on biodiversity.

The CBD is the most comprehensive agreement on biodiversity protection. Being a framework agreement and using several 'language softeners' pertaining to the state's capacity and appropriateness of action, it leaves the decisive role in its implementation to the level of national governments. Unlike some other treaties in this field, the CBD does not contain any definitive lists of species or sites to be protected, suggesting simply a list of indicative categories. The central obligations include strategic planning, identification and monitoring of biodiversity, *in-situ* conservation entailing a broad range of actions, sustainable use of biodiversity, public education and awareness, and environmental impact assessment. In addition to the provisions of this Convention as such, numerous thematic-specific guidelines, including those on forest biodiversity, have been adopted by the COPs, and some concepts that are not directly mentioned in the provisions, such as 'ecosystem approach' became primary framework of action almost inevitable for the implementation of this instrument.

The CITES regulates international trade in endangered species and follows a species-based conservation approach. The mechanism of protection of species under the CITES is based on listing the species into the three appendices, entailing various degrees of protection and procedures. Appendix I includes species threatened with extinction, the trade in specimens of which is possible only in exceptional circumstances based on the consent of relevant authorities and not for primarily commercial purposes. Appendix II species are not necessarily threatened with extinction but may become so unless the trade in their specimens is regulated; the procedure of trade in them requires consent of the relevant authorities (but unlike Appendix I species, the separate import permit is not required). Appendix III lists species designated by a particular State Party, which entails the need to grant export permits, however, based on a slightly less complex procedure than for Appendix II species. One of the peculiarities of the CITES in comparison with other biodiversity treaties is its well-developed compliance system.

The CMS is concerned with the protection of species that migrate from one state to another. Similarly to the CITES, the CMS uses a species-based conservation approach and lists species that require special protection. Appendix I includes migratory species in danger of extinction. The Range States of Appendix I species are obliged, in particular, to conserve and restore habitats of such species, to prevent or reduce factors that might further endanger such species and to prohibit taking of animals belonging to such species (with some exceptions). Appendix II lists species with unfavourable conservation status and those that will benefit from international cooperation and does not entail any specific obligations for the Range States, but suggests a possibility to conclude special agreements on the conservation of these species. Interestingly, the species might be simultaneously included in both Appendix I and Appendix II.

UNESCO helped to consolidate international efforts on the protection of remarkable natural sites, including by creating the Network of Biosphere Reserves and through the World Heritage Convention. According to the World Heritage Convention, the natural sites of outstanding universal value may be designated as natural heritage or mixed heritage. The criteria for the assessment of outstanding universal value include the presence of important natural habitats for *in-situ* conservation of biological diversity. The protection regime under this Convention includes national and international efforts, where states are primarily responsible for ensuring protection of the sites and their transmission to future generations. Within the Ukrainian Carpathians, several areas belong to the natural heritage Ancient and Primeval Beech Forests of the Carpathians and Other Regions of Europe, which represent significant ongoing ecological and biological processes in the development of forest ecosystems, are highly relevant for biodiversity protection and possess aesthetic value.

The Bern Convention is one of the key instruments on biodiversity protection in Europe. It aims at conserving wild flora and fauna and their natural habitats, paying special attention to the endangered and vulnerable species as well as natural habitats. It obliges states to introduce legislative and administrative measures and calls for special attention to the species listed in Appendices I and II, prohibiting their deliberate picking, collecting, cutting, uprooting, possession and sale (with some exceptions). It also requires special protection of migratory species listed in Appendices II and III. Based on a series of resolutions of the Standing Committee, a network of Areas of Special Conservation Interest, known as the Emerald Network, has been created in Europe. The reporting system and a case-file system have also been developed, with the latter enabling broad public participation. The Bern Convention also inspired the development of the EU biodiversity-related legislation.

The Carpathian Convention obliges parties to pursue policies on conservation, restoration and sustainable use of biodiversity in the Carpathians. It pays special attention to the natural and semi-natural habitats, their continuity and connectivity, protection of species characteristic of the Carpathians, endangered species, endemic species, and large carnivores. It also explicitly incorporates the ecosystem approach. Its Protocol on Conservation and Sustainable Use of Biological and Landscape Diversity and the Protocol on Sustainable Forest Management establish a set of norms most directly relevant to the protection of biodiversity of the forest ecosystems of the Ukrainian Carpathians.

The framework established by the provisions of the biodiversity treaty texts is extended and clarified by the strategic documents adopted by the Conference of the Parties. The Kunming-Montreal Global Biodiversity Framework adopted by the CBD COP is the current main global strategic document on biodiversity, which replaced the famous Aichi Biodiversity

Targets. The current strategic documents on the implementation of the CITES, CMS, Bern Convention and Carpathian Convention seek to reinforce the realisation of the Kunming-Montreal Global Biodiversity Framework in their respective contexts. The Carpathian Biodiversity Framework is the first distinct subregional biodiversity framework relying on the Kunming-Montreal Global Biodiversity Framework.

In the EU, the legislative basis for environmental protection is found in the key normative sources, including the Treaty on European Union, Treaty on the Functioning of the European Union, and Charter of Fundamental Rights of the European Union. The cornerstones of the EU biodiversity-legislation and policy are the Birds Directive (2009/147/EC) and Habitats Directive (92/43/EC), which form a legal basis for the Natura 2000 network that comprises 'special protection areas' under Birds Directive and 'special areas of conservation' under the Habitats Directive. In addition, the Environmental Action Programme adopted by the European Parliament and the Council of the European Union is the instrument for reflecting the EU's common agenda for environmental policy. It builds on the European Green Deal and is related to the EU Biodiversity strategy for 2030 as its core part. In addition, the sphere of forest biodiversity, there is a New EU Forest Strategy for 2030, the related Guidelines on Biodiversity-Friendly Afforestation, Reforestation and Tree Planting, Guidelines for Defining, Mapping, Monitoring and Strictly Protecting EU Primary and Old-Growth Forests, as well as a new regulation aimed at fighting deforestation and forest degradation.

Turning to the characterisation of the forest ecosystems of the Ukrainian Carpathians, some of these belong to the most preserved natural forests of Europe, hosting a wide variety of species, including large carnivores such as lynx, bear and wolf. Ukraine's share in the Carpathian ecoregion, being relatively small numerically, is significant for the forest biodiversity of this region. Within Ukraine, the Carpathians are situated in four administrative regions, mainly in Transcarpathia and Ivano-Frankivsk regions. The human settlements in the Carpathian region within Ukraine are characterised by a relatively low level of economic development, with some people relying on both logging and other uses of the forest for their subsistence and thus belonging to the category of forest-dependent communities. The society in the Ukrainian Carpathian region is characterised by a high level of religiosity with Christianity as a dominant religion (mostly the Ukrainian Greek-Catholic Church and the Orthodox Church of Ukraine). However, as the results of the interviews have shown, the connection between caring for the environment (in particular, forests) and Christian belief is not usually taken into account by the local residents (except for the initiative to reduce plastic in cemeteries promoted by the Ukrainian Greek-Catholic Church).

The legal and institutional landscapes of the biodiversity protection of forest ecosystems in the Ukrainian Carpathians, on the basis of Ukrainian legislation, are highly fragmented and complex. Several attempts to create strategic documents on biodiversity protection have been undertaken by Ukraine since regaining its independence in 1991. However, as of 2024, there is no comprehensive national biodiversity strategy or regional biodiversity strategies. Soon after the adoption of the Concept on biodiversity protection in 1997, envisaging the creation of a programme on biodiversity, the state policy switched to the subordination of the issue of biodiversity protection to the task of forming the ecological network. Another conceptual document covering the period of 2005 – 2025 again presupposed the creation of a programme on biodiversity. As of January 2025, however, this action has not been implemented.

The absence of a comprehensive biodiversity strategy or programme was mitigated by the adoption of the general strategy on environmental protection until 2030 and the accompanying action plan containing strategic points on biodiversity. For the forests specifically, there is a strategy incorporating biodiversity protection into forestry, covering commercially exploited forests. Moreover, there are specific strategic documents on the Carpathian region within Ukraine, including concepts or action plans on the implementation of the Carpathian Convention, the development of the Carpathian region and mountainous territories, and the protection of the beech forest ecosystems within the relevant UNESCO heritage sites. Each of the four Carpathian regions within Ukraine has adopted strategies for implementing certain aspects of the nationwide environmental legislation. Cross-border cooperation of Ukraine with the neighbouring states also includes preservation of the Carpathian forests. In addition, sectoral strategies in the areas of climate change, transport, tourism and urban planning directly or indirectly aim to enhance biodiversity protection of the forest ecosystems of the Ukrainian Carpathians. The need for the creation of a comprehensive national biodiversity strategy, however, remains, as does the need for further integration of biodiversity protection into all spheres of economic activity.

The biodiversity-related legislation in Ukraine applicable to the forests could be grouped on the basis of subject matter into two main categories:

nature protection legislation and legislation on forestry. The general framework of nature protection in Ukraine is outlined in the Law "On Environmental Protection". The protection of biodiversity by means of the creation of protected areas in their varied forms and legal regimes is regulated primarily by the Law "On Nature Reserve Fund". Protection of the flora or 'plant world' is addressed by the Law "On Plant World" and the Green Data Book of Ukraine. The fauna species or 'animal world' enjoy the protection based on the Law "On Animal World", and for some Carpathian species, particularly lynx, brown bear, and bison, separate action plans have been adopted. The endangered species of both flora and fauna are also protected by listing them in the Red Data Book of Ukraine. The important role of integration of biodiversity protection in economic activities is played by the relatively recently adopted laws on the EIA and the SEA, requiring assessment of impact on biodiversity concerning the planning of some developmental activities or documents of state planning.

The legislation on forestry is supposed to be codified by the Forest Code of Ukraine. However, it comprises many more laws and regulations, some of which establish a particular regime for the forest ecosystems in the Ukrainian Carpathians. In recent years, norms on forestry have witnessed significant amendments to incorporate biodiversity protection. The main procedure for taking biodiversity into account in commercial forestry activities is the procedure for forest organisation (management) planning, undertaken every 10 or 20 years, depending on certain parameters. For particularly valuable forests, the compartment method of this procedure is used. The inclusion of nature protection into this procedure partly relies on information on the location of flora and fauna species, which has to be obtained from the Ministry of Environmental Protection and partly has to be collected proactively. The identification of the Red Data Book species during this procedure may lead to the designation of new NRF sites or the enlargement of the ecological network. Importantly, it is stated that not only actions directly aimed at nature protection, but all planned forestry activities shall contribute to biodiversity conservation.

One of the recently introduced tools for biodiversity protection in commercial forestry is creation of protected areas to preserve biodiversity in forests serving the aim of protecting rare and endangered species including those listed in local lists, Red Data Book of Ukraine and protected by international treaties, breeding grounds of wild animals, and the oldest or notable trees and their groups. Creation of such areas limits logging, such as by exempting these areas from clear-cutting and the final stage of the gradual felling. Other tools for protecting biodiversity in forestry include the creation and preservation of the valuable gene fund, the prevention of genetic contamination of the gene pools of indigenous species and the prevention of invasions of introduced species into natural ecosystems, including during forest regeneration activities. Moreover, during all types of timber harvesting, felling or damaging of the rare and endangered species of trees and shrubs listed in the Red Data Book of Ukraine, of seed and plus trees, of hollow and oldest trees, and of trees with the nests of the rare bird species enlisted in the Red Data Book of Ukraine are not permitted. For the Carpathian forests, there are special rules on the main-use logging, which rely on the ecosystem approach and close-to-nature forestry. Furthermore, clear-cutting in the mountain fir-beech forests of the Carpathian region is outlawed. There are special provisions in the Rules for Improving the Quality Composition of Forests.

The following groups of actors shape biodiversity protection in the Carpathian region: state bodies and local self-government, non-governmental organisations, the business sector and individuals. Two primary state bodies are the Ministry of Environmental Protection and the State Forestry Agency. The administrations of the NRF sites, subordinate to the Ministry of Environmental Protection, undertake a wide range of actions on biodiversity protection, including keeping the comprehensive Chronicles of Nature book. The State Forestry Agency is the single largest forest user in Ukraine. As a result of recent reorganisation, the enterprise "Forests of Ukraine" was created in place of numerous smaller forestry enterprises. Since this reform, most of the Carpathian forests are governed by the Western Interregional Administration of Forestry and Hunting. Regional departments of ecology and natural resources and local self-governing bodies also have certain powers in biodiversity protection. However, greater clarity in their delimitation is required. The main governmental body in charge of ensuring compliance with the environmental legislation is SEI, but other law enforcement agencies may also play a role. The national and international NGOs are one of the leading driving forces of the development of biodiversity-protection legislation in Ukraine and monitoring compliance. The businesses and individuals may also influence biodiversity, both by encouraging and hindering its protection.

The analysis has allowed the identification of the following specific issues, which are particularly important for protecting forest biodiversity of the Ukrainian Carpathians: monitoring of biodiversity, creation of the ecological network, and preservation of the old-growth forests. Even though attempts to create a system of environmental monitoring, including biodiversity monitoring, have been undertaken in Ukraine for over 25 years, and some data is being collected, reform is needed to ensure adequate monitoring, which can serve as a basis for decision-making. The creation of the ecological network in Ukraine is a similarly lengthy and complicated process. One of the indicators of difficulties is the fact that 15 years have passed between the adoption of the Programme for the formation of an ecological network and the procedure for the inclusion of territories into it. A sub-issue warranting special attention in the context of the ecological network is the creation of the Emerald network in Ukraine. The Emerald network sites were nominated by Ukraine and officially adopted by the Standing Committee of the Bern Convention. The creation and operation of the Emerald network in Ukraine are also needed for implementing obligations stipulated in the Association Agreement between the EU and Ukraine. On the one hand, the Emerald network could be created in Ukraine based on the general legislation on the ecological network. However, its proper functioning necessitates the adoption of the specific law, which has been developed, but the adoption of which is being delayed for no clear reasons. The identification, designation and special protection of the old-growth forests (primeval, quasi-primeval and natural forests) in the Ukrainian Carpathians was invigorated by the implementation of the Carpathian Convention and the action of the NGOs. The designation and enhanced protection of these forests from logging is one of the priorities for ensuring the conservation of the Carpathian biodiversity.

The category of risks, threats, and challenges to the biodiversity protection of the Ukrainian Carpathians includes numerous parameters. Informed by globally identified risks, such as habitat loss, overexploitation, climate change, and invasive species, which have clear local manifestations in the Ukrainian Carpathians, it further encompasses the peculiarities of the functioning of the forestry sector and the NRF sites in Ukraine. Some of the most acute direct threats to biodiversity in the forest ecosystems of the Ukrainian Carpathians are illegal or unsustainable logging, often linked to corruption, and unsustainable developmental plans, such as those of building ski resorts and wind farms in the biodiversity-rich areas. In addition, there are institutional tensions and differences in the perception of forests among the key actors involved in biodiversity protection. Apart from the 'traditional' threats, the novel acute threat to the protection of biodiversity in the forests of the Ukrainian Carpathians is the Russian war of aggression. Even though Carpathian region is located relatively far away from the battlefield and has been almost spared from the direct hitting of missiles, the war affects action on biodiversity protection in numerous ways, including by limited access to information, limited capacity of public attention to Carpathian forests and draining the resources destined for nature protection to the defence needs.

The progress of Ukraine's implementation of its international obligations on biodiversity with respect to the Carpathian forests manifests itself in the recent legislative changes described above. The milestone achievements include the introduction of the procedures of the EIA and SEA, the provisions on primeval, quasi-primeval and natural forests, introduction of protected areas to preserve biodiversity, foundations of sustainable forestry and close-to-nature forestry in commercial forestry, extension of the NRF sites and designation of the Emerald network sites. At the same time, some of the key problems with implementation of the Ukraine's international obligations on biodiversity include lack of comprehensive biodiversity monitoring and inaccurate data, lack of integration of biodiversity protection into all of the relevant areas of life, lack of political support and understanding of the international biodiversity-related obligations among the executive power officials, limited financial, administrative and technical capacities as well as lack of coordination and clear division of powers on biodiversity protection between various institutions. In the context of the Bern Convention, one of the obstacles to implementing the obligations of the result under it is the absence of legislation that would define the status of the Emerald network in Ukraine and set an adequate protection regime. It is also advisable to align the approach to the formation of this network in Ukraine with the recommendations within the Bern Convention mechanism and the EU practices on the designation and functioning of the Natura 2000 network. Some of the further solutions on improvement of implementation of Ukraine's international obligations with respect to biodiversity include counteracting illegal logging in the primeval forests in the Carpathians, including by following the approach of the EU Regulation on deforestation-free supply chains, and investing in environmentally safe and sustainable tourist infrastructure. There is also a need for coordinated action on tackling invasive alien species, such as by preventing their deliberate introduction during reforestation activities.

Overall, there is a broad palette of best practices, recommendations and examples of useful strategies for biodiversity protection, which could be applied to the forest ecosystems of the Ukrainian Carpathians. For instance, the materials of the programmes of work on mountain biodiversity and on forest biodiversity within the CBD, the IUCN guidance on designing institutional and legal frameworks on invasive alien species, and results of various projects in the field of conservation and sustainable use of biodiversity under the auspices of the Carpathian Convention, such as on large carnivores, ecological connectivity and ecological corridors are potentially extremely useful for the Ukrainian policy-makers. Importantly, action on biodiversity has to align with a broader sustainable development paradigm; in particular, it is recommended that the reduction of biodiversity loss and environmental degradation coincide with poverty reduction in the local communities, improving human well-being and social equity.

Policy suggestions on biodiversity conservation further include establishing well-managed protected areas and those where genetic diversity is preserved by creating spaces where natural selection occurs freely, designating other types of areas directly or indirectly serving the purpose of biodiversity protection, promoting ecological connectivity and ecosystem restoration (including by rewilding), protecting primary forests and restoring conditions and parameters close to them in terms of forest structure, composition and functioning. In addition, one of the possible tools for generating greater public awareness and support of biodiversity-related action is the introduction of the monetary evaluation of the ecosystem services.

Within the Carpathian Convention, policy direction on forests includes promotion of the close-to-nature forest management, maintaining and enlarging forest cover, identifying and protecting natural and especially virgin (primeval) forests, ensuring productive functions of forests and their role in rural development, as well as protection and reintroduction of rare native forest tree species. It is further suggested to promote nature-based solutions to addressing climate change with a special focus on ecosystem-based adaptation.

What is also recommended in the context of forestry in Eastern Europe is increasing the level of management awareness of the uniqueness of the primary forests in the broader biogeographical context. Furthermore, in terms of enhancing the resilience of forests, the need for a shift in forest management approaches from focusing on timber extraction to broader approaches, as well as the increase of mixed forests as opposed to monoculture forests, is identified.

The examples from the two national nature parks located in Bavaria, Germany, provide some potentially useful for the Ukrainian Carpathians models of zonation of the protected areas, management goals, tourism and awareness-raising activities with the goal of 'leaving nature to its own devices', gradual and comprehensive monitoring of biodiversity, and ensuring respect of the rights of the local population and adjacent landowners.

It was established that there is a great potential for synergies among biodiversity-related legal norms and policies as well as those in interrelated spheres of climate change, human rights and tourism. Moreover, a broader category of environmental rule of law is important for implementing norms on biodiversity. Such synergies, however, are not always realised and acted upon, thus forming a future agenda rather than reflecting the current objective reality. For instance, despite climate change and biodiversity protection frameworks having been implicitly intertwined since the 1992 Rio conference, the interaction between these regimes remains quite complex and uneven. There is a possibility of conflict between the means used to achieve goals in both of these areas. Moreover, despite the ample efforts on integrating climate change into biodiversity-related laws and policies at an international level, the efforts on integrating biodiversity protection into the climate change agenda have been rather marginal. Such a situation requires close attention from the national governments in the formulation of international commitments and national policies that would aim at a synergetic impact. The interaction of tourism and biodiversity protection areas may also be either a synergetic or a detrimental one. Sustainable tourism, however, is capable of building synergies and enhancing efforts on biodiversity protection. There are numerous guidelines on the global, European and Carpathian levels to this extent, helping to direct the action of states and other actors to advance biodiversity protection through sustainable tourism.

There is a growing understanding of the interdependency between human rights and biodiversity. It is recognised that an environment of a certain quality (for which biodiversity is often a key) is necessary for the full enjoyment of a number of human rights, and that certain human rights are crucial for the protection of the environment. Accordingly, the creation and enforcement of effective legal and institutional frameworks on biodiversity ideally shall serve the purpose of both protecting the environment and human rights. State obligations at the intersection of human rights and biodiversity include both substantive and procedural ones. The former category comprises a general obligation to safeguard biodiversity and protect against environmental harm from private actors, as well as specific substantive obligations undertaken on the basis of international treaties on biodiversity. The procedural obligations are grounded in the civil and political rights in conjunction with the environmental context, such as those on access to environmental information, public participation in environmental decision-making, access to remedies for harm or protection of the environmental human rights defenders. The standalone substantive human right to a healthy environment that has been recently recognised on a global level particularly clearly ties human rights and biodiversity, as the component of 'healthy ecosystems and biodiversity' constitutes one of the elements of this right. Implementation of multilateral environmental agreements under the principles of international environmental law is required to promote this right.

The environmental rule of law, which partly overlaps with the human rights and biodiversity discourse, is vital for the functioning of the whole system of implementation of environmental norms in broader social, economic and governmental contexts. It entails a governance system where all persons are accountable to laws, which are clear and precise, equally enforced and independently adjudicated. Moreover, a clear division of powers and functions of different governmental agencies is needed, along with the promotion of the culture of compliance. The environmental rule of law also comprises tackling corruption, such as by increasing transparency and introducing independent auditing. The novel participatory tools for promoting environmental rule of law include 'citizen science', which could support decision-making and enforcement of biodiversity-related norms.

The results of our analysis of the ideas within the Christian environmental ethics suggest its great potential in constituting a moral underpinning of the biodiversity protection in the Ukrainian Carpathians. In the Catholic Social Teaching, for instance, biodiversity is called an "extraordinary richness for all of humanity", and the need to protect the heritage of forests by individuals and institutions is expressed. Furthermore, the maximisation of profits, blind to the ecological consequences, including "harm done to biodiversity", is criticised. In the Orthodox Church, causing the extinction of species, destruction of biodiversity and degrading the integrity of the earth through destruction of the natural forests are mentioned among the examples of sins. Some of the central ideas of Orthodox and Catholic environmental ethics alike include an understanding of creation (including biodiversity) as a gift entailing the responsibility to take care of it. This implies an active behaviour of keeping and preserving the creation as responsible stewards, coupled with self-restraint in the action towards it. Moreover, the notions of interconnectedness and interdependency of all things in the universe are voiced. The care for creation is considered to be not merely an economic and technological issue, but also a moral and spiritual issue, necessitating an inner change of heart and mind, which lies at the core of the effectiveness of the conservation projects. The potential benefit of Christian environmental ethics for the Ukrainian Carpathians may entail, for instance, its role in raising awareness of the moral dimension of the value of the Carpathian natural heritage and in providing some guidance on practical action, including encouragement to implement Ukraine's obligations under biodiversity treaties.

Finally, on the basis of the application of good practices and recommendations to the status quo of biodiversity protection in the Ukrainian Carpathians, we have identified the lines of change in the legal, policy, and ethical components for enhanced protection of the biodiversity of forest ecosystems of the Ukrainian Carpathians. These include adoption of the national biodiversity strategy and action plan, further integration of biodiversity protection into sectoral policies, such as on transport and construction, striving for enhancing synergies with the related areas such as climate action and human rights, promoting environmental rule of law including by ensuring legislative clarity and tackling corruption, improving biodiversity monitoring, enhancing ecological connectivity and effective *in-situ* conservation of biodiversity, restoration of ecosystems and application of the close-to-nature forestry and sustainable forest management approaches, placing the issue of biodiversity protection of the forest ecosystems into a broader social and economic development of the Carpathian region by taking into account alternative sources of income and employment opportunities of the local residents, allocating (as far as possible) sufficient funds for the functioning of the NRF sites and nature conservation in the Ukrainian Carpathians, and raising awareness on the value of the biodiversity of the forest ecosystems of the Ukrainian Carpathians by various means, including through the familiarisation with the ethical underpinning behind biodiversity protection in both secular and Christian environmental ethics.

Taken together, these results suggest that there is a complex, multifaceted and fragmented framework of biodiversity protection at the intersection of ethics, law, and policy applicable to the forest ecosystems of the Ukrainian Carpathians. It has witnessed particularly rapid development during the last decade. However, there remains significant room for future action in light of the identified recommendations.

In conclusion, the present thesis has gone some way towards enhancing our understanding of the biodiversity protection in the forest ecosystems of the Ukrainian Carpathians at the intersection of law, ethics and policy, proving its hypothesis as to the existence of both room for improvement and a broad range of tools to this extent. From the academic perspective, our results improve knowledge about the current stage of legislative norms, policies and ethics on biodiversity in forest ecosystems on a global, European, Carpathian, and Ukrainian levels (including regional approaches within Ukraine). In the academic domain of Public International Law, these results could be used for the purposes of teaching university-level courses on International Environmental Law, Nature Conservation Law and International Biodiversity Law. The exploration of the interaction of International Biodiversity Law with the related legal areas, in particular, Climate Change Law and International Human Rights Law as well as the ideas of Christian environmental ethics, including those of the Orthodox Church of Ecumenical Patriarchate and Catholic Social Teaching, in the context of environmental law and policy could serve as a basis for further scholarly inquiry. Moreover, the results on the implementation of international provisions in Ukraine and recent legislative developments on nature protection and forestry legislation applicable to the Ukrainian Carpathians could be incorporated to the study programme of the foresters, employees of the nature reserve fund institutions and civil servants (both in a university context and in an extracurricular setting). Possible practical uses of the results include consideration of the identified best practices, recommendations and suggested lines of change during the decision-making leading to the introduction of new policies and further development of the legislation underpinning biodiversity protection of the forest ecosystems of the Ukrainian Carpathians.

The present thesis could lay the foundation for future research on law, ethics, and policy focused on averting the global issue of biodiversity loss for the benefit of future generations and all life on our planet. It is hoped that this study may also reinvigorate the attention of various actors and lead to necessary action on the protection of the forest ecosystems of the Ukrainian Carpathians in line with the "think globally, act locally" motto.

BIBLIOGRAPHY

International treaties and EU legislation

"Charter of the United Nations," opened for signature June 26, 1945, *UNCIO* XV, p. 335, https://treaties.un.org/pages/ViewDetails.aspx?src=IND&mtdsg_no=I-1&chapter=1&clang=_en.

"Convention concerning the Protection of the World Cultural and Natural Heritage," opened for signature November 16, 1972, *United Nations Treaty Series* 1037 p. 151, https://whc.unesco.org/en/conventiontext/.

"Convention on Biological Diversity," opened for signature June 5, 1992, United Nations Treaty Series 1760 p. 79, https://treaties.un.org/pages/ViewDetails.aspx?src=TREATY&mtdsg_no=XXVII-8&chapter=27.

"Convention on International Trade in Endangered Species of Wild Fauna and Flora," opened for signature March 3, 1973, *United Nations Treaty Series* 993 p. 243, https://cites.org/eng/disc/text.php.

"Convention on the Conservation of European Wildlife and Natural Habitats," opened for signature September 19, 1979, *European Treaty Series* No. 104, https://rm.coe.int/1680078aff.

"Convention on the Conservation of European Wildlife and Natural Habitats," opened for signature September 19, 1979, *European Treaty Series* no. 104 https://www.coe.int/en/web/conventions/full-list?module=treaty-detail&treatynum=104.

"Convention on the Conservation of Migratory Species of Wild Animals," opened for signature June 23, 1979, *United Nations Treaty Series*, 1651, https://www.cms.int/en/convention-text.

"Framework Convention on the Protection and Sustainable Development of the Carpathians," opened for signature May 22, 2003, http://www.carpathianconvention.org/convention/framework-convention/.

"Kyoto Protocol to the United Nations Framework Convention on Climate Change," opened for signature December 11, 1997, *United Nations Treaty Series* 2303, p. 162, UN Doc FCCC/CP/1997/7/Add.1.

"New EU Forest Strategy for 2030," Communication from the Commission to the European Parliament, the Council, the European Economic and Social Committee and the Committee of the Regions, COM/2021/572 final, (July 16, 2021) https://eur-lex.europa.eu/legal-content/EN/ALL/?uri=COM%3A2021%3A572%3AFIN.

"Protocol on Conservation and Sustainable Use of Biological and Landscape Diversity," opened for signature June 19, 2008, http://www.carpathianconvention.org/convention/protocols/protocol-on-biodiversity/.

"Protocol on Sustainable Forest Management," opened for signature May 27, 2011, http://www.carpathianconvention.org/convention/protocols/protocol-on-sustainable-forest-management/.

"Protocol on Sustainable Tourism," opened for signature May 27, 2011, http://www.carpathianconvention.org/convention/protocols/protocol-on-sustainable-tourism/

"United Nations Framework Convention on Climate Change," opened for signature May 9, 1992, *United Nations Treaty Series* 1771, p. 107, https://treaties.un.org/pages/ViewDetailsIII.aspx?src=TREATY&mtdsg_no=XXVII-7&chapter=27&Temp=mtdsg3&clang=_en.

Association Agreement between the European Union and its Member States, of the one part, and Ukraine, of the other part, Document 22014A0529(01), *Official Journal of the European Union,* L 161, 29.5.2014, p. 3–2137, http://data.europa.eu/eli/agree_internation/2014/295/oj.

Charter of Fundamental Rights of the European Union, Document 12012P/TXT, *Official Journal of the European Union*, C 326, 26.10.2012, p. 391–407, http://data.europa.eu/eli/treaty/char_2012/oj.

Consolidated version of the Treaty on European Union, Document 12016M/TXT, *Official Journal of the European Union*, C 202/1, http://data.europa.eu/eli/treaty/teu_2016/oj.

Consolidated version of the Treaty on the Functioning of the European Union, Document 12016E/TXT, *Official Journal of the European Union*, C 202/1, http://data.europa.eu/eli/treaty/tfeu_2016/oj.

Council Directive 92/43/EEC of 21 May 1992 on the conservation of natural habitats and of wild fauna and flora, *Official Journal of the European Union,* L 206, 22.7.1992, p. 7–50, http://data.europa.eu/eli/dir/1992/43/oj.

Decision (EU) 2022/591 of the European Parliament and of the Council of 6 April 2022 on a General Union Environment Action Programme to 2030, PE/83/2021/REV/1, Document 32022D0591, *Official Journal of the European Union, L 114, 12.4.2022, p. 22–36*, http://data.europa.eu/eli/dec/2022/591/oj,.

Directive 2009/147/EC of the European Parliament and of the Council of 30 November 2009 on the conservation of wild birds, *Official Journal of the European Union*, L 20, 26.1.2010, p. 7–25, http://data.europa.eu/eli/dir/2009/147/oj.

European Commission, "Environment action programme to 2030", "EU Biodiversity Strategy for 2030: Bringing nature back into our lives," Communication from the Commission to the European Parliament, the Council, the European Economic and Social Committee and the Committee of the Regions, COM/2020/380 final, (May 20, 2020) https://eur-lex.europa.eu/legal-content/EN/TXT/?uri=celex%3A52020DC0380.

Regulation (EU) 2023/1115 of the European Parliament and of the Council of 31 May 2023 on the making available on the Union market and the export from the Union of certain commodities and products associated with deforestation and forest degradation and repealing Regulation (EU) No 995/2010, *Official Journal of the European Union*, L 150, 9.6.2023, p. 206–247, http://data.europa.eu/eli/reg/2023/1115/oj.

Regulation (EU) 2023/1115 of the European Parliament and of the Council of 31 May 2023 on the making available on the Union market and the export from the Union of certain commodities and products associated with deforestation and forest degradation and repealing Regulation (EU) No 995/2010.

Regulation (EU) 2024/1991 of the European Parliament and of the Council of 24 June 2024 on nature restoration and amending Regulation (EU) 2022/869, *Official Journal of the European Union, L, 2024/1991, 29.7.2024,* http://data.europa.eu/eli/reg/2024/1991/oj.

Laws of Ukraine

Constitution of Ukraine, Document 254k/96-VR, Bulletin of the Verkhovna Rada of Ukraine, No. 30, p. 141 (1996) https://zakon.rada.gov.ua/laws/show/254%D0%BA/96-%D0%B2%D1%80#Text [In Ukrainian: *Конституція України*, Документ 254к/96-ВР, Відомості Верховної Ради України (ВВР), № 30, ст. 141 (1996)].

"On Amending Certain Legislative Acts of Ukraine Regarding the Protection of Primeval Forests in Accordance with the Framework Convention on Conservation and Sustainable Development of the Carpathians," Law of Ukraine, Document 2063-VIII, Bulletin of the Verkhovna Rada of Ukraine, No. 37, p. 379 (2017) https://zakon.rada.gov.ua/laws/show/2063-19#n26; [In Ukrainian: "Про внесення змін до деяких законодавчих актів України щодо охорони пралісів згідно з Рамковою конвенцією про охорону та сталий розвиток Карпат", Закон України, Документ 2063-VIII, Відомості Верховної Ради № 37, ст. 379 (2017)].

"On Amendments to certain laws of Ukraine regarding the improvement and digitalisation of the environmental impact assessment procedure," Law of Ukraine, Document 3227-IX, Bulletin of the Verkhovna Rada of Ukraine, No. 84, p. 305 (2023) https://zakon.rada.gov.ua/laws/show/3227-20#Text; [In Ukrainian: "Про внесення змін до деяких законів України щодо удосконалення та цифровізації процедури оцінки впливу на довкілля," Закон України, Документ 3227-IX, Відомості Верховної Ради № 84, ст. 305 (2023)].

"On Amendments to Certain Legislative Acts of Ukraine Regarding the State Environmental Monitoring System, Environmental Condition Information (Environmental Information), and Information Support for Environmental Management," Law of Ukraine, Document 2973-IX, Bulletin of the Verkhovna Rada of Ukraine, No. 63, p. 208 (2023) https://zakon.rada.gov.ua/laws/show/2973-20#Text; [In Ukrainian: "Про внесення змін до деяких законодавчих актів України щодо державної системи моніторингу довкілля, інформації про стан довкілля (екологічної інформації) та інформаційного забезпечення управління у сфері довкілля," Закон України, Документ 2973-IX, Відомості Верховної Ради, № 63, ст. 208 (2023)].

"On Ecological Network of Ukraine," Law of Ukraine, Document 1864-IV, Bulletin of the Verkhovna Rada of Ukraine, No. 45, p. 502 (2004) https://zakon.rada.gov.ua/laws/show/1864-15#Text [In Ukrainian: "Про екологічну мережу України," Закон України, Документ 1864-IV, Відомості Верховної Ради України, № 45, ст. 502 (2004)].

"On Environmental Impact Assessment," Law of Ukraine, Document 2059-VIII, Bulletin of the Verkhovna Rada of Ukraine, No. 29, p. 315 (2017) https://zakon.rada.gov.ua/laws/show/2059-19#Text; [In Ukrainian: "Про оцінку впливу на довкілля," Закон України, Документ 2059-VIII, Відомості Верховної Ради № 29, ст. 315 (2017)].

"On Environmental Protection," Law of Ukraine, Document 1264-XII, Bulletin of the Verkhovna Rada of Ukraine, No.41, p. 546 (1991) https://zakon.rada.gov.ua/laws/show/1264-12#Text [In Ukrainian: "Про охорону навколишнього природного середовища," Закон України, Документ 1264-XII, Відомості Верховної Ради України № 41, ст. 546 (1991)].

"On Hunting Economy and Hunting," Law of Ukraine, Document 1478-III, Bulletin of the Verkhovna Rada of Ukraine, No. 18, p. 132 (2000) https://zakon.rada.gov.ua/laws/show/1478-14#Text; [In Ukrainian: "Про мисливське господарство та полювання," Закон України, Документ 1478-III, Відомості Верховної Ради України № 18, ст. 132 (2000)].

"On Nature Reserve Fund," Law of Ukraine, Document 2456-XII, Bulletin of the Verkhovna Rada of Ukraine, No. 34, p. 502 (1992), https://zakon.rada.gov.ua/laws/show/2456-12/conv#n12; [In Ukrainian: "Про природно-заповідний фонд України," Закон України, Документ 2456-XII, Відомості Верховної Ради України № 34, ст. 502 (1992)].

"On Strategic Environmental Assessment," Law of Ukraine, Document 2354-VIII, Bulletin of the Verkhovna Rada of Ukraine, No. 16, p. 138 (2018) https://zakon.rada.gov.ua/laws/show/2354-19#Text; [In Ukrainian: "Про стратегічну екологічну оцінку," Закон України, Документ 2354-VIII, Відомості Верховної Ради № 16, ст. 138 (2018)].

"On the Animal World," Law of Ukraine, Document 2894-III, Bulletin of the Verkhovna Rada of Ukraine, No. 14, p. 97 (2002), https://zakon.rada.gov.ua/laws/show/2894-14#Text; [In Ukrainian: "Про тваринний світ," Закон України, Документ 2894-III, Відомості Верховної Ради України № 14, ст. 97 (2002)].

"On the Fundamental Principles (Strategy) of the State Environmental Policy of Ukraine for the Period until 2030," Law of Ukraine, Document 2697-VIII, Bulletin of the Verkhovna Rada of Ukraine, No. 16, p. 70 (2019) https://zakon.rada.gov.ua/laws/show/2697-19#Text [In Ukrainian: "Про Основні засади (стратегію) державної екологічної політики України на період до 2030 року," Закон України, Документ 2697-VIII, Відомості Верховної Ради, № 16, ст. 70 (2019)].

"On the Fundamentals (Strategy) of the State Environmental Policy of Ukraine until 2020," Law of Ukraine, Document 2818-VI, Bulletin of the Verkhovna Rada of Ukraine, No. 26, p. 218 (2010) https://zakon.rada.gov.ua/laws/show/2818-17#Text [In Ukrainian: "Про Основні засади (стратегію) державної екологічної політики України на період до 2020 року," Закон України, Документ 2818-VI, Відомості Верховної Ради України, 2011, № 26, ст. 218 (2010)].

"On the Fundamentals (Strategy) of the State Environmental Policy of Ukraine until 2020," Law of Ukraine, Document 2818-VI, Bulletin of the Verkhovna Rada of Ukraine, No. 26, p. 218 (2010) https://zakon.rada.gov.ua/laws/show/2818-17#Text [In Ukrainian: "Про Основні засади (стратегію) державної екологічної політики України на період до 2020 року," Закон України, Документ 2818-VI, Відомості Верховної Ради України, 2011, № 26, ст. 218 (2010)].

"On the Plant World," Law of Ukraine, Document 591-XIV, Bulletin of the Verkhovna Rada of Ukraine, No. 22–23, p. 198 (1999), https://zakon.rada.gov.ua/laws/show/591-14#Text; [In Ukrainian: "Про рослинний світ," Закон України, Документ 591-XIV, Відомості Верховної Ради України, № 22–23, ст. 198 (1999)].

"On the prohibition of clear-cutting in the mountain fir-beech forests of the Carpathian region", Law of Ukraine, Document 1436-III, Bulletin of the Verkhovna Rada of Ukraine, No. 13, p. 99 (2000), https://zakon.rada.gov.ua/laws/show/1436-14#Text; [In Ukrainian: Закон України "Про заборону на проведення суцільних рубок у гірських ялицево-букових лісах Карпатського регіону," Документ 1436-III, Відомості Верховної Ради України (ВВР), № 13, ст. 99 (2000)].

"On the Red Data Book of Ukraine," Law of Ukraine, Document 3055-III, Bulletin of the Verkhovna Rada of Ukraine, No. 30, p. 20 (2002) https://zakon.rada.gov.ua/laws/show/3055-14#Text; [In Ukrainian: "Про Червону книгу України," Закон України, Документ 3055-III, Відомості Верховної Ради України № 30, ст. 20 (2002)].

Forest Code of Ukraine, Document 3852-XII, Bulletin of the Verkhovna Rada of Ukraine, No. 17, p. 99 (1994) https://zakon.rada.gov.ua/laws/show/3852-12#Text; [In Ukrainian: Лісовий кодекс України, Документ 3852-XII, Відомості Верховної Ради України № 17, ст. 99 (1994)].

Programme for the Formation of the National Ecological Network of Ukraine for 2000–2015, approved by the Law of Ukraine No. 1989-III, Document 1989-III, (September 21, 2000) https://zakon.rada.gov.ua/laws/show/1989-14#Text [In Ukrainian: Загальнодержавна програма формування національної екологічної мережі України на 2000–2015 роки, затверджено Законом України №1989-III, Документ 1989-III, (21 вересня 2000 року)].

Instructions, reports, regulatory acts and other documents of Ministries, other institutions, and departments

"Certain Issues of Reforming Forest Industry Management," Resolution of the Cabinet of Ministers of Ukraine No. 1003, Document 1003–2022-p, (September 7, 2022) https://zakon.rada.gov.ua/laws/show/1003-2022-%D0%BF#Text; [In Ukrainian: "Деякі питання реформування управління лісової галузі," Постанова Кабінету Міністрів України № 1003, Документ 1003–2022-п, (7 вересня 2022)].

"Certain Issues of Reforming Forest Industry Management" (2002); Regulations on the Western Interregional Administration of Forestry and Hunting Economy, approved by the Order of the State Forest Resources Agency of Ukraine No. 1006 (November 9, 2022) https://w.forest.gov.ua/upload/users_files/1/upload/traven%202023/Polozhennya%20pro%20ZMULMG.PDF; [In Ukrainian: Положення про Західне міжрегіональне управління лісового та мисливського господарства, затверджено наказом Державного агентства лісових ресурсів України № 1006 (9 листопада 2022)].

"Certain Issues of the Functioning of the State Environmental Monitoring System and Its Subsystems," Resolution of the Cabinet of Ministers of Ukraine No. 684, Document 684–2024-p (June 13, 2024) https://zakon.rada.gov.ua/laws/show/684-2024-%D0%BF#Text; [In Ukrainian: "Деякі питання функціонування державної системи моніторингу довкілля та її підсистем," Постанова Кабінету Міністрів України № 684, Документ 684–2024-п (13 червня 2024)];

"National Report on the State of the Environment in Ukraine in 2021," Ministry of Environmental Protection of Ukraine, https://mepr.gov.ua/wp-content/uploads/2023/01/Natsdopovid-2021-n.pdf; [In Ukrainian: "Національна доповідь про стан навколишнього природного середовища в Україні у 2021 році"], 85.

"On additional measures for the development of forestry, rational use of nature and conservation of objects of the nature reserve fund" Decree of the President of Ukraine, No. 381, Document 381/2017, (November 21, 2017) https://zakon.rada.gov.ua/laws/show/381/2017#Text; [In Ukrainian: "Про додаткові заходи щодо розвитку лісового господарства, раціонального природокористування та збереження об'єктів природно-заповідного фонду", Указ Президента України № 381, Документ 381/2017 (21 листопада 2017)].

"On Amending Certain Resolutions of the Cabinet of Ministers of Ukraine," Resolution of the Cabinet of Ministers of Ukraine No. 1224, Document 1224–2020-p, (December 9, 2020) https://zakon.rada.gov.ua/laws/show/1224-2020-%D0%BF#Text; [In Ukrainian: "Про внесення змін до деяких постанов Кабінету Міністрів України," Постанова Кабінету Міністрів № 1224, Документ 1224–2020-п, (9 грудня 2020)].

"On Approval of Methodological Guidelines for the Allocation and Assessment of Logging Areas, Issuance of Logging Tickets, and Inspection of Timber Harvesting Sites in the Forests of the State Forest Resources Agency of Ukraine," Order of the State Forest Resources Agency of Ukraine No. 9, Document v0009820–13, (January 1, 2013) https://zakon.rada.gov.ua/rada/show/v0009820-13#Text; [In Ukrainian: "Про затвердження Методичних вказівок з відведення і таксації лісосік, видачі лісорубних квитків та огляду місць заготівлі деревини в лісах Державного агентства лісових ресурсів України," Наказ Державного агентства лісових ресурсів України № 9, Документ v0009820–13, (21 січня 2013)]; "On Revocation of the Order of the State Forest Resources Agency from 21.01.2013 No. 9," Order of the State Forest Resources Agency of Ukraine No. 272, Document v0272820–13, (September 25, 2013) https://zakon.rada.gov.ua/rada/show/v0272820-13#Text; [In Ukrainian: "Про скасування наказу Держлісагентства України від 21.01.2013 № 9," Наказ Державного агентства лісових ресурсів України № 272, Документ v0272820–13, (25 вересня 2013)].

"On Approval of the Action Plan for the Conservation and restoration of the European bison (*Bison bonasus* L.) in Ukraine," Order of the Ministry of Environmental Protection No. 557, (December 28, 2022) https://mepr.gov.ua/nakaz-mindovkillya-557-vid-28-12-2022/; [In Ukrainian: "Про затвердження Плану дій щодо збереження та відтворення зубра (*Bison bonasus* L.) в Україні," Наказ Міністерства захисту довкілля та природних ресурсів України № 557, (28 грудня 2022)].

"On Approval of the Action Plan for the Conservation of the Brown Bear (*Ursus arctos* L.) in Ukraine," Order of the Ministry of Environmental Protection No. 679, (October 20, 2021) https://mepr.gov.ua/documents/pro-zatverdzhennya-planu-dij-shhodo-zberezhennya-vedmedya-burogo-ursus-arctos-l-v-ukrayini/; [In Ukrainian: "Про затвердження Плану дій щодо збереження ведмедя бурого (*Ursus arctos* L.) в Україні," Наказ Міністерства захисту довкілля та природних ресурсів України № 679, (20 жовтня 2021)].

"On Approval of the Action Plan for the Conservation of the Eurasian lynx (*Lynx lynx* L.) in Ukraine," Order of the Ministry of Environmental Protection No. 595, (September 16, 2021) https://mepr.gov.ua/documents/pro-zatverdzhennya-planu-dij-shhodo-zberezhennya-rysi-yevrazijskoyi-lynx-lynx-l-v-ukrayini/; [In Ukrainian: "Про затвердження Плану дій щодо збереження рисі євразійської (*Lynx lynx* L.) в Україні," Наказ Міністерства захисту довкілля та природних ресурсів України № 595, (16 вересня 2021)].

"On approval of the action plan for the implementation of the Concept of implementation of state policy in the area of climate change until 2030", Order of the Cabinet of Ministers of Ukraine No. 878-r, Document 878–2017-r (December 6, 2017), https://zakon.rada.gov.ua/laws/show/878-2017-%D1%80#Text; [In Ukrainian: "Про затвердження плану заходів щодо виконання Концепції реалізації державної політики у сфері зміни клімату на період до 2030 року," Розпорядження Кабінету Міністрів України № 878-р, Документ 878–2017-р, (6 грудня 2017)].

"On Approval of the List of Animal Species Subject to Special Protection in the Territory of Volyn Region," Order of the Ministry of Environmental Protection No. 140, (September 14, 2020) https://mepr.gov.ua/documents/pro-zatverdzhennya-pereliku-vydiv-tvaryn-shho-pidlyagayut-osoblyvij-ohoroni-na-terytoriyi-volynskoyi-oblasti/; [In Ukrainian: "Про затвердження Переліку видів тварин, що підлягають особливій охороні на території Волинської області," Наказ Міністерства захисту довкілля та природних ресурсів України №140, (14 вересня 2020)].

"On Approval of the List of Invasive Tree Species with a High Capacity for Uncontrolled Spread, Prohibited for Use in Forest Reproduction Processes," Order of the Ministry of Environmental Protection No. 184, Document z0641–23 (April 3, 2023), not in force since October 19, 2023, https://zakon.rada.gov.ua/laws/show/z0641-23#Text; [In Ukrainian: "Про затвердження Переліку інвазійних видів дерев із значною здатністю до неконтрольованого поширення, заборонених до використання у процесі відтворення лісів," Наказ Міністерства захисту довкілля та природних ресурсів України № 184, Документ z0641–23, (3 квітня 2023), Втрата чинності від 19 жовтня 2023].

"On Approval of the Lists of Animal Species Included in the Red Data Book of Ukraine (Animal World) and Animal Species Excluded from the Red Data Book of Ukraine (Animal World)," Order of the Ministry of Environmental Protection No. 29, (January 19, 2021) https://zakon.rada.gov.ua/laws/show/z0260-21#Text; [In Ukrainian: "Про затвердження переліків видів тварин, що заносяться до Червоної книги України (тваринний світ), та видів тварин, що виключені з Червоної книги України (тваринний світ), Наказ Міністерства захисту довкілля та природних ресурсів України № 29 (19 січня 2021)].

"On Approval of the Lists of Plant and Fungi Species Included in the Red Data Book of Ukraine (Plant World) and Plant and Fungi Species Excluded from the Red Data Book of Ukraine (Plant World)," Order of the Ministry of Environmental Protection No. 111 (February 2, 2021) https://zakon.rada.gov.ua/laws/show/z0370-21#Text; [In Ukrainian: "Про затвердження переліків видів рослин та грибів, що заносяться до Червоної книги України (рослинний світ), та видів рослин та грибів, що виключені з Червоної книги України (рослинний світ)," Наказ Міністерства захисту довкілля та природних ресурсів України № 111 (15 лютого 2021)]; "Is the Red Data Book of Ukraine stuck in a deadlock again?," Ukrainian Nature Conservation Group, February 10, 2022, https://uncg.org.ua/chervona-knyha-ukrainy-znov-u-hlukhomu-kuti/.

"On approval of the Procedure for maintaining the Unified Register of Strategic Environmental Assessment," Resolution of the Cabinet of Ministers of Ukraine No. 430, Document 430–2023-p, (May 2, 2023) https://zakon.rada.gov.ua/laws/show/430-2023-%D0%BF#Text; [In Ukrainian: "Про затвердження Порядку ведення Єдиного реєстру стратегічної екологічної оцінки," № 430, Документ 430–2023-п, (2 травня 2023)].

"On Approval of the Procedure for State Accounting of Rare and Endangered Species of Fauna and Flora Listed in the Red Data Book of Ukraine," Order of the Ministry of Environmental Protection No. 486, (October 9, 2012) https://zakon.rada.gov.ua/laws/show/z2031-12#n16; [In Ukrainian: "Про затвердження Порядку державного обліку рідкісних і таких, що перебувають під загрозою зникнення, видів тваринного і рослинного світу, занесених до Червоної книги України," Наказ Міністерства екології та природних ресурсів України від № 486 (09 жовтня 2012)].

"On Approval of the Regulations on the Carpathian Biosphere Reserve in a New Edition," Order of the the Ministry of Environmental Protection and Natural Resources of Ukraine No. 336, Document v0336737–11 (September 23, 2011) https://zakon.rada.gov.ua/rada/show/v0336737-11#Text; [In Ukrainian: "Про затвердження Положення про Карпатський біосферний заповідник у новій редакції," Наказ Міністерства екології та природних ресурсів України № 336, Документ v0336737–11 (23 вересня 2011)].

"On Approval of the Rules for Improving the Qualitative Composition of Forests, Conducting Other Logging Operations, and Performing Works Related and Unrelated to Forestry Management," Resolution of the Cabinet of Ministers of Ukraine No. 724, Document 724–2007-p, (May 12, 2007) https://zakon.rada.gov.ua/laws/show/724-2007-%D0%BF#Text; [In Ukrainian: "Про затвердження Правил поліпшення якісного складу лісів, проведення інших рубок та робіт, пов'язаних і не пов'язаних із веденням лісового господарства," Постанова Кабінету Міністрів № 724, Документ 724–2007-п, (12 травня 2007)].

"On Regulating Issues Related to the Special Use of Forest Resources," Resolution of the Cabinet of Ministers of Ukraine No. 761, Document 761–2007-p, (May 23, 2007) https://zakon.rada.gov.ua/laws/show/761-2007-%D0%BF#Text; [In Ukrainian: "Про врегулювання питань щодо спеціального використання лісових ресурсів," Постанова Кабінету Міністрів № 761, Документ 761–2007-п, (23 травня 2007)].

"On the establishment of the Working Group for preparing proposals on reforming the state environmental monitoring system in Ukraine in the area of "Biodiversity"," Order of the Ministry of Environmental Protection No. 527 (July 24, 2023) https://mepr.gov.ua/diyalnist/napryamky/bioriznomanittya/monitoryng-bioriznomanittya/; [In Ukrainian: "Про утворення Робочої групи з підготовки пропозицій щодо реформування державної системи моніторингу довкілля в Україні за напрямом "Біорізноманіття"," Наказ Міністерства захисту довкілля та природних ресурсів України № 527 (24 липня 2023)].

"On the merging of the draft laws of Ukraine: On the Program for the Formation of the National Ecological Network of Ukraine for 2000–2015 and On the National Program for the Conservation of Biological Diversity for 2000–2015," Resolution of the Verkhovna Rada of Ukraine, No. 1289-XIV, Document 1289-XIV (December 14, 1999) https://zakon.rada.gov.ua/laws/show/1289-14#Text [In Ukrainian: "Про об'єднання проектів Закону України про Програму формування національної екологічної мережі України на 2000–2015 роки і про Національну програму збереження біологічного різноманіття на 2000–2015 роки" Постанова Верховної Ради України №1289-XIV, Документ 1289-XIV (14 грудня 1999)].

"Public Report of the Head of the State Forest Resources Agency of Ukraine for 2022," State Forest Resources Agency of Ukraine, accessed September 20, 2024, https://forest.gov.ua/storage/app/sites/8/publich_zvit/publichnii-zvit-za-2022.pdf [In Ukrainian: "Публічний звіт голови Державного агентства лісових ресурсів України за 2022 рік," Державне агентство лісових ресурсів України].

"Report on the Implementation Status as of 2023 of the National Action Plan for Environmental Protection until 2025, approved by the Order of the Cabinet of Ministers of Ukraine from April 21, 2021 No. 443," Ministry of Environmental Protection and Natural Resources of Ukraine https://mepr.gov.ua/wp-content/uploads/2024/03/Rozmishhennya-Zvit-po-vykonannyu-NPD-za-2023.pdf [In Ukrainian: "Звіт про стан виконання у 2023 році Національного плану дій з охорони навколишнього природного середовища на період до 2025 року, затвердженого розпорядженням Кабінету Міністрів України від 21 квітня 2021 р. № 443," Міністерство захисту довкілля та природних ресурсів України].

"The Committee Proposes to Adopt as a Basis Draft Law No. 4480 on Amendments to Certain Legislative Acts of Ukraine Regarding the Protection of Primeval Forests in Accordance with the Framework Convention on the Protection and Sustainable Development of the Carpathians," The Committee of the Verkhovna Rada of Ukraine on Environmental Policy and Nature Management, October 26, 2016, https://komekolog.rada.gov.ua/news/main_news/73942.html [In Ukrainian: "Комітет пропонує прийняти за основу проект Закону №4480 про внесення змін до деяких законодавчих актів України щодо охорони пралісів згідно Рамкової конвенції про охорону та сталий розвиток Карпат," Комітет Верховної Ради України з питань екологічної політики та природокористування].

"The Draft Law On the Territories of the Emerald Network (4461 from 04.12.2020)," Verkhovna Rada of Ukraine, https://itd.rada.gov.ua/billInfo/Bills/Card/4847; [In Ukrainian: "Проект Закону про території Смарагдової мережі (4461 від 04.12.2020)"].

"The Report on Implementation of the Association Agreement between Ukraine and the European Union for 2023," Government Office for Coordination of European and Euro-Atlantic Integration of the Secretariat of the Cabinet of Ministers of Ukraine (Kyiv, 2024), https://www.kmu.gov.ua/storage/app/sites/1/18%20-%20Department/18%20-%20PDF/2024/03.2024/AA%20implementation%20report%20for%202023.pdf.

Action Plan for the Conservation of the Ukrainian Part of the UNESCO World Heritage Site "Ancient and Primeval Beech Forests of the Carpathians and Other Regions of Europe" and the Sustainable Development of Adjacent Territories, approved by the Order of the Cabinet of Ministers of Ukraine No. 892-r, Document 892–2018-r (November 21, 2018) https://zakon.rada.gov.ua/laws/show/892-2018-%D1%80#Text [In Ukrainian: План заходів щодо збереження української частини природного об'єкта всесвітньої спадщини ЮНЕСКО "Букові праліси і давні ліси Карпат та інших регіонів Європи" та сталого розвитку прилеглих до нього територій, затверджено розпорядженням Кабінету Міністрів України № 892-р, Документ 892–2018-р (21 листопада 2018)] [Action Plan for the Conservation of the UNESCO World Heritage Site 2018].

Action Plan for the Implementation of the National Transport Strategy of Ukraine for the Period until 2030, approved by the Order of the Cabinet of Ministers of Ukraine No. 321-r, Document 321–2021-r, (April 7, 2021) https://zakon.rada.gov.ua/laws/show/321-2021-%D1%80#Text; [In Ukrainian: План заходів з реалізації Національної транспортної стратегії України на період до 2030 року, затверджено розпорядженням Кабінету Міністрів України № 321-р, Документ 321–2021-р (7 квітня 2021)].

Action Plan for the Implementation of the Strategy for the Framework Convention on the Protection and Sustainable Development of the Carpathians for 2008–2020 in the Zakarpattia Region (February 5, 2008) https://view.officeapps.live.com/op/view.aspx?src=https%3A%2F%2Fecozakarpat.gov.ua%2Fwp-content%2Fpzf_ekomereja%2Fplan_strat.doc&wdOrigin=BROWSELINK [In Ukrainian: План заходів, спрямованих на реалізацію Стратегії виконання Рамкової конвенції про охорону та сталий розвиток Карпат на 2008–2020 роки по Закарпатській області (05 лютого 2008 року)].

Concept of the Conservation of Biological Diversity of Ukraine, approved by the Resolution of the Cabinet of Ministers of Ukraine No. 439, Document 439–97-p (May 12, 1997) https://zakon.rada.gov.ua/laws/show/439-97-%D0%BF#Text [In Ukrainian: Концепція збереження біологічного різноманіття України, затверджено постановою Кабінету Міністрів україни №439, Документ 439–97-п (12 травня 1997)].

Concept of the Development of Mountainous Areas of the Ukrainian Carpathians, approved by the Order of the Cabinet of Ministers of Ukraine No. 232-r, Document No. 232–2019-r (April 3, 2019) https://zakon.rada.gov.ua/laws/show/232-2019-%D1%80#Text; [In Ukrainian: Концепція розвитку гірських територій українських Карпат, схвалено розпорядженням Кабінету Міністрів України № 232-р, Документ 232–2019-р, (3 квітня 2019)].

Concept of the National Program for Biodiversity Conservation for 2005–2025, approved by the Resolution of the Cabinet of Ministers of Ukraine No. 675-r, Document No. 675–2004-r, (September 22, 2004) https://zakon.rada.gov.ua/laws/show/675-2004-%D1%80#Text; [In Ukrainian: Концепція Загальнодержавної програми збереження біорізноманіття на 2005–2025 роки, затверджено постановою Кабінету Міністрів України № 675-р, Документ 675–2004-р, (22 вересня 2004)].

Development Strategy of the Chernivtsi Region for the Period until 2027, approved by the decision of the session of the Chernivtsi Regional Council No. 2–31/20 (February 4, 2020), https://bukoda.gov.ua/storage/app/sites/23/uploaded-files/strategia-chernivetska-2027.pdf [In Ukrainian: Стратегія розвитку Чернівецької області на період до 2027 року затверджена рішенням сесії Чернівецької обласної ради № 2–31/20 (4 лютого 2020)].

Development Strategy of the Ivano-Frankivsk Region for 2021–2027, approved by the decision of the regional council No. 1381–34/2020 (February 21, 2020) https://www.if.gov.ua/storage/app/sites/24/documentu-2021/10-06-2021-strategiya-rozvitku-ivano-frankivskoi-oblasti-na-2021-2027-roki.pdf; [In Ukrainian: Стратегія розвитку Івано-Франківської області на 2021–2027 роки, затверджено рішенням обласної ради № 1381–34/2020 (21 лютого 2020)].

Development Strategy of the Lviv Region for the Period of 2021–2027, approved by the decision of the regional council No. 948 (December 24, 2019) https://loda.gov.ua/documents/49999; [In Ukrainian: Стратегія розвитку Львівської області на період 2021–2027 років, затверджено рішенням обласної ради № 948 (24 грудня 2019)].

Development Strategy of the Mountainous Areas of the Lviv Region for 2018–2022, Lviv Regional State Administration, Lviv Regional Council (Lviv, 2017) https://old.loda.gov.ua/upload/users_files/22/upload/Strategy_Lviv_region_mountians%20terytories%20565_str.pdf; [In Ukrainian: Стратегія розвитку гірських територій Львівської області на 2018–2022 роки, Львівська обласна державна адміністрація, Львівська обласна рада (Львів, 2017)].

I. I. Schmalhausen Institute of Zoology and WWF Ukraine, *Sixth National Report of Ukraine on the Implementation of the Convention on Biological Diversity: English version* (Kyiv, 2018) https://www.cbd.int/doc/nr/nr-06/ua-nr-06-en.pdf.

List of Rare, Endangered, and Typical Natural Plant Communities Subject to Protection and Included in the Green Data Book of Ukraine, approved by the Order of the Ministry of Environmental Protection No. 368, Document z0130–21, (December 17, 2020) https://zakon.rada.gov.ua/laws/show/z0130-21#n17; [In Ukrainian: Перелік рідкісних і таких, що перебувають під загрозою зникнення, та типових природних рослинних угруповань, які підлягають охороні і заносяться до Зеленої книги України, затверджено Наказом Міністерства захисту довкілля та природних ресурсів № 368, Документ z0130–21, (17 грудня 2020)].

Methodical Recommendations for Developing Projects for the Creation of Natural Areas and Objects of the Nature Reserve Fund of Ukraine, approved by the Order of the Ministry of Environmental Protection and Natural Resources of Ukraine No. 306, Document v0306737–18 (August 21, 2018) https://zakon.rada.gov.ua/rada/show/v0306737-18#Text; [In Ukrainian: Методичні рекомендації щодо розроблення проектів створення природних територій та об'єктів природно-заповідного фонду України, затверджено Наказом Міністерства екології та природних ресурсів України № 306, Документ v0306737–18 (21 серпня 2018)].

Methodical Recommendations on Conducting Strategic Environmental Assessment of Urban Planning Documentation, approved by the Order of the Ministry of Environmental Protection and Natural Resources of Ukraine No. 705, Document v0705926–23 (October 18, 2023) https://zakon.rada.gov.ua/rada/show/v0705926-23#Text; [In Ukrainian: Методичні рекомендації щодо здійснення стратегічної екологічної оцінки містобудівної документації, затверджено наказом Міністерства захисту довкілля та природних ресурсів України № 705, Документ v0705926–23, (18 жовтня 2023)].

Methodological Recommendations for Assessing Risks and Vulnerability of Socio-Economic Sectors and Natural Components to Climate Change, approved by the Order of the Ministry of Environmental Protection No. 386, Document v0386926–23, (June 3, 2023) https://zakon.rada.gov.ua/rada/show/v0386926-23#Text; [In Ukrainian: Методичні рекомендації для здійснення оцінки ризиків та вразливості соціально-економічних секторів та природних складових до зміни клімату, затверджено наказом Міністерства захисту довкілля та природних ресурсів України № 386, Документ v0386926–23 (03 червня 2023)].

Methodology for Determining the Classification of Forest Areas as Primeval Forests, Quasi-Primeval Forests, and Natural Forests, approved by the Order of the Ministry of Environmental Protection No. 161, Document z0707–18, (May 18, 2018) https://zakon.rada.gov.ua/laws/show/z0707-18#n14; [In Ukrainian: Методика визначення належності лісових територій до пралісів, квазіпралісів і природних лісів, затверджено наказом Міністерства екології та природних ресурсів України № 161, Документ z0707–18, (18 травня 2018)].

Methodology for Determining the Classification of Forest Areas as Primeval Forests, Quasi-Primeval Forests, and Natural Forests (2018); Methodology for Determining the Classification of Territories as Primeval Forest Nature Monuments, approved by the Order of the Ministry of Environmental Protection No. 162, Document z0707–18, (May 18, 2018) https://zakon.rada.gov.ua/laws/show/z0708-18#n14; [In Ukrainian: Методика визначення належності територій до пралісових пам'яток природи, затверджено наказом Міністерства екології та природних ресурсів України № 162, Документ z0708–18, (18 травня 2018)].

Ministry of Ecology and Natural Resources of Ukraine, "Biennial Report 2015–2016," https://rm.coe.int/biennial-report-ua-2015-2016/1680a86331.

Ministry of Ecology and Natural Resources of Ukraine, *Fifth national report of Ukraine to the Convention on Biological Diversity,* (Kyiv, 2015), https://www.cbd.int/doc/world/ua/ua-nr-05-en.pdf.

Ministry of Ecology and Natural Resources of Ukraine, *National Report of Ukraine on the Implementation of the Protocol on the Conservation and Sustainable Use of Biological and Landscape Diversity to the Framework Convention on the Protection and Sustainable Development of the Carpathians*, (Kyiv, 2017), http://www.carpathiaconvention.org/tl_files/carpathiancon/Downloads/02%20Activities/Biodiveristy/National%20report%20Biodiversity%20Ukraine.pdf.

Ministry of Ecology and Natural Resources of Ukraine, *Sixth National Report of Ukraine on the Implementation of the Convention on Biological Diversity* (Kyiv, 2018), https://www.cbd.int/doc/nr/nr-06/ua-nr-06-en.pdf.

Ministry of Environmental Protection and Natural Resources of Ukraine, *Alleged threats to the Emerald Network sites Skhidnyi Svydovets, Marmaroski ta Chyvchyno Hryniavski Hory and Carpathian Biosphere Reserve 2018/05 (Ukraine)*, Report by the Government, T-PVS/Files(2024)60, (Strasbourg, 2024) https://rm.coe.int/files60-2024-ukraine-skhidnyi-svydovets-gov-report-2787-7062-5290-1/1680b15226.

National Action Plan for Environmental Protection until 2025, approved by the Order of the Cabinet of Ministers of Ukraine No. 443-r, Document 443–2021-р (December 21, 2021) https://zakon.rada.gov.ua/laws/show/443-2021-%D1%80#n12 [In Ukrainian: Національний план дій з охорони навколишнього природного середовища на період до 2025 року, затверджено розпорядженням Кабінету Міністрів України № 443-р, Документ 443–2021-р (21 квітня 2021)].

National Transport Strategy of Ukraine for the Period until 2030, approved by the Order of the Cabinet of Ministers of Ukraine No. 430-r, Document 430–2018-r (May 30, 2018) https://zakon.rada.gov.ua/laws/show/430-2018-%D1%80#Text; [In Ukrainian: Національна транспортна стратегія України на період до 2030 року, схвалено розпорядженням Кабінету Міністрів України № 430-р, Документ 430–2018-р (30 травня 2018)].

Operational Action Plan for the Implementation in 2024–2026 of the Strategy for the Formation and Implementation of State Policy in the Sphere of Climate Change for the Period until 2035, approved by the Order of the Cabinet of Ministers of Ukraine No. 483-r, Document 483–2024-r, (May 30, 2024) https://zakon.rada.gov.ua/laws/show/483-2024-%D1%80#Text; [In Ukrainian: Операційний план заходів з реалізації у 2024–2026 роках Стратегії формування та реалізації державної політики у сфері зміни клімату на період до 2035 року, затверджено розпорядженням Кабінету Міністрів України № 483-р, Документ 483–2024-р, (30 травня 2024)].

Permanent Mission of Ukraine to the United Nations, *Communication by the State Forest Resources Agency of Ukraine on voluntary national contributions in the framework of implementation of the United Nations Strategic Plan for Forests for the period 2017–2030*, No. 4132/28–199–700 (May 4, 2018) https://www.un.org/esa/forests/wp-content/uploads/2018/10/Ukraine.pdf.

Procedure for Classifying Forests into Categories and Designating Specially Protected Forest Areas, approved by the Resolution of the Cabinet of Ministers of Ukraine No. 733, Document 733–2007-p, (May 16, 2007) https://zakon.rada.gov.ua/laws/show/733-2007-%D0%BF#n10; [In Ukrainian: Порядок поділу лісів на категорії та виділення особливо захисних лісових ділянок, затверджено постановою Кабінету Міністрів України, № 733, Документ 733–2007-п, (16 травня 2007)].

Procedure for Conducting Forest Management Planning, approved by the Resolution of the Cabinet of Ministers of Ukraine No. 112, Document 112–2023-p, (February 7, 2023) https://zakon.rada.gov.ua/laws/show/112-2023-%D0%BF#Text; [In Ukrainian: Порядок здійснення лісовпорядкування, затверджено постановою Кабінету Міністрів України № 112, Документ 112–2023-п, (7 лютого 2023)].

Procedure for Conducting the National Forest Inventory, approved by the Resolution of the Cabinet of Ministers of Ukraine No. 392, Document 392–2021-p, (April 21, 2021) https://zakon.rada.gov.ua/laws/show/392-2021-%D0%BF#n10; [In Ukrainian: Порядок проведення національної інвентаризації лісів, затверджено постановою Кабінету Міністрів України № 392, Документ 392–2021-п, (21 квітня 2021)].

Procedure for Establishing Protective Zones for Biodiversity Conservation in Forests, approved by the Resolution of the Cabinet of Ministers of Ukraine No. 499, Document 499–2023-p, (May 12, 2023) https://zakon.rada.gov.ua/laws/show/499-2023-%D0%BF#n10; [In Ukrainian: Порядок створення охоронних зон для збереження біорізноманіття у лісах, затверджено постановою Кабінету Міністрів України № 499, Документ 499–2023-п, (12 травня 2023)].

Procedure for Establishing Protective Zones for the Preservation of Objects Listed in the Red Data Book of Ukraine, approved by the Resolution of the Cabinet of Ministers of Ukraine No. 499, Document 499–2023-p, (May 12, 2023) https://zakon.rada.gov.ua/laws/show/499-2023-%D0%BF#n89; [In Ukrainian: Порядок створення охоронних зон для збереження об'єктів Червоної книги України, затверджено постановою Кабінету Міністрів України № 499, Документ 499–2023-п, (12 травня 2023)].

Procedure for including territories and objects in the lists of territories and objects of the ecological network, approved by the Resolution of the Cabinet of Ministers of Ukraine No. 1196, Document 1196–2015-p (December 16, 2015) https://zakon.rada.gov.ua/laws/show/1196-2015-%D0%BF#Text [In Ukrainian: Порядок включення територій та об'єктів до переліків територій та об'єктів екологічної мережі, затверджено постановою Кабінету Міністрів України № 1196, Документ 1196–2015-п, (16 грудня 2015)].

Procedure for Maintaining the State Forest Cadastre and Forest Inventory, approved by the Resolution of the Cabinet of Ministers of Ukraine No. 848, Document 848–2007-p, (June 20, 2007) https://zakon.rada.gov.ua/laws/show/848-2007-%D0%BF#Text; [In Ukrainian: Порядок ведення державного лісового кадастру та обліку лісів, затверджено постановою Кабінету Міністрів України, № 848, Документ 848–2007-п, (20 червня 2007)].

Procedure for Maintaining the Unified Register of Strategic Environmental Assessments, approved by the Resolution of the Cabinet of Ministers of Ukraine No. 430, Document 430–2023-p, (May 2, 2023) https://zakon.rada.gov.ua/laws/show/430-2023-%D0%BF#n10; [In Ukrainian: Порядок ведення Єдиного реєстру стратегічної екологічної оцінки, затверджено постановою Кабінету Міністрів України № 430, Документ 430–2023-п, (2 травня 2023)];

Programme of the Chronicles of Nature in Reserves and National Nature Parks, approved by the Order of the Ministry of Environmental Protection and Natural Resources of Ukraine and National Academy of Sciences of Ukraine No. 465/430, Document v465_737–02, (November 25, 2002) https://zakon.rada.gov.ua/rada/show/v465_737-02#Text; [In Ukrainian: Програма літопису природи для заповідників та національних природних парків, затверджено Наказом Міністерства екології та природних ресурсів України та Національної академії наук України № 465/430, Документ v465_737–02, (25 листопада 2002)].

Reform Support Team of the Ministry of Environmental Protection of Ukraine, *Environmental Monitoring: Analytical Note on the State and Prospects for the Development of the State Environmental Monitoring System*, (Kyiv, 2023) https://mepr.gov.ua/wp-content/uploads/2023/02/Monitoring-Green-Paper_15_02_2022.pdf; [In Ukrainian: Команда підтримки реформ Міндовкілля, *Моніторинг довкілля: Аналітична записка щодо стану та перспектив розвитку державної системи моніторингу довкілля*].

Regional Development Strategy of the Zakarpattia Region for the Period 2021–2027, approved by the decision of the regional council No. 1630 (December 20, 2019) with the changes based on the decision No. 1840 (October 1, 2020) https://carpathia.gov.ua/storage/app/sites/21/Economics/201001-1840p.pdf; [In Ukrainian: Регіональна стратегія розвитку Закарпатської області на період 2021–2027 років, затверджено рішенням обласної ради № 1630 (20 грудня 2019) зі змінами, внесеними рішенням від № 1840 (01 жовтня 2020)].

Regulation on the State Environmental Monitoring System, approved by the Resolution of the Cabinet of Ministers of Ukraine No. 391, Document 391–98-p, (March 30, 1998), https://zakon.rada.gov.ua/laws/show/391-98-%D0%BF#Text; [In Ukrainian: Положення про державну систему моніторингу довкілля, затверджено постановою Кабінету Міністрів України № 391, Документ 391–98-п (30 березня 1998)];

Regulations for Main-Use Logging in the Mountain Forests of the Carpathians, approved by the Resolution of the Cabinet of Ministers of Ukraine No. 929, Document 929–2008-p, (October 22, 2008) https://zakon.rada.gov.ua/laws/show/929-2008-%D0%BF#Text; [In Ukrainian: Правила рубок головного користування в гірських лісах Карпат, затверджено постановою Кабінету Міністрів України № 929, Документ 929–2008-п, (22 жовтня 2008)].

Regulations on the Green Data Book of Ukraine, approved by the Resolution of the Cabinet of Ministers of Ukraine No.1286, Document 1286–2002-p, (August 29, 2002), https://zakon.rada.gov.ua/laws/show/1286-2002-%D0%BF#Text; [In Ukrainian: Положення про Зелену книгу України, затверджено постановою Кабінету Міністрів України № 1286, Документ 1286–2002-п, (29 серпня 2002)].

Regulations on the Ministry of Environmental Protection and Natural Resources of Ukraine, approved by the Resolution of the Cabinet of Ministers of Ukraine No. 614, Document 614–2020-p, (June 25, 2020) https://zakon.rada.gov.ua/laws/show/614-2020-%D0%BF#n13; [In Ukrainian: Положення про Міністерство захисту довкілля та природних ресурсів України, затверджено постановою Кабінету Міністрів України № 614, Документ 614–2020-п, (25 червня 2020)].

Regulations on the State Environmental Inspectorate of Ukraine, approved by the Resolution of the Cabinet of Ministers of Ukraine No.275, Document 275–2017-p, (April 19, 2017) https://zakon.rada.gov.ua/laws/show/275-2017-%D0%BF#Text; [In Ukrainian: Положення про Державну екологічну інспекцію України, затверджено постановою Кабінету Міністрів України № 275, Документ 275–2017-п, (19 квітня 2017)].

Regulations on the State Forest Protection Service, Forest Protection of Other Permanent Forest Users, and Forest Owners, approved by the Resolution of the Cabinet of Ministers of Ukraine No. 976, Document 976–2009-p, (16 September 2009) https://zakon.rada.gov.ua/laws/show/976-2009-%D0%BF#Text; [In Ukrainian: Положення про державну лісову охорону, лісову охорону інших постійних лісокористувачів та власників лісів, затверджено постановою Кабінету Міністрів України № 976, Документ 976–2009-п, (16 вересня 2009)].

Regulations on the State Forest Resources Agency of Ukraine, approved by the Resolution of the Cabinet of Ministers of Ukraine No. 521, Document 521–2014-p, (October 8, 2014) https://zakon.rada.gov.ua/laws/show/521-2014-%D0%BF#n8; [In Ukrainian: Положення про Державне агентство лісових ресурсів України, затверджено постановою Кабінету Міністрів України № 521, Документ 521–2014-п, (8 жовтня 2014)].

Sanitary Rules in the Forests of Ukraine, approved by the Resolution of the Cabinet of Ministers of Ukraine No. 555, Document 555–95-p, (July 27, 1995) https://zakon.rada.gov.ua/laws/show/555-95-%D0%BF#Text; [In Ukrainian: Санітарні правила в лісах України, затверджено постановою Кабінету Міністрів України № 555, Документ 555–95-п, (27 липня 1995)].

State Programme for the Development of Cross-Border Cooperation for 2021–2027, approved by the Resolution of the Cabinet of Ministers of Ukraine No. 408, Document 408–2021-p, (April 14, 2021) https://zakon.rada.gov.ua/laws/show/408-2021-%D0%BF#Text; [In Ukrainian: Державна програма розвитку транскордонного співробітництва на 2021–2027 роки, затверджено постановою Кабінету Міністрів України № 408, Документ 408–2021-п, (14 квітня 2021)].

State Programme for the Development of the Ukrainian Carpathian Region for 2020–2022, approved by the Resolution of the Cabinet of Ministers of Ukraine No. 880, Document 880–2019-p (October 20, 2019) https://zakon.rada.gov.ua/laws/show/880-2019-%D0%BF#Text; [In Ukrainian: Державна програма розвитку регіону українських Карпат на 2020–2022 роки, затверджено постановою Кабінету Міністрів України № 880, Документ 880–2019-п, (20 жовтня 2019)].

State Strategy for Forest Management of Ukraine until 2035, approved by the Order of the Cabinet of Ministers of Ukraine No. 1777-r, Document 1777–2021-r (December 29, 2021) https://zakon.rada.gov.ua/laws/show/1777-2021-%D1%80#Text [In Ukrainian: Державна стратегія управління лісами України до 2035 року, схвалено розпорядженням Кабінету Міністрів України № 1777-р, Документ 1777–2021-р (29 грудня 2021)].

Strategy for Environmental Safety and Climate Change Adaptation for the Period until 2030, approved by the Order of the Cabinet of Ministers of Ukraine No. 1363-r, Document 1363–2021-r (October 20, 2021) https://zakon.rada.gov.ua/laws/show/1363-2021-%D1%80#Text; [In Ukrainian: Стратегія екологічної безпеки та адаптації до зміни клімату на період до 2030 року, схвалено розпорядженням Кабінету Міністрів України № 1363-р, Документ 1363–2021-р, (20 жовтня 2021)].

Strategy for the Development of Tourism and Resorts for the Period until 2026, approved by the Order of the Cabinet of Ministers of Ukraine No. 168-r, Document 168–2017-r, (March 16, 2017) https://zakon.rada.gov.ua/laws/show/168-2017-%D1%80#Text; [In Ukrainian: Стратегія розвитку туризму та курортів на період до 2026 року, схвалено розпорядженням Кабінету Міністрів України № 168-р, Документ 168–2017-р, (16 березня 2017)].

Strategy for the implementation of the Framework Convention on the Protection and Sustainable Development of the Carpathians, approved by the Order of the Cabinet of Ministers of Ukraine No. 11-r, Document 11–2007-r (January 16, 2007) https://zakon.rada.gov.ua/laws/show/11-2007-%D1%80#Text [In Ukrainian: Стратегія виконання Рамкової конвенції про охорону та сталий розвиток Карпат, схвалено розпорядженням Кабінету Міністрів України № 11-р, Документ 11–2007-р (16 січня 2007)].

Strategy for the implementation of the Framework Convention on the Protection and Sustainable Development of the Carpathians; See also: "Programme of Work on Mountain Biological Diversity," CBD, April 9, 2007, https://www.cbd.int/mountain/pow.shtml.

The Strategy for the Formation and Implementation of State Policy in the Sphere of Climate Change for the Period until 2035, approved by the Order of the Cabinet of Ministers of Ukraine No. 483-r, Document 483–2024-r, (May 30, 2024) https://zakon.rada.gov.ua/laws/show/483-2024-%D1%80#Text; [In Ukrainian: Стратегія формування та реалізації державної політики у сфері зміни клімату на період до 2035 року, схвалено розпорядженням Кабінету Міністрів України № 483 р, Документ 483–2024-р, (30 травня 2024)].

Documents of the international organisations, EU, and institutional mechanisms of the international treaties

"(Draft) Carpathian strategy for enhancing biodiversity and landscape conservation outside and inside protected areas," Centralparks, Deliverable D.T1.1.3, (2021) http://www.carpathianconvention.org/tl_files/carpathiancon/Downloads/03%20Meetings%20and%20Events/Implementation%20Committee/CCIC2021/1510C2FDCentralparks_DT1.1.3_draft%20Strategy%20biodiversity%20and%20landscape%20FULL%20Document.pdf.

"(Draft) Strategy for local sustainable tourism development based on natural and cultural heritage of the Carpathians," Centralparks, Deliverable D.T1.2.3 (2021), https://programme2014-20.interreg-central.eu/Content.Node/Centralparks/D.T1.2.3-Strategy-for-local-sustainable-tourism-development.pdf.

"15th Meeting of the Working Group on Biodiversity: 17–18 June 2024, Vienna, Austria," Carpathian Convention, accessed November 11, 2024, http://www.carpathianconvention.org/2024/03/19/15th-meeting-of-the-working-group-on-biodiversity/.

"Alleged threats to the Emerald Network sites Skhidnyi Svydovets, Marmaroski ta Chyvchyno-Hryniavski Hory and Carpathian biosphere Reserve," Bern Convention, May 2018, https://www.coe.int/en/web/bern-convention/-/alleged-threats-to-the-emerald-network-sites-skhidnyi-svydovets-marmaroski-ta-chyvchyno-hryniavski-hory-and-carpathian-biosphere-reserve.

"Background note for the moderated discussion on the implementation of the Carpathian Biodiversity Framework (CBF), to be held at the 15th meeting of the CC Working Group on Biodiversity on 17 June 2024," (2024) http://www.carpathianconvention.org/wp-content/uploads/2024/06/Background-note-for-the-moderated-discussion_CBF-implementation_WG-Biodiversity_17-June-.pdf.

"Carpathian Convention Guidance Document for Streamlining the Carpathian Biodiversity Framework into National Biodiversity Strategies and Action Plans (NBSAPs)", Secretariat of the Carpathian Convention, (2024) http://www.carpathianconvention.org/wp-content/uploads/2024/02/Guidance-Document_Streamlining-CBF-into-NBSAPs_FINAL-DRAFT-0702-.pdf.

"General Reports (2001–2004)," Convention on the conservation of European wildlife and natural habitats – 29th meeting of the Standing Committee (Bern, 23–26 November 2009), https://search.coe.int/democracy/eng?i=0900001680746c04.

"Guidelines on communication between protected areas and local communities in the Carpathians," Centralparks, Deliverable D.T1.3.3, (2021), http://www.carpathianconvention.org/tl_files/carpathiancon/Downloads/03%20Meetings%20and%20Events/Implementation%20Committee/CCIC2021/1510C3FDCentralparks_WPT1_Guidelines%20on%20communication_2021_04_26.pdf.

"Notification 2015–015: Tools, Guidance and Information Related to Biodiversity and Climate Change in the Context of the Expected Climate Agreement," CBD Executive Secretary, (February 2015) https://www.cbd.int/notifications/2015-015.

"Pan-European Biological and Landscape Diversity Strategy," approved by the Ministers of the Environment of the 55 states present at the Ministerial Conference "Environment for Europe" (Sofia, Bulgaria, 23 – 25 October 1995), https://www.cbd.int/doc/nbsap/rbsap/peblds-rbsap.pdf.

"Presumed threat to Emerald site "Polonina Borzhava" (UA0000263) from wind energy development," Case page, Bern Convention, accessed September 20, 2024, https://www.coe.int/en/web/bern-convention/-/presumed-threat-to-emerald-site-polonina-borzhava-ua0000263-from-wind-energy-development.

"*Progress indicators for measuring rights contemplated in the Additional Protocol to the American Convention on Human Rights in the Area of Economic, Social, and Cultural Rights, "Protocol of San Salvador"*, Working Group to examine the periodic reports of the States Parties to the Protocol of San Salvador, OAS, OEA/Ser.D/XXVI.11 (2015) https://www.oas.org/en/sedi/pub/progress_indicators.pdf.

"Reservations and Declarations for Treaty No.104 – Convention on the Conservation of European Wildlife and Natural Habitats (ETS No. 104)," Council of Europe Treaty Office, accessed December 30, 2024, https://www.coe.int/en/web/conventions/full-list?module=declarations-by-treaty&numSte=104&codeNature=0.

"The Lima 2014 Declaration on Biodiversity and Climate Change from Science to Policy-Makers, for Sustainable Development," delivered to the president of UNFCCC COP 20 (December 5, 2014) https://www.iai.int/admin/site/sites/default/files/THE_LIMA_2014_DECLARATION.pdf

8th WG Forest meeting, *Carpathian Convention Working Group on Sustainable Forest Management – Work Plan 2023–2026 implementing the Forest Protocol and its Strategic Action Plan*, CC/COP7/DOC13 (2022), http://www.carpathianconvention.org/cop7/docs/officialdocuments/CC_COP7_DOC13_%20WG%20Forest%20Work%20Plan%202023_2026%20FINAL.pdf.

Achieving functional biodiversity in the Danube-Carpathian Region by mainstreaming ecological connectivity, Declaration by EUSDR PA 4, EUSDR PA 5, EUSDR PA 6, Carpathian Convention, ICPDR, (2021) http://www.carpathianconvention.org/tl_files/carpathiancon/Downloads/02%20Activities/Biodiveristy/Connectivity%20Declaration_Final_with%20logos_f.pdf.

Carpathian Convention Working Group on Sustainable Forest Management, *Strategic Action Plan for the Implementation of the Protocol on SFM to the Carpathian Convention*, Presentation, (Zvolen, 2019), http://www.carpathianconvention.org/tl_files/carpathiancon/Downloads/03%20Meetings%20and%20Events/Working%20Groups/Sustainable%20Forest%20Management/7th%20meeting/presentations/Strategic%20Action%20Plan%20-Forest%20Protocol%20CC_M.Schwarz.pdf.

Carpathian Ministerial Conference, *Ministerial Declaration of the Carpathian Convention on the impact of war on the environment in Ukraine and the need for cooperation and assistance* (Rzeszów, November 2022), http://www.carpathianconvention.org/tl_files/carpathiancon/Downloads/03%20Meetings%20and%20Events/Others/Carpathian%20Ministerial%20Conference/Carpathian%20Ministerial%20Declaration_impact%20of%20war%20on%20Ukraine%20and%20the%20need%20for%20cooperation_FINAL.pdf.

CEM and IUCN, *Climate Mitigation and Biodiversity Conservation*, Technical Brief, UNFCCC COP 28 (November 2023) https://iucn.org/resources/information-brief/climate-mitigation-and-biodiversity-conservation.

CMS Secretariat, *Implementation of the Strategic Plan for Migratory Species 2015–2023*, UNEP/CMS/COP14/Doc.14.1 (2023).

Conference of the Parties, *Biodiversity and climate change related issues: advice on the application of relevant safeguards for biodiversity with regard to policy approaches and positive incentives on issues relating to reducing emissions from deforestation and forest degradation in developing countries; and the role of conservation, sustainable management of forests and enhancement of forest carbon stocks in developing countries*, CBD COP Decision XI/19 (2012).

Conference of the Parties, *Biological diversity and tourism*, CBD COP Decision V/25 (2000).

Conference of the Parties, *Capacity-building and development and technical and scientific cooperation*, CBD COP Decision 15/8 (2022).

Conference of the Parties, *Carpathian Biodiversity Framework, including a Carpathian Vision 2050*, CC/COP7/DOC7/ADOPTED, (Belgrade, 2023) http://www.carpathianconvention.org/cop7/docs/officialdocuments/CC%20COP7%20DOC7_Carpathian%20Biodiversity%20Framework_ADOPTED.pdf.

Conference of the Parties, *CITES compliance procedures*, CITES COP Resolution Conf. 14.3 (Rev. CoP19).

Conference of the Parties, *CITES compliance procedures*, Resolution Conf. 14.3 (Rev. CoP19).

Conference of the Parties, *CITES compliance procedures*, Resolution Conf. 14.3 (Rev. CoP19).

Conference of the Parties, *CITES Strategic Vision: 2008–2020*, CITES COP Resolution Conf. 16.3 (Rev. CoP17).

Conference of the Parties, *CITES Strategic Vision: 2021–2030*, CITES COP Resolution Conf. 18.3.

Conference of the Parties, *Conservation and sustainable use of biological and landscape diversity, Article 4 of the Carpathian Convention*, Decision COP7/9 (Belgrade, 2023), http://www.carpathianconvention.org/cop7/docs/officialdocuments/CC_COP7_DOC3_COP7%20DECISIONS_ADOPTED.pdf.

Conference of the Parties, *Cooperation among multilateral environmental agreements and other organizations*, CBD COP Decision IX/27 (2008).

Conference of the Parties, *Cooperation with other conventions and international organizations and initiatives*, CBD COP Decision VII/26 (2004).

Conference of the Parties, *Cooperation with other conventions and international organizations and initiatives*, CBD COP Decision X/20 (2010).

Conference of the Parties, *Cooperation with other conventions and international organizations*, CBD COP Decision 15/13 (2022).

Conference of the Parties, *Criteria and indicators for selection of virgin forests in the Carpathians*, adoped by the Decision COP4/4 Sustainable agriculture, rural development and forestry Article 7 of the Carpathian Convention (Mikulov, 2014) http://www.carpathianconvention.org/tl_files/carpathiancon/Downloads/03%20Meetings%20and%20Events/COP/2014_COP4_Mikulov/Follow%20Up/DOC13_Criteria_Indicators_virginforests_FINAL_26SEP.pdf.

Conference of the Parties, *Criteria for amendment of Appendices I and II*, CITES COP Resolution Conf. 9.24 (Rev. CoP17).

Conference of the Parties, *Digital sequence information on genetic resources*, CBD COP Decision 15/9 (2022).

Conference of the Parties, *Ecosystem approach*, CBD COP Decision V/6 (2000); Conference of the Parties, *Ecosystem Approach*, CBD COP Decision VII/11 (2004).

Conference of the Parties, *Education and public awareness*, CBD COP Decision V/17 (2000) §5.

Conference of the Parties, *Forest biological diversity*, CBD COP Decision IV/7 (1998).

Conference of the Parties, *Forest biological diversity*, CBD COP Decision VI/22 (2002); "Forest Biodiversity Programme of Work," CBD, July 27, 2012, https://www.cbd.int/forest/pow.shtml.

Conference of the Parties, *Forest biological diversity*, Decision IV/7, UNEP/CBD/COP/DEC/IV/7 (1998).

Conference of the Parties, *Forests and biological diversity*, CBD COP Decision II/9 (1995).

Conference of the Parties, *Guidelines for the Application of Certain Terms of the Convention*, UNEP/CMS/Resolution 02.02 (1988).

Conference of the Parties, *Guidelines on Biodiversity and Tourism Development*, CBD COP Decision VII/14 (2004).

Conference of the Parties, *Impact assessment, liability and redress*, CBD COP Decision V/18 (2000).

Conference of the Parties, *Implementation of the Carpathian Convention*, Decision COP7/1, http://www.carpathianconvention.org/cop7/docs/officialdocuments/CC_COP7_DOC3_COP7%20DECISIONS_ADOPTED.pdf.

Conference of the Parties, *Improving Ways of Addressing Connectivity in the Conservation of Migratory Species*, UNEP/CMS/Resolution 12.26 (Rev.COP13) (2020), https://www.cms.int/sites/default/files/document/cms_cop13_res.12.26_rev.cop13_e.pdf.

Conference of the Parties, *Incentive measures*, COP Decision III/18 (1996).

Conference of the Parties, *Kunming-Montreal Global Biodiversity Framework*, CBD COP Decision 15/4, CBD/COP/DEC/15/4 (2022) https://www.cbd.int/doc/decisions/cop-15/cop-15-dec-04-en.pdf.

Conference of the Parties, *Location of the Secretariat*, CBD COP Decision II/19 (1995).

Conference of the Parties, *Measures for implementing the Convention on Biological Diversity*, COP Decision IV/10 (1998).

Conference of the Parties, *Mechanisms for planning, monitoring, reporting and review*, CBD COP Decision 15/6 (2022).

Conference of the Parties, *Monitoring framework for the Kunming-Montreal Global Biodiversity Framework*, CBD COP Decision 15/5 (2022).

Conference of the Parties, *Mountain biological diversity*, CBD COP Decision VII/27 (2004).

Conference of the Parties, *Non-detriment findings*, CITES COP Resolution Conf. 16.7 (Rev. CoP17).

Conference of the Parties, *Operations of the Convention*, CBD COP Decision V/20 (2000), §10–16.

Conference of the Parties, *Paris Agreement*, UN Doc. FCCC/CP/2015/L.9/Rev/1 (December 12, 2015).

Conference of the Parties, *Preliminary consideration of components of biological diversity particularly under threat and action which could be taken under the Convention*, CBD COP Decision II/8 (1995).

Conference of the Parties, *Programme of work for terrestrial biological diversity: forest biological diversity*, CBD COP Decision III/12 (1996).

Conference of the Parties, *Programme of Work of the Carpathian Convention by sectors, 1 January 2024 – 31 December 2026,* Annex 1 to DECISION COP7/20, CC/COP7/DOC3/ADOPTED, (Belgrade, 2023), http://www.carpathianconvention.org/wp-content/uploads/2024/09/CC_COP7_Programme-of-Work.pdf, 35.

Conference of the Parties, *Progress report on the implementation of the programme of work for forest biological diversity*, CBD COP Decision V/4 (2000).

Conference of the Parties, *Progress report on the implementation of the programme of work for forest biological diversity*, CBD COP Decision V/4 (2000).

Conference of the Parties, *Report and recommendations of the third meeting of the Subsidiary Body on Scientific, Technical and Technological Advice, and instructions by the Conference of the Parties to the Subsidiary Body on Scientific, Technical and Technological Advice*, CBD COP Decision IV/1 (1998).

Conference of the Parties, *Report and recommendations of the third meeting of the Subsidiary Body on Scientific, Technical and Technological Advice, and instructions by the Conference of the Parties to the Subsidiary Body on Scientific, Technical and Technological Advice*, CBD COP Decision IV/1 (1998).

Conference of the Parties, *Resource mobilization*, CBD COP Decision 15/7 (2022).

Conference of the Parties, *Samarkand Strategic Plan for Migratory Species 2024–2032*, UNEP/CMS/Resolution 14.1 (2024).

Conference of the Parties, *Strategic Action Plan for the Implementation of the Protocol on Conservation and Sustainable use of Biological and Landscape Diversity*, UNEP/CC/COP4/DOC7 (Mikulov, 2014) http://www.carpathianconvention.org/tl_files/carpathiancon/Downloads/03%20Meetings%20and%20Events/COP/2014_COP4_Mikulov/WORKING%20DOCUMENTS/DOC7_Biodiversity%20Protocol%20SAP_Corrigendum.pdf.

Conference of the Parties, *Strategic Action Plan for the Implementation of the Protocol on Sustainable Forest Management*, UNEP/CC/COP4/DOC11/REV1 (Mikulov, 2014), http://www.carpathianconvention.org/tl_files/carpathiancon/Downloads/03%20Meetings%20and%20Events/COP/2014_COP4_Mikulov/Follow%20Up/DOC11_Forest%20SAP%20FINAL_26SepCOP4.pdf.

Conference of the Parties, *Strategic Plan For Migratory Species 2015–2023*, UNEP/CMS/Resolution 11.2 (2014).

Conference of the Parties, *Strategic Plan For Migratory Species 2015–2023*, UNEP/CMS/Resolution 11.2 (Rev.COP12) (2017).

Conference of the Parties, *Strategic Plan for the Convention on Biological Diversity*, CBD COP Decision VI/26 (2002).

Conference of the Parties, *Sustainable forest management, Article 7 of the Carpathian Convention,* Decision COP7/13, (Belgrade, 2023), http://www.carpathianconvention.org/cop7/docs/officialdocuments/CC_COP7_DOC3_COP7%20DECISIONS_ADOPTED.pdf, § 1–3, See also Conference of the Parties, Annex 1 to DECISION COP7/20, 36.

Conference of the Parties, *Sustainable use as a cross-cutting issue*, CBD COP Decision V/24 (2000).

Conference of the Parties, *The Strategic Plan for Biodiversity 2011–2020 and the Aichi Biodiversity Targets*, CBD COP Decision X/2, UNEP/CBD/COP/DEC/X/2 (2010).

Cristian R. Papp, Harald Egerer, Klaudia Kuraś and Gabriella Nagy, *International Action Plan on Conservation of Large Carnivores and Ensuring Ecological Connectivity in the Carpathians*, UNEP Vienna Programme Office – Secretariat of the Carpathian Convention, WWF Romania, CEEWeb, Eurac Research (2020) http://www.carpathianconvention.org/tl_files/carpathiancon/Downloads/02%20Activities/Large%20carnivores/CC%20COP6_DOC9P_Int%20Action%20Plan%20Large%20Carnivores%20and%20Ecological%20Connectivity_ADOPTED.pdf.

Department of Nature Conservation of the Ministry of Climate and Environment of Poland, *Impact of war on natural environment of the Carpathians in Ukraine*, report prepared by Zbigniew Niewiadomski (October, 2022), 22, https://www.gov.pl/attachment/9ed63b69-87d8-4c52-a74a-1c88385f5508.

European Parliament resolution of 11 February 2021 on the implementation of the EU Association Agreement with Ukraine (2019/2202(INI)), European Parliament, https://www.europarl.europa.eu/doceo/document/TA-9-2021-0050_EN.html.

FAO, *Guide to Implementation of Phytosanitary Standards in Forestry*, Second edition, FAO Forestry Paper No. 164. (Rome: FAO, 2024) https://doi.org/10.4060/cd3046en.

Finka, Maroš, Vladimír Ondrejička, Milan Husár et al. *Guidelines on How to Use Spatial Planning Tools in Integrative Management of Ecological Corridors*, Danube Transnational Programme ConnectGREEN Project "Restoring and managing ecological corridors in mountains as the green infrastructure in the Danube basin," (Banská Bystrica: State Nature Conservancy of the Slovak Republic, 2021) https://dtp.interreg-danube.eu/uploads/media/approved_project_output/0001/46/4bf6e34e0cc88332516e33e95333685adf014665.pdf.

Governing Council, *Advancing justice, governance and law for environmental sustainability*, Governing Council / Global Ministerial Environment Forum at its first universal session, Decision 27/9 (2013) https://wedocs.unep.org/bitstream/handle/20.500.11822/12221/Governing%20Council%20Decision%2027-2.pdf?sequence=1.

Group of Experts on Protected Areas and Ecological Networks, *The Emerald Network: A Network of Areas of Special Conservation Interest for Europe*, Explanatory document and compilation of relevant texts T-PVS/PA (2016) 4 (Strasbourg, 2016), https://rm.coe.int/168074669d.

Human rights and the environment, Human Rights Council Resolution 34/20, A/HRC/RES/34/20, (March 24, 2017) https://docs.un.org/en/A/HRC/RES/34/20.

Human rights and the environment, Human Rights Council Resolution 31/8, A/HRC/RES/31/8, (March 23, 2016) https://digitallibrary.un.org/record/836906?v=pdf.

IUCN SSC and Secretariat of the Carpathian Convention, *Proposal for a Concerted Action for the Eurasian Lynx (Lynx Lynx) Proposed for Listing on Appendix II (and I for L. l. balcanicus) of the Convention*, CMS, 14th Meeting of the Conference of the Parties, Samarkand, 12–17 February 2024, UNEP/CMS/COP14/Doc.32.3.4, https://www.cms.int/sites/default/files/document/cms_cop14_doc.32.3.4_proposal-ca-lynx-lynx_e_0.pdf.

IUCN World Conservation Congress 2020, *Ecological Connectivity Conservation in the Post-2020 Global Biodiversity Framework: From Local to International Levels*, WCC-2020-Res-073-EN (Marseille, 2020) https://portals.iucn.org/library/sites/library/files/resrecfiles/WCC_2020_RES_073_EN.pdf.

IUCN World Declaration on the Environmental Rule of Law, IUCN World Congress on Environmental Law in Rio de Janeiro (April 2016) https://iucn.org/sites/default/files/2022-10/world_declaration_on_the_environmental_rule_of_law_final_2017-3-17.pdf.

Kadlečík, Ján, ed. *Carpathian Red List of Forest Habitats and Species and Carpathian List of Invasive Alien Species (draft)*, BioREGIO Carpathians project, (Banská Bystrica: State Nature Conservancy of the Slovak Republic, 2014), http://www.carpathianconvention.org/tl_files/carpathiancon/Downloads/02%20Activities/RedListofSpecies_Habitats_AlienSpecies.pdf.

Keeton, William S., Sabine McCallum, Klaudia Kuras, and Harald Egerer. *Assessment of climate change risks and adaptation options for the Carpathian forests and their ecosystem services*, (Nairobi: United Nations Environment Programme, 2023), http://www.carpathianconvention.org/cop7/docs/officialdocuments/CC_COP7_DOC10_Assessment%20of%20climate%20change%20risks%20Carpathian%20forests%20FINAL.pdf.

Knox, John H. *Report of the Independent Expert on the Issue of Human Rights Obligations Relating to the Enjoyment of a Safe, Clean, Healthy and Sustainable Environment: Compilation of Good Practices*, Human Rights Council, Twenty-eighth Session, A/HRC/28/61 (February 3, 2015) https://docs.un.org/en/A/HRC/28/61.

Knox, John H. *Report of the Independent Expert on the issue of human rights obligations relating to the enjoyment of a safe, clean, healthy and sustainable environment*, Human Rights Council, Twenty-second Session, A/HRC/22/43 (December 24, 2012) https://docs.un.org/en/A/HRC/22/43.

Knox, John H. *Report of the Independent Expert on the issue of human rights obligations relating to the enjoyment of a safe, clean, healthy and sustainable environment*, Human Rights Council, Twenty-fifth session, A/HRC/25/53 (December 30, 2013) https://docs.un.org/en/A/HRC/25/53.

Knox, John H. *Report of The Special Rapporteur on the Issue of Human Rights Obligations Relating to the Enjoyment of a Safe, Clean, Healthy and Sustainable Environment*, Human Rights Council, Thirty-fourth Session, A/HRC/34/49 (January 19, 2017) https://documents.un.org/doc/undoc/gen/g17/009/97/pdf/g1700997.pdf.

Knox, John H. *Report of The Special Rapporteur on the Issue of Human Rights Obligations Relating to the Enjoyment of a Safe, Clean, Healthy and Sustainable Environment*, Human Rights Council, Thirty-seventh Session, A/HRC/37/59 (January 24, 2018) https://docs.un.org/en/A/HRC/37/59, § 2.

Knox, John H., *Human rights obligations relating to the enjoyment of a safe, clean, healthy and sustainable environment*, Report of the Special Rapporteur on the issue of human rights obligations relating to the enjoyment of a safe, clean, healthy and sustainable environment, A/73/188 (July 19, 2018) https://docs.un.org/en/A/73/188.

Kuraś, Klaudia. *WG Biodiversity Work Plan: COP7 Mandate, Review of the Progress in Implementation of the WG Biodiversity Work Plan 2021–2023 and Preparation Work Plan 2024–2026*, Secretariat of the Carpathian Convention (2024), http://www.carpathianconvention.org/wp-content/uploads/2024/06/2_-WG-Biodiversity-Work-Plan-2024-2026_Mandate_-15-WG-Biodiversity_K.Kuras_SCC.pdf.

Lawrence Jones-Walters and Bernard Fleming, *Presumed threat to Emerald Network site "Polonina Borzhava" from wind energy development (UA0000263) (Ukraine)*, Report of the Online Advisory Mission, Complaint on stand-by No. 2018/01, T-PVS/Files(2021)77, (Strasbourg, 2021) https://rm.coe.int/0900001680a460ce.

Nagy, Gabriella, Sergio Rejado Albaina, Valentina Delconte and Nella Sergejeva. *Guidelines for the Identification, Conservation, Restoration, and Management of Ecological Corridors in the Carpathian Ecoregion*, Danube Transnational Programme ConnectGREEN Project, (Budapest: CEEweb for Biodiversity, 2021), https://dtp.interreg-danube.eu/uploads/media/approved_project_output/0001/48/8970ecbfce8e1efb26e6d89be922dca9285d973e.pdf.

Nature knows no borders: transboundary cooperation – a key factor for biodiversity conservation, restoration and sustainable use, General Assembly Resolution 75/271, A/RES/75/271, April 20, 2021.

Okániková, Zuzana, Dušan Romportl, Adéla Kluchová et al., *Methodology for Identification of Ecological Corridors in the Carpathian Countries by Using Large Carnivores as Umbrella Species*, Danube Transnational Programme ConnectGREEN Project "Restoring and managing ecological corridors in mountains as the green infrastructure in the Danube basin" (Banská Bystrica: State Nature Conservancy of the Slovak Republic, 2021), https://dtp.interreg-danube.eu/uploads/media/approved_project_output/0001/46/b06b6e925fd510bee8d1ca23fff5b03424c513fa.pdf.

Parties to the CBD, *Cancun Declaration on Mainstreaming the Conservation and Sustainable use of Biodiversity for Well-being*, COP-13 Documents (Cancun, 2016) https://www.cbd.int/cop/cop-13/hls/cancun%20declaration-en.pdf;

Považan, Radoslav, and Ján Kadlečík, eds., *The Carpathian Ecosystem Services Toolkit*, Interreg CENTRAL EUROPE project Centralparks "Building management capacities of Carpathian protected areas for the integration and harmonisation of biodiversity protection and local socio-economic development", Deliverable D.T3.1.3. (Banská Bystrica: State Nature Conservancy of the Slovak Republic, 2021), https://programme2014-20.interreg-central.eu/Content.Node/Centralparks/D.T3.1.3-Carpathian-Ecosystem-Services-Toolkit-EN.pdf.

Preventing and Combating Corruption as it Relates to Crimes that Have an Impact on the Environment, Resolution 8/12, Conference of the States Parties to the United Nations Convention against Corruption, Eighth session (2019), https://www.unodc.org/corruption/en/cosp/conference/session8-resolutions.html.

Pritchard, Dave. *Proposal for Guidance on Detecting, Assessing, Reporting and Responding to Changes and Likely Changes in the Ecological Character of Emerald Network Sites*, Bern Convention Document T-PVS/PA(2018)13, (Strasbourg, 2018) https://rm.coe.int/proposal-for-guidance-on-detecting-assessing-reporting-and-responding-/16808db4e0.

Pritchard, Dave. *The Concept of the 'Ecological Character' of Sites in the Bern Convention/Emerald Network Context, and Options for Addressing Changes in Ecological Character,* Bern Convention Document T-PVS/PA(2017)8 (Strasbourg, 2017) https://rm.coe.int/the-concept-of-the-ecological-character-of-sites-in-the-bern-conventio/168073f68d.

Puentes Riaño, Astrid. *Overview of the implementation of the human right to a clean, healthy and sustainable environment,* Report of the Special Rapporteur on the human right to a clean, healthy and sustainable environment, A/79/270 (August 2, 2024) https://documents.un.org/doc/undoc/gen/n24/228/44/pdf/n2422844.pdf.

SBSTTA, *Agenda item 3.11: Economic valuation of biological diversity,* SBSTTA recommendation II/9 (1996).

SBSTTA, A *Background Report on Improving Forest Biodiversity Monitoring and Reporting,* UN Doc UNEP/CBD/SBSTTA/16/INF/25 (2012), 13.

SBSTTA, *Ecosystem approach: further elaboration, guidelines for implementation and relationship with sustainable forest management,* SBSTTA Recommendation IX/6 (2008) Annex II.

SBSTTA, *Measures taken for the conservation and sustainable use of mountain biological diversity,* UNEP/CBD/SBSTTA/8/6, CBD (2002), https://www.cbd.int/doc/meetings/sbstta/sbstta-08/official/sbstta-08-06-en.pdf.

SBSTTA, *Proposed elements for a programme of work on mountain biological diversity,* UNEP/CBD/SBSTTA/8/7, CBD (2002), https://www.cbd.int/doc/meetings/sbstta/sbstta-08/official/sbstta-08-07-en.pdf.

SBSTTA, *Status and trends of, and threats to, mountain biological diversity,* UNEP/CBD/SBSTTA/8/5, CBD (2002), https://www.cbd.int/doc/meetings/sbstta/sbstta-08/official/sbstta-08-05-en.pdf.

Secretariat of the Bern Convention, *Case-File System: Summary of General Procedures for the Processing of Complaints – a Resource for the Bern Convention Stakeholders,* T-PVS/Inf(2022)27 (Strasbourg, 2022), https://rm.coe.int/inf27e-2022-cfreflection-summary-of-general-procedures-for-processing-/1680a7bca7.

Secretariat of the Bern Convention, *Proposal to amend Appendices II and III of the Bern Convention of the Conservation of European Wildlife and Natural Habitats by moving the wolf (Canis lupus) from Appendix II to Appendix III,* Proposal by the European Union, T-PVS/Inf(2024)15, (Strasbourg, 2024) https://rm.coe.int/inf15e-2024-submission-on-behalf-of-the-european-union-of-a-proposal-f/1680b1e94e.

Secretariat of the CBD and World Tourism Organization, *Mainstreaming Biodiversity Into Tourism Development: Report on Status, Trends and Relevant Activities,* complement to CBD/COP/14/INF/1, (November 2018) https://www.cbd.int/tourism/doc/cop-14-tourism-background-document-en.pdf.

Secretariat of the CBD, *Managing Tourism and Biodiversity: User's Manual on the CBD Guidelines on Biodiversity and Tourism Development,* (Secretariat of the CBD, UNEP, 2007) https://www.cbd.int/doc/programmes/socio-eco/tourism/tourism-manual-en.pdf.

Secretariat of the CBD, *Tourism Supporting Biodiversity – A Manual on Applying the CBD Guidelines on Biodiversity and Tourism Development,* (Montreal: Secretariat of the CBD, 2015) https://www.cbd.int/tourism/doc/tourism-manual-2015-en.pdf.

Secretariat of the Convention on Biological Diversity, ed., *Handbook of the Convention on Biological Diversity*, prepared by Ruth Mackenzie, Sam Jonson and Martin Jenkins (London: Earthscan Publications, 2001), xvii.

Secretariat of the Convention on Biological Diversity, *Global Biodiversity Outlook 5* (Montreal, 2020) www.cbd.int/GBO5.

Sedy, Katrin, Christoph Plutzar, Florian Borgwardt et al. *A Methodology for Standardised Monitoring of Ecological Connectivity: Guidelines for the Analysis of Structural and Functional Connectivity*, Danube Transnational Programme DTP3–314–2.3 SaveGREEN project, (Vienna: Environment Agency Austria, 2022) https://dtp.interreg-danube.eu/uploads/media/approved_project_output/0001/56/dc86e1c6e3dac3299b3b411262b93dcd0210f85f.pdf.

Standing Committee, *Recommendation No. 16 (1989) of the standing committee on areas of special conservation interest*, (June 9, 1989) https://search.coe.int/democracy?i=0900001680746c25.

Standing Committee, *Recommendation No. 14 (1989) of the standing committee on species habitat conservation and on the conservation of endangered natural habitats*, (June 9, 1989) https://search.coe.int/democracy?i=09000016807464c9.

Standing Committee, *Recommendation No. 213 (2021) of the Standing Committee, adopted on 3rd December 2021, on the presumed threat to Emerald Network site "Polonina Borzhava" from wind energy development (UA0000263) (Ukraine)*, (Strasbourg, 2021) https://rm.coe.int/2021-rec-213e-polonina-borzhava/1680a4c2c4.

Standing Committee, *Resolution No. 1 (1989) of the standing committee on the provisions relating to the conservation of habitats*, (June 9, 1989) https://search.coe.int/democracy?i=0900001680746be2.

Standing Committee, *Resolution No. 3 (1996) concerning the setting up of a pan-European Ecological Network*, (January 26, 1996), https://search.coe.int/democracy?i=09000016807467d3;

Standing Committee, *Resolution No. 8 (2012) of the Standing Committee, adopted on 30 November 2012 on the national designation of adopted Emerald sites and the implementation of management, monitoring and reporting measures*, (November 30, 2012), https://rm.coe.int/1680746515.

Standing Committee, *Three Dimensional Road Map for Achieving a Fully Operational Emerald Network in 7 Countries of Central and Eastern Europe and the South Caucasus*, Document agreed at the Final Conference of the EU/CoE Joint Programme "Emerald Network of Nature Protection Sites, Phase II" and compiled by Mr Dave Pritchard T-PVS/PA (2016) 10 (Strasbourg, 2016) https://rm.coe.int/16807464ae.

Standing Committee, *Updated list of officially adopted Emerald Network sites (December 2021)*, T-PVS/PA(2021)11, (Strasbourg, 2021) https://rm.coe.int/pa11e-2021-updated-list-officially-adopted-emerald-sites-final/1680a4be3d.

Standing Committee, *Updated list of officially adopted Emerald Network sites (December 2023)*, T-PVS/PA(2023)08, (Strasbourg, 2023) https://rm.coe.int/draft-list-of-adopted-emerald-network-sites/1680ad54a1.

Standing Committee, *Vision for the Bern Convention for the Period to 2030*, Document prepared by the Mr Dave E Pritchard, T-PVS(2021)14 ((Strasbourg, 2021), https://rm.coe.int/tpvs14e-2021-vision-final/1680ada0f0.

The human right to a clean, healthy and sustainable environment, General Assembly Resolution 76/300, A/RES/76/300 (July 28, 2022) https://digitallibrary.un.org/record/3983329?v=pdf.

The human right to a clean, healthy and sustainable environment, Human Rights Council Resolution 48/13, A/HRC/RES/48/13 (8 October 2021), undocs.org/en/A/HRC/RES/48/13.

Transforming our world: the 2030 Agenda for Sustainable Development, General Assembly Resolution 70/1, A/RES/70/1 (25 September 2015) (www.un.org/ga).

Trouwborst, Arie. *Obligations of Bern Convention Parties Regarding the Conservation of Candidate and Adopted Emerald Network Sites: A Legal Analysis*, Document prepared on behalf of the Bern Convention, T-PVS/PA(2020)07, (Strasbourg, 2020) https://pure.uvt.nl/ws/portalfiles/portal/58698518/Emerald_Network_obligations_2020.pdf.

UNEP Governing Council, *Rationalization of International Conventions on Biological Diversity*, Decision 14/26, proceedings of the Governing Council at its 14th session, UNEP/GC/DEC/14/26 (1987).

UNEP/CMS Secretariat, *Connectivity and the Post-2020 Biodiversity Framework: An Introduction*, Fact Sheet (June 2019) https://www.cms.int/sites/default/files/publication/fact_sheet_connectivity_new.pdf.

UNEP/CMS Secretariat, *Connectivity and the Post-2020 Biodiversity Framework: Elements for New Goals and Targets*, Fact Sheet (August 2019) https://www.cms.int/sites/default/files/publication/fact_sheet_connectivity_2.pdf.

UNESCO World Heritage Centre, *Operational Guidelines for the Implementation of the World Heritage Convention*, WHC.17/01 (2017).

United Nations Conference on Environment and Development, *Forest Principles: Non-legally Binding Authoritative Statement of Principles for a Global Consensus on the Management, Conservation and Sustainable Development of All Types of Forests* A/CONF.151/26/Rev.1(Vol.I) (1992) https://digitallibrary.un.org/record/160453?v=pdf.

United Nations Conference on Environment and Development, *Rio Declaration on Environment and Development*, A/CONF.151/26 Vol. I (1992) https://www.un.org/en/development/desa/population/migration/generalassembly/docs/globalcompact/A_CONF.151_26_Vol.I_Declaration.pdf.

United Nations Decade on Ecosystem Restoration (2021–2030), General Assembly Resolution 73/284, A/RES/73/284 (March 1, 2019) https://documents.un.org/doc/undoc/gen/n19/060/16/pdf/n1906016.pdf.

United Nations Decade on Ecosystem Restoration, *Ecosystem Restoration Playbook: A Practical Guide To Healing The Planet*, developed for World Environment Day 2021, https://wedocs.unep.org/bitstream/handle/20.500.11822/35858/ERP.pdf?sequence=1&isAllowed=y.

United Nations Environment Assembly of the United Nations Environment Programme, *Political Declaration of the Special Session of the United Nations Environment Assembly to Commemorate the Fiftieth Anniversary of the Establishment of the United Nations Environment Programme*, UNEP/EA.SS.1/4 (March 2022) https://documents.un.org/doc/undoc/gen/k22/007/72/pdf/k2200772.pdf.

United Nations Environment Programme, *Environmental Rule of Law: Tracking Progress and Charting Future Directions*, (Nairobi: UNEP, 2023), https://doi.org/10.59117/20.500.11822/43943.

United Nations Environment Programme, *Environmental Rule of Law: Tracking Progress and Charting Future Directions*, 79; See an example from the US *San Antonio Bay Estuarine Waterkeeper v. Formosa Plastics Corp.*, No. 6:17-CV-0047 (S.D. Tex. 2019).

United Nations Environment Programme, *Human Rights and Environmental Rule of Law*, Asia Pacific Issue Brief: SDG16 (March 2021) https://wedocs.unep.org/bitstream/handle/20.500.11822/35408/SDG16.pdf.

United Nations Environment Programme, *Stockholm Declaration: Declaration on the Human Environment* (1972) https://wedocs.unep.org/bitstream/handle/20.500.11822/29567/ELGP1StockD.pdf?sequence=1&isAllowed=y

United Nations, *Report of the United Nations Conference on the Human Environment,* UN Doc A/CONF.48/14/Rev.1 (Stockholm, 5–16 June, 1972), https://digitallibrary.un.org/record/523249?v=pdf.

World Commission on Environment and Development, *Report of the World Commission on Environment and Development "Our Common Future"* A/42/427, New York, NY: UN Headquarters, August 4, 1987, available from https://digitallibrary.un.org/record/139811?v=pdf.

World Tourism Organization, *The Integration of Biodiversity in National Tourism Policies*, (Madrid: UN Tourism, 2024) https://doi.org/10.18111/9789284424900.

Judicial decisions and arbitral awards

Case №260/1058/19, Case file number: К/9901/25888/20, Date of entry into force: 24.04.2024 https://reyestr.court.gov.ua/Review/118599491.

Case №260/771/19, Case file number: К/990/26571/22; Date of entry into force: 10.08.2023 https://reyestr.court.gov.ua/Review/112757712.

Case №907/801/20 Date of entry into force: 10.07.2024 https://reyestr.court.gov.ua/Review/120623796.

Commission v France C-2220/99 [2001] ECR I-5831.

Commission v France C-96/98 [1999] ECR I-8531.

Gentini case (Italy v Venezuela) (1903) 10 RIAA 551.

Indigenous Communities of the Lhaka Honhat (Our Land) Association v. Argentina, February 6, 2020, Inter-American Court of Human Rights, https://www.corteidh.or.cr/docs/casos/articulos/seriec_400_ing.pdf.

Iron Rhine Arbitration (Belgium v Netherlands) (2005), Permanent Court of Arbitration ICGJ 373, Award of 24 May 2005.

Landelijke Vereniging tot Behoud van de Waddenzee and Nederlandse Vereniging tot Bescherming van Vogels v Staatssecretaris van Landbouw, Natuurbeheer en Visserij, C-127/02 [2004] ECR I-07405.

Legality of the Threat or Use of Nuclear Weapons (Advisory Opinion), ICJ Rep 226, ICGJ 205 (1996).

The Environment and Human Rights, Advisory opinion OC-23/17 of November 15, 2017, requested by the Republic of Colombia, Inter-American Court of Human Rights, https://corteidh.or.cr/docs/opiniones/seriea_23_ing.pdf.

Scientific, educational-methodological, and specialized literature published in Cyrillic

Didukh, Yakiv et al., ed, *Green Book of Ukraine* (Kyiv, Alterpres, 2009), https://komekolog.rada.gov.ua/uploads/documents/36467.pdf [In Ukrainian: Яків Дідух et al. (під заг. ред.), *Зелена книга України*, (Київ, Альтерпрес, 2009)].

Dovhanych, Yaroslav, and V. Y. Dovhanych, "The monitoring system of mammals in the Carpathian Biosphere Reserve," *Monitoring and conservation of biodiversity in Ukraine: Applied aspects of biodiversity monitoring and conservation, Series* "Conservation Biology in Ukraine" Issue 16, Vol. 3 (2020): 66–69, https://uncg.org.ua/wp-content/uploads/2020/05/T3_WEB_MonOchBioriz_Konference_2.pdf; [In Ukrainian: Ярослав Довганич, В. Я. Довганич, "Система моніторингу ссавців у Карпатському біосферному заповіднику," *Моніторинг та охорона біорізноманіття в Україні: Прикладні аспекти моніторингу та охорони біорізноманіття*, Серія: "Conservation Biology in Ukraine," Вип. 16. Т. 3 (2020): 66–69].

Khymynets, Volodymyr. "Carpathian region in the context of sustainable development of Ukraine," *Scientific Bulletin of Uzhhorod National University*, Series 'Economics' No.3 (Part3) (2012): 40–45, https://dspace.uzhnu.edu.ua/jspui/handle/lib/23763 [In Ukrainian: Володимир Химинець, "Карпатський регіон у контексті сталого розвитку України," *Наук. вісник УжНУ*, Серія 'Економіка' № 37(Частина 3) (2012): 40–45].

Moskalenko, Yurii. "The "Chronicle of Nature" program for reserves and national parks of Ukraine – what is wrong with it?" *Monitoring and conservation of biodiversity in Ukraine: Applied aspects of biodiversity monitoring and conservation, Series* "Conservation Biology in Ukraine" Issue 16, Vol. 3 (2020): 91–106, https://uncg.org.ua/wp-content/uploads/2020/05/T3_WEB_MonOchBioriz_Konference_2.pdf; [In Ukrainian: Юрій Москаленко, "Програма Літопису природи заповідників і національних природних парків України – що з нею не так?" *Моніторинг та охорона біорізноманіття в Україні: Прикладні аспекти моніторингу та охорони біорізноманіття*, Серія: "Conservation Biology in Ukraine," Вип. 16. Т. 3 (2020): 91–106].

Parnikoza, Ivan, Volodymyr Sesin, and Volodymyr Boreiko, "History, current state and perspectives of conservation of European bison (*Bison bonasus* L.) in Ukraine," *Proceedings of the Theriological School*, Issue 10 (2010): 137–149, http://www.terreco.univ.kiev.ua/_media/library/bizon/pts10-35-parnikoza-bison-3ed.pdf; [In Ukrainian: Іван Парнікоза, Володимир Сесін, та Володимир Борейко, "Історія, сьогодення та перспективи збереження популяції зубра (*Bison bonasus* L.) в Україні," Праці Теріологічної школи, Випуск 10 (2010):137–149].

Pohorila, Nataliia, and Ihor Soloviy, eds, *Carpathian forests as a resource and common good* (Lviv: UCU, 2022) [In Ukrainian: Наталія Погоріла та Ігор Соловій (ред.), *Карпатські ліси як ресурс і спільне благо* (Львів: УКУ, 2022)].

Poluda, Anatolii et al,. eds, *Encyclopaedia of migratory species of wild animals of Ukraine (Kyiv, 2018),* https://mepr.gov.ua/wp-content/uploads/2023/05/Entsyklopediya-migruyuchyh-vydiv-dykyh-tvaryn-Ukrayiny-3.pdf, 235 [In Ukrainian: Анатолій Полуда et al. (під заг. ред.), *Енциклопедія мігруючих видів диких тварин України*, (Київ, 2018)].

Sheliah-Sosonko, Yurii et al., eds, *Green Book of Ukraine. Forests* (Kyiv: Naukova dumka, 2002), https://nature.land.kiev.ua/green-book-02.pdf [In Ukrainian: Юрій Шеляг-Сосонко et al. (під заг. ред.), *Зелена книга України. Ліси*, (Київ, Наукова думка, 2002)].

Shutiak Sofiia. *Analysis of Ukraine's Implementation of the Framework Convention on the Protection and Sustainable Development of the Carpathians* (Committee of the National Association of Advocates of Ukraine on Agrarian, Land, and Environmental Law, 2024) https://unba.org.ua/assets/uploads/publications/publications/%D0%90%D0%BD%D0%B0%D0%BB%D1%96%D0%B7_%D0%B2%D0%B8%D0%BA%D0%BE%D0%BD%D0%B0%D0%BD%D0%BD%D1%8F_%D0%A3%D0%BA%D1%80%D0%B0%D1%97%D0%BD%D0%BE%D1%8E_%D0%A0%D0%B0%D0%BC%D0%BA%D0%BE%D0%B2%D0%BE%D1%97_%D0%BA%D0%BE%D0%BD%D0%B2%D0%B5%D0%BD%D1%86%D1%96%D1%97_2024.pdf [In Ukrainian: Софія Шутяк, *Аналіз виконання Україною Рамкової конвенції про охорону та сталий розвиток Карпат* (Комітет НААУ з питань аграрного, земельного та довкілевого права, 2024)].

Vasyliuk, Oleksiy. *The Status of Reflection in Ukraine's Programmatic Documents and the Implementation of the Provisions of the UN Convention on Biological Diversity*, Analytical Report, (Kyiv, October 2017), https://www.undp.org/ukraine/publications/implementing-un-convention-biological-diversity-ukraine [In Ukrainian: Олексій Василюк, *Стан відображення в програмних документах України та стану реалізації положень Конвенції ООН про охорону біологічного різноманіття*, аналітичний звіт].

Zinko, Y., M. Malska, M. Ivanyk, S. Blagodyr, "Tourism in the Carpathian Region:Threat to the Environment and Ways of Sustainable development," *Visnyk of the Lviv University*, Series Geography 45 (2014): 443–451, [In Ukrainian: Ю. Зінько, М. Мальська, М. Іваник, С. Благодир, "Туризм у Карпатському Регіоні: Загрози для Довкілля та Способи Сталого Розвитку," *Вісник Львівського Університету*, Серія Географічна 45, (2014): 443–451].

Scientific, educational-methodological, and specialized literature published in Latin script

Ahuja, Naysa, et al. "Advancing Human Rights through Environmental Rule of Law." In *Human Rights and the Environment: Legality, Indivisibility, Dignity and Geography*, edited by James R. May and Erin Daly, 13–33. Cheltenham: Edward Elgar Publishing, 2019.

Almond, R.E.A., M. Grooten and T. Petersen, eds. *Living Planet Report 2020 – Bending the Curve of Biodiversity Loss.* Gland: WWF, 2020, https://f.hubspotusercontent20.net/hubfs/4783129/LPR/PDFs/ENGLISH-FULL.pdf.

Ball, Terence. "Deep Ecology," *Encyclopedia.com.* (May 2018), https://www.encyclopedia.com/environment/encyclopedias-almanacs-transcripts-and-maps/deep-ecology.

Barral, Virginie. "The Principle of Sustainable Development." In *Principles of Environmental Law*, edited by Ludwig Krämer and Emanuela Orlando, 103–114. Cheltenham: Edward Elgar Publishing, 2018.

Bashta, Andriy-Taras, *Bat population status survey in the Ukrainian Carpathians Mts. (Ukraine)*, Final report. Lviv: Bat Research and Protection Group, 2007, https://ruffordorg.s3.amazonaws.com/media/project_reports/03.06.05%20Detailed%20Final%20Report.pdf

Bastmeijer, Kees, "Ecological restoration in international biodiversity law: a promising strategy to address our failure to prevent?" In *Research Handbook on Biodiversity and Law*, edited by Michael Bowman et al., 387–413. Cheltenham: Edward Elgar Publishing, 2016.

Benedict XVI. *Caritas in Veritate* (2009), https://www.vatican.va/content/benedict-xvi/en/encyclicals/documents/hf_ben-xvi_enc_20090629_caritas-in-veritate.html.

Benson, David, Viviane Gravey, and Andrew Jordan, "Environmental Policy." In *European Union Politics*, edited by Michelle Cini and Nieves Perez-Solorzano Borragan. 6th ed. 373–386. Oxford: Oxford University Press, 2012.

Bevz, Olena. "Legal Regulation of the Emerald Network: National and Global Aspects," *Journal of Vasyl Stefanyk Precarpathian National University*, 5, no. 2 (2018): 91–98, https://doi.org/10.15330/jpnu.5.2.91-98.

Birnie, Patricia W., Alan E. Boyle, and Catherine Redgwell. *International Law and the Environment.* 3d ed. Oxford: Oxford University Press, 2009.

Bodansky, Daniel M. "International Law and the Protection of Biological Diversity." *Vanderbilt Journal of Transnational Law*, 28 Issue 4 (October 1995): 623–634.

Bondaruk, G., et al.. *Legal Framework of Biodiversity Protection in Forest Sector of Ukraine: Analysis and Prospects.* Lviv: WWF, 2013.

Bossert, Leonie N. and Lena M. Schlegel. „Anthropozentrismus (in) Der Krise: Warum Probleme Nicht Mit Der Denkweise Gelöst Werden Können, Die Sie Auch Hervorgerufen Hat." *GAIA – Ecological Perspectives for Science and Society* 31, no. 1 (31 March 2022): 14–18, https://doi.org/10.14512/gaia.31.1.5.

Bosworth, Andrew, et al. *Ethics and biodiversity.* Ethics and Climate Change in Asia and the Pacific (ECCAP) Project, Working Group 16 Report. UNESCO Bangkok, 2011.

Bowman, Michael, and Catherine Redgwell, *International Law and the Conservation of Biological Diversity.* International Environmental Law and Policy Series. London: Kluwer Law International, 1996.

Bowman, Michael, Peter Davies, and Catherine Redgwell, *Lyster's International Wildlife Law*, 2nd ed. Cambridge: Cambridge University Press, 2010.

Bowman, Michael, Peter G. G. Davies, and Edward Goodwin. *Research Handbook on Biodiversity and Law.* Cheltenham: Edward Elgar Publishing, 2016.

Bowman, Michael. "Biodiversity, Intrinsic Value, and the Definition and Valuation of Environmental Harm." In *Environmental Damage in International and Comparative Law: Problems of Definition and Valuation*, edited by Michael Bowman, and Alan Boyle, 41- 62. Oxford: Oxford University Press, 2002.

Boyle, Alan E. "The Convention on Biological Diversity." In *The Environment after Rio: International Law and Economics*, edited by Luigi Campiglio *et al.*, 1. publ, International Environmental Law and Policy Series, 111 – 130. London: Graham & Trotman/Martinus Nijhoff, 1994.

Boyle, Alan. "Environment and Human Rights." In *Max Planck Encyclopedia of Public International Law*, edited by Rüdiger Wolfrum, 446–55. Oxford: Oxford University Press, 2012.

Brennan, Andrew, and Norva Y. S. Lo. "Environmental Ethics", *The Stanford Encyclopedia of Philosophy* (Summer 2024 Edition), edited by Edward N. Zalta and Uri Nodelman (Fall 2023). Metaphysics Research Lab, Stanford University, 2024, https://plato.stanford.edu/archives/sum2024/entries/ethics-environmental/.

Burns, Charlotte, and Neil Carter. "Environmental Policy." In *The Oxford Handbook of the European Union*, edited by Erik Jones, Anand Menon, and Stephen Weatherill, 511–525. Oxford: Oxford University Press, 2012.

Cantarello, Elena, et al. "Shaping and Enhancing Resilient Forests for a Resilient Society," *Ambio* 53, no. 8 (August 2024): 1095–1108, https://doi.org/10.1007/s13280-02 4-02006-7.

Cardesa-Salzmann, Antonio. "Monitoring and compliance mechanisms." In *Biodiversity and Nature Protection Law*, edited by Elisa Morgera and Jona Razzaque, 455–467.Cheltenham: Edward Elgar Publishing, 2017.

Chazdon, Robin L. "Protecting Intact Forests Requires Holistic Approaches." *Nature Ecology & Evolution* 2, no. 6 (April 2018): 915, https://doi.org/10.1038/s41559-018-05 46-y.

Cheng, Bin. *General Principles of Law as Applied by International Courts and Tribunals.* London: Stevens, 1953, reprinted 2006.

Conradie, Ernst M. "Christianity: An ecological critique of Christianity and Christian critique of ecological destruction." In *Routledge Handbook of Religion and Ecology*, edited by Willis Jenkins, Mary Evelyn Tucker, and John A. Grim, 70 – 78. Abingdon New York (N. Y.): Routledge Earthscan from Routledge, 2017.

Dalton, Daniel, Vanessa Berger, Hanns Kirchmeir et al. *A Framework For Monitoring Biodiversity In Protected Areas And Other Effective Area-Based Conservation Measures: Concepts, Methods And Technologies*, IUCN WCPA Technical Report Series No. 7. Gland: IUCN, 2024, https://portals.iucn.org/library/sites/library/files/documents/PATRS-007-En.pdf.

de Klemm, Cyrille, and Clare Shine. *Biological Diversity Conservation and the Law.* Gland, Switzerland and Cambridge, UK: IUCN, 1993.

de Sadeleer, Nicolas. "European Union in Biodiversity and Nature Protection Law." In *Biodiversity and Nature Protection Law*, edited by Elisa Morgera and Jona Razzaque, 413–428. Cheltenham: Edward Elgar Publishing, 2017.

Dias, Braulio Ferreira de Souza, and Kathryn Garforth. "Historical perspectives on the challenge of biodiversity conservation." In *Biodiversity and Nature Protection Law*, edited by Elisa Morgera and Jona Razzaque, 13–30. Cheltenham: Edward Elgar, 2017.

Dierks, Jan. „Holismus." In *Handbuch Umweltethik*, edited by Konrad Ott, Jan Dierks, and Lieske Voget-Kleschin, 177–182. Stuttgart: J.B. Metzler Verlag, 2016.

Dizdarevic, Azra. "Convention on International Trade in Endangered Species of Wild Fauna and Flora 1973." In *Multilateral Environmental Treaties*, edited by Malgosia Fitzmaurice, Attila Tanzi, and Angeliki Papantoniou, 67–80. Cheltenham: Edward Elgar Publishing, 2017.

Duclos, Joshua S. *Wilderness, Morality, and Value* (Lanham (Md.): Lexington books, 2022.

Ecumenical Patriarch Bartholomew. *On Earth as in Heaven: Ecological Vision and Initiatives of Ecumenical Patriarch Bartholomew*, edited by John Chryssavgis, Orthodox Christianity and Contemporary Thought. New York: Fordham University Press, 2012, https://doi.org/10.1515/9780823292257.

Edward, David A. O., and Robert C. Lane, *Edward and Lane on European Union Law*. Cheltenham, UK Northampton, MA, USA: Edward Elgar, 2013.

Egede, Edwin. "Common Heritage of Mankind." In *Oxford Bibliographies Online: International Law*, ed. Anthony Carty (July 2014), https://doi.org/10.1093/obo/9780199796953-0109.

Eser, Uta. „Mit Umweltethik Gegen Pandemien? Zum Unterschied von Ethik Und Politik." *GAIA – Ecological Perspectives for Science and Society* 30, no. 4 (16 December 2021): 223–226, https://doi.org/10.14512/gaia.30.4.3.

Eser, Uta. „Naturschutz." In *Handbuch Umweltethik*, ed. Konrad Ott, Jan Dierks, and Lieske Voget-Kleschin, 44–48. Stuttgart: J.B. Metzler Verlag, 2016.

Fady, Bruno, and Magda Bou Dagher Kharrat. "To conserve biodiversity, create spaces where natural selection is allowed free rein." *Nature* 633, 36 (September 2024): 36, *doi:* https://doi.org/10.1038/d41586-024-02854-z.

Faith, Daniel P. "Biodiversity." In *The Stanford Encyclopedia of Philosophy*, edited by Edward N. Zalta and Uri Nodelman, (Fall 2023). Metaphysics Research Lab, Stanford University, 2023, https://plato.stanford.edu/archives/fall2023/entries/biodiversity/.

Fodella, Alessandro. "Mountain biodiversity." In *Biodiversity and Nature Protection Law*, edited by Elisa Morgera and Jona Razzaque, 161–174. Cheltenham: Edward Elgar Publishing, 2017.

Fosci, Mattia, and Tom West, "In Whose Interest? Instrumental and Intrinsic Value in Biodiversity Law." In *Research Handbook on Biodiversity and Law*, edited by Michael Bowman, Peter G. G. Davies, and Edward Goodwin, 55–77. Cheltenham: Edward Elgar Publishing, 2016.

Francis. *Laudato Si'* (2015), https://www.vatican.va/content/francesco/en/encyclicals/documents/papa-francesco_20150524_enciclica-laudato-si.html.

Gillespie, Alexander. "Ethical Considerations." In *The Oxford Handbook of International Environmental Law*, edited by Lavanya Rajamani and Jacqueline Peel, 2nd ed. 217–232. Oxford: Oxford University Press, 2021.

Gillespie, Alexander. *Conservation, Biodiversity and International Law,* New horizons in environmental and energy law. Cheltenham: Edward Elgar, 2011.

Gillespie, Alexander. *International Environmental Law, Policy, and Ethics*, 2nd ed. Oxford: Oxford University Press, 2014.

Glowka Lyle, et al. *A Guide to the Convention on Biological Diversity: A Contribution to the Global Biodiversity Strategy.* IUCN Environmental Policy and Law Paper 30. Gland Cambridge: IUCN the World Conservation Union, 1994.

Gruber, Stefan. "Convention concerning the Protection of the World Cultural and Natural Heritage 1972." In *Multilateral Environmental Treaties*, edited by Malgosia Fitzmaurice, Attila Tanzi, and Angeliki Papantoniou, 60–66. Cheltenham: Edward Elgar Publishing, 2017.

Hardmeier, Christian, and Konrad Ott. „Biblische Schöpfungstheologie." In *Handbuch Umweltethik*, edited by Konrad Ott, Jan Dierks, and Lieske Voget-Kleschin, 183–189. Stuttgart: J.B. Metzler Verlag, 2016.

Harrison, Paula, et al. "Linkages between Biodiversity Attributes and Ecosystem Services: A Systematic Review." *Ecosystem Services* 9 (September 2014): 191–203, https://doi.org/10.1016/j.ecoser.2014.05.006.

Harrop, Stuart R., and Diana J. Pritchard, "A Hard Instrument Goes Soft: The Implications of the Convention on Biological Diversity's Current Trajectory," *Global Environmental Change* 21, no. 2 (May 2011): 474–480, https://doi.org/10.1016/j.gloenvcha.2011.01.014.

Hilty, Jodi, et al. *Guidelines for Conserving Connectivity through Ecological Networks and Corridors*, edited by Craig Groves. Gland: IUCN, 2020, https://doi.org/10.2305/IUCN.CH.2020.PAG.30.en.

Hockings, Marc, Sue Stolton, Fiona Leverington et al. *Evaluating Effectiveness: A Framework for Assessing Management Effectiveness of Protected Areas*, 2nd ed. Gland and Cambridge: IUCN, 2006, https://portals.iucn.org/library/efiles/documents/pag-014.pdf.

Hrynyk, Yehor, Andrii Biletskyi and Amanda Cabrejo le Roux, "How corruption threatens the forests of Ukraine: Typology and case studies on corruption and illegal logging," *Environmental Corruption Deep Dive Series*, Working Paper 43. Basel: Basel Institute on Governance, 2023, baselgovernance. org/publications/deepdive1-ukraine.

Hrynyk, Yehor, Kateryna Harbarchuk, and Petro Tiestov. "Biodiversity in the Rear of Ukraine: What has Changed in Nature Protection in 2022–23? UNCG (November 2023), https://uncg.org.ua/en/wp-content/uploads/2023/11/EN_compressed.pdf.

Humphreys, Stephen. "Against Future Generations," *European Journal of International Law* 33, no. 4 (December 2022): 1061–92, https://doi.org/10.1093/ejil/chac068.

Hunter, David, James Salzman, and Durwood Zaelke, *International Environmental Law and Policy*, 6th ed., University Casebook Series. (St. Paul, MN: Foundation Press, 2022).

Jaret, Amanda, and Frank Pasquale. "The Ethical, Legal, and Political Significance of Laudato Si'." In *Care for the World: Laudato Si' and Catholic Social Thought in an Era of Climate Crisis*, edited by Frank Pasquale, 1–22. Cambrige: Cambrige University Press, 2019.

John Paul II. *Solicitudo Rei Socialis* (1987), https://www.vatican.va/content/john-paul-ii/en/encyclicals/documents/hf_jp-ii_enc_30121987_sollicitudo-rei-socialis.html.

Kelly, Anthony. *Laudato Si: An Integral Ecology and the Catholic Vision*. Adelaide: ATF Press, 2016.

Kingston, Suzane. "Environmental Policy." In *The Law of the European Union*, edited by Pieter Jan Kuijper et al., 5th ed. 1165–1184. Alphen aan den Rijn, the Netherlands: Wolters Kluwer, 2018.

Kiss, Alexandre and Shelton, Dinah L. *International Environmental Law*, 3rd ed. Ardsley, NY: Transnational Publishers, 2004.

Kiss, Alexandre Charles, and Dinah L. Shelton. *Guide to International Environmental Law*. Leiden: Nijhoff, 2007.

Knox, John H., and Ramin Pejan. "Introduction." In *The Human Right to a Healthy Environment*, edited by John H. Knox and Ramin Pejan, 1–16. Cambridge: Cambridge University Press, 2018.

Köck, Mathilde, et al. *Integrated management of biological and landscape diversity for sustainable regional development and ecological connectivity in the Carpathians*, BioREGIO Carpathians project. Sarajevo: ProPrint, 2014, BioREGIOCarpathians_FINALPublication.compressed.pdf.

Koester, Veit. "Environmental principles and concepts in biodiversity treaties." In *Principles of Environmental Law*, edited by Ludwig Krämer and Emanuela Orlando, 538–554. heltenham: Edward Elgar, 2018).

Kolodezhna, Valeria. "Protecting the environment in times of war: An interview with environmentalist Yehor Hrynyk," *UWEC*, 14 (2023): 33–37, https://uwecworkgroup.info/protecting-the-environment-in-times-of-war-an-interview-with-environmentalist-yehor-hrynyk/.

Kostiushyn, Vasiliy, Serhii Gubar, and Volodymyr Domashlinets, *Strategy for Developing the Monitoring of Biodiversity in Ukraine*. Kyiv: ECNC-European Centre for Nature Conservation, National Ecological Centre of Ukraine, 2009.

Krämer, Ludwig, and Emanuela Orlando, "Introduction to Volume VI." In *Principles of Environmental Law*, edited by Ludwig Krämer and Emanuela Orlando, 1–10. Cheltenham: Edward Elgar Publishing, 2018.

Krebs, Angelika, and Bernard Williams. *Ethics of Nature: A Map*, Perspektiven Der Analytischen Philosophie 22, Berlin: W. de Gruyter, 1999.

Król, Wiesław, et al., eds. *Carpathian List of Endangered Species*. Vienna : Krakow: WWF International Danube-Carpathian Programme; Institute of Nature Conservation, Polish Academy of Sciences, 2003, https://archive.nationalredlist.org/files/2012/08/Carpathian-List-of-Endangered-Species-2003.pdf.

Lewis, Melissa, and Arie Trouwborst, "Bonn Convention on the Conservation of Migratory Species of Wild Animals 1979." In *Multilateral Environmental Treaties*, edited by Malgosia Fitzmaurice, Attila Tanzi, and Angeliki Papantoniou, 25–34.Cheltenham: Edward Elgar Publishing, 2017.

Lier, Markus, et al. "The New EU Forest Strategy for 2030: A New Understanding of Sustainable Forest Management?," *Forests* 13, no. 2 (February 2022): 245, https://doi.org/10.3390/f13020245.

Limon, Marc. "The Politics of Human Rights, the Environment, and Climate Change at the Human Rights Council: Toward a Universal Right to a Healthy Environment?." In *The Human Right to a Healthy Environment*, edited by John H. Knox and Ramin Pejan, 189–214. Cambridge: Cambridge University Press, 2018.

Lovejoy, Thomas E. "Biodiversity: An Inordinate Fondness for Living Things." In *Routledge Handbook of Religion and Ecology*, edited by Willis Jenkins, Mary Evelyn Tucker, and John A. Grim, 249–256. Abingdon New York (N. Y.): Routledge Earthscan from Routledge, 2017.

Maljean-Dubois, Sandrine, and Matthieu Wemaëre. "Biodiversity and Climate Change," In *Biodiversity and Nature Protection Law*, edited by Elisa Morgera and Jona Razzaque, 295–308. Cheltenham: Edward Elgar Publishing, 2017.

Martin, Gilles J. "Principles and Rules." In *Principles of Environmental Law*, edited by Ludwig Krämer and Emanuela Orlando, 13–22. Cheltenham: Edward Elgar Publishing, 2018.

Meinard, Yves, Sylvain Coq, and Bernhard Schmid. "The Vagueness of 'Biodiversity' and Its Implications in Conservation Practice." In *From Assessing to Conserving Biodiversity: Conceptual and Practical Challenges*, edited by Elena Casetta, Jorge Marques da Silva, and Davide Vecchi, 353–374. Cham: Springer International Publishing, 2019.

Michallet, Isabelle. "Equity and the interests of future generations." In *Principles of Environmental Law*, edited by Ludwig Krämer and Emanuela Orlando, 150–160. Cheltenham: Edward Elgar Publishing, 2018.

Millennium Ecosystem Assessment. *Ecosystems and Human Well-being: Biodiversity Synthesis*. Washington, DC: World Resources Institute, 2005, https://www.millenniumassessment.org/documents/document.354.aspx.pdf.

Morgera, Elisa, and Elsa Tsioumani. "Yesterday, Today, and Tomorrow: Looking Afresh at the Convention on Biological Diversity." *Yearbook of International Environmental Law* 21, no. 1 (1 January 2010): 3–40, https://doi.org/10.1093/yiel/yvr003.

Morgera, Elisa. "The Ecosystem Approach and the Precautionary Principle." In *Biodiversity and Nature Protection Law*, edited by Elisa Morgera and Jona Razzaque, 70–80. Cheltenham: Edward Elgar Publishing, 2017.

Norenko, Kateryna, Petro Testov and Oleksiy Vasyliuk. *Forest territories for wild nature: new policy of forest management*. Kyiv: EPL, 2018, http://epl.org.ua/wp-content/uploads/2018/07/Green-paper_forests_ENG_cover.pdf.

Oguamanam, Chidi. "Biodiversity, Biosafety and Bioprospecting." In *Routledge Handbook of International Environmental Law*, edited by Erika J. Techera et al., 2nd ed. 101–115. London: Routledge, Taylor & Francis Group, 2021.

Ollino, Alice. *Due Diligence Obligations in International Law.* Cambridge University Press, 2022, https://doi.org/10.1017/9781009053082.

O'Neill, John. "The Varieties of Intrinsic Value" *The Monist*, 75, Issue 2, (April 1992): 119–137, https://doi.org/10.5840/monist19927527.

Pankiv, Natalia, and Oksana Roik, "Sustainable Development of Tourism in The Carpathian Region." In *Modern Aspects of Science,* 21-th volume of the international collective monograph. Czech Republic: Mezinárodní Ekonomický Institut, 2022, http://perspectives.pp.ua/public/site/mono/monography-21.pdf.

Peel, Jacqueline. "Precaution." In *The Oxford Handbook of International Environmental Law*, edited by Lavanya Rajamani and Jacqueline Peel, 2nd ed. 302–318. Oxford: Oxford University Press, 2021.

Potthast, Thomas, und Margarita Berg. „Biodiversität." In *Handbuch Umweltethik*, edited by Konrad Ott, Jan Dierks, and Lieske Voget-Kleschin, 240–246. Stuttgart: J.B. Metzler Verlag, 2016).

Pounds, J. Alan, Michael P. L. Fogden, and John H. Campbell. "Biological Response to Climate Change on a Tropical Mountain," *Nature* 398, no. 6728 (April 1999): 611–615, https://doi.org/10.1038/19297.

Rayfuse, Rosemary. "Biological Resources." In *The Oxford Handbook of International Environmental Law*, edited by Daniel Bodansky, Jutta Brunnée, and Ellen Hey, 1st ed. 362–393. Oxford: Oxford University Press, 2012.

Rosenberger, Michael. *Christian Ethics of Creation*, Baden-Baden: Nomos, 2022.

Sabatini, Francesco M., et al. "Protection Gaps and Restoration Opportunities for Primary Forests in Europe," *Diversity and Distributions* 26, no. 12 (December 2020): 1646–1662, https://doi.org/10.1111/ddi.13158.

Sandifer, Paul A., Ariana E. Sutton-Grier, and Bethney P. Ward. "Exploring Connections among Nature, Biodiversity, Ecosystem Services, and Human Health and Well-Being: Opportunities to Enhance Health and Biodiversity Conservation," *Ecosystem Services* 12 (April 2015): 1–15, https://doi.org/10.1016/j.ecoser.2014.12.007.

Sands, Philippe, Jacqueline Peel, Adriana Fabra, and Ruth MacKenzie, *Principles of International Environmental Law*, 4th ed. Cambridge: Cambridge University Press, 2018.

Sarkar, Sahotra. "What Should 'Biodiversity' Be?" In *From Assessing to Conserving Biodiversity: Conceptual and Practical Challenges*, edited by Elena Casetta, Jorge Marques da Silva, and Davide Vecchi, 375 – 399. Cham: Springer International Publishing, 2019.

Sarkar, Sahotra. *Biodiversity and Environmental Philosophy: An Introduction.* Cambridge, UK: Cambridge University Press, 2005.

Savaresi, Annalisa. "Forest Biodiversity." In *Biodiversity and Nature Protection Law*, edited by Elisa Morgera and Jona Razzaque, 203–214. Cheltenham: Edward Elgar Publishing, 2017.

Schaefer, Jame, and Tobias Winright, ed. *Environmental Justice and Climate Change: Assessing Pope Benedict XVI's Ecological Vision for the Catholic Church in the United States*, Lanham, MD: Lexington Books, 2013.

Schlingemann, Lynn, et al., ed, *Combating Wildlife and Forest Crime in the Danube-Carpathian Region*. UN Environment – Eurac Research – WWF, 2017, https://wwfint.awsassets.panda.org/downloads/combating_wildlife_and_forest_crime_in_the_danube_carpathian_region_report_2017_1.pdf.

Schrader-Frechette, Kristin. "Environmental Ethics." In *The Oxford Handbook of Practical Ethics*, ed. Hugh LaFollette, 188–215. Oxford: Oxford University Press, 2003.

Scotford, Eloise. *Environmental Principles and the Evolution of Environmental Law*. London, Oxford: Bloomsbury Publishing Hart Publishing, 2017.

Shelton, Dinah. "Nature in the Bible," *Man and the Environment: Essays In Honor of Alexandre Kiss,* (Frison-Roche, 1998): 63–79, https://ssrn.com/abstract=1028357.

Shine, Clare, Nattley Williams, and Lothar Gündling. *A Guide to Designing Legal and Institutional Frameworks on Alien Invasive Species*. IUCN Environmental Policy and Law Paper 40, Gland and Cambridge: IUCN, 2000.

Smaliychuk, Anatoliy, and Uli Grabener, eds, *Natural forests of Ukrainian Carpathians*. Lviv: Carty i Atlasy, 2018.

Spracklen, Benedict D., and Dominick V. Spracklen. "Identifying European Old-Growth Forests Using Remote Sensing: A Study in the Ukrainian Carpathians." *Forests* 10, no. 2 (5 February 2019): 127, https://doi.org/10.3390/f10020127.

Stone, Christopher D. "Do Morals Matter? The Influence of Ethics on Courts and Congress in Shaping U.S. Environmental Policies," *U.C. Davis Law Review* 37 (1) (November 2003)): 13–51, https://environs.law.ucdavis.edu/sites/g/files/dgvnsk15356/files/media/documents/ENV-27-1-stone.pdf.

Stone, Christopher D. "Ethics and International Environmental Law." In *The Oxford Handbook of International Environmental Law*, edited by Daniel Bodansky, Jutta Brunnée, and Ellen Hey, 1st ed. 291–312. Oxford: Oxford University Press, 2012.

Subbotina, Natalia. "The Perspective of SDGs and CST on Biodiversity in the Context of the Protection of Forest Ecosystems in the Ukrainian Carpathians." *Analecta of the UCU: Theology* 9 (2022): 183–199, doi: 10.47632/2075-4817-2022-9-183-199.

Subbotina, Natalia. "Ukraine's Implementation of the Key Obligations Under the Convention on Biological Diversity: Challenges and Prospects for the Forest Ecosystems." *Journal of the Ukrainian Free University: Academia Iuniora*, 3 (2023).

Sushyk, Olha. "Legal Framework of Wildlife Protection on the Area of Natura 2000 (Emerald Network) on Wind Energy Site: Case of Ukraine." *Studia Iuridica Lublinensia* 30, no. 3 (16 September 2021): 207–225, https://doi.org/10.17951/sil.2021.30.3.207-225.

Tanaka, Yoshifumi. *The International Law of the Sea*, 2nd ed. Cambridge: Cambridge University Press, 2015.

Taylor, Prue. "Common heritage of mankind and common concern of humankind." In *Principles of Environmental Law*, edited by Ludwig Krämer and Emanuela Orlando, 303–322. Cheltenham: Edward Elgar Publishing, 2018.

Techera, Erika J. "Species-based conservation." In *Biodiversity and Nature Protection Law*, edited by Elisa Morgera and Jona Razzaque, 97–109. Cheltenham: Edward Elgar Publishing, 2017.

Toepfer, Georg. "On the Impossibility and Dispensability of Defining 'Biodiversity'." In *From Assessing to Conserving Biodiversity: Conceptual and Practical Challenges*, edited by Elena Casetta, Jorge Marques da Silva, and Davide Vecchi, 341–351. Cham: Springer International Publishing, 2019.

Trouwborst, Arie and Jens-Christian Svenning. "Megafauna Restoration as a Legal Obligation: International Biodiversity Law and the Rehabilitation of Large Mammals in Europe" *Review of European, Comparative & International Environmental Law 31*, no. 2 (July 2022): 182–198, https://doi.org/10.1111/reel.12443.

Trouwborst, Arie. *Restoring what is broken: Wildlife law in an era of ecological emergency, eye-opening science, and maturing morality*. Inaugural address.Tilburg University, 2024.

Trouwborst, Arie. "Conserving European Biodiversity in a Changing Climate: The Bern Convention, the European Union Birds and Habitats Directives and the Adaptation of Nature to Climate Change." *Review of European Community & International Environmental Law* 20, no. 1 (April 2011): 62–77, https://doi.org/10.1111/j.1467-9388.2011.00700.x.

Trouwborst, Arie. "Megafauna Restoration as an Obligation – the Role of Law in Rehabilitating Europe's Large Mammals." Rewilding symposium: people, policies, practice, video from 62:30, Wageningen University and Research Public Library, 29 September 2022, https://wur.yuja.com/V/Watch?v=260217&node=1323158&a=2135271602.

Trouwborst, Arie. "Transboundary Wildlife Conservation in A Changing Climate: Adaptation of the Bonn Convention on Migratory Species and Its Daughter Instruments to Climate Change." *Diversity* 4, no. 3 (25 June 2012): 258–300, https://doi.org/10.3390/d4030258.

Verschuuren, Jonathan. "Sustainable Development and the Nature of Environmental Legal Principles." *Potchefstroom Electronic Law Journal*, 9, no. 1 (2006): 1–57, https://ssrn.com/abstract=899537.

Vogt, Markus. *Christliche Umweltethik: Grundlagen und zentrale Herausforderungen*. Freiburg: Herder, 2022.

Welsch, Wolfgang. *Homo mundanus: jenseits der anthropischen Denkform der Moderne*. Weilerswist: Velbrück Wissenschaft, 2012.

Wiener, Jonathan B. "Precautionary Principle." In *Principles of Environmental Law*, edited by Ludwig Krämer and Emanuela Orlando, 174–185. Cheltenham: Edward Elgar Publishing, 2018.

Wiersema, Annecoos. "Wildlife." In *The Oxford Handbook of International Environmental Law*, edited by Lavanya Rajamani and Jacqueline Peel, 2nd ed. 554–573. Oxford: Oxford University Press, 2021.

Willmore, Christine. "Sovereignty, conservation and sustainable use." In *Biodiversity and Nature Protection Law*, edited by Elisa Morgera and Jona Razzaque, 31–43. Cheltenham: Edward Elgar Publishing, 2017.

Wolfslehner, Bernhard, and Stefanie Linser. *European Forest Indicators at a Glance*. Forest Europe Background Paper and Contribution to the European Forest Alliance (EFA), (November 2023), https://foresteurope.org/wp-content/uploads/2024/03/European-forest-biodiversity-indicators-at-a-glance.pdf.

Yamin, Farhana. "Biodiversity, Ethics and International Law." *International Affairs (Royal Institute of International Affairs 1944-)* 71, no. 3 (July 1995): 529–546, https://doi.org/10.2307/2624839.

Yzquierdo, Marine. "The 1992 Convention on Biological Diversity." In *Multilateral Environmental Treaties*, edited by Malgosia Fitzmaurice, Attila Tanzi, and Angeliki Papantoniou, 9–24. Cheltenham: Edward Elgar Publishing, 2017.

Scientific, analytical, and statistical information published on the Internet

"About Species+." Species+. Accessed September 20, 2024. https://speciesplus.net/about.

"About Us." Ukrainian State Project Forest Management Production Association. Accessed September 20, 2024. https://lisproekt.gov.ua/objednannja; [In Ukrainian: "Про нас." Українське державне проектне лісовпорядне виробниче об'єднання].

"Ancient and Primeval Beech Forests of the Carpathians and Other Regions of Europe." UNESCO. Accessed September 20, 2024. https://whc.unesco.org/en/list/1133/.

"Ancient and Primeval Beech Forests of the Carpathians and Other Regions of Europe." UNESCO. Accessed September 24, 2024. https://whc.unesco.org/en/list/1133/.

"Background." Convention on Biological Diversity. October 13, 2023. https://www.cbd.int/reports/national.shtml.

"Barometer statistics per country: Ukraine." Emerald Barometer Dashboard. Accessed September 20, 2024. https://tableau-public.discomap.eea.europa.eu/views/EmeraldBarometerdashboard/Barometerstatisticspercountry?%3AshowAppBanner=false&%3Adisplay_count=n&%3AshowVizHome=n&%3Aorigin=viz_share_link&%3AisGuestRedirectFromVizportal=y&%3Aembed=y.

"Biodiversity Monitoring." Nationalparkvervaltung Berchtesgaden. Accessed November 11, 2024. https://www.nationalpark-berchtesgaden.de/english/research/monitoring/biodiversity/index.htm.

"Biodiversity." Carpathian Convention. Accessed September 20, 2024. http://www.carpathianconvention.org/topics/biodiversity/.

"Biodiversity." OECD. Accessed November 11, 2024. https://www.oecd.org/en/topics/biodiversity.html.

"Biosphere reserves – Ukraine." UNESCO. Accessed September 20, 2024. https://www.unesco.org/en/mab/map?f%5B0%5D=countries%3A501c7f7d-f0c7-5ac3-a3e8-86ec665c6528&f%5B1%5D=dataset_filters%3A6c254c17-2986-4f89-aa10-17d38a33454c&f%5B2%5D=regions%3A53da4dd6-bdd0-433d-bbb3-476f12b4cc32&hub=66369#toggle-facets.

"Biosphere Reserves." UNESCO. Accessed September 20, 2024. https://www.unesco.org/en/mab/map?hub=66369.

"Carpathian Biodiversity Framework." CBD. October 14, 2023. https://www.cbd.int/article/carpathian-biodiversity-framework.

"Carpathian Biosphere Reserve." Bern Convention. Accessed September 20, 2024. https://www.coe.int/en/web/bern-convention/-/carpathian-biosphere-reserve.

"Carpathian Biosphere Reserve." Bern Convention. Accessed September 20, 2024. https://www.coe.int/en/web/bern-convention/-/carpathian-biosphere-reserve.

"Carpathian," UNESCO. Accessed September 20, 2024, https://www.unesco.org/en/mab/carpathian?hub=66369.

"Centralparks: Draft Carpathian Strategy for Enhancing Biodiversity and Landscape Conservation Outside and Inside Protected Areas." Centralparks (2021). http://www.carpathianconvention.org/tl_files/carpathiancon/Downloads/03%20Meetings%20and%20Events/Implementation%20Committee/CCIC2021/1510C1FCentralparks%20WPT1%20draft%20Biodiversity%20strategy_factsheet.pdf.

"Checklist of CITES Species: Ukraine." CITES. Accessed September 20, 2024. https://checklist.cites.org/#/en/search/country_ids%5B%5D=211&cites_appendices%5B%5D=I&cites_appendices%5B%5D=II&cites_appendices%5B%5D=III&output_layout=alphabetical&level_of_listing=0&show_synonyms=1&show_author=1&show_english=1&show_spanish=1&show_french=1&scientific_name=&page=1&per_page=20.

"Climate Change." CBD. Accessed November 11, 2024. https://www.cbd.int/forest/CC.shtml.

"Common Declaration on Environmental Ethics." Common Declaration of John Paul II and the Ecumenical Patriarch His Holiness Bartholomew I. June 10, 2002. https://www.vatican.va/content/john-paul-ii/en/speeches/2002/june/documents/hf_jp-ii_spe_20020610_venice-declaration.html.

"Conservation and Restoration of the European Bison." Department of Ecology and Natural Resources of the Lviv Regional State Administration. February 25, 2020, https://deplv.gov.ua/2020/02/25/zberezhennya-ta-vidnovlennya-populyacziyi/; [In Ukrainian: "Збереження та відновлення популяції зубра європейського." Департамент екології та природних ресурсів Львівської обласної державної адміністрації].

"Conservation of Biological Diversity." Western Interregional Administration of Forestry and Hunting Economy Hunting Management. Accessed September 20, 2024, https://w.forest.gov.ua/activities_recreation; [In Ukrainian: "Збереження біологічного різноманіття." Західне міжрегіональне управління лісового та мисливського господарства].

"Convention on Biological Diversity: Status." United Nations, https://treaties.un.org/pages/ViewDetails.aspx?src=TREATY&mtdsg_no=XXVII-8&chapter=27#1.

"COP Decisions." Carpathian Convention. Accessed September 20, 2024. http://www.carpathianconvention.org/cop/.

"COP15: Final Text of Kunming-Montreal Global Biodiversity Framework." Convention on Biological Diversity. December 27, 2022. https://www.cbd.int/article/cop15-final-text-kunming-montreal-gbf-221222.

"Countering Illegal Logging." WWF-Ukraine. Accessed September 20, 2024. https://wwf.ua/our-work/forest/fight-illegal-logging/#stages-t2-l1; [In Ukrainian: "Протидія нелегальним рубкам"].

"Department of Nature Reserve Fund and Biodiversity." Ministry of Environmental Protection of Ukraine. Accessed September 20, 2024. https://mepr.gov.ua/pro-nas/struktura/departament-pryrodno-zapovidnogo-fondu-ta-bioriznomanittya/; [In Ukrainian: "Департамент природно-заповідного фонду та біорізноманіття." Міністерство захисту довкілля та природних ресурсів України].

"Designation and Review Process." UNESCO. Accessed September 20, 2024. https://www.unesco.org/en/mab/wnbr/designation.

"East Carpathians." UNESCO. Accessed September 20, 2024. https://www.unesco.org/en/mab/east-carpathians-0?hub=66369;

"Ecological Connectivity." CMS. Accessed November 11, 2024. https://www.cms.int/en/topics/ecological-connectivity.

"Ecosystem Approach." CBD. Accessed November 11, 2024. https://www.cbd.int/forest/ecosystem.shtml.

"EcoSystem." Ministry of Environmental Protection of Ukraine. https://eco.gov.ua/; [In Ukrainian: "ЕкоСистема"].

"Emerald Network." UNCG. Accessed September 20, 2024. https://uncg.org.ua/emerald/ [In Ukrainian: "Мережа Емеральд"].

"Environment Action Programme to 2030." European Commission. Accessed September 20, 2024. https://environment.ec.europa.eu/strategy/environment-action-programme-2030_en.

"Environment." Mission of Ukraine to the European Union. April 15, 2021. https://ukraine-eu.mfa.gov.ua/en/2633-relations/galuzeve-spivrobitnictvo/ohorona-dovkillya.

"Environmental Implementation Review." European Commission. Accessed September 20, 2024. https://environment.ec.europa.eu/law-and-governance/environmental-implementation-review_en.

"Environmental Protection." Government Portal. Accessed September 20, 2024. https://www.kmu.gov.ua/en/yevropejska-integraciya/coordination/environmental-protection.

"Environmental Rule of Law." United Nations Environment Programme. Accessed November 11, 2024. https://www.unep.org/explore-topics/environmental-rights-and-governance/what-we-do/promoting-environmental-rule-law-0.

"Environmental Rule of Law: First Global Report." United Nations Environment Programme. July 6, 2019. https://www.unep.org/resources/assessment/environmental-rule-law-first-global-report#:~:text=The%20UN%20Environment%20report%20found,widespread%20species%20and%20habitat%20loss.

"Environmental Rule of Law: Tracking Progress and Charting Future Directions." United Nations Environment Programme. November 22, 2023. https://www.unep.org/resources/publication/environmental-rule-law-tracking-progress-and-charting-future-directions.

"EUDR Forum in Ukraine: Results and Prospects." Forest Stewardship Council (FSC). March 27, 2024. https://www.ua.fsc.org/ua-en/newsfeed/eudr-forum-in-ukraine-results-and-prospects.

"Explanation for the Public." Ministry of Environmental Protection of Ukraine. Accessed September 20, 2024. https://mepr.gov.ua/diyalnist/otsinka-vplyvu-na-dovkillya/roz-yasnennya-predstavnykam-gromadskosti/ [In Ukrainian: "Роз'яснення представникам громадськості"].

"Explanation Regarding the "Quiet Season" During Martial Law." State Forest Resources Agency of Ukraine. April 4, 2022. https://forest.gov.ua/news/rozyasnennya-shchodo-sezonu-tishi-u-period-voyennogo-stanu [In Ukrainian: "Роз'яснення щодо "сезону тиші" під час дії воєнного стану." Державне агентство лісових ресурсів України].

"Fighting deforestation and forest degradation." European Union. Accessed December 31, 2024. https://eur-lex.europa.eu/legal-content/EN/LSU/?uri=CELEX:32023R1115#:~:text=The%20regulation%20sets%20out%20binding%20rules%20for%20European,to%20greenhouse%20gas%20emissions%20and%20global%20biodiversity%20loss.

"Forestry Reform: What Does the Creation of a Single SE "Forests of Ukraine" Provide for?" State Forest Resources Agency of Ukraine. September 7, 2022. https://forest.gov.ua/en/news/reforma-lisovoho-hospodarstva-shcho-peredbachaie-stvorennia-iedynoho-dp-lisy-ukrainy.

"Forests." WWF-Ukraine. Accessed September 20, 2024. https://wwf.ua/our-work/forest/; [In Ukrainian: "Ліси"].

"Framework Convention." Carpathian Convention. Accessed September 20, 2024. http://www.carpathianconvention.org/convention/framework-convention/.

"Gap Analysis: Ukraine." EU Forest Crime Initiative. Brussels: WWF, August 2020. https://wwfeu.awsassets.panda.org/downloads/_____1_1_1_1_1.pdf?2432466/forest-crime-analysis-ua; [In Ukrainian: "Аналіз прогалин: Україна," Ініціатива ЄС щодо лісової злочинності].

"Geographical Location." Carpathian Heritage. Accessed September 20, 2024. http://carpathian-heritage.org.ua/ua/geograph; [In Ukrainian: "Географічне розташування." Карпатська спадщина].

"Global Partnership on Ecological Connectivity (GPEC)." CMS. Accessed November 11, 2024. https://www.cms.int/en/page/global-partnership-ecological-connectivity-gpec.

"Good Practices in the Carpathian Countries." Secretariat of the Carpathian Convention. Accessed November 11, 2024. http://www.carpathianconvention.org/mountain-biodiversity/.

"High-Level Roundtable: Strengthening Action for Change: Synergistic Solutions to the Climate Crisis, Nature Loss, Desertification, and Pollution." IISD. October 28, 2024. https://enb.iisd.org/strengthening-action-change-synergistic-solutions?utm_medium=email&utm_campaign=ENB%20Update%20-%2031%20October%202024&utm_content=ENB%20Update%20-%2031%20October%202024+CID_35d33d96f3210bf077aded2aa5f841d2&utm_source=cm&utm_term=Strengthening%20Action.

"History of the Convention." Carpathian Convention. Accessed September 20, 2024. http://www.carpathianconvention.org/convention/history/.

"Hurry up to Save the Lynx." WWF-Ukraine. Accessed September 20, 2024. https://specials.wwf.ua/lynx?fbclid=IwZXh0bgNhZW0CMTAAAR2GCSDA0ss5fmDsFy6b4vMRpnl7_NUv7GGHSrp4Lv8Vr6tmixTXxiTvyGA_aem_AaqTGGx0LF6CnkpKfMmjK08Ej0mjeq-GQrgNPpAxuade8wc-Lhn48-_EBExBGEbR3MZRKTO99sQvWqatxrphCuiR; [In Ukrainian: "Не барись врятувати рись"].

"Illegal Sanitary Logging in the Carpathians! Now – Vyhodsky Forest Enterprise." UNCG. December 7, 2020. https://uncg.org.ua/vyhodskyj-lishosp/; [In Ukrainian: "Незаконні санітарні рубки у Карпатах! Тепер – Вигодський лісгосп"].

"Inputs to the Process of Revising and Updating the CBD Strategic Plan 2002–2010." Convention on Biological Diversity. March 29, 2017. https://www.cbd.int/sp/inputs/.

"Institutions of the Bern Convention." Bern Convention. Accessed September 20, 2024. https://www.coe.int/en/web/bern-convention/institutions.

"International Partnership for Sustainable Development in Mountain Regions (Mountain Partnership)." United Nations Department of Economic and Social Affairs. Accessed November 11, 2024. https://sdgs.un.org/partnerships/international-partnership-sustainable-development-mountain-regions-mountain.

"Invasive Alien Species." CBD. Accessed November 11, 2024. https://www.cbd.int/invasive.

"IUCN at UN Biodiversity Conference CBD COP16." IUCN. October 21, 2024. https://iucn.org/cbdcop16.

"IUCN Category II – National Park." UNEP WCMC. Last updated December 24, 2020. https://tinyurl.com/4cswa7dz.

"Joint Liaison Group." CBD. November 13, 2017. https://www.cbd.int/cooperation/liaison.shtml.

"Judicial Protection of the Svydovets Particularly Valuable Massif." EPL. February 24, 2024. https://epl.org.ua/announces/sudovyj-zahyst-osoblyvo-tsinnogo-masyvu-svydovets/. [In Ukrainian: "Судовий захист особливо цінного масиву Свидовець"].

"LECA." Interreg Central Europe. Accessed November 11, 2024. https://www.interreg-central.eu/projects/leca/#.

"Liaison Group of Biodiversity-related Conventions." CBD. January 20, 2022. https://www.cbd.int/blg/.

"Maintenance of the State Cadastre of Plant World of Ukraine." Ministry of Environmental Protection of Ukraine. Accessed September 20, 2024. https://mepr.gov.ua/diyalnist/napryamky/bioriznomanittya/chervona-knyga-ukrayiny/vedennya-derzhavnogo-kadastru-roslynnogo-svitu-ukrayiny/; [In Ukrainian: "Ведення Державного кадастру рослинного світу України"].

"Management of Protected Areas." Ministry of Environmental Protection of Ukraine. Accessed September 20, 2024. https://mepr.gov.ua/diyalnist/reformy/upravlinnya-pryrodoohoronnymy-terytoriyamy/; [In Ukrainian: "Управління природоохоронними територіями," Міністерство захисту довкілля та природних ресурсів України].

"Management." Nationalparkvervaltung Berchtesgaden. Accessed November 11, 2024. https://www.nationalpark-berchtesgaden.de/english/nature/national_park/management/index.htm.

"Monitoring set up under the Bern Convention." Bern Convention. Accessed September 20, 2024. https://www.coe.int/en/web/bern-convention/monitoring.

"National Reports on the State of the Environment in Ukraine." Ministry of Environmental Protection of Ukraine. https://mepr.gov.ua/diyalnist/napryamky/ekologichnyj-monitoryng/natsionalni-dopovidi-pro-stan-navkolyshnogo-pryrodnogo-seredovyshha-v-ukrayini/; [In Ukrainian: "Національні доповіді про стан навколишнього природного середовища в Україні"].

"National Reports." Convention on Biological Diversity. Accessed September 20, 2024. https://www.cbd.int/reports.

"Natura 2000: The Largest Network of Protected Areas in the World." European Commission. Accessed September 20, 2024. https://environment.ec.europa.eu/topics/nature-and-biodiversity/natura-2000_en.

"Nomination file 1133: Executive Summary." Ukraine, Slovak Republik (2007). https://whc.unesco.org/uploads/nominations/1133.pdf.

"Open Data." Ministry of Environmental Protection of Ukraine. Accessed September 20, 2024. https://mepr.gov.ua/diyalnist/vidkryti-dani/ [In Ukrainian: "Відкриті дані," Міністерство захисту довкілля та природних ресурсів України].

"Ostap Semerak: The Association Agreement requires the Swift Implementation of the Birds and Habitats Directives in Ukraine." Government Portal. March 13, 2018. https://www.kmu.gov.ua/news/ostap-semerak-ugoda-pro-asociaciyu-vimagaye-yaknajshvidshogo-vprovadzhennya-v-ukrayini-ptashinoyi-ta-oselishnoyi-direktivi; [In Ukrainian: "Остап Семерак: Угода про асоціацію вимагає якнайшвидшого впровадження в Україні Пташиної та Оселищної директиви." Урядовий портал].

"Over 200 Hectares of Forests in the "Arshytsia" Mountain Range are to Be Granted Protected Status at the National Level." WWF. March 28, 2024. https://www.wwf.mg/?13339891/More-than-200-hectares-of-forests-in-the-Arshytsia-mountain-range-are-to-be-granted-protected-status-at-the-national-level; [In Ukrainian: "Понад 200 га лісів гірського масиву "Аршиця" мають отримати охоронний статус на загальнодержавному рівні"].

"Preparations for the Post-2020 Biodiversity Framework." Convention on Biological Diversity. Accessed September 20, 2024. https://www.cbd.int/conferences/post2020.

"Preservation of Primeval Forests." WWF-Ukraine. Accessed September 20, 2024. https://wwf.ua/our-work/forest/unique-forests/; [In Ukrainian: "Збереження пралісів"].

"Preservation of Primeval Forests." WWF-Ukraine. Accessed September 20, 2024. https://wwf.ua/our-work/forest/unique-forests/.

"Preventing, Halting and Reversing Loss of Nature." United Nations Decade on Ecosystem Restoration 2021 – 2030. Accessed November 11, 2024. https://www.decadeonrestoration.org/.

"Programmatic Links." CBD. Accessed November 11, 2024. https://www.cbd.int/forest/plinks.shtml.

"Programme of Work on Mountain Biological Diversity." CBD. September 4, 2007. https://www.cbd.int/mountain/pow.shtml.

"Protected Areas – an Overview." CBD. Accessed November 11, 2024. https://www.cbd.int/protected/overview.

"Protected Areas in the Carpathians." Carpathian Integrated Biodiversity Information System. Accessed November 11, 2024. https://ccibis.org/protected-areas-in-the-carpathians/.

"Rare Species." WWF-Ukraine. Accessed September 20, 2024. https://wwf.ua/our-work/wildlife/; [In Ukrainian: "Рідкісні види"].

"Red Data Book of Ukraine." Diia. Accessed September 20, 2024. https://data.gov.ua/dataset/b5cdb316-6074-4ef3-a0c5-463ff3a72e68; [In Ukrainian: "Червона книга України," Дія].

"Reference documents." Bern Convention. Accessed September 20, 2024. https://www.coe.int/en/web/bern-convention/documents1.

"Regulation on Deforestation-free Products." European Commission. Accessed September 20, 2024. https://environment.ec.europa.eu/topics/forests/deforestation/regulation-deforestation-free-products_en.

"Religiosity, Trust in the Church, Confessional Affiliation and Inter-Church Relations in Ukrainian Society (November, 2023)." Razumkov Centre. December 28, 2023. https://razumkov.org.ua/en/research-areas/surveys/religiosity-trust-in-the-church-confessional-affiliation-and-inter-church-relations-in-ukrainian-society-november-2023.

"SaveGREEN: Safeguarding the Functionality of Transnationally Important Ecological Corridors in the Danube Basin." Interreg Danube Transnational Programme. Accessed November 11, 2024. https://dtp.interreg-danube.eu/approved-projects/savegreen.

"Selected PAs Have the Necessary Planning Documents for their Development." Support to Nature Protected Areas in Ukraine. Accessed September 20, 2024. https://snpa.in.ua/en/english-diyalnist-proektu/diyalnist-proektu-1/.

"Special Rapporteur on the Human Right to a Clean, Healthy and Sustainable Environment." OHCHR. Accessed November 11, 2024. https://www.ohchr.org/en/special-procedures/sr-environment.

"State Cadastre of Animal World." Diia. Accessed September 20, 2024. https://data.gov.ua/dataset/mepr_04; [In Ukrainian: "Державний кадастр тваринного світу," Дія].

"State Cadastre of Territories and Objects of the Nature Reserve Fund of Ukraine. Boundaries of the territories and objects of the Nature Reserve Fund of Ukraine (Dataset for 2023)." Diia. Accessed September 20, 2024. https://data.gov.ua/dataset/mepr_05; [In Ukrainian: "Державний кадастр територій та об'єктів природно-заповідного фонду. Межі територій та об'єктів природно-заповідного фонду України (Набір даних за 2023-й рік)." Дія].

"Support for Protected Areas in the Carpathians." Frankfurt Zoological Society. Accessed September 20, 2024. https://fzs.org/en/support/support-for-protected-areas-in-the-carpathians/.

"Sustainable Forest Management." Carpathian Convention. Accessed November 11, 2024. http://www.carpathianconvention.org/topics/sustainable-forest-management-2/.

"Sustainable Forest Management." Ministry of Environmental Protection of Ukraine. Accessed September 20, 2024. https://mepr.gov.ua/diyalnist/reformy/stale-vedenny a-lisovogo-gospodarstva/; [In Ukrainian: "Стале ведення лісового господарства." Міністерство захисту довкілля та природних ресурсів України].

"Sustainable Use of Biodiversity." CBD. Accessed November 11, 2024. https://www.cbd.i nt/sustainable.

"Svydovets 2023: Fighting for Wildlife Amid the War." Free Svydovets Initiative Group, 2023. https://freesvydovets.org/wp-content/uploads/2023/02/svydovets2023_en_co mpressed.pdf.

"Svydovets." Initiative group "Free Svydovets". Accessed November 11, 2024. https://free svydovets.org/en/.

"The Birds Directive." European Commission. Accessed September 20, 2024. https://en vironment.ec.europa.eu/topics/nature-and-biodiversity/birds-directive_en.

"The Cabinet of Ministers Believes that Biological Research in the Forest is not Necessary!" UNCG. February 2, 2023. https://uncg.org.ua/biolohichni-doslidzhenn ia-v-lisi/ [In Ukrainian: "Кабмін вважає, що біологічні дослідження в лісі не потрібні!"].

"The Carpathian Convention Implementation Committee." Carpathian Convention. Accessed September 20, 2024. http://www.carpathianconvention.org/organization/o rganizational-structure/.

"The Cassation Administrative Court Has Once Again Postponed the Hearing of the Case Concerning the Svydovets Resort." EPL. August 15, 2024. https://epl.org.ua/an nounces/kasatsijnyj-administratyvnyj-sud-znovu-vidklav-rozglyad-spravy-po-kur ortu-svydovets/ [In Ukrainian "Касаційний адміністративний суд знову відклав розгляд справи по курорту Свидовець"].

"The European Green Deal Sets Out How to Make Europe the First Climate-Neutral Continent by 2050, Boosting the Economy, Improving People's Health and Quality of Life, Caring for Nature, and Leaving No One Behind." European Commission. December 11, 2019. https://ec.europa.eu/commission/presscorner/detail/en/ip_19_6 691.

"The Great Carpathian Land Grab: How oligarchs are using Ukraine's war economy to get hold of one of Europe's last great wilderness areas." Bruno Manser Fonds, European Cooperative Longo Maï and the Free Svydovets Group. April 2024. https:/ /freesvydovets.org/wp-content/uploads/2024/04/Great_Carpathian_Land_Grab_E ng_web-1.pdf.

"The Habitats Directive." European Commission. Accessed September 20, 2024. https:/ /environment.ec.europa.eu/topics/nature-and-biodiversity/habitats-directive_en.

"The Ministry of Environmental Protection is Launching a Test Version of the Unified Register of Strategic Environmental Assessments," The Ministry of Environmental Protection of Ukraine, May 23, 2023, https://mepr.gov.ua/mindovkillya-zapuskaye -testuvannya-novoyi-poslugy-strategichnu-ekologichnu-otsinku-mozhna-zamovyt y-na-ekosystemi/ [In Ukrainian: "Міндовкілля запускає тестову версію Єдиного реєстру стратегічної екологічної оцінки," Міністерство захисту довкілля та природних ресурсів України].

"The National Nature Park "Boykivshchyna"." Boykivshchyna National Nature Park. Accessed September 20, 2024. https://boikivshchyna-park.in.ua/; [In Ukrainian: Національний природний парк «Бойківщина»].

"The Presidency of the Carpathian Convention." Carpathian Convention. Accessed September 20, 2024. http://www.carpathianconvention.org/organization/organizational-structure/.

"The Progress in Creation of the Emerald Network in Ukraine: Policy Brief." EPL. October 18, 2023. https://epl.org.ua/eco-analytics/stan-stvorennya-smaragdovoyi-merezhi-v-ukrayini/#.

"The Project is on Pause but is Helping Parks." Support to Nature Protected Areas in Ukraine. Accessed November 11, 2024. https://snpa.in.ua/en/english-diyalnist-proektu/diyalnist-proektu-1/.

"'There is no Kolomoyskyi in Bukovel at all'. Who currently owns the most famous Ukrainian resort." *NV*. June 27, 2023, https://biz.nv.ua/ukr/markets/bukovel-komu-naspravdi-nalezhit-nayvidomishiy-kurort-ukrajini-rozsliduvannya-nv-50334936.html; [In Ukrainian: "«У Буковелі Коломойського немає взагалі». Кому зараз належить найвідоміший український курорт." *NV*. 27 червня 2023].

"Today, the Supreme Court protected the Picturesque Mountain Ranges From the Mega-Resort Svydovets." October 9, 2024. https://epl.org.ua/announces/sogodni-vs-zahystyv-malovnychi-girski-hrebty-vid-mega-kurortu-svydovets/ [In Ukrainian: "Сьогодні ВС захистив мальовничі гірські хребти від мега-курорту Свидовець"].

"Tracking Economic Instruments and Finance for Biodiversity 2024." OECD. October 18, 2024. https://www.oecd.org/en/data/insights/data-explainers/2024/10/Tracking-Economic-Instruments-and-Finance-for-Biodiversity-2024.html.

"Trees Cannot Scream: How Unsustainability and Illegality are Destroying the Forests of the Ukrainian Carpathians." Free Svydovets Group, Bruno Manser Fonds and European Cooperative Longo Maï. 2021. https://freesvydovets.org/en/.

"Ukraine." The Convention on Wetlands. Accessed November 11, 2024. https://www.ramsar.org/country-profile/ukraine.

"Ukraine." UNEP/EUROBATS. Accessed September 20, 2024. https://www.eurobats.org/about_eurobats/parties_and_range_states/ukraine.

"UN Common Approach to Biodiversity." CEB. Accessed November 11, 2024. https://unsceb.org/un-common-approach-biodiversity.

"We are Being Thanked for the Victory: the Ministry of Environmental Protection's Order on the List of Invasive Tree Species Prohibited for Use Has Been Repealed." Society of Foresters of Ukraine. October 27, 2023. https://tlu.kiev.ua/pro-nas/novini-zakhodi/novina/article/nam-djakujut-za-peremogu-vtrativ-chinnist-nakaz-mindovkillja-pro-perelik-invaziinikh-vidiv-derev-zabo.html [In Ukrainian: "Нам дякують за перемогу: втратив чинність наказ Міндовкілля про перелік інвазійних видів дерев, заборонених до використання." Товариство лісівників України].

"We Support the Ministry of Environmental Protection's Order Approving the List of Invasive Tree Species Prohibited in Forest Reproduction." WWF-Ukraine. July 27, 2023. https://www.wwf.mg/?11403791/pproval-of-a-list-of-invasive-tree-species; [In Ukrainian: "Підтримуємо наказ Міндовкілля про затвердження переліку інвазійних видів дерев, заборонених у відтворенні лісів"].

"What is the Emerald Network and Why is it Important for Ukrainians?" Ecodiya (Ecoaction). June 24, 2022. https://ecoaction.org.ua/emerald-ua.html; [In Ukrainian: "Що таке Смарагдова мережа і чому вона потрібна українцям," Екодія];

"What We Do." Ukrainian Nature Conservation Group (UNCG). Accessed September 20, 2024. https://uncg.org.ua/en/activities/.

"What We Do." WWF-Ukraine. Accessed September 20, 2024. https://wwf.ua/.

"Working Groups." Carpathian Convention. Accessed September 20, 2024. http://www.carpathianconvention.org/organization/working-groups/.

"WWF-Ukraine Does Not Support Draft Law 9516, Which Contradicts Ukraine's European Integration Commitments." WWF-Ukraine. March 13, 2024. https://www.wwf.mg/?13182666/WWF-Ukraine-does-not-support-draft-law-9516-which-contradicts-Ukraines-European-integration-commitments [In Ukrainian: "WWF-Україна не підтримує законопроєкт 9516, який суперечить євроінтеграційним зобов'язанням України"].

Arustamian, Eduard. "Protected Areas System in the Ukrainian Carpathians." *Protected Areas – Cornerstones of Ecological Connectivity in the Carpathians and Beyond International Conference*, Visegrád, Hungary, 28–30 September 2021. https://keep.eu/api/project-attachment/49664/get_file/.

Bolokhovets, Yurii. "Branches of the State Enterprise "Forests of Ukraine" Have Received Nearly 10,000 Electronic Logging Tickets." Facebook. February 15, 2024. https://www.facebook.com/permalink.php?story_fbid=pfbid02Bpd6gMRB3r3BpcoCRbwn1rffPuq4j7VYbqWBXjC2ocQWYNcYfP9u9MnwL3M4SjFdl&id=100010028957829; [In Ukrainian: Юрій Болоховець, "Філії ДП "Ліси України" отримали майже 10 тисяч електронних лісорубних квитків"].

Bolokhovets, Yurii. "The leadership of the Carpathian Forest Office has changed." Facebook. February 27, 2024. https://www.facebook.com/permalink.php?story_fbid=pfbid02kAdkVnFiaoh9fqcnWjvjsADmu43U3qWs7thjprDw3CpmxCAYPCKKzA4Ec33siY6Ul&id=100010028957829; [In Ukrainian: Юрій Болоховець, "У Карпатський лісовий офіс змінилося керівництво"].

Boreiko, Volodymyr. "'Forest Reform' – A Road to Nowhere." Interfax-Ukraine. August 30, 2023. https://interfax.com.ua/news/blog/931888.html; [In Ukrainian: Володимир Борейко, "'Лісова реформа' – шлях нікуди," Інтерфакс-Україна].

Catechism of the Catholic Church. Vatican City (1997). https://www.vatican.va/archive/ENG0015/_INDEX.HTM.

De Haas, Arend. "Impact of Rewilding on Ecosystem Resilience." Rewilding Academy, accessed November 11, 2024. https://rewilding.academy/impact-of-rewilding-on-ecosystem-resilience/.

Earthsight. *Complicit In Corruption: How billion-dollar firms and EU governments are failing Ukraine's forests*. Report (July 2018). https://fe8a03e2-1131-44e7-a06a-fb468c2a30d4.filesusr.com/ugd/624187_673e3aa69ed84129bdfeb91b6aa9ec17.pdf.

EUROPARC Federation. *The Charter.* European Charter for Sustainable Tourism in Protected Areas. EUROPARC Federation, 2010. https://www.europarc.org/wp-content/uploads/2015/05/2010-European-Charter-for-Sustainable-Tourism-in-Protected-Areas.pdf.

Hordiienko, Yuliia. "The Threat to Ukrainian Forests Amid War: Ukraine Eases Logging Rules in the Carpathians." Misto vechirne. May 22, 2022. https://mistovechirne.in.ua/zagroza-ukrayinskym-lisam-v-umovah-viyny-v-ukrayini-sproshchuyut-pravyla-rubok-v-karpatah; [In Ukrainian: Юлія Гордієнко. "Загроза українським лісам в умовах війни: в Україні спрощують правила рубок в Карпатах." Місто вечірнє].

Informace o Lesích. "Close to Nature Management in Carpathian Forests – as Viewed by Czech Foresters." Video. YouTube. May 26, 2023. https://www.youtube.com/watch?v=U8Y3gS-ZZZI&ab_channel=Informaceoles%C3%ADch.

Kondracki, Jerzy A. "Carpathian Mountains." *Encyclopedia Britannica.* Last updated September 13, 2024. https://www.britannica.com/place/Carpathian-Mountains.

Mayrand, Nick. "Theologians praise suggestion to add 'ecological sins' to Catholic catechism." Crux. November 20, 2019. https://cruxnow.com/church-in-the-usa/2019/11/theologians-praise-suggestion-to-add-ecological-sins-to-catholic-catechism.

Minarchenko, Valentyna. "Maintenance of the State Cadastre of Plant World of Ukraine." Report on Scientific Research Work. Accessed September 20, 2024. https://mepr.gov.ua/wp-content/uploads/2023/05/Cadastr2018.pdf; [In Ukrainian: Валентина Мінарченко. "Ведення Державного кадастру рослинного світу України." Звіт про науково-дослідну роботу].

Nationalparkverwaltung Bayerischer Wald. *Forschung im Nationalpark.* August 2022. https://www.nationalpark-bayerischer-wald.bayern.de/service/downloads/doc/broschuere/forschung_im_nationalpark_2022.pdf.

Pontifical Council for Justice and Peace. *Compendium of the Social Doctrine of the Church.* 2004. https://www.vatican.va/roman_curia/pontifical_councils/justpeace/documents/rc_pc_justpeace_doc_20060526_compendio-dott-soc_en.html.

Protsenko, Leonid. "The current state of the development of the Emerald Network in Ukraine 2009–2015." Presentation. Accessed September 20, 2024. https://wwfeu.awsassets.panda.org/downloads/emerald_network_protsenko.pdf; [In Ukrainian: Проценко, Леонід. "Сучасний стан розбудови Смарагдової мережі в Україні 2009–2015"].

Rozvod, Serhii. "Prospects and Risks of Voluntary Forest Certification in the Context of the Ongoing Reform of Ukraine's Forestry Sector." Presentation for the Ukrainian Forest Platform. February 2023. https://cdn.prod.website-files.com/62b33cda52fedd6ad62d4c22/63f3db3c82cd3bdabbb773a6_Sergey%20%20%20Rozvod.ppt.pdf; [In Ukrainian: Розвод, Сергій. "Перспективи та ризики добровільної лісової сертифікації в умовах сучасного реформування лісової галузі України." Презентація для Української лісової платформи];

Rusyn, Mariana. "In Transcarpathia it has been forbidden to visit forests." July 21, 2023. Suspilne Uzhhorod. https://suspilne.media/534129-na-zakarpatti-zaboronili-vidviduvati-lisi-2/ [In Ukrainian: Русин, Мар'яна. "На Закарпатті заборонили відвідувати ліси." Суспільне Ужгород].

SDG Academy. "How SDG 15 Links With Other SDGs." Video by Jeffrey D. Sachs. August 6, 2019. https://sdgacademylibrary.mediaspace.kaltura.com/media/How+SDG+15+Links+With+Other+SDGs/1_j0kpb2iw.

Synod of Bishops for the Pan-Amazon Region. *The Amazon: New Paths for the Church and for an Integral Ecology*. Final document. October 26, 2019. http://secretariat.synod.va/content/sinodoamazonico/en/documents/final-document-of-the-amazon-synod.html.

Ukraine Biodiversity Analysis (Assessment) Team. *Ukraine Biodiversity Analysis*. prepared by ECODIT for USAID/Ukraine. June, 2017. https://www.brucebyersconsulting.com/wp-content/uploads/2017/07/Ukraine-Biodiversity-Analysis-Report-Final-as-Posted-on-DEC.pdf.

ANNEXES

Annex A. List of typical questions for a semi-structured interview

Part 1: Interviews in Ukraine

Local Residents

1. What ethical stance do local residents take, do they belong to Christian communities, how important is religion in their behavior, do they share the ideas of the social teaching of the Catholic Church or Orthodox teaching regarding environmental protection and biodiversity in particular.
2. Is the local Christian community involved in any form of biodiversity conservation? If their churches articulated these ideas better, would their attitudes and way of life change?
3. How do local residents use the forest and how do they perceive it (only as a resource, as a valuable ecosystem that needs to be preserved for future generations, etc.)
4. What do local residents do, what do they earn and live on, what role do the forest and mountains play in this?
5. What factors influence the behavior of residents of your locality regarding biodiversity conservation? What has more influence on behavior regarding forest use – religious-ethical factors or adherence to legislation? Are these factors relevant at all, or do others (local customs, superstitions, etc.) prevail.
6. Do you think that the problem of biodiversity loss is relevant for the forest near your locality / for the Carpathians? What factors negatively affect local ecosystems (based on your own experience, what can you say about the local forest, what condition is it in, has anything changed in recent years, decades)?
7. Have you seen wild animals in the local forest? How often do you encounter them / did you encounter them before, has anything changed in recent years, decades)?
8. Have you seen signs of deforestation? Who is cutting it down? Who is in charge of the local forest? Who takes care of it? Are you aware of corruption problems, illegal logging, etc. (in the nearby forest, in the Carpathians in general)?

9. What should be done to protect the local nature from destruction (for example, other areas of employment and sources of income, subsidies, awareness, etc.)?

Local Government Employees

1. What are the sources of income for the community, what role do the forest and mountains play in this?
2. How does local self-government participate in biodiversity conservation or in the management or use of forest resources?
3. What are the risks to local biodiversity?
4. How is waste disposal carried out, do some of them end up in / affect the local forest?
5. Do you know anything about the problems with logging in local forests? Is there a corruption factor?
6. What is the community's ethical approach to biodiversity, what is the role of religion in this (perhaps just statistically – how religious is the community, which denomination dominates)?
7. What needs to be changed (what policies to implement) to improve the protection of local biodiversity / the Carpathians in general?

Forestry employees (forestries, forestry enterprises, State Forestry Agency and regional administrations)

1. Is biodiversity monitoring carried out in your forestry / forestry enterprise / region / Carpathians?
2. Is biodiversity taken into account during economic activities (how exactly)?
3. What other priorities of the forestry enterprise / (...) may interfere (conflict with) biodiversity conservation?
4. What are the risks to biodiversity conservation inherent in the local forest / the Carpathians in general?
5. Are there signs of corruption at any level affecting the condition of the local forest / the Carpathians in general (how does it manifest, examples)?
6. Does your forestry enterprise / (...) have an anti-corruption program? Are any real measures being taken to implement it (if so, name examples).
7. What measures are being taken in your forestry enterprise / (...) to conserve biodiversity?

8. Institutional questions: who is the forestry enterprise / (...) subordinate to, who does it report to, how are decisions made, how is financing carried out, where do the profits go, can this be viewed online, what are the problems?
9. How familiar are you with the norms of international conventions and Ukrainian legislation regulating biodiversity conservation (on a scale from 1 to 5, where 1 is minimal and 5 is very good)?
10. Does Christian faith (or the ideas of the social teaching of churches) matter to you when making decisions about forest use? How do you perceive the forest (only as a resource, as a valuable ecosystem that needs to be preserved for future generations, etc.)?
11. What needs to be changed (what policies to implement) to improve biodiversity conservation in your forestry / forestry enterprise / region / the Carpathians in general?

Employees of Nature Reserve Fund Objects

1. Is biodiversity monitoring carried out in (...)? How exactly? If not, how would it be appropriate to carry it out? What facilitates this, what hinders it?
2. What rare species of flora and fauna are found in (...), what exactly needs special protection at the species and ecosystem levels (...).
3. What risks to biodiversity can you name? (list from Millenium Assessment / Living Planet Index – which of these risks are most / least relevant).
4. What measures are being taken to conserve biodiversity in your (...) (both habitat-based approach and species-based approach)? What measures would be appropriate to take. What problems arise, what factors hinder the implementation of measures (if any)?
5. Is there an impact of corruption on biodiversity (if so, what kind, negative or positive, examples)?
6. Institutional questions: how is management carried out, to whom are they subordinate and accountable, how is financing carried out, can this be viewed online? /
7. What needs to be changed (what policies to implement) to improve biodiversity conservation in your Nature Reserve Fund object / the Carpathians in general?

Employees of Non-Governmental Environmental Organizations (EPL, Ecoaction, etc.), experts, activists

1. How exactly is your organization involved in the conservation of Carpathian biodiversity?
2. Is biodiversity monitoring carried out in the Carpathians (by whom? how)? If not, how would it be appropriate to carry it out (what exactly to monitor, who should do it)?
3. What risks to Carpathian biodiversity can you name (which of them are the main ones, list from Millenium Assessment and Living Planet Index – which of these risks are most / least relevant for Carpathian forest ecosystems, how do they manifest, examples)?
4. Is corruption a factor affecting Carpathian biodiversity (how does it affect, negatively or positively, how does it manifest)?
5. How do you assess the institutional structure (management, financing) of forestry enterprises, Nature Reserve Fund objects, is there anything that needs to be changed, what exactly?
6. How do you assess Ukrainian legislation on biodiversity conservation (is there anything that needs to be added, changed)?
7. Is the religion of the local population a factor affecting biodiversity conservation?
8. What measures, policies should be implemented to conserve Carpathian biodiversity?

Part 2: Interviews in Bavaria

1. What measures are taken to conserve or preserve forest biodiversity in your national park?
2. How is biodiversity monitored?
3. How is forest protection carried out, and how is it financed?
4. How is the park divided into zones, and are there differences in the level of protection provided to these zones?
5. What uses of the forest are allowed and practised in your national park?
6. What environmental education activities are being carried out?
7. Are measures taken for climate change adaptation (in the context of biodiversity conservation)?

Annex B. Anonymised categories of interviewees (grouped chronologically)

5.9.2022, certain settlement in the Kosiv district, Ivano-Frankivsk region, Ukraine

Local resident, L1
Local resident, L2
Local resident, local councillor, L3 (A)
Local resident, village head, L4 (A)
Local resident, sawmill owner, L5 (B)
Local resident, L6
Local resident, L7
Local resident, L8

6.9.2022, several settlements in the Kosiv district, Ivano-Frankivsk region, Ukraine

Local resident, L9
Local resident, L10
Local resident, scientific employee of NNP "Hutsulshchyna", L11 (N)
Local resident, settlement mayor, L12 (A)
Local resident, deputy settlement mayor, L13 (A)
Local resident, L14
Local resident and employee of NNP "Hutsulshchyna", L15 (N)

7.9.2022, Ivano-Frankivsk, Ukraine

High-ranking civil servant, Ivano-Frankivsk Regional Forestry and Hunting Economy Authority, F16 (A)

8.9.2022, Ivano-Frankivsk region, Ukraine

Forester in the Carpathians, F17

12.9.2022, Lviv, Ukraine

High-ranking civil servant, Lviv Regional Forestry and Hunting Economy Authority, F18 (A)
Civil servant, Lviv Regional Forestry and Hunting Economy Authority, F19 (A)

19.9.2022, Munich, Germany

Former civil servant, State Forestry Agency F24 (A)

21.9.2022, Munich, Germany

Former press secretary of the forest enterprise in Ivano-Frankivsk region F20

27.9.2022, online

Yehor Hrynyk, forest policy expert at the NGO "Ukrainian Nature Conservation Group"

28.9.2022, online

Oksana Omelchuk, specialist of the climate department, NGO "Ecodiya" (Ecoaction)

29.9.2022, online

Bohdan Kuchenko, environmental scientist, NGP "Environment-People-Law"

11.12.2023, online

Research and monitoring employee, Berchtesgaden National Park

18.12.2023, Grafenau, Germany

Orsolya Decker, nature conservation and research employee, Bavarian Forest National Park

Kristin Biebl, ranger, Bavarian Forest National Park

Annex C. Extract from the UNESCO World Heritage List Property Ancient and Primeval Beech Forests of the Carpathians and Other Regions of Europe

Areas of the Ukrainian Carpathians, designated as natural heritage sites, belonging to the transnational property Ancient and Primeval Beech Forests of the Carpathians and Other Regions of Europe.[1377]

ID	Name & Location	Coordinates	Property	Buffer Zone
1133quater-001	Chornohora	N48 8 25 E24 23 35	2,476.8 ha	12,925 ha
1133quater-002	Kuziy-Trybushany	N47 56 52.08 E24 8 10.07	1,369.6 ha	3,163.4 ha
1133quater-003	Maramarosh	N47 56 12 E24 19 35	2,243.6 ha	6,230.4 ha
1133quater-004	Stuzhytsia – Uzhok	N49 4 55.16 E22 35 1.69	2,532 ha	3,615 ha
1133quater-005	Svydovets	N48 11 21 E24 13 37	3,030.5 ha	5,639.5 ha
1133quater-006	Uholka – Shyrikyi Luh	N48 18 22 E23 41 46	11,860 ha	3,301 ha
1133quater-064	Gorgany	N48 28 19 E24 17 58	753.48 ha	4,637.59 ha
1133quater-067	Synevyr – Darvaika	N48 0 0 E23 0 0	1,588.46 ha	312.32 ha
1133quater-068	Synevyr – Kvasovets	N48 23 6 E23 42 46	561.62 ha	333.63 ha
1133quater-069	Synevyr – Strymba	N48 27 11 E23 47 48	260.65 ha	191.14 ha
1133quater-070	Synevyr – Vilshany	N48 21 20 E23 39 36	454.31 ha	253.85 ha
1133quater-071	Zacharovanyi Krai – Irshavka	N48 27 9 E23 5 23	93.97 ha	1,275.44 ha
1133quater-072	Zacharovanyi Krai – Velykyi Dil	N48 25 21 E23 9 42	1,164.16 ha	

1377 "Ancient and Primeval Beech Forests of the Carpathians and Other Regions of Europe," UNESCO, accessed September 24, 2024, https://whc.unesco.org/en/list/1133/.